Issues in Business Ethics

Volume 43

Series editors
Wim Dubbink, Department of Philosophy, School of Humanities,
Tilburg University, Tilburg, Netherlands
Mollie Painter-Morland, College of Business Law & Social Sciences,
Nottingham Business School, Nottingham, UK

More information about this series at http://www.springer.com/series/6077

Domènec Melé • Martin Schlag

Editors

Humanism in Economics and Business

Perspectives of the Catholic Social Tradition

 Springer

Editors
Domènec Melé
IESE Business School
University of Navarra
Barcelona, Spain

Martin Schlag
Markets, Culture and Ethics
  Research Center
Pontifical University of the Holy Cross
Rome, Italy

ISSN 0925-6733   ISSN 2215-1680   (electronic)
Issues in Business Ethics
ISBN 978-94-017-9703-0   ISBN 978-94-017-9704-7   (eBook)
DOI 10.1007/978-94-017-9704-7

Library of Congress Control Number: 2015932141

Springer Dordrecht Heidelberg New York London

Printed on acid-free paper

Springer Science+Business Media B.V. Dordrecht is part of Springer Science+Business Media (www.springer.com)

Foreword

The impact of globalization and technological change on job creation and social welfare is reframing the question of the firm and its role in society. At the same time, the notion that the firm's purpose is to achieve the maximum economic efficiency and its goal is to maximize shareholder value is being reviewed and reassessed. This combination of factors has fueled a great debate on the role of companies in market-based economies and society, and this debate is far from finished. A basic question underlying this debate is the notion of the person that scholars and practitioners use in business and economics.

At a deeper level one can see that a simplified and rather limited view of the person is at the root of dominant notions – maximizing personal utility, maximizing shareholder value, separation of economic good and personal virtue, a disconnection between personal good and common good, among others – that, implicitly or explicitly, have shaped our thinking about economics, finance and management. It seems increasingly clear that without a comprehensive notion of the person that respects human dignity, the development of modern capitalism is not sustainable, and effective leadership in modern companies would become an impossible task.

The book on Catholic Social Teaching-based Christian Humanism that Professors Domènec Melé and Martin Schlag have edited addresses several relevant challenges. The first is how to better define a notion of humanism based on Christianity that could be effective in promoting a positive notion of the human person and his or her motivations, as well as the treatment of this in economics, management and leadership literature. Their proposals do not come only from a refined theoretical system, but combine theology, philosophy, economics and management contributions. They also offer a helpful historical perspective on the concepts proposed, in particular, the different notions around the concept of humanism.

Some of the chapters included in this book do a very good job in reshaping this notion and explain why a comprehensive view of the person is a pre-condition for the respect for each individual, a better foundation for human rights and a more sustainable approach to social and economic development. They also provide a more solid bedrock for business ethics, based upon the dignity of the person and his or her rights. They take into account some interesting requirements of stakeholder theory and corporate social responsibility but go beyond these.

This book also provides a fresh approach to cross-disciplinary work. A purely economic or sociological approach to some of the current challenges are not enough to understand individuals or society sufficiently well, because there are too many missing links. There is a widely-felt perception today in social sciences that cross-disciplinary efforts are indispensable if we want to make a better case for hypotheses, theories and models of individual and social behavior, and also to better understand these phenomena in contemporary society. Melé and Schlag offer us a good portfolio of authors and approaches, with different backgrounds, whose notions and models will be most helpful in refining the notion of humanism and introducing it more effectively in management and leadership models and in action.

IESE Business School   Jordi Canals
University of Navarra
Navarra, Spain

Contents

Abbreviations (Documents of Catholic Social Teaching)

CA   *Centesimus Annus* (1991), Encyclical Letter of Pope John Paul II on the Social and Economic Order on the Hundredth Anniversary of *Rerum Novarum*.[1]

CCC   Catechism of the Catholic Church (1997).

CL   *Christifideles Laici* (1988), Apostolic Exhortation of Pope John Paul II on the Vocation of the Lay Faithful.

CSDC   *Compendium of the Social Doctrine of the Church* (2004), ed. by the Pontifical Council for Justice and Peace.

CV   *Caritas in Veritate* (2009), Encyclical Letter of Pope Benedict XVI on Integral Human Development in Love and Truth.

DCE   *Deus Caritas Est* (2005) Encyclical Letter of Pope Benedict XVI on Christian Love and Its Requirements.

DH   *Dignitatis Humanae*, Second Vatican Council – Declaration on Religious Freedom, promulgated by Pope Paul VI.

EG   *Evangelii Gaudium* (2013), Apostolic Exhortation of Pope Francis.

EJFA   *Economic Justice for All* (1986), Pastoral Letter on Catholic Social Teaching focused on the US Economy, Washington. http://www.usccb.org/upload/economic_justice_for_all.pdf

FR   *Fides et Ratio* (1998), Encyclical Letter of Pope John Paul II on the Relationship of Faith and Reason.

GS   *Gaudium et Spes* (1965), Second Vatican Council – Pastoral Constitution on the Church in the Modern World, promulgated by Pope Paul VI.

LE   *Laborem Exercens* (1981), Encyclical Letter of Pope John Paul II on Human Work.

LF   *Lumen Fidei* (2013), Encyclical Letter of Pope Francis on Faith.

LG   *Lumen Gentium*, Second Vatican Council – Dogmatic Constitution on the Church, promulgated by Pope Paul VI.

---

[1] This and all the other documents mentioned here are available at www.vatican.va

LP   *Libertas* (1888), Encyclical Letter of Pope Leo XIII, on the Nature of Human Liberty.

MM   *Mater et Magistra* (1961), Encyclical Letter of Pope John XXIII on Christianity and Social Progress.

PP   *Populorum Progressio* (1967), Encyclical Letter of Pope Paul VI on the Development of Peoples.

PT   *Pacem in Terris* (1963), Encyclical Letter of Pope John XXIII on Human Rights and the Social Order.

QA   *Quadragesimo Anno* (1931), Encyclical Letter of Pope Pius XI on Reconstruction of the Social Order.

RM   *Redemptoris Missio* (1990), Encyclical Letter of John Paul II on the Mission of the Church.

RN   *Rerum Novarum* (1891), Encyclical Letter of Pope Leo XIII, on Capital and Labor Relationship.

SRS   *Sollicitudo Rei Socialis* (1987), Encyclical Letter of Pope John Paul II on the Development of Peoples.

VS   *Veritatis Splendor* (1993), Encyclical Letter of John Paul II on Christian Morals.

List of Authors

Antonio Argandoña is Professor of Economics and holder of "la Caixa" Chair of Corporate Social Responsibility and Corporate Governance, IESE Business School, University of Navarra. He is a member of the Royal Academy of Economics and Finance, chairperson of the Professional Ethics Committee of the Catalan Economics Association, a member of the Anti-Corruption Committee of the International Chamber of Commerce (Paris) and of the Committee of Control and Transparency of the FC Barcelona. He has been a member of the Executive Committee of the European Business Ethics Network (EBEN) and Secretary General of EBEN-Spain.

Ericka Costa (Ph.D. in Business Economics) is Assistant Professor of Accounting at the University of Trento (Italy) and Research Fellow in the EURICSE – European Research Institute of Cooperatives and Social Enterprises. Since 2006 she has been a member of the EBEN and CSEAR networks. Her research interests are the investigation of Sustainability Accounting and Corporate Social Responsibility both for profit and non-profit organizations. She has written a number of chapters in books, and articles and papers which have been accepted for national and international journals and conferences.

Geert Demuijnck is Professor of Business Ethics at EDHEC Business School (France). He also holds an academic appointment at the Catholic University of Louvain-la Neuve (Belgium). He is associate member of the Hoover Chair of economic and social ethics (Louvain-la-Neuve). He serves on the Executive Committee of the European Business Ethics Network (EBEN). Educated in philosophy, economics and politics, he has published on business ethics, economic ethics and social policy. He is member of the ethics committee of two major European companies.

Markus Krienke (Dr. in Theology and Habilitation, Munich, Germany) is Professor of Modern Philosophy and Social Ethics at the Theological Faculty of Lugano (Switzerland). He is holder of the "Rosmini Chair" (www.cattedrarosmini.org)

and is Guest Lecturer at the Pontifical Lateran University of Rome. He is the editor of the book series "La Rosminiana", a collaborator with the Foundation Konrad Adenauer, and a member of the scientific committee of various scientific journals. His scientific interests are ethics in the economy, Catholic liberalism, the ethics of human rights and the European philosophy of the nineteenth century.

Arnd Küppers Vice Director of the Catholic Centre for Social Sciences of the German Episcopal Conference in Mönchengladbach. He studied Theology, Philosophy and Law in Bielefeld, Bonn and Freiburg. He holds a doctorate in Theology from the Albert-Ludwigs-University in Freiburg. From 2003 to 2010 he served as Assistant Professor for Catholic Social teaching at the University of Freiburg.

Elena Lasida is a Professor at the faculty of social and economic sciences of Institut Catholique (Paris), where she is in charge of the master programme "Economie solidaire et logique du marché" (solidarity economy and market mechanisms). She is missioned by the episcopal commission Justice and Peace France to work on the relation between economics and theology, in particular focusing in sustainability and social economy.

Miguel A. Martínez-Echevarría is Professor of Philosophy of Economics and History of Economic Thought in the School of Economics of the University of Navarra, where he was Dean from 1987 to 1992. A Doctor in Physical Sciences, he was Visiting Scholar in Harvard University. He is an Academic Member of the Royal Academy of Economic and Financial Sciences; Ordinary Member of Francisco de Vitoria Economics Investigations Institute of Madrid; a Member of the Humanism and Business Institute of the University of Istmo, Guatemala, and a Member of the Anthropology and Ethics Institute of the University of Navarra. He has authored some 100 academic publications, mainly related to the philosophy of work and management, and the history of economic thought. In 2008 he founded the Politic Economic and Philosophy Research Group in University of Navarra.

Domènec Melé (Ph.D. in Industrial Engineering and in Theology) is Professor and holder of the Chair of Business Ethics at IESE Business School, University of Navarra, Spain. Over the last 25 years, he has researched and written extensively on the areas of business ethics, business in society and Catholic Social Thought. He has authored, co-authored or edited 12 books, including *Business Ethics in Action* (Palgrave 2009), *Management Ethics* (Palgrave 2012) and *Human Development in Business. Values and Humanistic Management in the Encyclical "Caritas in Veritate"* (Palgrave 2012). In addition, he has published over 50 scientific chapters and articles in referred journals and some 20 case studies. Professor Melé serves as section editor of *Journal of Business Ethics* and on several editorial boards of scientific journals, and has been guest or co-guest editor of seven special issues of journals in his field.

Michael Naughton is the holder of the Alan W. Moss Endowed Chair in Catholic Social Thought at the University of St. Thomas (Minnesota) where he is a Full Professor with a joint appointment in the departments of Catholic Studies (College of Arts and Sciences) and Ethics and Law (Opus College of Business). He is the Director of the John A. Ryan Institute for Catholic Social Thought, at the Center for Catholic Studies, which examines Catholic social thought in relation to business theory and practice. He is the author and editor of nine books and over 30 articles. He currently serves as Board Chair for Reell Precision Manufacturing, a global producer of innovative torque solutions for transportation, consumer electronics, and medical and office automation products.

Kemi Ogunyemi holds a degree in Law from University of Ibadan, Nigeria; an LLM from University of Strathclyde, UK; and MBA and Ph.D. degrees from Lagos Business School, Pan-Atlantic University, Nigeria. She leads sessions on business ethics, managerial anthropology and sustainability management at Lagos Business School and is the Academic Director of the School's Senior Management Programme. Her consulting and research interests include personal ethos and organizational culture, responsible leadership and sustainability, and work-life ethic. She has authored over 20 articles, case studies and book chapters, and the book titled *Responsible Management: Understanding Human Nature, Ethics and Sustainability*. Kemi worked as director, team lead and mentor in various projects of the Women's Board (ECS) before joining LBS. She is a member of BEN-Africa and EBEN, and was part of the faculty team that developed the UNGC-PRME Anti-Corruption Toolkit.

Tommaso Ramus is Assistant Professor in Business Ethics at School of Business and Economics, Catholic University of Portugal. He received an M.Sc. in Business Administration (University of Trento, Italy) and a Ph.D. in Business Administration from University of Bergamo (Italy). He collaborates with the European Research Institute on Cooperative and Social Enterprises (Italy). His research focuses on social entrepreneurship, corporate social responsibility and organizational legitimacy.

Luis Romera is a Professor of Metaphysics and the Rector of the Pontifical University of the Holy Cross in Rome as well as President of the Rectors' Conference of the Roman Pontifical Universities. He holds a Doctorate of Philosophy from the University of Navarra, a degree in Geology from the University of Barcelona and a degree in Theology from the University of Navarra. He currently serves as a member of the Pontifical Academy of St. Thomas Aquinas in Rome. Professor Romera's teaching has focused on the foundations of metaphysics, comparing classic and relevant contemporary authors, with a special emphasis on Heidegger, and he has participated in numerous meetings and public debates on current issues connected with practical philosophy, such as multiculturalism, relativism and professional ethics. He has also authored numerous publications, including *Finitudine e trascendenza* (*Finitude and Transcendence*), EDUSC, Rome 2006; *L'uomo e il mistero di Dio*

(*Man and the Mystery of God*), EDUSC, Rome 2008; *Introduzione alla domanda metafisica* (*Introduction to the Metaphysical Question*), Armando, Rome 2003; *Ripensare la metafisica* (Rethinking Metaphysics), Armando, Rome 2005; and *Dalla differenza alla trascendenza in Tommaso d'Aquino e Heidegger* (*From Difference to Transcendence in Thomas Aquinas and Heidegger*), Marietti, Genova-Milano 2006.

Lloyd E. Sandelands teaches business administration and psychology at the University of Michigan in Ann Arbor. He studies the social and spiritual aspects of life today, especially in business. He is the author of *Feeling and Form in Social Life* (1998, Rowman and Littlefield), *Male and Female in Social Life* (2001, Transaction), *Thinking about Social Life* (2003, University Press of America), *Man and Nature in God* (2005, Transaction), *An Anthropological Defense of God* (2007, Transaction), *God and Mammon* (2010, University Press of America), and *The Nuptial Mind* (2012, University Press of America).

Martin Schlag is Professor at the Pontifical University Santa Croce (PUSC) in Rome, where he teaches Moral Theology and Social Ethics. At the University he co-founded the Research Center "Markets, Culture and Ethics", of which he presently is director. He has authored numerous publications. His latest book is *La dignità umana come principio sociale* (*Human Dignity as Social Principle*) published by EDUSC, 2013. He also co-edited the book *Free Market and the Culture of the Common Good*, published by Springer, 2012.

Jens Zimmermann is Professor in the Humanities and Canada Research Chair for Interpretation, Religion, and Culture at Trinity Western University, British Columbia, Canada. He has published articles and books on philosophy, theology, and literary theory. His most recent publications are *Humanism and Religion: A Call for the Renewal of Western Culture* (Oxford University Press 2012) and *Incarnational Humanism* (InterVarsity Press, 2012).

Chapter 1
Christian Humanism in Economics and Business

Domènec Melé and Martin Schlag

Abstract Humanism places the person at the origin, the center and the end of society and of every activity within it. A comprehensive view of the human being and the centrality of the person, which characterizes humanism, can make a valuable contribution to our society and, in particular, to the economic and business world. Humanism proposed by the Catholic tradition sees the person as a perfectible being, called to self-development. This calling makes full sense within a transcendent humanism, which gives to man his greatest possible perfection. Humanism challenges economic and business activity and their management. In the last part, the editors explain the structure of this book and introduce the authors of this collective work and their respective contributions.

Keywords Catholic tradition • Christian humanism • Economic activity • Humanism • Secular humanism

In the last decade an increasing interest has emerged regarding humanism in economics and business activities. Previously some attention was paid to humanist economics (e.g., Bowen 1972), humanizing the workplace (e.g., Meltzer and Wickert 1976; Mire 1976) and humanism in business (Llano et al. 1992). At the turn of this century humanistic management was presented as a challenge (Melé 2003a) and certain scholars showed interest in this topic (see, e.g., authors in the collective work edited by Spitzeck et al. (2009a)). After the financial crisis the necessity for a more humanistic approach to economics and business has become increasingly evident.

D. Melé (✉)
IESE Business School, University of Navarra, Barcelona, Spain
e-mail: mele@iese.edu

M. Schlag
Markets, Culture and Ethics Research Center, Pontifical University
of the Holy Cross, Rome, Italy
email: schlag@pusc.it

© Springer Science+Business Media Dordrecht 2015
D. Melé, M. Schlag (eds.), *Humanism in Economics and Business*,
Issues in Business Ethics 43, DOI 10.1007/978-94-017-9704-7_1

1

Humanistic management has been central in various recent conferences and other academic events[1]; think tanks, research centers and chairs have emerged recently,[2] prestigious journals have included articles on this matter,[3] and a number of books[4] on this topic have been published. Some practitioners are also stressing the necessity to humanize business (Cottet and Grant 2012) or proposing the humanizing of different aspects of corporate activity (technology, production, consumption, selling strategy, and so on). Recently, Andreu and Rosanas (2012) have launched a *Manifesto to Humanize the Firm*, which includes, among others, a number of practical pledges such as: viewing the company as a community of people, not a money-making machine; breaking with the concept of human beings as mere instruments and considering that the company must serve the people with whom it interacts, not vice versa; upholding corporate values that promote friendship, loyalty, identification and enthusiasm and building a community around these shared values, and creating a culture of learning within the organization.

---

[1] The Academy of Management, the largest organization of management academics and practitioners, in its annual meeting, usually includes a caucus on humanistic management and other events related to humanistic management. In addition, papers on humanistic business and management are usually presented at the annual meetings of the Society for Business Ethics and the European Business Ethics Network. IESE Business School, University of Navarra, has promoted a number of conferences specifically related to humanism in business. These include the following: "Business and Management: Towards More Human Models and Practices" (Barcelona, May 16–17, 2008), "Facing the Crisis: Towards a More Humanistic Synthesis" (Barcelona, May 13–15, 2010), First Colloquium on Christian Humanism in Economic and Business (Barcelona, January, 20, 2010) and "Humanizing the Firm and Management Profession" (Barcelona, June 27–28, 2011), Second International Colloquium on Christian Humanism in Economics and Business (Barcelona, October 24–25, 2011) co-organized by the Pontifical University of the Holy Cross, Rome. The Third International Colloquium on Christian Humanism in Economics and Business was in Washington (October 22–23, 2012). This was hosted by the Catholic University of America and the Markets, Culture and Ethics Research Center of the Pontifical University of the Holy Cross and with the collaboration of the Chair of Business Ethics of IESE Business School. In addition, the International Symposia on Catholic Social Thought and Management Education, established in 1991 and organized by St. Thomas University and other Catholic institutions, have often included topics related to humanism in management.

[2] Thus, the Aspen Institute of Humanistic Studies, international nonprofit organization founded in 1950. The Institute of Enterprise and Humanism (University of Navarra), Humanistic Management Network, the Humanistic Management Center (University of St. Gallen, Switzerland), Research Center "Markets, Culture and Ethics" (Pontifical University of the Holy Cross, Rome), Chair of Humanistic Management (University of Pavia, Italy), Crèdit Andorrà Chair of Markets, Organizations, and Humanism (IESE Business School, University of Navarra, Barcelona). This latter School also hosts a Permanent Seminar on humanizing the firn and humanist management.

[3] Hirschman (1986), Verstraeten (1998), Melé (2003a, b, 2012a), Lurie (2004), Moore (2005), Rosanas (2008), Pirson and Lawrence (2010), Sandelands (2009), Maak and Pless (2009), Haroon and Nisar (2010), Laurent Martínez et al. (2011), Aranzadi (2011), Spitzeck (2011), Grassl and Habisch (2011), Melé (2012a), Costa and Ramus (2012), Acevedo (2012), Gangopadhyay (2012), among others.

[4] E.g., Spitzeck et al. (2009a, b), Von Kimakowitz et al. (2011), Amann et al. (2011), Dierksmeier (2011), von Kimakowitz et al. (2011), Melé and Dierksmeier (2012), Rosanas and Ricart (2012), Schlag and Mercado (2012) and Melé (2012b).

A number of contributions related with humanizing business have come from churches and some social movements. From the Catholic Church, these include, among others, the Focholar movement of "Economy of Communion", the Jesuits' concern for social justice, and the importance of the unity of life and the sanctification of human work in Christian mangers, promoted by Opus Dei. In different ways, these include the application of the humanism of Catholic social teaching in understanding the firm and its management, and in promoting more just conditions in the economic and social context.

This book is in line with the movement undertaken to humanize management, economics and business. Most articles included in this volume were presented in the Second International Colloquium on Christian Humanism in Economics and Business which took place in Barcelona, Spain, on October 24–25, 2011 at IESE Business School, co-chaired by the editors of this volume. Other articles have been added by invitation.

As Pope Francis recognizes, values of an authentic Christian humanism can be found in the Christian substratum of certain peoples – most of all in the West (EV 68). However, we belief that such humanism needs a serious reinforcement. The genesis of this book is our strong conviction that Christian Humanism, and especially that proposed by the Catholic tradition, can make a valuable contribution to our society and, in particular, to the economic and business world. It provides a comprehensive view of the human being and places the person at the origin, the center and the end of society and of every activity within it, including economics and business.

Given such a comprehensive view, it could be sufficient to talk of "Humanism", instead of "Christian Humanism" or "Catholic Humanism". Nevertheless, in an academic work like this, there are several other reasons for adding "Christian" or "Catholic" to the substantive "Humanism". The first is that the concept of humanism can be understood with different meanings. This is the case of outstanding scholars coming from a variety of philosophical positions. Jean-Paul Sartre (2007 [1945]), for instance, proposed a humanism based on an individualistic and atheistic existentialism. In contrast, Jacques Maritain (1973/1936) defended an integral humanism, within the Catholic tradition.

The second reason is that Humanism has been often presented in opposition to Christianity and any other religions, and explicitly excludes any faith-based knowledge. One of the contributors to this book (Martínez-Echevarria) explains the genesis of "humanism" developed in Modernity and attempts to demonstrate the intrinsically individualistic and atheistic dimension entailed in this vision, which, obviously, is foreign to Christianity. This position is still held nowadays by some who introduce themselves as defenders of "Secular Humanism".

The question is whether or not a secularist humanism is a truly human humanism or if rather it leads us to a certain pseudo-humanism, making the human being less human. Depriving the human being of any knowledge derived from divine revelation leaves unanswered the more radical questions of human existence, including the search of meaning for human life (Frankl 1963). In contrast, the openness to the Absolute provides a full meaning for life. In words of Pope Paul VI, "there is no true humanism but that which is open to the Absolute, and is conscious of a vocation which gives human life its true meaning." (1987, PP hereafter, 42)

The centrality of the human being, which characterizes humanism, should not ignore that he or she is a perfectible being, called to self-development. This calling makes full sense within a transcendent humanism, which gives to man his greatest possible perfection: this is the highest goal of personal development (PP 16).

Christian humanism includes many propositions of secularist humanism but completes them with some other important elements, as some authors discuss in this work.

A third reason is that "Christian Humanism" emphasizes both human values and evangelical values, which include the former. Christianity is indeed fully open to human values and encourages acquiring virtues based on such values. This is the recommendation of the Bible (1966): "whatever is true, whatever is honorable, whatever is just, whatever is pleasing, whatever is pure, whatever is commendable, if there is anything excellent and if there is anything worthy, think about these things." (*Phil* 4:8) However, the Christian view is centered on love that transcends justice and a merely human horizon of values. Love is a crucial virtue, which gives support, inspires and harmonizes all other virtues: "love binds everything together in perfect harmony" (*Col* 3:14).

Love (charity) is paramount in Christianity, but truth is too: charity "rejoices in the truth" (*1 Cor* 13:6). It might surprise followers of other religions to discover how central human reason is to Christian faith. Christian faith excludes anything irrational from its creed: Christians must only believe what is true. Reason, therefore, has always been highly cherished in the Catholic and other Christian traditions as a means to search for the truth. However, it is not the only means to reach it. There is another source for achieving true knowledge – a Person: Jesus Christ, who calls himself "the way, the truth, and the life." (*Jn* 14:6) Based on several biblical texts (*Ex* 33:18; *Ps* 27:8–9; 63:2–3; *Jn* 14:8; *1 Jn* 3:2) this double source for truth is expressed by Pope John Paul II in his declaration that: "Faith and reason are like two wings on which the human spirit rises to the contemplation of truth; and God has placed in the human heart a desire to know the truth—in a word, to know himself— so that, by knowing and loving God, men and women may also come to the fullness of truth about themselves." (1998 –FR hereafter, introductory words).

Of course, this implies that there is novelty in the faith. However, it is worth noting that faith is not "i-rrational" but "supra-rational". Faith does not alienate human reason or damage its full development (FR 45ff). On the contrary, the radical separation of faith and reason impoverishes both. Faith provides inspiration for reflection, and it is reasonable in its contents. This reasonableness of the Christian faith makes a fruitful dialogue with such religious and philosophical approaches and traditions possible, which in their turn are open to rational dialogue. In his contribution, Prof. Romera discusses this problem within the current cultural context, defending the role of reason, without destroying faith, and that of faith without eliminating reason.

Evangelical values revolve around "love in truth" (Benedict XVI 2009, CV hereafter) and present a solid base for a rich humanism. Thus, they provide a clear point of reference in our contemporary society and culture, where there is a widespread tendency to identify love with feeling and to relativize truth. Pope Benedict XVI defended that the greatest service to development, then, is a Christian humanism affirms that "practising love in truth helps people to understand that adhering to the values of Christianity is not merely useful but essential for building a good society and for true integral human development." (CV 4). He adds that the greatest service to development "is a Christian humanism" (CV 78).

A last remark before introducing the respective chapters of this book is that Christian-Catholic Humanism has an implicit and explicit ethical content, extensible to Corporate Social Responsibility. However, its approach differs substantially from certain current business and management doctrines which see ethics or corporate responsibility exclusively as a means to avoid risks and to obtain profits. This is the case, for instance of the concept "Creating Shared Value" formulated by Michael Porter (Porter and Kramer 2011), which lacks consideration of the dignity of human beings and the intrinsic value of a responsible behavior. In contrast, Christian Humanism emphasizes both of these, without regarding profits as a motive to respect human dignity nor for ethical behavior. However, this does not entail that Christian Humanism has no relevant economic consequences in the middle and long-term.

Understanding Christian Humanism

The previous remarks may justify the length of the first part of the book which is devoted to gaining an understanding of Christian-Catholic Humanism. Let us briefly introduce the chapters which try to achieve this goal. **Martin Schlag** discusses how Christian Humanism has developed over the centuries in the Catholic Church. He focuses on the question of how a concept of inclusive secularity –a necessary correlate to Christian humanism– formed. Setting out from the creation of man and woman in God's image, he analyses how the early Christian writers, known as Fathers of the Church, wrought a conceptual social revolution and were firmly rooted in the conviction of the unity between nature and grace. The Second Vatican Council was paramount for the formation of the concept of Christian humanism, which was developed further by the postconciliar Popes.

This piece is followed by an essay by **Luis Romera,** who – as has been said – examines the concept of Christian Humanism within contemporary culture. Firstly he analyses the cultural trends which determine the fundamental attitudes of current society. Secondly, he examines the meaning of humanism, in order to indicate the ultimate reasons for which the humanism of our time needs Christianity. He argues that Christian faith offers a set of ideas that have proven to be essential for the recuperation of humanism. In addition, Christianity fosters attitudes in the person that direct him or her towards forms of social action (economic-business, political, juridical, familiar, etc.) that are effectively oriented towards humanism. Last, but not least, Prof. Romera points out that Christianity offers hope, precisely because of its transcendent and soteriological character.

These points are complemented by the work of **Jens Zimmermann,** who warns against the pervasiveness of equating humanism with secularism. He points out how important it is to understand the religious roots that gave birth to our Western understanding of human nature and its corresponding institutions. He argues, in dialogue with other positions, that Christian humanism is a foundational element of Western culture and constitutes the soul of our educational ideal. It is not by denying or belittling the Christian origins of humanism but by fully grasping their content that we can overcome the separation of reason and faith. Moreover, he believes that an in-depth understanding of Christian humanism can help dispel the worries of those that believe that religion is inherently dogmatic and intolerant. Jens Zimmermann proposes that Christian Humanism is at the foundations of Western culture.

This first part of the book concludes with a chapter written by **Markus Krienke**, in which he proposes rethinking the concept of liberty. This would open new perspectives for Christian Humanism. In an innovative interpretation of the Encyclical *Caritas in veritate*, Krienke tries to overcome the impasse between libertarianism and communitarianism with the consideration of those more foundational relationships in which human liberty is articulated: those of the family and the transcendent. The question he answers in an affirmative sense is whether our concept of liberty in society can be rethought beginning from this ethical foundation implied in Christian Humanism.

Christian Humanism and Economic Activity

The second part of this book focuses on the relationship between Christian-Catholic Humanism on one hand, and economics and business on the other; inquiring into how to humanize economics and business. This part begins with an essay by **Miguel A. Martínez-Echevarría** where he discusses whether or not Christian Humanism makes sense within economic activity. He holds that a "humanist" individualism, which emerged with Modernity, has had an enormous influence in economic thought. This vision can be seen as an "anthropological inversion". He concludes by defending the position, that a Christian conception of man might produce a more realistic and practical view of the economy.

In the next chapter, **Domènec Melé** presents three key concepts of Catholic humanism for economic activity: human dignity, human rights, and human development, holding that these three elements are at the core of Christian Humanism within Catholic teaching. He examines the roots of human dignity and some precedents of the modern concept of human rights and stresses the important role played by the Judeo-Christian tradition. This author argues that in the later nineteenth century the Papacy became a great advocate of basic labor rights. Nowadays, the Catholic Church, along with other Christian confessions, openly defends human rights in its social teachings, although it questions claims she considers to be contrary to or without a sound anthropological and ethical foundation. Prof Melé discusses how Catholic social teaching understands human dignity, rights and development, with some implications in common topics regarding business activity.

Christian Humanism made an important contribution to the Social Market Economy developed in Germany after the Second World War and is still present in this and other European countries. Early ordoliberal economists of the Freiburg School of Economics (Ludwig Erhard, Walter Eucken, Franz Böhm, Wilhelm

Röpke, Alexander Rüstow, and others) heavily inspired the Social Market Economy. As **Arnd Küppers** explains in his contribution, the Freiburg School presents genuine and fundamental Christian elements. Ordoliberal thinkers have the firm conviction, that a free economic (and political) system needs a constitutional order, the rules of which hold the competitors in a market within certain limits, thus guaranteeing the maintenance of a free and fair competition. They developed a personalistic and humanistic outline of a socio-economic order, at the centre of which stands the human person and his or her inalienable rights, including the social rights. It emphasizes both the personal responsibility of each individual and solidarity in the social community. Küppers concludes by stating that "the Christian elements of the concept of Social Market Economy are not only accidental, but rather are essential."

If Christian Humanism can influence one's understanding of the markets and the economy, as is the case with Social Market Economics, as noted above, why can't it have an influence in developing business models? Using a model inspired by Christian Humanism, the Italian *"Economia Aziendale"*, **Ericka Costa** and **Tommaso Ramus** argue that, in fact, it can. In this model the business firm is seen as a community of persons, and its *raison d'être* as a service to human needs. The authors discuss this model linking it with Catholic Social Teaching. They conclude that the firm as an organization is not aimed exclusively at profit-maximization: Profit has an instrumental character. *Economia Aziendale* refers to the common good of the members of all business organizations, which requires enabling everyone involved in the organizational activity to flourish as a human being. Indirectly it serves the common good of society. In some way, *Economia Aziendale* covers all forms of economic organizations, be they for-profit, not-for profit or publicly owned.

The third part focuses more specifically on business. The centrality of the person is highlighted by **Lloyd Sandelands** in his contribution. Applying the Christian Humanism proposed by Catholic social teaching he holds that "the business of business is the human person". He does not deny that business should create wealth for its owners, but he strongly defends the position that persons are not assets to deploy on behalf of owners, and it is morally wrong to treat them as such. He reminds us of eight social principles proposed by Catholic social teaching that both correct and enlarge the shareholder-centered ethic of much current business thinking, and discusses some practical implications of these for management.

An important point is how the business firm should be understood. **Michael Naugthon** proposes that we should "think institutionally" about business in a way that promotes a humanistic philosophy for management informed by Christian Humanism and more specifically by the Catholic social tradition. In his essay he describes the *nature* of a business on a continuum between an "association of individuals" and a "community of persons" and the various shadings in between. Prof. Naughton discusses and accepts as compelling the notion that the nature of business is a "community of persons" and then sets out the principle of the common good as its purpose. He explain how the common good views the institutional goods that are particular to a business (good goods, good work, good wealth), and how these goods are ordered to true human development (ordering principles, goods held in common, virtues).

On his part, **Antonio Argandoña** considers Christian Humanism from a different perspective. He questions whether a Christian manager should be different and why. He considers the Scriptures and documents of Catholic social teaching trying to understand what makes the Christian who works as an entrepreneur different and what advantages or disadvantages being a Christian brings about. He argues that religion sheds light for a deeper understanding of business and its orientation toward people. Likewise, it provides the manager with a wider view of business and helps him or her to understand reasons for ethical behavior, along with the spiritual and ascetic means necessary.

Last, but not least, the third part concludes with a chapter authored by **Geert Demuijnck, Kemi Ogunyemi** and **Elena Lasida,** which discusses three cases studies on business and management practices influenced by Catholic humanism. The first of these deals with a medium size company where the owner-manager has a solid Catholic education and a great sense of integrity and discipline. This company shows policies and practices of high quality in treating people, acting with justice, care and promoting the development of managers and employees. The second case is about a small enterprise organized according to the principles of the 'Economy of Communion'. In this case, Catholic humanism has particular characteristics which are reflected in particular management and business practices, as well as in all internal and external relations. A different approach is presented in the last case, about a retail company which started as a small shop and is now a large organizations. From the very beginning the founders, who had profound Catholics convictions, introduced a number of innovative practices based on Catholic social teaching. While the business was growing they gradually clarified the ethical responsibilities of their company through an ongoing discussion on particular issues in an ethical committee. In this way, the company has reached high ethical standards which are rooted in the religious and ethical motivations of their leaders and influenced by Catholic teachings.

While the book is not an exhaustive guide to Catholic humanism in economics and business, the topics selected are significant and cover a variety of key topics. Hopefully, it will serve a variety of purposes and people, including Catholic and other Christian institutions which offer courses on Economics, Business Ethics and Corporate Social Responsibility. It also provides materials for seminars for doctoral students and executives. In addition, inasmuch as Catholic social teaching is offered to everybody of good will, this volume may well be useful to those who are interested in humanistic management and humanizing business. It also serves to explain the Catholic position on economic and business activity and how Catholicism understands the foundations of business ethics.

References

Acevedo, Alma. 2012. Personalist business ethics and humanistic management: Insights from Jacques Maritain. *Journal of Business Ethics* 105: 197–219.

Amann, Wolfgang, Michael Pirson, Claus Dierksmeier, Ernst Von Kimakowitz, and Heiko Spitzeck (eds.). 2011. *Business schools under fire. Humanistic management education as the way forward*. New York: Palgrave Macmillan.

Andreu, Rafael, and Josep M. Rosanas. 2012. Manifiesto for a better management. A rational and humanist view. In *Towards a new theory of the firm. Humanizing the firm and the management profession*, ed. J.M. Rosanas and J.E. Ricart, 109–150. Madrid: Fundación BBVA.

Aranzadi, Javier. 2011. The possibilities of the acting person within an institutional framework: Goods, norms, and virtues. *Journal of Business Ethics* 99: 87–100.

Bible, The Holy. 1966. *New revised standard version*. Catholic Edition. Princeton: Scepter.

Benedict XVI. 2009. *Encyclical Letter 'Caritas in veritate'*. Available at: http://www.vatican.va/holy_father/benedict_xvi/encyclicals/documents/hf_ben-xvi_enc_20090629_caritas-in-veritate_en.html

Bowen, Howard R. 1972. Toward a humanist economics. *Journal of Economics and Business* 11: 9–24.

Costa, Ericka, and Tommaso Ramus. 2012. The Italian economia aziendale and catholic social teaching: How to apply the common good principle at the managerial level. *Journal of Business Ethics* 106: 103–116.

Cottet, Jamie, and Maddie Grant. 2012. *Humanize: How people-centric organizations succeed in a social world*. Upper Saddle River: Pearson.

Dierksmeier, C. 2011. *Humanistic ethics in the age of globality*. New York: Palgrave Macmillan.

Frankl, Viktor Emil. 1963. *Man's search for meaning: An introduction to logotherapy* (Earlier title, 1959: From Death-Camp to Existentialism. Originally published in 1946 as Ein Psycholog erlebt das Konzentrationslager). New York: Washington Square Press.

Gangopadhyay, Somnath. 2012. Humanizing work and work environment: A challenge for developing countries. *Work* 43: 399–401.

Grassl, Wolfgang, and André Habisch. 2011. Ethics and economics: Towards a new humanistic synthesis for business. *Journal of Business Ethics* 99: 37–49.

Haroon, Muhammad, and Mansoor Nisar. 2010. Humanizing stakeholders interaction: As a part of corporate responsibility, interdisciplinary. *Journal of Contemporary Research in Business* 1: 160–178.

Hirschman, E.C. 1986. Humanistic inquiry in marketing research: Philosophy, method, and criteria. *Journal of Marketing Research* 23(3): 237–249.

John Paul II. 1993. *Encyclical-Letter- 'Fides et ratio', on the relationship between faith and reason*. Available at: http://www.vatican.va/holy_father/john_paul_ii/encyclicals/documents/hf_jp-ii_enc_14091998_fides-et-ratio_en.html

Llano, Alejandro, Rafael Alvira, Tomás Calleja, Miguel Bastons, and Cruz Martinez Esteruelas. 1992. *El humanismo en la empresa*. Madrid: Rialp.

Lurie, Yotam. 2004. Humanizing business through emotions: On the role of emotions in ethics. *Journal of Business Ethics* 49(1): 1–11.

Maak, Thomas, and Nicola Pless. 2009. Business leaders as citizens of the world. Advancing humanism on a global scale. *Journal of Business Ethics* 88: 537–550.

Maritain, Jacques. 1973[1936]. *Integral humanism*. Notre Dame: University of Notre Dame Press. Original: L'humanisme intégral (Aubier, París, 1936).

Martínez, Laurent, Laura Leticia, Jorge Loza López, Juan Laurent, and Juan Francisco Rosales. 2011. Competitiveness and humanistic productivity. *Advances in Competitiveness Research* 19: 74–84.

Melé, Domènec. 2003a. The challenge of humanistic management. *Journal of Business Ethics* 44: 77–88.

Melé, Domènec. 2003b. Organizational humanizing cultures: Do they generate social capital? *Journal of Business Ethics* 45: 3–14.

Melé, Domènec. 2012a. The firm as a "community of persons": A pillar of humanistic business ethos. *Journal of Business Ethics* 106: 89–101.

Melé, Domènec. 2012b. *Management ethics: Placing ethics at the core of good management*. New York: Palgrave MacMillan.

Melé, Domènec, and Claus Dierksmeier (eds.). 2012. *Human development in business. Values and humanistic management in the in the encyclical "Caritas in Veritate"*. New York: Palgrave – MacMillan.

Meltzer, H., and Frederic R. Wickert. 1976. *Humanizing organizational behavior*. Springfield: Thomas.

Mire, Joseph. 1976. Humanizing the workplace. *Labor Studies Journal* 1: 219–223.

Moore, Geoff. 2005. Humanizing business: A modern virtue ethics approach. *Business Ethics Quarterly* 15: 237–255.

Paul VI. 1967. *Encyclical-Letter 'Populorum Progressio'*, on people development. Available at: http://www.vatican.va/holy_father/paul_vi/encyclicals/documents/hf_p-vi_enc_26031967_populorum_en.html

Pirson, Michael, and Paul Lawrence. 2010. Humanism in business – towards a paradigm shift? *Journal of Business Ethics* 93: 553–565.

Porter, M.E., and M. Kramer. 2011. Creating shared value. How to reinvent capitalism and unleash a wave of innovation and growth. *Harvard Business Review* 89(1/2): 62–77.

Rosanas, Josep. 2008. Beyond economic criteria: A humanistic approach to organizational survival. *Journal of Business Ethics* 78: 447–462.

Rosanas, Josep M., and Joan E. Ricart (eds.). 2012. *Towards a new theory of the firm. Humanizing the firm and the management profession*. Madrid: Fundación BBVA.

Sandelands, Lloyd. 2009. The business of business is the human person: Lessons from the catholic social tradition. *Journal of Business Ethics* 85: 93–101.

Sartre, Jean-Paul. 2007[1945]. *Existentialism is a humanism*: Translated by Carol Macomber, introduction by Annie Cohen-Solal; notes and preface by Arlette Elkaïm-Sartre ; edited by John Kulka. New Haven: Yale University Press.

Schlag, Martin, and Juan A. Mercado (eds.). 2012. *Free markets and the culture of the common good*. Heidelberg/New York/Berlin: Springer.

Spitzeck, Heiko. 2011. An integrated model of humanistic management. *Journal of Business Ethics* 99: 51–62.

Spitzeck, Heiko, Wolfgang Amann, Michael Pirson, Shiban Khan, and Ernst V. Kimakowitz (eds.). 2009a. *Humanism in business – State of the art. A reflection on humanistic values in today's business world*. Cambridge: Cambridge University Press.

Spitzeck, H., M. Pirson, W. Amann, S. Khan, and E. Von Kimakowitz (eds.). 2009b. *Humanism in business. Perspectives on the development of a responsible business society*. Cambridge, UK: Cambridge University Press.

Verstraeten, Johan. 1998. From business ethics to the vocation of business leaders to humanize the world of business. *Business Ethics: A European Review* 7: 111–124.

Von Kimakowitz, E., H. Spitzeck, M. Pirson, C. Dierksmeier, and W. Amann (eds.). 2011. *Humanistic management in practice*. New York: Palgrave Macmillan.

Part I
Understanding Christian Humanism

Chapter 2
The Historical Development of Christian-Catholic Humanism

Martin Schlag

Abstract We live in times of cultural and anthropological uneasiness, and, to some extent, of crisis. Unemployment, economic injustice, public debt, the civilization of death, and the demographic winter are menacing our Western civilization. Simultaneously, Christian faith, as a result of its historical development, is now capable of offering its contribution when it is most needed. We are in a *kairos*. The contribution of Christian–Catholic humanism does not only consist in giving "meaning" to the good we do and the evil we suffer, but it also demands conversion, transformation, a cleansing of our culture from the evil aspects in our lives. Christian humanism is a positive and strengthening injection into the life streams of our society, which joins forces with people of all religions as well as with secular humanists who do not believe but do not exclude religion from the public sphere. This humanism is capable of releasing an influx of positive energy and potentialities for the future integral development of mankind.

Keywords Catholic social teaching • Humanism • Historical-doctrinal developments of Christian humanism • Secularism

A certain sensation of crisis or decline in Europe, but also in the United States, and in general within the Western World, can hardly be overlooked. This has to do, first and foremost, with material reasons: with the economic crisis that is simultaneously a social and political one. It is, however, also a cultural and an anthropological crisis: our societies seem to lack the energy to regenerate their strength and zeal in tackling our common problems in a sustainable and socially responsible way, for instance, not by increasing public or private debt for consumer goods but through private enterprise and investment. The uneasiness that our continual progress might be slowing down and or that the Western culture might be found weak in confrontation with other cultures has been expressed in various ways. From an historical perspective, Niall Ferguson has pointed out

M. Schlag (✉)
Markets, Culture and Ethics Research Center, Pontifical University of the Holy Cross,
Rome, Italy
e-mail: schlag@pusc.it

© Springer Science+Business Media Dordrecht 2015
D. Melé, M. Schlag (eds.), *Humanism in Economics and Business*,
Issues in Business Ethics 43, DOI 10.1007/978-94-017-9704-7_2

how the neglect of those cultural elements, which made the West great in the past, has led to its present decline (Ferguson 2011). Furthermore, Charles Taylor, in his magnificent historical narrative covering the same time period, has analyzed the deeper philosophical and cultural reasons that create the malaises of modernity and its "unquiet frontiers" (Taylor 2007, in particular 299–321 and 711–727). Generally speaking, there is a renewed awareness of the importance of culture for social life and of the need to defend it against destruction from within and from without (cf. e.g. Scruton 2007). In this context, it is interesting to note that authors who formerly excluded religious arguments from public debates or from the public sphere in general are now changing their position: in a "post-secularist" society, they affirm, we must reconsider the importance of religion as a catalyst of social cohesion and altruist energy (Habermas and Ratzinger 2006; Habermas 2011). Authors who want to "rethink secularism" in a way that includes religion in the public arena (Calhoun et al. 2011) are actually engaging suggestions, made by previous communitarian thinkers, that our society needs a nucleus of values shared in freedom, fundamental values capable of self-regeneration (cf. for instance Etzioni 2006).

This assertion that religions, including the Christian faith, contribute to human flourishing, to culture, and to social life, has been challenged by secular or exclusive humanism, the *weltanschauung* which holds that religion, instead of furthering human happiness on earth, actually impedes it. Secular humanism excludes a dimension of transcendence and the idea of a transformation of human nature, limiting the conception of human fulfillment to purely immanent, inner-worldly achievements and satisfactions. Secular humanism and Christian faith are therefore contradictory approaches to achieving human flourishing. However, in a very balanced manner, Charles Taylor has demonstrated that both the Christian faith and an exclusive humanism strive to address the same human problems and needs. Taylor does not stop with stating their common objective but continues his analysis by indicating which difficulties each approach encounters (Taylor 2007, 594–772). Taylor's arguments can be interpreted as an attempt of intellectual disarmament of the two conflicting positions, an attempt at opening eyes on both sides to the inner weaknesses of their own arguments and at the same time pointing out some of the positive contributions of the Christian faith to solving the malaises of modernity.

In this chapter, I do not wish to go into the merits and demerits of the arguments pro- and contra- secular humanism. Rather, I will attempt to present an historical study concerning Christianity's withdrawal from the world and the subsequent possible self-negation of its humanist fruits, as could be the case if the world is erroneously seen primarily as a sphere of temptation and of evil. Only if it presupposes and uses a concept of inclusive secularity can Christianity contribute to culture and human flourishing. Such an inclusive secularity comprehends an understanding of God, the faith, the Church and the believing person that includes God in the world, and the world and earthly affairs in faith. Christian humanism needs the concept of inclusive secularity in order to serve man and society.

Various definitions for Christian humanism have been offered. For example, Shaw argues that "Christian humanism is the interest in human persons and the positive affirmation of human life and culture which stems from the Christian faith." It shares a concern for the human person with secular humanism but differs from it in that it finds the font and the end of all human powers in the Holy Trinity (Shaw et al. 1982, 23). Franklin and Shaw also state that "Christian humanism is a way of looking at human existence, including public life, from the standpoint of classical Christian faith" (Franklin and Shaw 1991, 204). For the purposes of this chapter, Christian humanism signifies the contribution of Christian faith to human happiness on earth, not only in heaven, and specifically the contribution of Christian faith to social ethics. The particular emphasis of this chapter will be upon the means by which we have arrived at the contemporary Catholic concept of Christian humanism and the difficulties that had to be overcome. This process will therefore be studied, as it were, from inside the Church in such a manner that those who are not necessarily acquainted with the Church can profit from this internal perspective.

The Foundations

The whole of the Christian faith deals with God's relationship to mankind. The Bible is God's revelation of himself, and of his love for us, which led him to create and to redeem us, and to finally grant us everlasting life. Hence, faith is not theory or speculation alone; it is life. Life through, with and in God, life as an individual, life in the family, in our communities and in society. This means that in and of itself the Judeo-Christian faith is dynamic. Knowledge alone is not sufficient for belief; nor is the faith adequately understood when viewed as a simple code of conduct. It is an encounter with Jesus Christ, a dialogue with God, a community with people in the richness and variety of individual historical circumstances (cf. Benedict XVI 2005, 1).

The Bible describes man and women as "God's image and likeness" (Gen 1:26–28). Within the context of the neighboring Egyptian and Mesopotamian myths of man's formation, this biblical passage is one of breathtaking beauty and audacity: it elevates the whole of humanity to the royal dignity of God's representative in the government of creation. The surrounding religions conceived man in general as the gods' slave, condemned to toil and hardship. In their accounts, only the king was venerated as the national god's image whereas in the Bible, every man and every woman is created with great dignity, receives God's blessing and vocation, and is meant to be God's partner in a conversation full of peace and trust (cf. Schlag 2013, 50–62).

After man's sin, the Biblical God does not negate this great dignity but rather guides his people along a path of salvation, creating a chosen people and offering them a Covenant they can freely accept or reject (Ex 19:5–8). God respects our freedom; he does not force his commandments on us but gently persuades us to choose the path of life (Dt 30:15–16; Tabet 2005). Freedom, this important dimension of Christian humanism, and in particular of the Catholic tradition, is taken up by the message of the New Testament through the centrality it bestows on love, especially of the poor and underprivileged: One can love only in freedom.

The New Testament is the Good News about Jesus of Nazareth, the Christ of faith. Its texts proclaim a faith in the transforming power of God who has raised Jesus from the dead and placed him at his right hand. The most important message about man and Christian humanism in the New Testament is Jesus himself. In him, we understand God's original idea of human existence in love and holiness (Childs 1993, 579f). This is resplendent in the letters of St. Paul, who proclaims God's power in resurrecting Christ and restoring our dignity in Christ. Everything in Paul is about Christ, God's true image, in whom we have regained our filiation and our likeness with God. Anthropology and therefore Christian humanism are central for Paul (Dunn 1998, 53; Schlag 2013, 69–78).

The Fathers of the Church continued along this line, connecting the idea of man's creation in the image of God with the social principle of human dignity, an idea of fundamental importance in the societies of their time, as it is in ours. In so doing, they inverted the pyramid of honor in pagan society: dignity was no longer conquered by prowess in battle and through merits recognized by the Senate, but was rather granted to all by God, independently of the social standing of the person involved. Even slaves and the poor possessed the dignity of the children of God (See Tertullian 1954, 481; Theophilus of Antioch 2004, 2,18). Gregory of Nyssa argued that slavery was contrary to human dignity, and St. John Chrysostom passionately defended the poor because of their dignity. In his characteristic turn to interiority, Augustine of Hippo rethought the Trinity from the mode of spiritual cognisance thus introducing the notion of relationship into the idea of human dignity. His path to the knowledge of the Triune God departs from psychology, thus firmly placing man and woman, as equalling possessing a human soul, on the same natural level (Schlag 2013). The whole Tradition of the early Church clearly believed in the preeminence of human nature over that of the animals (Volp 2006). Based on these foundations, Christian humanism has flowed through the centuries like a stream, sometimes permeating culture vigorously, sometimes hidden in a subterranean bed.

Medieval Developments

Certain aspects of Christian humanism were obscured by the medieval confusion of spiritual and temporal power, and the Catholic Church regained its spiritual purity from involvement in temporal power only at the end of the nineteenth century (Balthasar 1989, 207–220). However, it should be recalled that during the Middle Ages, Scholastic teachers, especially Thomas Aquinas, maintained the spirit of the Fathers as regards the unity of nature and grace; this essential element for the formation of the Catholic concept of Christian secularity and humanism cannot be neglected. Divine grace, faith in God and religious life do not destroy or condemn our natural human and bodily inclinations as evil. To the contrary, they presuppose, heal, and elevate them (Aquinas 1999, I-II, q. 111). Divine commandments do not unhinge natural justice: what is just by human standards is also valid and binding in the realm of conscience and in the ecclesial sphere (Porter 2002, 284). Consequently, from this perspective, the Christian religion cannot be seen as a sort of privileged sphere exempted from earthly standards; instead, it respects and affirms inner-worldly affairs.

This unity began to disintegrate with the advent of the philosophical school of nominalism, particularly with the introduction of William of Ockham's conception of moral obligation. Ockham believed that it was contrary to God's almighty power to be limited by nature. The goodness of our human actions, he thought, could not stem from what we thought was appropriate to nature but from God's sovereign will alone. What God commanded was good, whatever it was. In other words, God did not command things because they were good, but because he demanded them they were good, even if it were murder, adultery or theft. What is good is therefore not to be known through man's nature and through the world he inhabits, but through God's will alone, manifested to us through revelation (see Pinckaers 1995, 241–253). Such an approach severs the intrinsic connection between faith and secular activities. It does not make the world evil, but the goodness of the world is not inherent. Moral goodness is conferred by God's will from outside, extrinsically, and afterwards.

This line of thought influenced the Protestant reformers who saw their position confirmed by the late works of St. Augustine, especially by his anti-Pelagian polemics which underscored the sinfulness of human nature. However, the Reformers also rediscovered the importance of daily life and of professional work as a Divine calling to a full Christian life. This is probably the Reformers' most important and lasting contribution to Christian humanism.

Overcoming Obstacles

Protestantism's affirmation of the common priesthood of all the baptized and its program of general improvement for all Christians led the Reformers to abolish the "hierarchy of complementarity" (Taylor 2007, 179–189). The concept of a "hierarchy of complementarity" expresses the idea that there were specific states with their own particular functions. This notion pervaded medieval feudal society: the knights defended everyone, the monks prayed and sanctified themselves for everyone, and the peasants worked for and fed everyone. These states mutually complemented one another, relating to each other in a vertical hierarchy. Protestantism, on the other hand, sought to eliminate the idea of a special state of perfection, i.e. the notion of certain Christians being somehow superior to others or having to follow higher standards of Christian life than others. For the Reformers, the necessity of eliminating this idea implied the need to destroy the ministerial priesthood and the religious orders.

The Council of Trent (1545–1563) reacted to such a claim by defending the ministerial priesthood and religious vocations. It was the holiness of her priests and religious, living in the world and ministering to the laity, but for whom the world was seen as a temptation, as an obstacle or at least a distraction from religious duties and tasks, which became the primary concern of the Church. In this manner, the role of the laity was allowed to fade into the background. The Christian laity and their activity in the world were considered to be the object of pastoral care of ordained ministers, not the subject or bearer of the Church's mission in the world. The formation of a Catholic concept of Christian humanism or inclusive secularity was obviously hindered by such an approach, an obstacle that the Church had to overcome at the Second Vatican Council.

The other obstacle in the process of forming a Catholic concept of Christian humanism was the comprehensible reaction of shock by the Church to the French Revolution. The humiliation, vexation and imprisonment of the Pope, the persecution and murder of priests, nuns and devout Catholics, and the confiscation of Church property by liberal revolutionaries instilled a deep resentment in the Church's magisterium against political and economic liberalism and against some of the important elements of modern society, such as democracy, popular sovereignty, and liberal human rights (Rhonheimer 2012, 134–185). In such historic circumstances, Traditionalism, yearning for the past union of Throne and Altar, seemed to be closer to the Catholic position. With its romantic backlash against enlightened rationalism, Traditionalism sought a return to medieval forms of economic life and organization. Such proposals, however, could hardly do justice to the needs of the emerging economic phenomena, addressing these phenomena with the instruments of ages past. Modern industry with its thousands of workers in one firm requires forms of organization different from those used by the much smaller units of production found in former times. For instance, even in its moments of glory and maximum expansion in the fifteenth century, the Medici bank had no more than sixty employees! (Roover 1974, 153).

Wisely, Leo XIII, undeceived by appearances, did not choose the Traditionalist version of social ethics. Instead, he based his social teaching on human nature, not on history. Human nature is not subject to the changes and circumstances of historical development but is surprisingly uniform throughout the ages. Thus it permits a metahistorical analysis, offering a foundation for ethics and law that places them above the contingencies of concrete and specific social organizations *hic et nunc*. Leo XIII's choice reflects his general revival of Thomism as official Church teaching, for natural law theory is an important element of Thomas's moral theology (cf. e.gr. Aquinas 1999, I-II, q. 94). By basing Catholic social teaching on human nature and formulating it in terms of natural law, Pope Leo XIII carefully avoided the two extremes of his time: both the Liberalism of the Enlightenment and of the French Revolution as well as the romantic reaction of Traditionalism. For the cause of Christian humanism, the Pope's positioning had clear advantages: it confirmed the centrality of the human person over any other consideration, either structural or historical. The human person, her essence and needs, form the starting point of all ethical reflection.

However, within time, the limits of the method of natural law in social teaching also became apparent. As the foundation of *individual* ethics, human nature is valid and useful. Throughout the centuries, the basic elements of individual nature have not changed: all human beings since the beginning of mankind have a body and a soul, they possess the same passions, strive for love and to be loved, they suffer illness and death, etc. The natural inclinations, which we bear in our being, do not essentially change; therefore, they can be used as permanent basis for ethical reflection. As regards *social organization*, however, such an endeavor becomes much more difficult, if not impossible. There are, of course, certain elements in our being that refer also to the common life: We are relational beings, hence we neither flourish nor develop our humanity outside of a community. However, on the political level, historical forms of social organization fluctuate heavily. States can be organized as monarchies, aristocracies, democracies, or as mixtures of these forms; governments can be centralized or decentralized, they can possess different degrees of power, etc. Applying the methodology of natural law to socio-ethical analysis can thus prove to be misleading. From what "nature of the State" or from which "nature of government" should social ethics be deduced? This does not mean that attempts at establishing social norms on a parallelism between "social" and natural bodies have not existed: as a natural human being has only *one* head, monarchism contended, thus a State as social body must possess one head; or, non-democratic corporatism deduced, as a living organism coordinates different organs for the wellbeing of the whole, thus the different elements of society must cooperate in an organic unity (Uertz 2005). Corporatism includes the opposing social forces (for instance, workers and owners) in one social body, forcing them to cooperate by renouncing their individual interests. Such a stance made it difficult to appreciate the liberal democratic constitutional model that accepts the existence of the antagonistic forces of individual interests but harnesses them to the achievement of the common good by a system of checks and balances. Moreover, using the deductive method in social ethics can obstruct the idea of the autonomy of earthly affairs, i.e. of the existence of social principles proper to the political, economic, and other spheres. Since the notion of deduction presupposes the knowledge of higher norms by which, through their application to circumstances, one can discover specific norms, only somebody who pretends to possess the whole of practical knowledge and wisdom can claim to be able to legislate on every aspect of social life. Catholic social teaching before Vatican II was not completely free of such an attitude: the laity had to seek all orientation of an ethical kind in the Church's Magisterium, the possibility of constructive dialogue and mutual enrichment between the Magisterium and the laity, as later established by the Pastoral Constitution *Gaudium et spes*, was excluded. Incompatible with the concept of true Christian secularity, such an attitude was also an obstacle for Christian humanism. In reality, it denies the possibility of Christian humanism itself since secularity as such and historical development and progress are not seen as bearers of ethical meaning in their own right. Rowland has characterized the general neoscholastic atmosphere before Vatican II as the attempt to maintain a truth without history. Certainly, this must also be understood as a reaction against the modernism that stressed history without truth (Rowland 2008, 2).

    In any case, the uneasiness with this state of theological affairs in the period before the Second Vatican Council coincided with the explicit use and forceful application of the expression "Christian humanism" by Jacques Maritain, a very influential Catholic thinker. The challenge posed by Marxist, or in general atheist, humanism, whether humanism can be Christian, was taken up by Maritain and inverted. The question is not whether Christianity enriches human life (this is presupposed and taken for granted by Maritain against Marxism and atheism), but whether "humanism" is a sufficient expression of the greatness of Christianity. As Maritain formulates it: Is a heroic humanism possible? Only if it *is* possible, can Christianity let itself be involved in a project of humanism. Humanism, generally speaking is what renders man more truly human, manifesting his original greatness by encouraging him to participate in everything in nature and in history that will enrich him. In fact, however, "humanist" periods seem to be opposed to heroic times. These periods ignore superhuman ideals, choosing human mediocrity, and, full of benevolence, propose as an ideal what all other people do. The Christian ideal, in contrast, consists in heroism or sanctity. These expressions seem to be incompatible. However, they are not, for if we do not transcend ourselves in the aspiration to heroism, we are not fully human (Maritain 1996, 153–156). The new Christian humanism, Maritain emphasized, would be a new form of secular sanctity in the world (Maritain 1996, 229–231).

In the era in which we live, Maritain's formulations are as acute as ever. In greater measure in Europe than in the United States, Christianity is denied recognition as an important source of cultural identity. The Preamble of the Treaty of Lisbon, for instance, when describing the inheritance from which Europe draws its inspiration, opposes humanism to religion. This has been denounced as an attempt of imposing the French version of *laicité* on the rest of Europe, regardless of the different cultural traditions therein (Weiler 2004).

Another important thinker, Henri de Lubac, although wary of the expression Christian humanism, responded in turn to the challenge of atheist humanism. He actually suggested dropping the "equivocal, perhaps in fact too weak, expression 'Christian humanism', or (…) reserv(ing) it for designating certain forms, certain more or less debatable successes offered us by history" (Lubac 1995, 400). Simultaneously, de Lubac underscored the great relevance of Christianity for man: the Gospel is good news for man. "Christianity does not deny man in order to affirm God. Nor does it seek a compromise between them" (Lubac 1995, 400). According to de Lubac, atheist humanism is essentially anti-human. The rejection of God means the annihilation of the human person (cf. Lubac 1995, 12). "It is not true, as is sometimes said, that man cannot organize the world without God. What is true is that, without God, he can ultimately only organize it against man. Exclusive humanism is inhuman humanism. (…) Thus faith in God, which nothing can tear from the heart of man, is the sole flame in which our hope, human and divine, is kept alive" (Lubac 1995, 14). De Lubac hence anticipated central ideas of what was to be the Pastoral Constitution *Gaudium et spes*: the theme of the centrality of Christ who fully reveals man to man and the belief in God without whom secularity would lose its transcendental foundation.

Leading up to the Second Vatican Council, there were also German speaking scholars who made use of the term that is the object of our study. Gustav Gundlach (see Rauscher 1988) did not use the expression "Christian humanism," but the analogous Latin concept "humanum", which he considered to be the foundation of society, when and insofar as humanism is founded on God and human conscience (Gundlach 1964, vol. 1, 420–424). This volume contains essays written over the course of 40 years, well before the Council. Otherwise, humanism falls ill. This conception clearly included the notion of transcendence.

In a manner more explicit than that of de Lubac, Johannes Messner applied the concept of Christian humanism to social ethics. Messner described the history of his time as the result of the struggle of collectivist socialism against individualist capitalism. As a way out of these "social heresies" (Messner 1964, 289), Messner proposed the Christian program of social reform. He was thus a representative of that tradition in Catholic social ethics, which understood itself as a "third path": the reasonable middle line between two extremes. Messner refers to Christian humanism as the most important philosophical foundation of this third path, which is defined by Christian social principles (Messner 1964, 333–336). He correctly points out that Christian humanism is a relatively new philosophical concept, originating from the Christian opposition against secular and especially Marxist humanism. Based on the Christian revelation, but not part of it, our concept was designed with the purpose of countering the social heresies. Unlike de Lubac, Messner does not seem to include the supernatural dimension in his understanding of Christian humanism: Christian revelation only strengthens our knowledge of the natural moral law and of natural religion, and thus gives us certainty about human dignity. "Christian humanism is the interpretation of human nature which is the basis of modern Christian social teaching and reform. On principle, it is known by human reason alone but reinforced by Revelation" (Messner 1964, 334). Oswald von Nell-Breuning, one of the most influential German social ethicists both before and after the Second Vatican Council, went yet another step further in removing the transcendent character of Christian humanism. He explicitly denied that Christian social teaching had any specifically Christian content. It was called Catholic merely because of its origin in the Magisterium of the Church or in the teaching of professors of theology (Nell-Breuning 1990, 156f).

Here Nell-Breuning seems to confirm an observation made by John Milbank on the difference between the French Nouvelle Théologie and the transcendental Thomism of Karl Rahner and the German school in general. Simplifying Milbank's analyses, this scholar says that the German theologians naturalize the supernatural; the French, on the contrary, supernaturalize the natural. The thrust of their theology is towards a recovery of a pre-modern sense of the Christianized person as the fully real person (Milbank 1998, 208). This, as I have tried to show, is the concept closest to the Fathers of the Church and Thomas Aquinas. Even though I cannot agree with Milbank's overall conception, especially his rejection of the existence of secular spheres as such, there is something important in his observation: Something specifically Christian does exist in social ethics. These specific elements are: charity, the virtues of the Sermon on the Mount, the exemplary moral function of Christ's death on the Cross and his victorious Resurrection from the ultimate human defeat, death. Not all of this can be expounded here. However, it is important to show that leading up to the Second Vatican Council, regarding Christian humanism, there was a tension between a supernatural, soteriological vision of human nature and a slightly different conception. This tension reemerged after the Council in the debates on liberation theology.

One other German theologian deserves to be specially mentioned: Joseph Höffner, whose textbook on Christian social ethics appeared in 1962 in its first edition. In it, Höffner expressed the tenets of Christian humanism in a balanced way, giving room both to the autonomy of the economic laws of free markets, and to the specific contribution of Christian Revelation (social theology) (Höffner 1997, 20–23). The binomial "Christian humanism" does not appear; however, the sum of his work manifests the conviction that Christ's message is not limited to seeking eternal bliss beyond this world. Very much to the contrary, the Christian faith aims at transforming society and the economy through Jesus' core teachings on justice and charity (see Nothelle-Wildfeuer 2010).

On a practical level, St. Josemaría Escrivá played an important role as spiritual leaven in the preparation of the Second Vatican Council, creating a pastoral institution, Opus Dei, that implanted Christian humanism in the hearts and lives of many Catholics. His teaching on the universal calling to holiness in the midst of the world, on the "professional vocation", and on the unity of religious and social life, to name a few, are important contributions to the formation of a Catholic concept of Christian humanism and secularity (cf. Burkhart and López 2010).

It was these abovementioned currents of thought as well as other elements, such as the influence of Pope John XXIII and authors like Pietro Pavan, that facilitated the theological fermentation leading up to the Second Vatican Council and the process of mutual rapprochement of Church and modernity that took place in the documents of this ecumenical Church assembly.

Christian Humanism at the Second Vatican Council

The Second Vatican Council was of paramount importance for Christian humanism. It overcame a certain tendency of self-exclusion of the Christian faith from the world through a "full immersion" of faith in secularity, without, however, accepting the privatization or the secularization of the Christian faith.

The humanism propounded by the Second Vatican Council is a Theo- and Christocentric humanism that includes God in the world as its Creator and fully inserts the world in the faith as a constitutional element of a Christian's calling to holiness through baptism. These teachings are expressed in several of the Council's documents, especially in the Constitutions *Lumen gentium*, On the Mystery of the Church, *Gaudium et spes*, On the Church in the Modern World, and the Declaration *Dignitatis humanae*, On the Right to Social and Civil Freedom in Matters Religious.

Lumen gentium proclaims the universal calling to holiness of all the baptized, including those who live and work in the world and in secular professions and married family life, in other words, the laity. The Council defines these latter as characterized by "their secular nature". It is worth citing the passage:

> the laity, by their very vocation, seek the kingdom of God by engaging in temporal affairs and by ordering them according to the plan of God. They live in the world, that is, in each and in all of the secular professions and occupations. They live in the ordinary circumstances of family and social life, from which the very web of their existence is woven. They are called there by God that by exercising their proper function and led by the spirit of the Gospel they may work for the sanctification of the world from within as a leaven. (LG, 31)

In other words, temporal affairs and their ordering through honest work are God's vocation for the laity. They are not only the circumstances in which their lives, willy-nilly, are situated, but the very matter in which their holiness consists. Ordained ministers are not the primary actors on the stage of life, but serve the entire People of God through the sacraments.

The title of *Gaudium et spes*, the Church in the Modern World, expresses the Council's intention of placing the message of Christ in the midst of the world, of society, and of all human activities. The Pastoral Constitution defines the relationship between faith and society as a pastoral program or challenge, in other words, as a cultural task of Christians in civil society. It is the Church's *magna charta* of Christian humanism: the Church is in the world and for the world, because "nothing genuinely human fails to raise an echo" (GS 1) in the hearts of Christ's disciples. Those laity which are well-educated and zealous are especially called to lift up their voices in defense of human dignity, to place care for the poor and the underprivileged at the center of the economy, to proclaim Christ and the faith in the public arena. *Gaudium et spes* explicitly denominates this endeavor to construct a better world in truth and justice as a "new humanism" (GS 55). The Church has discovered her place in the civil society, but she has not accepted and cannot accept the privatization or marginalization of faith since faith possesses a social and public dimension (cf. Casanova 1994). The Church acknowledges the differentiation of modern society into autonomous spheres of earthly affairs, but she is convinced that God, as Creator, is an intrinsic element of these affairs, which are thus not governed only by their inner logic and rationality but also by God's laws (GS 36). One modern understanding of the word "secular" is a sphere emptied of all theological referents. In Christian thought, creation never meant, and cannot mean, secular in this sense. Thus, sin is not a part of secularity. It distorts what is truly human and secular. *Gaudium et spes* therefore addresses Christians who engage these fields of human activity, on two different levels, which become apparent by the structure of the document itself: it expounds certain social *principles* in its first part, and their *application* to the varying historical and social circumstances in the second (GS, footnote 1). Throughout, *Gaudium et spes* opts for an attitude of dialogue between faith and the world. The exclusive stance of mere deduction of norms from higher principles of faith is abandoned in order that the Church might learn from the world, and not only teach it. However, so the Pastoral Constitution, in the light of Christian faith the Church is able to offer the world the unique service of orientation. By interpreting the facts of secular life as divine gifts, they receive their true meaning in a context of salvation.

The Declaration *Dignitatis humanae* proclaims the civic right of individuals and communities to religious freedom. It is a reflection and consequence of having chosen civil society as the Church's "habitat". It is not the State's task to decide on religious questions, and the government should therefore not interfere in these matters. However, the Declaration presupposes a positive attitude of the public authorities towards religion. Thus the Declaration on religious freedom is like the cornerstone of the Second Vatican Council's social teaching, maintaining and closing the span of the arch. Reaching from the individual Christian's baptismal calling to the social mission of the whole Church in civil society, the role of government as positively neutral had to be clarified. Without this clarification, the arch could not have borne its own weight: the laity have to be free to act according to their own well educated conscience, free from State interference, in order to play their role in civil society; and at the same time, the Church must fully accept this element of liberal constitutionalism, rooted in the tradition of early Christianity.

All that has been said so far about the Second Vatican Council is no more than a very cursory summary of some of its more salient points, understood to be of great importance for the modern Catholic concept of Christian humanism. The Council has made it clear that Christians must feel and act as what they are, citizens in this world, contributors to human progress, and constructors of society in its diverse social articulations (culture, family, economy, politics, international relations, etc.). Simultaneously, in the same line of logic, ordinary work and the human endeavors of earthly progress are not alien or indifferent to God. On the contrary, they are of great interest to the Kingdom of God (GS 39). In them we continue God's work of creation and redemption, spreading "justice, peace and joy in the Holy Spirit" (Rm 14:17) in all walks of life.

It has been noted that the texts of the Second Vatican Council were certainly written with great optimism, an optimism which in hindsight might not seem completely justified (Sander 2005). Hittinger, in fact, has pointed out that Catholic social teaching was not prepared for the possibility that the rule of law could also mean "state neutrality on the ontological grounds of rights", or even a prohibition against the state, under the pretext of rights-language, adopting an adequate anthropology. This makes comprehensible the attitude of Pope John Paul II who, in his encyclical *Evangelium vitae,* views the development of Western political reality as a history of "betrayal". Describing this history, the Pontiff speaks of "conspiracy", a poisoning of the culture of rights, and a violation of the principles of the constitution which were their boast (Hittinger 2007, 32).

However this may be, two things must be affirmed as regards our topic of Christian humanism:

1. The idea of Theo- and Christocentric humanism, so forcefully proposed by the Second Vatican Council, especially in its Pastoral Constitution, has not been abandoned by the Popes after the Council. On the contrary, it has become a continuous thread running throughout Papal enunciations. The positive references to Christian humanism remain as acute as ever, reflecting an unabated human need. Since the Second Vatican Council, the Catholic Church has taken an anthropological turn: the human being is the path of the Church, and Christ the redeemer and revealer of man.

2. From *Gaudium et spes* onwards, the term humanism is closely linked to the social concern for a just and charitable world. This receives its strongest affirmation in Pope Paul VI' encyclical *Populorum progressio*, On the Development of Peoples. Christian humanism includes social concern for the poor, the underprivileged, and the developing countries.

Leaving aside the criticism leveled against it from an economic point of view (affirmative: Nell-Breuning 1967; negative: Bauer 2009, 94–108), we can state that the encyclical *Populorum progressio* links Christian humanism with the concern for development in a manner that has continued to characterize social teaching. Published shortly after the end of the Second Vatican Council, the encyclical *Populorum progressio* can be seen as a kind of Papal interpretation of what *Gaudium et spes* meant by binding humanism to the notion of a better world: humanism is not merely earthly progress but directs man towards God through all of his actions. Citing Maritain and De Lubac, Pope Paul VI wrote:

> The ultimate goal (of the developing countries) is a full-bodied humanism. And does this not mean the fulfillment of the whole man and of every man? A narrow humanism, closed in on itself and not open to the values of the spirit and to God who is their source, could achieve apparent success, for man can set about organizing terrestrial realities without God. But 'closed off from God, they will end up being directed against man. A humanism closed off from other realities becomes inhuman.'
>
> True humanism points the way toward God and acknowledges the task to which we are called, the task which offers us the real meaning of human life. Man is not the ultimate measure of man; in fact, man becomes truly man only by transcending himself as Pascal affirmed: 'Man infinitely surpasses man.' (Paul VI 1967, n. 42)

The Modern Development of Christian Humanism in the Magisterium of the Catholic Church

Theologically speaking, the lasting contribution of Paul VI to Christian humanism is its identification with the vocation to an integral human development including transcendence and dedication to God. In this manner, Pope Paul VI endeavored to overcome "salvific individualism", an endeavor taken up by all successive Popes, and explicitly by Benedict XVI in the encyclical *Spe salvi*, where he again quotes De Lubac (Benedict XVI 2007b, n. 13) and by Pope Francis (Francis 2013, n. 89). This entails the double discovery of economic injustice as a problem and of love and humanity as a social principle. Little wonder that it was Pope Paul VI who created the expression "civilization of love" (Paul VI 1976, 709) to designate the true civilization to which we should aspire.

John Paul II followed in the footsteps of his predecessors, although it might be more adequate to say that due to his experience before and during the Second Vatican Council, Card. Wojtyla, the later St. Pope John Paul II, was already on the same wave-length as John XXIII and Paul VI.

Before the Second Vatican Council had even started, Card. Wojtyla had already made an important contribution to its later deliberations and to the thrust of its teaching. In his preliminary statement (such statements had been requested from all bishops and representatives of other Catholic institutions), Wojtyla suggested putting Christian humanism at the center of the Council's reflections. "At the end of 2,000 years of Christian history, the world had a question to put to the Church: What was Christian humanism and how was it different from the sundry other humanisms on offer in late modernity? What was the Church's answer to modernity's widespread 'despair (about) any and all human existence'?" (Weigel 1999, 159)

In fact, the Council took up this idea, which was in the general cultural air of the epoch, and made it the central theme of its texts. In the speech, with which he concluded the deliberations of the Council, Paul VI referred to the "horrible anticlerical" challenge posed by secular humanism. The Council, so the Pope said, had proposed "our own new type of humanism": a humanism that honors and serves humanity without divorcing man from God. To the contrary, "(…) a knowledge of God is a prerequisite for a knowledge of man as he really is, in all his fullness." The Council's anthropological turn becomes apparent in Pope Paul VI's conclusive words: "our humanism becomes Christianity, our Christianity becomes centered on God; in such sort that we may say, to put it differently: a knowledge of man is a prerequisite for a knowledge of God" (see Paul VI 1965). Some interpreted this anthropological turn in a radical, political way, thus reducing Christian humanism to an inner-worldly political program of liberation, as in some strands of the theology of liberation. In fact, one of the challenges to Christian humanism faced by Wojtyla immediately after his election as Pope was liberation theology, which at that time was heavily influencing Catholicism both in Latin America and in Europe. The new Pope John Paul II took the occasion of his first trip to Mexico in January 1979 to address this growing concern (Weigel 1999, 281–287). An application of the Second Vatican Council's Christian humanism to the social problems of the exploited and impoverished populations of Latin America, John Paul II's speeches announced the truth about the human being, made in God's image. Over and against the materialistic and atheistic reductions of Marxism, Christian humanism is the "foundation of the Church's social doctrine, in which men and women were not the victims of impersonal historical or economic forces but the artisans of society, economy, and politics" (Weigel 1999, 285). Due to its fundamentally flawed anthropology, true liberation cannot be found by means of Marxism. Rather, it is the salvation offered by Christ which makes possible a liberation wrought by "transforming, peacemaking, pardoning, and reconciling love" (Weigel 1999, 285). Like Paul VI before him, John Paul II linked Christian humanism with social concern. Like Paul VI, John Paul II also began his pontificate with a programmatic encyclical, the 1979 *Redemptor hominis*, The Redeemer of Man, in which he proclaimed Christian humanism as the foundational concept and guiding idea of his pontificate.

As Bishop of Rome, John Paul II incessantly repeated the central Christological passage of *Gaudium et spes* (inspired by Lubac 1988, 339f): "Christ, the final Adam, by the revelation of the mystery of the Father and His love, fully reveals man to man himself and makes his supreme calling clear" (GS 22). From his first encyclical to his last publication, John Paul II sees man and Christian humanism through the eyes of Christ. In 1979, he wrote:

> This, as has already been said, is why Christ the Redeemer 'fully reveals man to himself'. If we may use the expression, this is the human dimension of the mystery of the Redemption. In this dimension man finds again the greatness, dignity and value that belong to his humanity. In the mystery of the Redemption man becomes newly "expressed" and, in a way, is

newly created. He is newly created! 'There is neither Jew nor Greek, there is neither slave nor free, there is neither male nor female; for you are all one in Christ Jesus' (Gal 3:28). The man who wishes to understand himself thoroughly-and not just in accordance with immedi-ate, partial, often superficial, and even illusory standards and measures of his being-he must with his unrest, uncertainty and even his weakness and sinfulness, with his life and death, draw near to Christ. He must, so to speak, enter into him with all his own self, he must "appropriate" and assimilate the whole of the reality of the Incarnation and Redemption in order to find himself. (John Paul II 1979, n. 10)

In 2005, the year of his death, John Paul II summed up his life's experience in these words: "Christ alone, through his humanity, reveals the totality of the mystery of man. (…) The primary and definitive source for studying the intimate nature of the human being is therefore the Most Holy Trinity" (John Paul II 2005, 125). "The dignity proper to man (…) is based not simply on human nature, but even more on the fact that, in Jesus Christ, God truly became man" (John Paul II 2005, 126). The anthropological revolution was therefore Christological in character (John Paul II 2005, 127).

That Christian humanism was the driving theme of his pontificate was not only palpable in Catholic social teaching, as has already been said, but also in John Paul II's emphasis on the anthropological dimension and meaning of Christian revela-tion: "Christian humanism, which reflected the permanent truths built into human nature, could speak to the turmoil in the human heart that atheistic humanism had created" (Weigel 1999, 614). The implications of Christian humanism could there-fore be unfolded in the manifold aspects of human existence where human dignity is always at stake or affected: the family, culture, the economy, politics, religion, etc. John Paul II was especially sensitive to the different cultures that shape nations. Peoples have a right to their culture in order to become a nation. This right is a ques-tion of the "humanistic perspective of man's development" (John Paul II 2005, 96).

With this understanding, Christian humanism is capable of welcoming the secu-lar world as the space where Christian life unfolds and as the matter in which its holiness consists. Christians are called to affirm all earthly realities that are worthy, even though they may seem exteriorly unconnected with sacral or religious mean-ing. However, Christian humanism possesses a cleansing, purgative side as well. I intentionally repeat, that sin is not a constitutive element of secularity; on the con-trary, it destroys the original goodness of the world. During John Paul II's lengthy pontificate, the somber shadows of sin in Western civilization became increasingly apparent: the killing of innocent human beings at the beginning and the end of life, the disintegration of marriage as an indissoluble covenant between one man and one woman, economic injustice in the intentional exclusion and exploitation of entire portions of the human family, unabating wars and bloodshed in all parts of the globe, and, especially in the Western world, a general lack of hope and spiritual tiredness, which we could call a collective acedia. Against these "new barbarisms set loose in the world by absolutized fragments of truth," (Weigel 1999, 863) John Paul II preached Christian humanism, a teaching about the whole man that satisfies his yearning for the absolute, found in God alone. As an answer to the cultural situ-ation of Western civilization John Paul II proposed a "new evangelization," a pro-gram of cultural transformation (cf. George 2009, 20–23). As culture is the sum of all the elements that shape social life, and man's life is to a great extent social and related to others, transforming culture means accepting what is good in it and cleansing it of its evil, demonic aspects through arguments and the positive example of one's own life. Here again Christian humanism is immediately engaged: what does the Christian faith have to say to the manifold problems afflicting mankind? How does the Church, as Christ's lasting presence on earth, contribute to overcoming them?

John Paul II therefore encouraged the publication of The *Compendium of the Social Doctrine of the Church* (Pontifical Council of Justice and Peace 2005), which summarizes the social encyclicals and other social teachings of the Catholic Church. It makes humanism central, by affirming that the Compendium proposes *"to all men and women a humanism that is up to the standards of God's plan of love in history, an integral and solidary humanism* capable of creating a new social, economic and political order, founded on the dignity and freedom of every human person, to be brought about in peace, justice and solidarity" (n. 1999, emphasis in the original).

Pope Benedict XVI was also fully aware of these challenges and felt committed to developing the Christian humanism so forcefully promoted by his predecessor. However, he used the *term* sparingly and usually quoting from his predecessors. His most characteristic contribution to the *notion and concept* of Christian humanism was indirect, consisting in his continual insistence upon the unity of faith and reason. Atheist or secular humanism considers Christianity to be incapable of producing any real form of humanism, either because Christian faith is thought to alienate man from humanity or because the Christian moral demands are accused of being unrealistic. Thus, belief is understood to be irrational, or worse, a humiliation of man. In response, Benedict XVI points out that biblical faith is a "profound encounter of faith and reason", "an encounter between genuine enlightenment and religion." Faith helps to positively overcome "the self-imposed limitation of reason to the empirically falsifiable", with the dangers of manipulation implied therein, most notably the fact that scientific knowledge without ethics can turn against man himself. Humanism needs an openness towards faith in order to broaden the concept of reason and its application (Benedict XVI 2006). Although this does not imply that a person without faith necessarily has a limited concept of reason, it does mean that an intellectual position, which positively and *a priori* excludes the possibility of transcendence, is lacking in an anthropological sense. With this confidence in the intellect, the first Christian apologists turned to those currents of pagan philosophy open to transcendence in order to explain Christian faith and did not hesitate to use their findings and concepts. However, it should be noted that they did not turn to pagan religion, nor did they strive to impose a revealed religious law on society. "Instead, (Christian faith) has pointed to nature and reason as the true sources of law – and to the harmony of objective and subjective reason, which naturally presupposes that both spheres are rooted in the creative reason of God" (Benedict XVI 2011). This recurrent idea of Pope Benedict XVI when dealing with the topic of politics asserts the need of reason for faith in order to avoid distortions through ideologies and utopia; faith needs reason as well, in order to avoid falsification through fundamentalism and incommunicability. It is a two-way process. Within this relationship, Christian faith does not propose specific technical solutions, even less does it aspire to power. Rather, as Pope Benedict XVI suggested, "that the world of reason and the world of faith – the world of secular rationality and the world of religious belief – need one another and should not be afraid to enter into a profound and ongoing dialogue, for the good of our civilization" (Benedict XVI 2010). Specifically within his encyclical *Deus caritas est*, Benedict XVI referred to this service of faith to political and social reason as an "indirect duty" that consists in contributing "to the purification of reason and to the reawakening of those moral forces without which just structures are neither established nor prove effective in the long run" (Benedict XVI 2005, n. 29).

That Benedict XVI linked these considerations with the notion of Christian humanism becomes apparent in his last encyclical, the social encyclical *Caritas in veritate*. Therein we encounter the same desire to unite faith and reason in the economic and social spheres at the service of integral human development. Without God's help, we are unable to bring about progress and authentic integral humanism. "The greatest service to development, then, is a Christian humanism that enkindles charity and takes its lead from truth, accepting both as a lasting gift from God" (Benedict XVI 2009, n. 78). In the line of his predecessors since the Second Vatican Council, Benedict XVI re-proposed Christian humanism as the solution for the different crises that are rocking our economies: the "ideological rejection of God and an atheism of indifference, oblivious to the Creator and at risk of becoming equally oblivious to human values, constitute some of the chief obstacles to development today. A humanism, which excludes God is an inhuman humanism. Only a humanism open to the Absolute can guide us in the promotion and building of forms of social and civic life — structures, institutions, culture and ethos — without exposing us to the risk of becoming ensnared by the fashions of the moment" (Benedict XVI 2009, n. 78; cf. also Benedict XVI 2007a).

This formulation of Pope Benedict XVI's social teaching addresses the needs of the "new evangelization" as a program of cultural transformation. It underscores the contribution of the Christian faith to the search for discovering what is good and true in society and for mankind. His encyclicals, furthermore, two of his three encyclicals dealing with aspects of this divine virtue, visibly posit the main accent on charity. Christian charity has been and is the most convincing argument for Christian humanism. Only love is credible, only love can move hearts, and for this reason, Christian charity will be the decisive argument in the program of cultural transformation that the new evangelization requires. Pope Francis is putting this program into practice, more through gestures and deeds than words. Despite the apparent differences in style, there is a deep continuity between Benedict XVI and his successor Francis in their emphasis on the centrality of charity. Both affirm that charity is the beginning and source of Christian culture and humanism. Charity is the central element of Christian moral teaching, which is not confined to charitable relationships among individuals. The social dimension is essential to it: Christian faith, morality, and charity unfold and crystallize in culture. Charity, however, becomes distinctively Christian through its preferential option for the poor and marginalized. Jesus was very clear in saying that we do nothing different from Pagans if we love only the rich and wealthy. On this view, Pope Francis' appeal for a "poor church for the poor" is a central – and very attractive – element of Christian humanism and of the transformation of culture through evangelization.

References

Aquinas, Thomas. 1999. *Summa Theologiae*, (Cinisello Balsamo: San Paolo, 1999, third edition). In English, *The Summa Theologica*. 2nd, rev. ed. 22 vols., trans. by the Fathers of the English Dominican Province, (London: Burns, Oates & Washbourne, 1912–36). Reprint in 5 vols., (Westminster, MD: Christian Classics, 1981).

Balthasar, Hans Urs von. 1989. *Der antirömische Affekt*. Einsiedeln/Trier: Johannes Verlag.

Bauer, Peter. 2009. *From subsistence to exchange and other essays*. Princeton: Princeton University Press.

Benedict XVI. 2005. Encyclical *Deus caritas est*. Acta Apostolicae Sedis 98(2006): 217–252.

Benedict XVI. 2006. Lecture at the University of Regensburg September 12th, 2006. *Acta Apostolicae Sedis* 98(2006): 728–739.

Benedict XVI. 2007a. Address to the participants in the First European Meeting of University lecturers June 23, 2007. *Acta Apostolicae Sedis* 99(2007): 704–707.

Benedict XVI. 2007b. Encyclical *Spe salvi* on Christian Hope. *Acta Apostolicae Sedis* 99(2007): 985–1027.

Benedict XVI. 2009. Encyclical *Caritas in veritate*. *Acta Apostolicae Sedis* 101(2009): 641–709.

Benedict XVI. 2010. Address at Westminster Hall September 17th, 2010. *Acta Apostolicae Sedis* 102(2010): 635–639.

Benedict XVI. 2011. Speech at the German Parliament September 22nd, 2011. *Acta Apostolicae Sedis* 103(2011): 663–668.

Burkhart, Ernst, and Javier López. 2010. *Vida cotidiana y santidad en la enseñanza de San Josemaría*, Estudio de teología espiritual, vol. 1. Madrid: Rialp.

Calhoun, Craig, Mark Juergensmeyer, and Jonathan Van Antwerpen. 2011. *Rethinking secularism*. Oxford: Oxford University Press.

Casanova, José. 1994. *Public religions in the Modern World*. Chicago/London: The University of Chicago Press.

Childs, Brevard S. 1993. *Biblical theology of the old and new testaments. Theological reflection on the Christian Bible*. Minneapolis: Fortress Press.

Dunn, James D.G. 1998. *The theology of Paul the Apostle*. Grand Rapids/Cambridge: William B. Eerdmans.

Etzioni, Amitai. 2006. *The new golden rule. Community and morality in a democratic society*. New York: HarperCollins.

Ferguson, Niall. 2011. *Civilization: the west and the rest*. London/New York: Allen Lane.

Francis, Pope. 2013. Apostolic exhortation *Evangelii Gaudium*. Acta Apostolicae Sedis 105(2013): 1019–1137.

Franklin, R. William, and Joseph M. Shaw. 1991. *The case for Christian Humanism*. Grand Rapids: William B. Eerdmans.

George, Francis. 2009. *The difference God makes. A Catholic vision of faith, communion, and culture*. New York: The Crossroad Publishing Company.

Gundlach, Gustav. 1964. *Die Ordnung der menschlichen Gesellschaft*, hrsg von der Katholischen Sozialwissenschaftlichen Zentralstelle Mönchengladbach, 2 Vols. Köln: Bachem.

Habermas, Jürgen. 2011. "The political": The rational meaning of a questionable inheritance of political theology. In *The power of religion in the public sphere*, ed. Eduardo Mendieta and Jonathan Van Antwerpen, 15–33. New York: Columbia University Press.

Habermas, Jürgen, and Joseph Ratzinger. 2006. *The dialectics of secularization. On reason and religion*. San Francisco: Ignatius Press.

Hittinger, Russell. 2007. Introduction to modern Catholicism. In *The teachings of modern Roman Catholicism on law, politics, and human nature*, ed. John Witte Jr. and Frank S. Alexander, 1–38. New York: Columbia University Press.

Höffner, Joseph. 1997. *Christliche Gesellschaftslehre*, ed. Lothar Roos. Kevelaer: Butzon & Bercker (first edition 1962).

John Paul II. 1979. Encyclical *Redemptor hominis. Acta Apostolicae Sedis* 71: 257–324.

John Paul II. 2005. *Memory and identity. Personal reflections*. London: Weidenfeld & Nicolson.

Lubac, Henri, de. 1988. *Catholicism. Christ and the common destiny of man*. San Francisco: Ignatius Press.

Lubac, Henri, de. 1995. *The drama of atheist humanism*. San Francisco: Ignatius Press (original Le Drame de l'humanisme athée, Paris 1944).

Maritain, Jacques. 1996. *Integral humanism, freedom in the modern world, and a letter on independence*, ed. Bird Otto. Notre Dame: University of Notre Dame Press (Originally published in 1936).

Messner, Johannes. 1964. In *Die Soziale Frage im Blickfeld der Irrwege von gestern*, ed. der Sozialkämpfe von heute und der Weltentscheidungen von morgen, Innsbruck/Wien/München: Tyrolia (7th edition; first edition 1928).

Milbank, John. 1998. *Theology and social theory. Beyond secular reason*. Oxford: Blackwell (first published 1990).

Nell-Breuning, Oswald von. 1967. *Einleitung zur Enzyklika "Populorum progressio" über die Entwicklung der Völker*, 7–14. Trier: Paulinus – Verlag.

Nell-Breuning, Oswald von. 1990. In *Den Kapitalismus umbiegen. Schriften zu Kirche, Wirtschaft und Gesellschaft. Ein Lesebuch*, ed. Friedhelm Hengsbach. Düsseldorf: Patmos.

Nothelle-Wildfeuer, Ursula. 2010. Das sozialethische Anliegen von Joseph Höffner – zehn Thesen. In *Freiburger Schule und Christliche Gesellschaftslehre*, ed. Nils Goldschmidt and Ursula Nothelle-Wildfeuer, 1–22. Tübingen: Mohr Siebeck.

Paul VI. 1965. *Address during the last general meeting of the second Vatican Council*, 7 Dec 1965. http://www.vatican.va/holy_father/paul_vi/speeches/1965/documents/hf_p-vi_spe_19651207_epilogo-concilio_en.html

Paul VI. 1967. Encyclical *Populorum progressio on the development of peoples. Acta Apostolicae Sedis* 59: 257–299.

Paul VI. 1976. Message world day for peace 1977. *Acta Apostolicae Sedis* 68: 707–714.

Pinckaers, Servais. 1995. *The sources of Christian ethics*. Washington, DC: Catholic University of America Press.

Pontifical Council of Justice and Peace. 2005. *Compendium of the social doctrine of the Church*. Vatican: Libreria Editrice Vaticana.

Porter, Jean. 2002. The virtue of justice (IIa IIae, qq. 58–122). In *The ethics of Aquinas*, ed. Stephen J. Pope, 272–286. Washington, DC: Georgetown University Press.

Rauscher, Anton (ed.). 1988. *Gustav Gundlach 1892–1963*. Paderborn: Schöningh.

Rhonheimer, Martin. 2012. *Christentum und säkularer Staat*. Herder: Geschichte/Gegenwart/Zukunft. Freiburg/Basel/Wien.

Rowland, Tracey. 2008. *Ratzinger's faith. The theology of Pope Benedict XVI*. Oxford: Oxford University Press.

Roover, Raymond de. 1974. The development of accounting prior to Luca Pacioli according to the account books of medieval merchants. In *Business, banking, and economic thought in late medieval and early modern Europe*, ed. Julius Kirshner, 119–181. Chicago/London: The University of Chicago Press.

Sander, Hans-Joachim. 2005. Theologischer Kommentar zur Pastoralkonstitution über die Kirche in der Welt von heute. In *Herders Theologischer Kommentar zum Zweiten Vatikanischen Konzil*, ed. Peter Hünermann and Bernd Jochen Hilberath, 581–886. Freiburg/Basel/Wien: Herder.

Schlag, Martin. 2013. *La dignità dell'uomo come principio sociale. Il contributo della fede cristiana allo Stato secolare*. Rome: edusc.

Scruton, Roger. 2007. *Culture counts. Faith and feeling in a world besieged*. New York: Encounter Books.

Shaw, Joseph M., R.W. Franklin, Harris Kaasa, and Charles W. Buzicky (eds.). 1982. *Readings in Christian humanism*. Minneapolis: Augsburg.

Tabet, Miguelangel. 2005. Fondamenti di un'etica politica alla luce di Lv 19. In *Teologia ed etica politica*, ed. Ángel Rodriguez Luño and Enrique Colom, 115–134. Vatican: Libreria Editrice Vaticana.

Taylor, Charles. 2007. *A secular age*. Cambridge, MA/London: Harvard University Press.

Tertullian. 1954. *Adversus marcionem*, Corpus Christianorum Series Latina, vol. 1, 441–720. Turnhout: Brepols. (Originally 3rd century)

Theophilus of Antioch. 2004. *A Autólico*, edited by J.P. Martin, Fuentes Patrísticas 16, Greek and Spanish, Madrid: Ciudad Nueva. (Originally 2nd century)

Uertz, Rudolf. 2005. *Vom Gottesrecht zum Menschenrecht. Das katholische Staatsdenken in Deutschland von der Französischen Revolution bis zum II. Vatikanischen Konzil (1789–1965)*. Paderborn: Schöningh.

Volp, Ulrich. 2006. *Die Würde des Menschen. Ein Beitrag zur Anthropologie in der Alten Kirche*, "Supplements to Vigiliae Christianae", Leiden-Boston: Brill.

Weigel, George. 1999. *Witness of hope. The biography of Pope John Paul II*. New York: HarperCollins.

Weiler, Joseph H.H. 2004. *Ein Christliches Europa. Erkundungsgänge*. Anton Pustet: Salzburg/München.

Chapter 3
Christian Humanism in the Context of Contemporary Culture

Luis Romera

Abstract Christian Humanism has a long tradition in the Catholic thought. However, a significant number of academics and fellow citizens would either appear perplexed or bluntly confess that they do not understand such a term. Such a response would warn us that this point of view is considered alien to contemporary sensibilities. In order to gain a comprehension of "Christian Humanism" in general, and Catholic humanism in particular, this article will examine the concept within contemporary culture in two stages. First, it will analyze the two cultural trends determining the fundamental attitudes of the current society. Second, following upon such an exercise, it will examine the meaning of humanism, in order to indicate the ultimate reasons for which the humanism of our time needs Christianity.

Keywords Contemporary culture • Cultural trends • Christianity • Christian humanism • Humanism

Pausing to reflect upon the meaning of Christian Humanism within the context of this book presupposes that both the immediate comprehension of such a term as well as its social and economic application cannot be taken for granted. Moreover, I believe that it would not be strange if, faced with the question concerning the relevance of an approach to personal life and life in society from the perspective of Christian Humanism, a not insignificant number of our colleagues and fellow citizens would either appear perplexed or bluntly confess that they do not understand such a term. Their response would warn us that this point of view is considered alien to contemporary sensibilities. In order to gain a comprehension of the term, "Christian Humanism," and to consider whether it has a meaning and is justified as a framework to inspire and influence economic action and business conduct, one of the best and most certain strategies would be to direct our attention to Benedict XVI's encyclical, *Caritas in veritate* (2009) Nevertheless, rather than turning to

L. Romera (✉)
Pontifical University of the Holy Cross, Rome, Italy
e-mail: romera@pusc.it

© Springer Science+Business Media Dordrecht 2015
D. Melé, M. Schlag (eds.), *Humanism in Economics and Business*,
Issues in Business Ethics 43, DOI 10.1007/978-94-017-9704-7_3

33

such a document of undoubted scope and intellectual rigor, I propose taking a step back and limiting this discussion to addressing some of the presuppositions that will allow us access to a comprehension of Christian Humanism in the context of the contemporary culture. Such a passage will allow us to highlight its relevance and focus upon the arguments for its justification. I will attempt this undertaking in two stages. In the first stage, we will analyze the two cultural trends determining the fundamental attitudes of the current society. In the second, following upon such an exercise, we will examine the meaning of humanism, in order to indicate the ultimate reasons for which the humanism of our time needs Christianity.

As a final remark, I should note that this chapter is aimed at sketching a conceptual framework within which we can develop those reflections of a practical nature presented within the other chapters of this book. For this reason, the discussion is concerned only with a general panorama, leaving to other colleagues those considerations that deal specifically with economics and business.

Humanism and Contemporary Society

Why is it necessary to revisit the question of humanism? At first sight, one could object that, all things considered, Western societies are constantly, although perhaps implicitly, referring to an inherited humanism, which gives meaning to the basic attitudes and social praxis that govern everyday life. The great cultural battles of modernity, that have forged our mentality and configured our society, are the fruit of certain claims, justified by human rights. Fundamentally, these battles consisted in the demand for rights, that is, in something that is due to the human being because of his inviolable dignity. In the end, the claims to personal liberty in social and political environments, with the right to think for oneself, to express one's own ideas, of association, to vote and thus to participate in government, to own property and to take on productive and commercial initiatives; the claims to social justice, to education, to a minimum salary that avoids the conditions of poverty, of access to indispensable medical care, the guarantee of an old age without embarrassment; the claims to equality in order to participate in social dynamics and to enter into the working world, etc., specify the unconditional right to the recognition of personal dignity that each human being deserves, and that falls to each human being, inasmuch as he is human.

As Taylor (2004) has highlighted, social praxis are made possible by an implicit common understanding of society that allows one to assume attitudes and behaviors for everyday life according to meaningful criteria. He has named this common understanding of society, "social imaginaries". Social imaginaries are inherited concepts, received through different medium, by which the culture found in society is transmitted and re-elaborated in dialogue with one's peers; they shape that horizon in which we freely and rationally move. In Taylor's opinion, the current society is characterized by three social forms consolidated and sustained by means of concepts elaborated during modernity: the market economy, popular sovereignty and the public sphere. The latter, the public sphere, is that space to which all citizens have access and in which the opinions that dictate the criteria of legitimacy for social life are rationally – at least in principle - shaped through dialogue.

Modernity constitutes a historical period of enormous social transformations, which have decisively influenced the novel conception of that state that has arisen and been consolidated: urbanization, geographical discoveries, the development of the sciences, technological advancements, the market economy, the industrial revolutions, the progressive generalization of information, and in these last decades, the computer. A culture that places the subject at the center underlies and is simultaneously configured by the complex intertwining of these phenomena. At its roots, modernity possesses an overwhelming interest for the human being, precisely because it considers him irreducible to the rest of the realities that populate our world. Man is gifted with intelligence and liberty, with an interior world constituted by ideas, ambitions, decisions, feelings, projects and hopes, disappointments and corrections, which make him irreducible to objectivity – to something that can be thoroughly understood by scientific observation – and that distinguish him from the "merely natural," as studied by physics, chemistry, and biology. Over and above mathematical formulations derived from empirical observations and the determinisms that modern science identifies in nature, the human being presents himself as one who rationally investigates and who freely plays the protagonist of his own life. The identity of each man and each woman does not come from an ecological and social context that precedes them. Although this context plays an important role in life, the person is generated by his own ideas, his liberty, the relationships that he establishes on his own. The human being is always an "I" capable of expressing himself, of directing himself explicitly to a "you", of creating and of introducing in the course of time those intentional novelties that shape culture and constitute history.

The understanding of the human being consolidated throughout modernity demonstrates explicit classical and Christian roots. Upon this basis, core elements of modern anthropologies have been developed that lead to a conception of man in which his particular dignity is realized; from this point, the declarations of human rights have been elaborated. The modern conception of man leads to sanctioning his inalienable and irreplaceable protagonism in regard to his own life, in virtue of his reason and liberty. On the one hand, the dignity of the person entails the affirmation of the initiative of each person in his own life, that the decisive element of individual identity does not arise from the social structure in which one is found or from certain personal qualities, but from the person's ideas and actions: in a word, his liberty. On the other hand, the dignity of the human person requires a conception of society that guarantees the sovereignty of each and every citizen, allowing them to determine the direction of society.

Modernity and the Project of Emancipation

Hence, modern humanism, in the first place, recognizes that the human being is irreducible; in the second place, it situates this irreducible element in his rationality, liberty, and interiority (that which is called *subjectivity*); and, in the third place, it concludes with the affirmation of his dignity, from which it obtains a series of social consequences with political and economic implications. It is clear that we must add another aspect: the modern focus of humanism opts progressively for that perspective which characterized the Enlightenment. An analysis of this point would require a historical, conceptually detailed tour, upon which we cannot embark. Briefly put, the comprehension of subjectivity moves from a conception in which interiority – reason, liberty, intimacy – speaks in itself of an immanence open to transcendence, to an approach in which subjectivity is understood in the light of a project of emancipation. I will try to explain this idea synthetically.

The human being bespeaks immanence, because he is self-conscious and decides about himself. His reason, his liberty, his interior world speak to us of a being that possesses self-consciousness and self-determination, a being that refers to himself, with an interior life, that is configured in its intimacy: immanence. However, he is a being whose immanence opens constitutively to that which transcends him. For this reason, he is capable of innovative work, of developing culture and of developing himself, of directing himself to a "you," and of establishing personal relationships. Interpersonal relationships – intersubjectivity – require immanence and transcendence: only an "I" conscious of himself and who decides about himself – open to himself –is capable of directing himself to another subject – of opening himself to otherness – and of establishing authentic personal relationships, in the measure in which they include the recognition of the other and of liberty. Understanding man by means of the immanent-transcendent binomial brings us to two conclusions. In the first place, it must be accepted that the human being cannot realize himself if he is not open to relationships with others; in other words, that individualism leads to a human being diminished in his humanity, or that ego-centrism or mere self-reference is far from guaranteeing and encouraging the formation of one's identity. They rather imply self-alienation (Spaemann 2006). In second place, there is the realization that the human being, in his irreducibility, through his constitution and, more specifically, through his teleological orientation, refers to the Transcendent.

The project of emancipation characteristic of the Enlightenment approaches, on the contrary, interprets the irreducible element of man in terms of self-sufficiency, at least as a claim and as an ideal, so that immanence is overwhelmingly understood as self-referentiality. The dignity of the human being entails, from this perspective, the necessity of a sovereignty exempt from any dependence, whether it is manifested in the rational sphere or that of liberty. Emancipation signifies not only the eradication of those things that restrict liberty but also the overcoming of any connection, necessity, or insufficiency. In regard to reason, the project of emancipation is the pretension to intellectually assume only those ideas that present themselves as transparent – clearly and distinctly – to reason, ideas that impose themselves by means of immediate evidence in a naturally intuitive intellectual act or that can be deduced from an incontrovertible principle. This kind of reason assumes the Kantian lemma *sapere aude* (meaning "dare to be wise", or more precisely "dare to know") in the perspective of a "critical reason," emancipated from that which is considered extraneous, for example, faith or tradition. As is logical, the consequent interpretation of faith and tradition in this approach, as alien or at least extrinsic to reason, presupposes an idea of intelligence that the twentieth century has revealed to be inconsistent.

The critical reason of the Enlightenment is self-limiting, in the measure in which it is uniquely restricted to an exercise of a series of intellectual acts, discarding others that, in different circumstances, we understand as fixed values. At the margin of mathematics, the human being must confront such intellectual acts constantly with ideas, concepts, judgments, values – indispensable in the working world, in relationships with others, in regard to personal dilemmas of liberty, etc. – that are not presented as diaphanous notions, but as concepts which must be studied in depth. These are ideas that we have received from the tradition that precedes us, from a culture that supplies a conceptual baggage with which we arrive in the world and that we actively assume, in a certain critical manner. However, such an idea of "critical" signifies acts of discernment by means of reflection, dialogue, personal experience, and not the utopian pretension to dispense with all that does not originate from an individualist and exiled reason, that begins with oneself and accepts exclusively that which one has deductively constructed. Modern critical reason has passed through different stages and is expressed by different figures or paradigms: rationalist reason, empiricist reason, Kantian transcendental reason, idealist reason, historical reason. The intrinsic dynamism of Enlightenment reason – that which has been denominated *the dialectic of Enlightenment* – has generated within itself a disposition of suspicion that will end by turning against its own constructions (Horkheimer and Adorno 2002). For this reason, modernity has been conducive to thought such as that of Nietzsche and Heidegger and concludes with the typical postmodern deconstructivist attitude. From the claim of certainty and totality in the context of a reason that seeks to provide for its own foundations, we pass to skepticism of the concepts that modern reason has elaborated. Postmodernity criticizes the modern pretension to reach an absolute truth in an absolute, or infallible, manner, or, in other words, to construct, by means of ideas, a rational system that contains all of truth in a complete and transparent mode. This modern pretension has revealed itself to be utopic: the finite reason of the human being – with his fragility, his historical context, his dependencies – is incapable of making an absolute truth in an absolute manner. When it attempts to do so, the human being easily creates an ideology; and an ideology consists, in the end, in an absolutized unilateral vision. The social application of ideologies, precisely because they stem from a partial concept of man and of society judged to be absolute and exhaustive, has created political regimes whose violence have ripped apart the history of the last century. The critique of these ideologies, per se necessary, leads us to a fork in the road: either we overcome these ideologies in the measure in which intelligence opens unto a less-restricted vision of man, or we radicalize its attitude of emancipated-critique, concluding with an, at times, cynical skepticism. Postmodernity has been overwhelmingly oriented towards the second possibility.

Consequently, emancipation is finally directed towards a modality of reason that in place of constructing ideas, de-constructs concepts: it dismantles and unmasks the hidden presuppositions (that it usually interprets as paradoxes) upon which these concepts have been built, in order to deprive them of the force of conviction and of value. Postmodernity rejects the "great narratives" of metaphysics or of any ethics that does not limit itself to guaranteeing the procedures of dialogue, but rather aspires to present binding content.

Postmodern Culture

What is the result? A culture suspicious in regard to the possibilities of reason leads to a scientific-technical exercise of intelligence, in which the modality of reason that makes social consensus possible and that is subject to being accepted in terms of truth and falsehood, where these words signify, "rationally acceptable or not," follows the protocol of justification that society or the scientific circles establish. In other words, throughout modernity there has been a progressive reduction of intelligence to its scientific exercise – which is always partial in the measure in which it adheres methodologically to physics or biology or psychology – and to instrumental reason, which focuses upon identifying the means in order to reach, efficaciously and efficiently, its established objectives, while ignoring an enunciation of the ends. Even today there remains a tendency, in the programs of formation for the different faculties and schools, to concede a preeminence, which in some cases becomes hegemony, to instrumental reason. The analyses necessary for decision-making and the evaluation of results, however, are rather the task of practical reason. Obviously, instrumental and technical reason is necessary for the action and progress of humanity; the problem occurs when such reasoning becomes exclusive.

The link between positivism and a positivist vision of the nature is evident. Scientific reason permits us to acquire knowledge whose valor is indubitable; nevertheless, to consider it as the only modality of rationality intellectually reliable entails a threat to humanism. Thus, the observation of Benedict XVI: "Where positivist reason considers itself the only sufficient culture and banishes all other cultural realities to the status of subcultures, it diminishes man, indeed it threatens his humanity" (\Benedict XVI 2011). The domination of instrumental reason is the first phenomenon that I wanted to address. The second concerns the comprehension of liberty pulsating throughout various contemporary attitudes, called more or less accurately postmodern.

In my opinion, postmodernity is situated in an ambivalent or dialectic mode in respect to modernity. On the one hand, it recognizes its debt to modern ideals; on the other hand, it criticizes them. Concretely, it rejects the modern pretension to achieve truth; however, it assumes the project of emancipation. This duality in regard to modernity entails the claim for a liberty without "external" bonds, self-sufficient in its order and autonomous. The term, "auto-nomos" indicates that it is a law unto itself. However, if practical reason is reduced to the instrumental, instead of *recognizing* its own normativity, it *decides* upon a normativity coherent with its own opinions, and thus liberty finds itself without any criteria for orientation, except for that of utility. A subjectivity that determines itself by claiming ethical autonomy does not recognize truths and goods proper to the human being but establishes what is good or evil in function of its aims. This conception of liberty, that presupposes the absence of objective and binding ethical concepts, implies relativizing ethics and necessitates ethical neutrality in society. However, ethical neutrality in society signifies that in human relations – that which constitutes a society – authenticity or inauthenticity, properly speaking, are not possible. This has been made quite clear, for example, in the numerous arguments brandished in the debates concerning the definition of marriage or the family. Without truth or goods proper to human relations, these remain at the mercy of individual interests, generating an individualist society and depriving public debates of an objective point of reference to which democratic dialogue should aspire, a reference without which the human being is deprived of critical recourses before those who determine the "politically correct" and before his own inclinations. Without truth or ethics, liberty becomes vague, to the benefit of cultural trends or sentimentalism devoid of reason.

In brief, within contemporary society, we are witnessing a series of approaches to personal life as well as social and political claims that are based upon an experience of liberty lacking a veracious point of reference. Intelligence is focused upon its technical–instrumental aspect and the properly human – those profound attitudes before oneself and others, relations, emotions, that which has to do with the meaning of existence and happiness, etc. – is often left in the hands of a sentimentalism unprotected by the discernment of the intellect or is interpreted and determined in function of those personal interests that spontaneously arise in those who lack the resources to judge their interests. Ethics, on the contrary, allows one to discern the exercises of liberty that are authentically human from those that alienate the persons who perform them. These latter exercises of liberty are alien to the identity of man, in the measure in which (1) they are opposed to his being, (2) they marginalize, tyrannize, or suppress others, those who are without voice or strength to defend their rights. Without ethics, liberty finds itself without normative criteria, criteria that are binding because they refer to that which distinguishes an authentically human act from an inhuman one, that which alienates from that which realizes.

The Enlightenment dialectic has conditioned the evolution of an idea of man, consolidated in modernity, which is moving towards a culture that risks blurring that which is specifically human. The idea of a self-sufficient and emancipated subjectivity finishes by leading towards positivist stances in which the preponderance of the scientific vision of man is affirmed, leading to the inversion of those terms which gave birth to modernity: "The dominion of all of nature under the subject, master of himself, culminates justly in the dominion of blind objectivity, that is to say, in nature" (Horkheimer and Adorno 2002, 56). In other words, the restriction of reason to one of its modes of thinking leads to a series of cultural implications that affect the idea of the human being: "In strict relationship with all of this, a radical reduction of man has taken place, considered a simple product of nature and as such not really free, and in himself susceptible to be treated like any other animal. Thus, an authentic overturning of the point of departure of this culture has come about, which started as a claim of the centrality of man and his freedom. Along the same lines, ethics is brought within the confines of relativism and utilitarianism with the exclusion of every moral principle that is valid and in itself binding" (Benedict XVI 2006).

The regression to which Enlightenment dialectic thought is directed, inducing the eclipse of humanism, does not exhaust all of the hermeneutics of modernity. Upon a classical-Christian basis, modern thought has elaborated other possible approaches to the great principles of humanity within the areas of law, political philosophy, economy, anthropology, management, and many others. Nevertheless, one can confirm that in crucial sectors of culture and of society we have arrived at a crisis of humanism. In this respect, Belardinelli indicates, that "nevertheless, it is as well true that the Enlightenment, in which our institutions and our liberal-democratic culture was formed, lives principally the pathos of the truth and that, as on the other hand Nietzsche had already intuited, if this pathos disappears, we risk the disappearance of the Enlightenment as well" (2009, 7). For this reason, "far from constituting the foundation of a liberal and democratic culture, relativism constitutes its malaise, the threshold of a radical functionalism" (2009, 9). Lübbe (2007) argues in similar terms.

Recovering Humanism

The determining approach to humanism that characterizes the important currents of modernity has lead to these two phenomena which we have already elaborated: a tendency to the predominance of instrumental reason in the field of praxis, and the exercise of liberty at the margin of objective criteria that would allow one to distinguish those acts of authentically human liberty from those that on the contrary alienate, inasmuch as they are opposed to the identity of man. In the case of the preeminence of instrumental reason, the rational analyses that are directed towards the action or its evaluation substitute the centrality of the person with the notions of the functional and efficient. In the case of a liberty deprived of an ethics with content, the legitimacy of a personal option is justified by appealing to the right to satisfy the desires of one's autonomous subjectivity, as understood above. These two phenomena call into question humanism itself. The problem does not reside in the multiple expressions of modern humanism as such, but in the unilateral manner of understanding practical reason and personal liberty that has led to the subjective approach.

Scientific reason has made evident progress, allowing for the development of much more human conditions in essential aspects of life which no one could sanely be disposed to disregard: "The positivist approach to nature and reason, the positivist world view in general, is a most important dimension of human knowledge and capacity that we may in no way dispense with. But in and of itself it is not a suffi-cient culture corresponding to the full breadth of the human condition" (Benedict XVI 2011) This notwithstanding, to concentrate exclusively upon scientific reason has meant that, as stated time and time again, today we possess an immense knowledge concerning man – but we do not know who he is. The sciences offer partial perspectives; however, they lack an integral understanding of who we are. Instrumental and technical reason, for its part, is adapt for those specific fields within which it is applied, and within which it has been demonstrated to be irreplaceable. While indubitably allowing for a certainty concerning actions exclusively from a specific perspective, such reason neglects other dimensions of the same action. The result is the lack of both a wholistic (sapiential) vision of the human being as well as an absence of a praxis considered within the totality of its dimensions and in the light of the entire person, without being limited to the point of view of its quantitative yield. Such a vision corresponds to ethics.

The specific nature of ethics consists in offering a consideration of the totality of the action, in its relation with the totality of the person. This enables the judgment of actions in terms of humanity or inhumanity. To ethics fall the strict protection, preservation, and promotion of the human; from here it receives, on the one hand, its binding character and, on the other, its insistence upon taking initiative. Ethics possesses a deontological and normative (legal) dimension, in the measure that it warns against those actions that de-humanize man. However, ethics is not exhausted therein. Essential as well to ethics is (1) encouraging the human, by identifying those great goods of existence (the ethics of goods), (2) operating practical discernment before concrete goods and evils (prudence), and (3) encouraging attitudes and behaviors that allow one to rationally and stably tend towards such goods (virtue ethics) (Polo 2008). Ethics indicates how to be better human beings; this is the intrinsic connection between ethics and humanism. From the point of view of practical reason, recuperating humanism means a return to ethics in its exercise as practical reason. As is evident, in ethics, humanism does not end with practical reason: there are other dimensions that are indispensable and that have to do with interpersonal relationships in general, with aesthetics, with religion, etc. However, ethics is the condition of possibility for all of these and frequently the first step towards recuperating the meaning of the human in praxis, the theme of this conference. On the other hand, practical reason lives by means of a series of presuppositions that provide the content for speculative reflection; this reflection focuses upon these presuppositions, clarifies them, elaborates their content more profoundly, and judges them. If they are shown to be insufficient, it will be necessary to open them up unto either other dimensions of reality or the human being that is either absent or only partially present in such presuppositions. Thus, theoretical reason is indispensable for the ethical exercise of practical reason.

The predominance of instrumental reason concretely conditions the spontaneous manner by which agents understand society. Such a comprehension is made explicit *a posteriori* in the scientific analyses of social phenomena, in the hermeneutic of the same, and in the theories that sociology elaborates upon such foundations. The hegemony of instrumental reason, inasmuch as it is an alleged sign of modernity or the modernization of a society, is reinforced in those schools of sociology that examine society in the light of the systems theory (Luhmann 1992). From this perspective, society consists in an ensemble of subsystems – political, economic, juridical, festive, academic, familiar, etc. – each of which is autonomous: each possesses its own environment, its own laws and codes, its own praxis. Each system is governed according to specific rules guaranteeing its subsistence and growth. Each one possesses its own language and specific standards of conduct: its own logic. To know how to conduct oneself therein presupposes understanding such a logic; he who is most fluent in such a logic, respecting it and at the same time using it creatively, will have greater success.

A system is self-referential: it seeks stability and growth; it relates to the external as with an essential setting for its own continuity. However, that external is kept at a distance and seen only in function of its contribution. Approaching society from this perspective entails an interpretation that allows for the different interconnections between the various subsystems which are, however, autonomous, each one of them with its own specific instrumental rationality. Consequently, within this framework, ethics is the rigidly human that remains at the margins of the system. The human constitutes the environment or the means by which the system may maintain relationships, however it remains extrinsic. "It is maintained that the market has its own rules, politics its own games, the media possesses its own logic, etc. The human subject fluctuates in the environment of the social system. The human is identified with the necessities, the desires, dreams, – good or evil – of a subject that is perceived and represented as external and undetermined with respect to organized social relationships" (Donati 2009, 82). In this way, strictly speaking, an "inhuman" society is generated, in which women and men are considered from the perspective of systems, or functionally: they perform functions and are treated as variables in a formula to be calculated.

It is clear that the paradigm of the self-referential system and the predominance of instrumental reason can be applied, beyond the economy as such, to business. In this framework, human beings are collocated within their various administrative, labor, investment, consumption, or supply functions and are considered in terms of these functions and their short, medium, or long-term performance; in a word, the functional consideration prevails. Common sense rebels against such a vision of this kind and vindicates the necessity to overcome the unilateral nature of such proposals in order to open up onto a more human consideration of the different environments of society, of business specifically, in which the human is not treated as extrinsic, as something with which the system enters into relation in order to survive although external to the system itself, but rather as something intrinsic: its essence. In this respect, Donati notes: "A social form is human when the social relations in which it consists are produced by subjects reciprocally oriented to one another upon the basis of a supra-functional meaning. A social form is not human if and when the subjects are not oriented to one another (because relationships do not exist, but are pure reactivity or affirmations of individuality), if and when the meaning of actions is only functional" (Donati 2009, 133). Without a humanist approach to life, to society, and to action, the human being risks losing himself. Recuperating humanism presupposes developing an ethical vision of society and of existence, in which ethics is not seen as a code imposed upon a business (or upon a researcher or a politician), conditioning the range of his liberty for valid reasons that originate from outside of the business world, but as something which is intrinsic to the business in the measure in which the business bespeaks humanity.

A brief excursus upon the experience of human existence as such, and not merely some of its dimensions, can serve to illustrate this point. The experience of every person testifies that existence presents itself to us as a personal task that cannot be handed onto another or renounced: the task of being. We could express this by saying that for the human being to exist means the demand of self-realization, that is to say, the necessity of becoming fully oneself. Existence does not present itself to us as a program already written, capable of being "learned" and adapted, which is, however, already definitively outlined. Existence has been left in the hands of each of us and that which is in play therein is existence as such – the person of each one – and not only one of its dimensions, such as the professional sphere. On the other hand, the experience of humanity demonstrates that the complete realization of such a task is not guaranteed; history and modernity testify to worthwhile lives, the biographies of people who have achieved being human beings in an excellent way and others, unfortunately, men and women who have lost themselves in drugs or in violence, to mention two brief examples.

Instrumental reason as much as a personal liberty at the margin of ethical criteria leave the human being lacking the necessary capacities to confront his existence as such, with the evident risk of directing his life towards a loss of self instead of a successful existence. On the one side, the hegemony of instrumental reason impedes an integral self-orientation, provoking a fragmented interiority in virtue of the tensions that arise between the different spheres of life (family, work, hobbies, etc.).[1] On the other hand, personal liberty without ethics generates a society of individualists, of citizens who are closed within a self-referential nature of their own interests or desires and thus forget that man only realizes himself fully, in as much as he is person, in authentic human relationships with others: in the family, in friendship, with solidarity, in a society in which the human person is truly committed to the common good.

Humanism demands that the focus of attention should be upon the person, and this requires an ethical discernment and entrepreneurial initiative. It is necessarily from such a position that, in contrast to ideas and attitudes that champion an exercise of liberty at the margin of the criteria of truth and authenticity, "without subtracting anything from the centrality of the human person – or even more, fully valuing the person -, the impulse to come out of the narrow semantics of self-referential individualism, of ethical neutrality, and of the consequent relativism grows." (Belardinelli 2009, 92–93)

What does it concretely mean to overcome the "inhuman" vision of business by maintaining that ethics is found at the center of business action? In the first place, as we have said, this means that ethics – the human – is not extrinsic, imposed or juxtaposed to the economic-business realm. Instrumental reason addresses certain

---

[1] This problematic is addressed, particularly in regard to the promotion of work-family relationships, by the study of Chinchilla and Moragas (2008).

dimension of business action; ethics, ethical reason, enters into a thorough study of the same. In the second place, this means that ethics is not limited to warning against inhuman orientations, attitudes or decisions (natural law ethics), but also inspires the acting subject towards self-growth and to the realization of the growth of the other persons involved in the business (virtue ethics). Ethics hence encourages the development of the human in society, hastening to contribute to the common good by means of the production of tangible and intangible goods (ethics of goods).[2]

In this sense, it is clear that it would be reductive to restrict ethics to resolve deontological questions of the kind: is this action permissible? Ethics goes much further: it encourages and promotes the good for the acting subject and the *stakeholders* of a business as well as society in general: in a word, the common good. Ethics encourages creativity; the ethical man and woman discover that ethics is intrinsic to business activity, because business is intrinsically human: it is the place of the promotion of the human being, in regard to both the actions accomplished and the results obtained. For this reason, ethical attitudes have positive repercussions on the economic performance of business as long as ethics is not instrumentalized to such an end. In this case, ethics would be lost since, as Kant affirmed, the person can never used as an instrument.

It is the task of ethics to confront the question of the ends and hence fundamental motivations. Ethics engenders an attitude that seeks the good of the human being as the fundamental end. That is why in regard to business activity, motivations are generally of an objective nature, either extrinsic (quantifiable benefits) or intrinsic (intangible goods that refer to the growth of the person and his transcendental dimension). At times, the two types of motivations come into conflict, sometimes simply because the intangible motivations are marginalized due to an exclusive use of instrumental reason. The ethical vision penetrates the different motives, seeks a harmony between them, and inspires initiative to promote the goods that develop the human being, goods that concern interpersonal relationships, the growth of each one as person, material (physical and psychological) wellbeing, the common good.

Christian Humanism

In light of these reflections, one intuits that practical reason of an ethical nature is required in order to promote humanism. However, why are we speaking of Christian humanism? What can Christianity contribute in this regard? As is evident, an adequate treatment of this question requires a development that greatly exceeds the time at our disposition. For this reason, I will limit the discussion to three indications, appealing to an author who, although his thought is not considered Christian,

---

[2] For a synthetic vision of how it is possible to consider the relationship between virtues and business action, see Argandoña (2011).

has recently rediscovered the value of religion and, more specifically, that of Christianity. I am referring to the latest publications of Habermas.

To begin, it should not be forgotten that all of society possesses cultural roots, in which the fundamental ideas of the culture and the basic attitudes that give meaning to the actions therein are grounded: the manner of behaving, those institutions that reflect and consolidate the acting and the relationships of men and women, the ideas of just and unjust, and responding to those meanings that are generally understood or implied, but which are no less important. This cultural humus is intrinsically linked to certain ideas concerning man, the meaning of existence and that transcendence which possesses a religious character or origin. Thus, there are authors who speak of a theological matrix of society in order to refer to the determining influence that religious ideas have held in the construction of society, subsequently warning of the danger implied by a hasty or uncritical marginalization of these ideas (Donati 2010).

In the most recent work of Habermas, we can recognize at least three decisive contributions of Christianity to the edification of a society that promotes humanism at its most basic level.[3] In the first place, Christianity offers to the understanding of man a reservoir of ideas that permit the elaboration of an ethics with depth and range, that is, with meaning and a solid foundation. "Postmetaphysical thinking is ethically modest in the sense that it is resistant to any generally binding concept of the good and exemplary life. Holy scriptures and religious traditions, by contrast, have articulated intuitions concerning transgression and salvation and the redemption of lives experienced as hopeless, keeping them hermeneutically vibrant by skillfully working out their implications over centuries. This is why religious communities… can preserve intact something that has been lost elsewhere and cannot be recovered through the professional knowledge of experts alone" (Habermas 2008, 110). This author observes that an ethics of contents that possesses existential scope and promotes a more human society is an ethics that is not limited to the deontological aspect, but rather is elaborated from an idea of the *good life* in contrast to a detestable existence. For this reason, Habermas states, a vision of a metaphysical nature in regard to the human being, which, as we have noted, post-modern culture lacks, is necessary.

Ethics presupposes a constitutive or essential identity of the being, according to which each woman and each man is a human being, with an inviolable dignity, but also with a teleology and liberty present both to oneself and to others. Positivism logically entails a positivist vision of nature, an exclusive vision that impedes the recognition of an "essence" of the human being with specific normative implications consequent upon his dignity. "Man too has a nature that he must respect and that he cannot manipulate at will. Man is not merely self-creating freedom. Man does not create himself. He is intellect and will, but he is also nature, and his will is rightly ordered if he respects his nature, listens to it and accepts himself for who he is, as one who did not create himself. In this way, and in no other, is true human

---

[3] I presented a more complete vision of Habermas' position in Romera (2009).

freedom fulfilled" (Benedict XVI 2011). To reintroduce a vision of metaphysical significance assumes overcoming the dichotomy between being and good-value-obligation, typical of a positivist approach to reason and to nature, as diffused in common parlance (such as the positivist mentality in the juridical camp).[4] Christianity, for its part, has conserved and transmitted throughout the centuries an intellectually rigorous idea of the human being, important for life, which promotes humanism, precisely because it does not lose sight of his religious dimension. For this reason, the Christian faith offers an ensemble of ideas that are showing themselves to be essential for the recuperation of humanism.

In second place, Christianity facilitates attitudes in the person that direct him towards social action (economic-business, political, juridical, familiar, etc.) that is effectively oriented towards humanism. All of democracy is sustained – Habermas notes – upon the basis of "a solidarity that cannot be legally imposed", a solidarity necessary in order that citizens participate in social, economic, and political life "not only in their enlightened self-interest but also with a view to promoting the common good" (Habermas 2008, 9). For the Christian, the truly human existence is that in which man does not limit himself to not committing evil, but rather promotes the good of his neighbor. The Christian does not remain passive before the situation or the condition of others; on the contrary, he exerts himself positively, with initiative, in order to do the good. Christianity encourages attitudes that cannot be induced by legal statutes but that are essential for the society that would be authentically human.

In the third place, Christianity offers hope, precisely because of its transcendent and soteriological character. "Secular languages that simply eliminate what was once there leave behind only irritation. Something was lost when sin became guilt. The desire for forgiveness is, after all, still closely connected with the unsentimental wish to undo other injuries as well. We are truly unsettled by the irreversibility of any suffering that has been caused - that injustice to those innocents who have been mistreated, degraded and murdered, that goes beyond any measure of restitution within the power of man. The lost hope of resurrection has left behind a palpable emptiness" (Habermas 2001, 24–25). Humanism means that the person does not remain outside of the different spheres in which he passes his life. For this reason, the great themes of existence have an enormous repercussion upon the motivations that lead us to act and that determine how we behave, even if at first sight this is not perceived: experience demonstrates the decisive influence of the quality of the person upon the quality of his work. The existential is not alien to professional praxis. The Christian idea of transcendence and the relationship of man with God leads to a recognition of the irreducibility of the religious in our understanding of the human being, which permits us, on the one hand, to recognize an ultimate reference point of truth and of the good that is unconditioned, and on the other hand, to open ourselves to a hope that transcends the difficulties of existence. For both reasons,

---

[4] The repercussions of the aforementioned in regard to making decisions have been highlighted by Melé (2011).

Christianity promotes humanism and facilitates a society that aims with optimism towards the future.

The reflections that we have outlined constitute a series of indications requiring a much more extensive development and, above all, an exposition in regard to economic and business action. As we noted at the beginning, this second aspect will be seen in greater detail and more practically in the following sessions, in order to obtain a more complete vision of that which we are seeking. From the consideration of praxis, one better understands the potential of Christian humanism for the contemporary context.

References

Argandoña, A. 2011. Las virtues en una teoria de la acción humana. In *La persona al centro del Magistero sociale della Chiesa*, ed. Schlag Requena, 49–71. Roma: Edusc.

Belardinelli, S. 2009. *L'altro Illuminismo. Politica, religion e funzione pubblica della verità*. Catanzaro: Rubbetino.

Benedict XVI .2006. Speech to the participants in the Fourth National Ecclesial Convention. Verone, Oct 19. http://www.vatican.va/holy_father/benedict_xvi/speeches/2006/october/documents/hf_ben-xvi_spe_20061019_convegno-verona_en.html. Accessed 21 Mar 2013.

Benedict XVI. 2009. Encyclical letter 'Caritas in veritate'. http://www.vatican.va/holy_father/benedict_xvi/encyclicals/documents/hf_ben-xvi_enc_20090629_caritas-in-veritate_en.html. Accessed 21 Mar 2013.

Benedict XVI .2011. Address to the Bundestag. Berlin, Sept 22. http://www.vatican.va/holy_father/benedict_xvi/speeches/2011/september/documents/hf_ben-xvi_spe_20110922_reichstag-berlin_en.html. Accessed 21 Mar 2013.

Chinchilla, Nuria, and Maruja Moragas. 2008. *Masters of our destiny*. Pamplona: Eunsa.

Donati, P. 2009. *La società dell'umano*. Genova/Milano: Marietti.

Donati, P. 2010. *La matrice teologica della società*. Catanzaro: Rubbetino.

Habermas, J. 2001. *Glauben und Wissen*. Suhrkamp: Frankfurt am Main.

Habermas, J. 2008. *Between naturalism and religion: Philosophical essays*. Cambridge: Polity Press.

Horkheimer M, Adorno TW. 2002. Dialectic of enlightenment: Philosophical fragments. Ed. G.S. Noerr. Trans. E. Jephcott. Stanford University Press: Stanford. Originally published in 1947.

Lübbe, H. 2007. *La politica dopo l'Illuminismo*. Catanzaro: Rubbettino.

Luhmann, N. 1992. *Beobachtungen der Moderne*. Opladen: Westdeutscher Verlag. English translation: *Observations on modernity*. Stanford: Stanford University Press.

Melé, D. 2011. Toma de decisiones: unidad, primacía de la ética e interdependencia dimensional. In *La persona al centro del Magistero sociale della Chiesa*, ed. Schlag Requena, 203–220. Roma: Edusc.

Polo, L. 2008. *Ethics. A modern version of its classic themes*. Manila: Sinag-Tala.

Romera, L. 2009. Ragione e religion nella società post-secolare. *Sociologia e politiche sociali* 12(1): 23–41.

Spaemann, R. 2006. *Persons: The difference between 'someone' and 'something'*. Oxford/New York: Oxford University Press.

Taylor, C. 2004. *Modern social imaginaries*. Durham/London: Duke University Press.

Chapter 4
Being Human, Becoming Human: Christian Humanism as a Foundation of Western Culture

Jens Zimmermann

Abstract Recent debates about human dignity and the role of religion within democratic, constitutional societies in Europe and North America demonstrate a deterioration of secularism and the need to retrieve the religious, Christian humanist roots of our culture. After demonstrating the necessity to recover a metaphysical framework for answering the question of our humanity and society's ultimate purpose, and for regaining a synthesis of reason and faith, this chapter offers a reconstruction of Christian humanism for the renewal of Western culture based on patristic, medieval and Renaissance roots, modern theology (both Protestant and Catholic), and hermeneutic philosophy. While non-Christians share intrinsically in this ideal as those created in God's image, the chapter concludes, that renewal of a humanistic ethos depends first of all on Christians' living out the belief that God became flesh to make us truly human.

Keywords Humanistic cultural ethos • Habermas • Religion • Secularism • Western culture

Western Culture in general and European culture in particular display signs of a profound and lasting identity crisis. One indication of this loss of cultural identity is the ongoing debate about integrating immigrants into European countries. English, German, and French politicians have now declared the death of multiculturalism as a viable the leading social model for integration.[1] To some degree, of course, such statements are certainly political theater and grandstanding, motivated by a desire to capitalize on the frustration of voters. For this purpose, cultural minorities, such as Moslems become convenient scapegoats for all manners of social problems and cultural unease. At the same time, however, the general dissatisfaction within a number of European countries over their current cultural situation does point to a deep insecurity about the foundations of modern, pluralistic societies. The positive

---

[1] Theologians such as Kardinal Walter Kasper, who are concerned about cultural developments, share this verdict. In his *Stuttgarter Rede Zu Europa*, Kasper concludes that "Multikulti, that is the co-existence of parallel societies has failed Europe-wide" (Kasper 2007, 24).

J. Zimmermann (✉)
Trinity Western University, Langley, British Columbia, Canada
e-mail: jensz@twu.ca

© Springer Science+Business Media Dordrecht 2015   49
D. Melé, M. Schlag (eds.), *Humanism in Economics and Business*,
Issues in Business Ethics 43, DOI 10.1007/978-94-017-9704-7_4

reception of many books, such as Thilo Sarrazin's *Germany Abolishes Itself* (*Deutschland Schafft Sich Ab*), are symptoms of a crisis of identity and meaning that already exists within German culture and is merely exacerbated, but not caused, by the confrontation with other cultures.

Another symptom of this identity crisis of Western culture is our universities in which higher education is increasingly reduced to the tangible results of practical research and job-creation. Not only in North America, with its native tendency toward pragmatism and self-improvement, but also in Europe, the spiritual cradle of humanist education, the human sciences are fighting for their survival. Human scientists, it is said, do not produce anything tangible, cannot fight deadly diseases, and fail to increase the gross national product. Somehow, the humanistic ideals of wisdom and character formation have been lost. Our universities teach us how to live longer and produce greater wealth, but we no longer learn anything about what we should live for or what we should spend our money on.

Both of these examples of a cultural identity crisis in Western culture indicate the loss of a transcendent framework of meaning that goes beyond merely practical or political considerations for human action. The essential question behind our educational crisis, as well as behind discussions about integration and the unity of Europe, is a question of identity and purpose. The real issue is the foundational question of what it means to be human, that is, *who we are* and *for what purpose we exist as society and as culture.* We are dealing with the question of our common human identity, with our being human and becoming human. Especially in academic discussions, the desire for a cultural identity is sometimes rejected as exclusivist and as inimical to intercultural dialogue. But do not intercultural dialogue and integration demand just such an identity? For example, when we talk about the integration of a child into a family, we naturally assume a family identity, deriving from a certain history, values and traditions. In the same way, cultural integration also assumes an existing cultural identity based on historically developed social structures and traditions. In short, without cultural identity we have neither dialogue nor integration. Moreover, a modern democratic society, with its concept of a sovereign people, already requires a strong communal sense and a common purpose. The democratic process is not an end it itself but requires a common, freely chosen goal, together with mutual trust and cooperation in achieving this end (Taylor 2009a, 1158). Yet this kind of cultural ethos cannot exist on the sole basis of pragmatic or political expediency. Examining and sustaining a people's culture inevitably involve metaphysical, and, ultimately, religious considerations. In the case of Western, European societies, our vision of humanity and of a humanistic education, with its values of freedom, equality, and solidarity, arises predominantly from Judeo-Christian roots, and we cannot understand who we are and what we live for without understanding these religious roots (Taylor 2009a, 1151). It is true, of course, that during medieval times and also in the Renaissance, Moslem scholars played an important role in Western intellectual history; it is also true that the three monotheisms share a number of important beliefs and throughout their shared history could thus "disagree meaningfully" (Lewis 1993, 6). Since, however, the crucial impulses for modern ideas of human freedom, personhood, and democracy clearly depended on Christian developments of Jewish theology, the case sometimes made for an "Islamo-Christian civilization" lacks convincing historical evidence (Bulliet 2004, 5–7).

Without denying Islamic influence on the formation of Western culture, I want to argue that understanding the identities of European cultures requires a solid grasp of their religious roots, and these roots can be described as "Christian Humanism." Just such an understanding of Europe's religious roots is made difficult, however, because the European consciousness, at least as represented by many intellectuals and politicians, remains profoundly ambivalent, indeed uncomfortable, about the topic of religion. The sociologist José Casanova rightly speaks in this context of Europe's "fear of religion" (Casanova 2009a, 28). I am convinced that the identity crisis of Western cultures derives at least in part from this fear of religion, and that this fear is caused in turn by a certain ideology, namely the ideology of secularism. Before we analyze this ideology, however, we have to probe even more deeply into the origins of this anxiety about religion to expose its structural heart. For the heart of this secularism consists in the separation of reason and transcendence. As modern human beings, we are supposed to think post-metaphysically.[2] Such post-metaphysical thinking rejects transcendent, objective realities that could provide a moral compass and admits only an immanent framework within which human reason creates its own values. In contrast to ancient philosophers, post-metaphysical thinkers no longer believe in an objective rational or moral order to which our thinking has to conform. This modern dismissal of any real correspondence between being and transcendence, between being and spirit, and thus between being and the divine, constitutes a radical and decisive break with the conceptions of humanity that dominated our self-understanding from the ancient world well into the nineteenth century. The German philosopher Hegel is perhaps the last great thinker who still held to the ancient idea of our participation in a transcendent reality as "an ontological core in which all things share and which intrinsically links them to one another" (Dupré 2008, 116). Without such an ontological synthesis, language, art, poetry, indeed all the human disciplines of knowledge, lose the vital link that makes them truthful expressions of reality.

This break with the onto-theological tradition characterizes modern, post-metaphysical thinking. Indeed, Europe's crisis of identity and of its humanistic educational ideal originates with this modern denial of the link between consciousness and transcendence, that is, with the separation of reason and faith. As long as we define reason as essentially independent of faith, we can understand neither our own Christian roots nor talk intelligently about the religious convictions of other cultures with whom we interact economically and politically. We require a better,

---

[2] The German philosopher Hans Jürgen Habermas employs this term to indicate "agnostic positions that strictly distinguish between belief and knowledge, without claiming the validity of one particular religion (as in modern apologetics) or to deny religious traditions any possible cognitive content (as does scientism)." Acceptable for public discourse, however, are only religious truths that can convince those outside a particular religious community (Habermas 2009b, 384).

broader conception of reason, one that is intrinsically open toward religious transcendence, and one that does not force us into the separation of knowledge and meaning, of fact and (moral) value on the one hand, or into the conflation of morality and biology on the other.

I will do three things to illustrate and back up my argument for a broader conception of reason for recovering the humanistic ethos of Western culture. First, we will look at the current German discussion about the role of religion within constitutional democracy to show the prevalence and effect of separating reason and faith. Second, we will examine the ideology of secularism underlying this separation. Third, we will finish by arguing that the humanistic educational ideal of Europe cannot be maintained without its Christian roots.

Religion and Democratic Society

As we turn to the German discussion about religion and constitutional democracy, our goal is to see whether the prevalent post-metaphysical framework with its separation of reason and faith can assess the role of religion in a modern, pluralistic society. More specifically, we are concerned with the concept of "constitutional patriotism" (*Verfassungspatriotismus*), in which constitutional values such as human dignity and human rights are separated from their religious roots in order to declare them to be religiously neutral, universal rights. The basic motivation of this claim is sound. It is indeed an important achievement of the modern constitutional state that its laws do not compel us to agree with the particular religious sources that gave rise to them. In this sense, it is immaterial whether one agrees either with the Judeo-Christian origins of human dignity and equality or with their enshrining in the constitution, as long as one observes their legal expressions (Krech 2007, 146). This distinction between a value and a formal law is important because it protects politics from the dominance of ideology, including religious ideology (Krech 2007, 149). Yet this protective mechanism itself becomes an ideology when it also claims that the democratic process itself is the only legitimate basis for the values that support the democratic state. Jürgen Habermas, for example, argues that, "[what] unites a nation of constitutional citizens—in contrast to a folk-nation—is not a pre-given substrate, but a shared context of possible communication" (Habermas 1996, 189).

Habermas' reference to a "folk-nation" makes clear that his anxiety about the religious foundations of a society's unity stems from the European experience with totalitarian regimes, whose communistic and fascistic nationalisms have left deep scars on Europe's collective consciousness. The devastating consequences of the quasi-religious visions of Aryan supremacy and of communistic eschatological hopes have burdened especially the German historical consciousness to such a degree that any social consensus rooted in a transcendent source is instinctively rejected. Because of this background, any talk about the "Christian occident," a Christian cultural ethos, or about the Christian roots of Europe is perceived to threaten the constitutional and purely formal basis on which it is believed a pluralistic society alone will flourish (Pera 2009, 106). This separation of value consensus and constitutional rights also explains why it is legitimate to express one's patriotism for the constitution, whereas an equally passionate adherence to the religious roots of human dignity or Europe's humanistic ethos is condemned as dangerous fanaticism.

Yet we cannot evade the question of origins. World religions root universal values in transcendent reality, but where do values originate for the modern, secular European? Again, Habermas answers this question for us: "After the religious foundation [for values] has lost validity, the cognitive content of the moral language game can be reconstructed only with reference to the will and reason of its participants" (Habermas 2009a, 315). In other words, if we want to be modern, progressive, liberal and able to function in a constitutional state, our reason can no longer appeal to any religious, transcendent, or "onto-theological" foundation for the values that guide us.

But does not this narrowing of reason to the immanent by definition reduce those informed by religious worldviews to second rate citizens and to dubious partners in political negotiations? Moreover, we can neither understand nor sustain Western ideals and institutions if we accept such a post-metaphysical concept of reason with its separation of reason and faith.

This lack of self-understanding occurs every time champions of secular constitutional patriotism are confronted with statements that do not separate clearly between constitution and religious tradition. And such statements do not even have to come from Islamic radicals or American evangelical fundamentalists. All it takes to unleash a storm of indignation from constitutional patriots is the repetition of a historical commonplace by politicians such as the German chancellor, Angelika Merkel, who mentioned the Judeo-Christian view of human beings made in the image of God as the foundation of the German constitution. Many constitutional patriots felt that making such a religious value the basis of a democratic state contravened the religious neutrality of the state. For example, the well-known politician and jurist Wolfgang Lieb protested passionately, "No, Madame chancellor, *I* feel beholden to the humanistic ideal of what it means to be human, and as constitutional patriot I adhere to the vision for humanity of the constitution and not to a Christian vision. Am I, therefore, out of place" (Gorges 2010)?

This passionate affirmation of constitutional patriotism illustrates the deep-seated separation of reason and faith among educated Europeans, for whom religion is, by definition, the enemy of freedom, tolerance, reason and humanity. The constitutional patriot assumes that the value neutral state is incompatible with religious values. Moreover, the presumed opposition between humanism and a Christian view of our humanity in Lieb's statement shows us how the instinctive separation of reason and faith distorts cultural history. For secular humanism with its high confidence in human abilities for moral progress clearly derives from an earlier Christian humanism. But before I say more about this Christian humanism, we now move to the second part of my argument by probing the ideology of secularism that lies at the heart of these issues.

Secularism as Ideology

For an assessment of our current cultural problems, it is important to understand that secularism is neither based on scientific facts nor is it common sense, but it constitutes a worldview. Indeed, secularism is an ideology whose definition of universal reason excludes religious truths from public, legal, and political discourse. In his work, *A Secular Age*, the Canadian philosopher Charles Taylor has described the historical development of this specifically Western ideology from its Christian humanistic roots to the Deism and the French Revolution. By showing the ideological character of secularism, Taylor exposes the illusion that secularism is simply a value neutral way of assessing reality (Taylor 2007).[3] The secularist creed requires the separation of reason and faith, a dualism that Taylor, along with postmodern philosophies, has demonstrated to be untenable (Taylor 2007, 314–319). In stark contrast to its supposedly disinterested rationality, secularism rests on the belief that human progress necessitates the demise of religion. Taylor calls this the "subtraction narrative of secularism," and he exposes the powerful narrative imagery of this myth. According to the secularist story, the mature human being leaves the irrational childhood of religious superstition and walks, erect and free, into the rising sun of an enlightened, humane rationality. Once this story has been internalized, any return to religion will "naturally" appear as a regress toward the dark and infantile beginnings of humanity.

For those who inhabit this subtraction narrative, the sociological fact that religion never really receded is immaterial. In other words, the currently much-discussed "return of religion" is a phenomenon that arises itself from the subtraction narrative. In other words, the experience that religion had already been banished from rational thought but now has in some manner returned, did never really correspond to a social reality, neither globally nor in all of Europe; rather, the return of religion, or the notion of a post-secular society expresses the sentiments of those who already inhabit the secularist narrative and thus expected religions' continual diminishment (Joas 2004, 124). Based on this internalized story, many educated Europeans instinctively link religion to intolerance and irrationality. They regard religious convictions as irreconcilable with rational thought and therefore as dangerous for the democratic state (Casanova 2009b).[4] Non-Western cultures, however, are not historically conditioned in the same way, and the Western fear of religion is rather foreign to them. Thus Pope Benedict is quite right to worry that the ideology of secularism with its separation of reason and faith provides a poor starting point for much needed inter-cultural dialogue, because the majority of the world's cultures cannot quite comprehend our separation of faith and reason (Benedict XVI 2007, 55).

---

[3] *A Secular Age*. Taylor also summarizes his criticism of the Enlightenment *mythos* in a more recent dialogue with Habermas (See, Taylor 2011, 34–59, 53).

[4] Taylor believes, on the contrary, that religion plays an important part in democratic societies (Taylor 2009b).

To be fair, however, we must acknowledge that secularism itself has undergone an important self-critique in recent decades. This self-correction was partially caused by the direct confrontation with deeply religious cultures such as Islam, and also by the visible expansion of Christianity in Asia and Africa (Jenkins 2007). But, more importantly, philosophical criticism from within has exposed secularism as an inadequate foundation for modern democratic societies. Again, Jürgen Habermas exemplifies this self-critical turn of secularism. In his early work *Theory of Communicative Action*, Habermas still embraced secularism's ambition to replace religion through secular, communicative reason; but since about 2001, Habermas has admitted religion to be a necessary source for social values in a post-secular society, and he has become the main secular champion for the dialogue between secular and religious reasoning (Junker-Kenny 2011, 136).

At least in part, this changed attitude may be attributed to the influence of hermeneutic philosophy. Guided by hermeneutic philosophy, Habermas rejected the outmoded view that detached, verifiable observation is the only valid basis for human knowledge. Insight into the reality of things does not come from mere data transfer, but requires the intuitive integration of information into a larger, tradition-dependent framework of meaning. Moreover, a large swath of human experience remains inaccessible to the scientific standard of repeat verifiability. The German philosopher, Martin Heidegger, had famously pointed out the limitations of scientific objectivism with the provocative phrase, "science does not think" (Heidegger 1992, 349). Habermas himself uses the related expression "the brain does not think" to indicate the limits of scientific objectivism. To be sure, observation and verification are important tools for scientific research, but even science depends on imagination and tradition. But especially when we are dealing with questions concerning wisdom and the purpose of human existence, science cannot really help us.

Based in part on this hermeneutic theory of truth, Habermas's post-metaphysical reasoning is also post-secular, and essentially open towards religious insights. Yet at the same time, Habermas continues to hold that within a post-metaphysical framework, members of a democratic society must rely fully on the democratic process and the formation of a common societal will for the development of the social norms within a society. The question is, whether a process based on the exclusion of transcendence can actually truly acknowledge and be inspired by ideas from religious frameworks that insist on transcendent realities. On the positive side, Habermas' emphasis on public debate requires the rejection of any dogmatism or fundamentalism of any kind, be it philosophical, theological or scientific (Habermas 2009b, 31). While Enlightenment philosophy still assumed "the role of an inspector" who "tests and approves the truth content of the world religions," post-secular reason enters into an open dialogue with religions and is prepared to learn from them. According to Habermas, secular reason needs this dialogue in order to cleanse itself from its own pathological and defeatist tendencies, as represented by the postmodern denial of universal reason or by scientistic rationalism (Habermas 2009b, 30).[5] Moreover,

---

[5] "'wissenschaftsgläubiger Naturalismus' und postmoderne 'Zuspitzung der Dialektik' der Aufklärung sind Zeichen dieses Defätismus".

he argues that religion also provides us with a sensibility and language for human phenomena, such as moral failings and forgiveness, which are essential for our life together, but which are absent from secular reason (Habermas 2005, 137).

Without denying in the least the positive aspects in Habermas' post-secular perspective, I do think that his remarkable criticism of secularism does not go far enough. For his post-metaphysical reasoning still operates on a basic opposition between transcendence and immanence. Christianity, however, arguably the most important shaper of social values in Western culture, has overcome this separation with the belief that God has become human in the incarnation. This teaching has deeply influenced the Western vision of what it means to be human. While claiming religion as an important resource for secular reasoning, Habermas, because of his dogmatic insistence that for a post-metaphysical worldview no possible synthesis of reason and faith can exist, misses the great potential of this particular Christian resource for uniting reason and faith (Reder and Schmidt 2008, 28). Modern philosophy, he claims, can no longer take recourse to a transcendent point of view (Habermas 2009a, 312) but knows only "natural reason". What, however is "natural reason?" The one that excludes transcendence? On whose authority is this natural? These kinds of questions reveal an essential weakness in the self-criticism of secular reason. For certainly what the word "natural" means is itself a matter of interpretation. For Habermas, "natural reasoning" stands for communicative action by which moral norms are rationally deduced from our social interactions. These rationally achieved values are religiously neutral and precede religious norms, which, for the purpose of public use and for the benefit of the constitutional state, have to be translated into the language of public rational discourse (Habermas 2005, 138).[6]

In short, a discourse ethic based on public reason remains the normative ideal and true source of public values, while religion is at best another valuable source, but one that requires translation into the primary discourse of public secular reason. This position, however, is plausible only if Habermasian discourse ethics was really a neutral basis for ethics, which it is not.[7] For example, the conception of personhood assumed by Habermas – an essential human dignity and the recognition of the other as equal dialogue partner – is a moral, indeed religiously founded, pre-political notion, that does not derive from discourse ethics but precedes it (Pera 2009, 107). Now, Habermas knows very well that his supposedly purely rationally-derived human values depend on religious roots. He himself refers repeatedly to the Judeo-Christian idea of the *imago dei*, of humanity as created in the image of God, as the foundation of human rights and as protection against the excesses of genetic

---

[6] Habermas is sensitive enough to insist that this demand for translation should not give the religious citizen the impression that his religion is relegated to the private sphere (Habermas 2001, 34).

[7] On this point, Charles Taylor remarks correctly that Habermas's distinction between a public political and a religiously motivated morality "would be more credible, if one had a watertight secular argument for rights. And this explains probably the difference between Habermas and myself on this point. He finds a secure foundation in a discourse ethic which I, unfortunately, consider fairly unconvincing" (Taylor 2011, 54).

engineering. Yet whenever his dependency on a religious tradition is pointed out to him, Habermas withdraws to a "purely philosophical approach" that is not tied to religious experience.[8]

Indeed, Habermas assumes simply as a matter of course that natural reason recognizes the cognitive value of religious traditions in their universal essence and then cleanses them from their religious particularity in preparation for their public consumption. Is it not the case, however, that Habermas' secular "natural reason" (Kalisch 2007, 29) acknowledges the biblical view of humanity as a universal truth only because he himself is already looking at it through a Christian lens (Pera 2009, 115)? Neither the German constitution nor secular reason is in fact self-sufficient, but each is a product of Christian imagination in the broadest sense, and can be neither comprehended nor sustained without this context.

Moreover, Habermas misjudges the nature of many religions, when he names inter-human dialogue as the only source of self-formation. He overlooks the important role in religion of dialogue with the divine other, as conducted in Christianity through bible reading, prayer, liturgy, preaching and sacrament. Apparently, this dialogue with God is not a legitimate aspect of self-formation and hence of reason for Habermas.

A related problem is that Habermas's insistence on translating religious values tends to split the religious citizen into two selves. At least his writing often conveys the impression that the religious self has to think separately from the public self (Junker-Kenny 2011, 107). This separation divides religious citizen from the innermost motivational power inherent in their religious values. In the case of the Christian faith, for example, Christian citizens (ideally) respect other members of society because, they, like themselves, participate in the living image of God in Christ, something they are reminded of every time Christ's incarnation, death, and resurrection are announced in church. The Christian citizen's solidarity derives not from an abstract, constitutional value of human rights, but from the intimate association of God with humanity in the incarnation celebrated by Christians every Sunday at the Eucharistic table. At the heart of her faith, the Christian is called to imitate God's love for human beings in Christ. To accept this participation as the engine for concrete human solidarity, however, violates the non-metaphysical, immanent frame imposed on us by constitutional patriots. Yet neither this non-metaphysical framework of post-secular nor the fear of religion that motivates it is necessary. Why not try another approach? Why not conceive the relation of religion and society from a religious perspective? This takes us to the final part of my presentation, namely to the humanistic roots of Western culture.

---

[8] Habermas argues that "secular reasons belong to a context of assumptions – in this case to a philosophical approach, which is distinguished from any kind of religious tradition by the fact that it doesn't require membership in a community of believers." For Habermas, religious reasoning depends on sharing in a specific religious tradition and community, while secular reason does not depend on tradition or faith (Taylor and Habermas 2011, 61).

Religion as Foundation for a Humanistic Cultural Ethos

The European, humanistic ideal of education provides a good illustration of the need to acknowledge the reciprocal relation between reason and faith. For when we examine the cultural roots of this humanistic ideal, we find that humanism begins with the Christian religion. We may be surprised by this claim, but analyzing historical source texts shows us that the Western humanistic ethos arose from a certain interpretation of the Christian faith by the early church. In what follows, I want to show that at the heart of Christian dogma lies a foundational humanistic impulse, and I believe that recovering this basic impulse can help us overcome the separation of reason and faith in post-secular thought and thus help us to address our currently identity crisis.

Indeed, Habermas himself has pointed us to the beginnings of the European humanistic ethos, namely the creation of humankind in the image of a personal, utterly sovereign creator God. We find this concept first in Judaism and Islam later adopted the same view (See, Küng 2004, 118; Rahman 1989, 5 and 65ff). Yet it is only with Christianity and its unique doctrine of God's becoming human that the *imago dei* becomes the foundation for a Christian humanism that in turn contributed significantly to the formation of European cultures. The heart of the Christian faith and thus of Christian humanism is God's incarnation in Jesus the Christ as the authoritative exemplar of what it means to be truly human, because early Christian theologians regarded Christ as the perfect image of God.

In contrast to Wolfgang Lieb's claim we heard earlier, this Christian idea of human nature cannot be opposed to a secular humanistic ideal because it is its very foundation. It is a common error to assume that humanism is by definition atheistic, secular humanism. Christians and atheists alike make this mistake; ironically, this is one of the few things on which they agree. The pervasiveness of equating humanism with secularism shows us how important it is to understand the religious roots that gave birth to our Western understanding of human nature and its corresponding institutions. Christian humanism is a foundational element of Western culture and constitutes the soul of our educational ideal. It is not by denying or belittling the Christian origins of humanism but by fully grasping their content that we can overcome the separation of reason and faith. Moreover, I believe that an in-depth understanding of Christian humanism can help dispel the worries of our religiously tone-deaf fellow citizens that religion is inherently dogmatic and intolerant. For contrary to Habermas's well-meant efforts, we will not re-establish the value of religion for democratic society by translating religious language into secular, post-metaphysical vocabulary in order to avoid the threat of religious fanaticism. A case in point is the Christian teaching of the incarnation. Only when we go to the full depth of Christology will we understand the importance of this teaching for the humanistic ethos of Western culture.

But surely, before Christianity, there were other humanisms? Indeed there were, but even these precursors of Christian humanism were never secularist. Already in its Greek and Roman beginnings, humanism had a metaphysical and even religious flavour. The Greek ideal educational ideal of παιδεία, which was later subsumed into the Roman concept *humanitas*, assumed that humanity existed within a divine, meaningful cosmos that provided the natural moral norms to which one must conform through education. Cicero's educational principles, which already carry the label *studia humanitatis*, adopted Greek anthropology. Reason (Ratio) and Language (Logos) allow human beings to develop beyond the merely instinctual life of their animal nature toward a community based on reason and virtue.[9] It is, to cite Cicero, "no insignificant manifestation of nature and reason that man is the only animal with a sense of order, decency, and continence in word and deed" (Cicero 1913, 14 [1.iv]).

Genuine humanity thus demands the cultivation of our spirit through literature and poetry because in them wisdom and virtue acquired through generations are deposited and passed on. Cicero's educational programme, therefore, already contains in a nutshell the educational principles of renaissance humanism (Buck 1987, 26),[10] which also subordinated knowledge and science to the attainment of true humanity (Cicero 1913, 156–157 [1.xliv]). Despite minor differences among ancient philosophies, we can thus make the general claim that ancient humanism pursued true humanity through soul formation (Buck 1987, 24).[11] As the intellectual historian Werner Jaeger has shown, however, the actual birth of Western humanism consisted in the adaptation and transformation of neo-Platonic philosophy by the church fathers. Using the theological filter of the incarnation, these early Christian theologians transformed Greco-Roman humanism into an image of humanity more familiar to us, that is, into the free, independently valuable individuals, who are nonetheless oriented toward human solidarity and neighbourly responsibility.

The Old Testament idea of a radically transcendent, personal creator God introduced important changes into the immanent worldview of Plato, Aristotle and ancient Stoic philosophy. Only a sovereign creator God who is utterly independent of the cosmos enables the contingency of the world and establishes human freedom and creativity in response to this deity. Jewish monotheism opposed itself to the myriad of capricious nature gods, to an indifferent, deterministic cosmos, and to an impersonal world soul, and offered instead the foundational notions of individual human dignity and freedom based on a personal I-Thou relation between the sovereign creator God and mankind. In contrast to Roman humanism, Judaism permitted neither a tribe nor the state to become a sacred entity that could demand our self-sacrifice for its cause. But only the Christian incarnation joins this radical transcendent God permanently to the world and to humanity. Of course, the Old Testament is replete with the presence of God in creation through theopanies and the interventions of divine power, but only in the incarnation does God irrevocably and physically tie himself in total solidarity to humanity. Only here divine wisdom and reason

---

[9] Cicero adopted from the Greek Stoa the teaching that "men are born for the sake of men, that they may be able mutually to help one another" (Cicero 1913, 22 [1.vii]).

[10] (See also, Nauert 2006, 12).

[11] For Cicero, "the cultivation of the soul is the nourishment of 'humanitas': cultus animi humanitatis cibus" (Cicero 1913, 156–157 [1.xliv]).

itself become human, and do so in a sacrificial event that provides a living divine
example and concrete definition of humanity as love for others. Like no other event,
God's identification with humanity to the point of death establishes the dignity and
the responsibility of our humanity (Balthasar 1967, 274).

The history of humanism, therefore, begins with Christology, that is, with the
interpretations of the incarnation offered by the apostles and the church fathers.
More specifically, humanism begins with the patristic claim that God became human
so that humanity could regain its god-likeness. The church father Irenaeus von Lyon
(135–202) is especially known for his interpretation of the incarnation as the reca-
pitulation of humanity through the god-man Jesus, who is the archetype, the original *imago dei*, according to whom God has designed humanity from the very first.
This idea is common among early Christian theologians, from Clement of Alexandria
to Athanasius and Augustine, who still repeats the common patristic formula that,
"the Son of God became the Son of Man, so as to make the sons of men into sons of
God" (Augustine 1990, 372).[12] For the Latin West, it is especially Augustine who
gathers the entire arsenal of pagan and Judeo-Christian educational tools to construct a Christian educational programme with the goal to attain god-likeness. Early
theologians used the word "divinization" for this process, a word that even Martin
Luther later used.[13] In a certain sense, therefore, the apotheosis of humanity is not at
all a secular humanistic boast, for the first people who talked about the divinization
of the human were the Christians. It is true, of course, that the Christian idea of
divinization takes up an earlier Platonic conception of assimilation to the divine.
One early Eastern Theologians, Basil of Caesaria, for example, simply adopts
Platonic vocabulary from the *Timaeus*: "but those conscious of the goal of our calling realize that we are *to become like God, as far as this is possible for human
nature*" (Basil 2005, 16). Yet this Platonic motif of becoming godlike undergoes a
radical transformation at Christian hands. Neither gnostic dualism with its attendant
mystical elitism nor the pursuit of virtue for its own sake becomes the mark of true
humanity, but rather communion with God and love of neighbour.[14]

Christianity also contributed to Western consciousness the idea of humanity's
moral progress. Many early theologians believed that without the fall humanity
would have naturally become like Christ, the archetypical human. Participation in

---

[12] See also Augustine's related statement that our salvation depends more on the incarnation of God
than on the mighty deeds wrought by him while on this earth: "Instead, we should rejoice and be
in wonder that our Lord Jesus Christ was made man, rather than that he, as God, performed divine
deeds among men. Our salvation, after all, depends more on what he was made on our behalf, than
on what he did among us" (Augustine 1990, 305).

[13] The German terms are "vermenschet" and "vergottet" respectively. Martin Luther, *D. Martin
Luthers Werke. Kritische Gesasmtausgabe, 58 volumes* Weimar, 1883, 20:229,30. Cited as a 1526
sermon in: (Marquart 2000, 185).

[14] David Sedley has shown convincingly for modern readers what was common knowledge among
ancient readers of Plato (including his Christian interpreters), namely that the goal of Plato's philosophy is "*homoiōsis theōi kata to dunaton*", to become like God as far as possible (See, Sedley
1999, 316ff). For the use and adaptation of this Greek ideal in the New Testament see: (Kooten
2008, 93–219).

the resurrected god-man had put humanity back on course toward this goal. For the fathers, the goal of Christian education was becoming truly human according to the archetype who had revealed himself in the incarnation as love for others.

The incarnation, death and resurrection of the god-man Jesus also inspired early Christians with hope for the unity of the human race, a hope often falsely believed to originate with Enlightenment humanism. The church fathers reminded Christians that the Eucharist especially celebrates the truth that in Christ all of humanity had been gathered up and unified beyond any national, racial and ethnic boundaries. They did, of course, differentiate between Christians and non-Christians, but this separation was not absolute. For participation in Christ connected every believer with humanity as a whole, and thus every human being becomes a neighbour for whom Christ died.

The basic motif of divinization as the goal of human knowledge carries over into the Christian humanism of the Middle Ages. Not only monastic but also scholastic humanism is shaped by this idea. The impressive systematization of all existing human knowledge by medieval scholastics was motivated by the desire to restore the kind of total knowledge mankind was believed to have had before the fall. Encouraged by the incarnation, Scholasticism also fostered trust in human reason based on its connection to divine reason to a degree that remains unequalled by any other culture. The belief in a rational universe and a correspondent human rationality capable of exploring this universe informed the entire scholastic enterprise and laid the foundation of Western science. It is true that scholasticism's aspirations for comprehensive knowledge eventually failed, and failed in part for lack of empirical observation, but the scholastic enthusiasm for rational logic nonetheless provided the foundation of the Enlightenment and of our universities.[15]

Finally, we move to Christian humanism in the Renaissance. The Renaissance is often viewed as a radical break from medieval humanism, as the liberation of human thought from its religious shackles, and as the first autonomous steps of Promethean man, who had always desired emancipation from God but only now found an opportunity to do so. This interpretation of the Renaissance as precursor to secularism may well confirm the lasting effect of the secularist subtraction narrative – that man's progress demands the demise of religion—on our interpretation of cultural history, but this view does not correspond to the historical facts. Renaissance research, especially in the 1970s and 1980s, has corrected this distorted view by showing that Renaissance humanism was essentially a Christian humanism. Historical research affirms that "from the time of Petrarch to that of Milton, the Christian humanists represent the main tradition of Western culture" (Dawson 2010, 32). The goal of this Christian humanism was the Christianization of society, which

---

[15] By recognizing the intrinsic rather than merely sacramental value of nature, scholastic humanism of the twelfth and thirteenth centuries, despite different metaphysical presuppositions, laid the groundwork for the scientific developments of the nineteenth and twentieth centuries (See, Southern 1995, 21).

also explains why many Renaissance humanists explicitly argued against secularization and against the separation of theology and philosophy (Southern 2001, 466).[16]

When we look at the educational ideal of Renaissance humanism, we find once again that god-likeness was the goal of human learning. When humanists such as Petrarch Coluccio Salutati, Lorenzo Valla, Marsilio Ficino, Giovanni Pico della Mirandola, Pietro Pomponazzi (and many others) describe human nature, they always refer to God who has become human and to the perfection of the *imago dei* in mankind. In short, the educational ideal of the Renaissance is not a precursor to secular humanism but builds on the Christian Platonism of the church fathers. Humanistic education is basically ascent to godlikeness through overcoming our lower, egoistic instincts. Education is still motivated by Christian anthropology, as one can see in the following citation from Pico dela Mirandolla (1463–94), whose important text *Oratio de hominis dignitate* is often falsely interpreted as a proto-secularist manifesto. Rather than proclaiming the independence of man from God, Pico uses the ancient Christian deification language based on the incarnation: "But just as all of us, who have obeyed God less than the devil, whose sons we are according to the flesh, have degenerated from human beings to animals, so we are also in the New Adam, Jesus Christ, who fulfilled the will of the Father and con-quered our spiritual vices by his blood, [God's] sons according to the spirit. By grace are we regenerated through the [god]-man, and adopted as sons of God."[17]

Thus for Renaissance humanism too, education aimed at attaining god-likeness. And even more strongly than Augustine, Renaissance humanists emphasized the role of language and rhetoric for self-knowledge. Once again, the incarnation played an important role in supporting this emphasis. Plato's problem of how the transcen-dent forms could manifest themselves ontologically without loss of being finds its solution in the incarnation, in which radical transcendence resides within being without any loss. On this incarnational basis, human reason, language and rhetoric can serve as reliable vehicles for divine and universal truths that illumine being itself and human existence.[18] The Renaissance ideal of education with its emphasis on self-knowledge through language and literature persists well into the eighteenth century, when the university professor Giambattista Vico has to defend Christian humanism against the rising Cartesian, rationalistic epistemology. Long before scientific positivism became the reigning paradigm for knowledge in modernity Vico complains about the narrowing of human rationality through a rationalism that many mistook "for the very voice of nature." In his more recent defense of the human sciences, Hans-Georg Gadamer recalls the importance of the incarnation for a humanistic model of truth beyond the extremes of rationalism and historicism.

---

[16] For example, Trinkaus shows that the Italian humanist Marcilio Ficino (1433–99) "wished to combat secularism as such, and he also was opposed to the separation of the study of philosophy in the universities' arts faculties from the exposition of revelation based on faith."

[17] *Commentary on Genesis* as qtd. in: (Trinkaus 1995, 517).

[18] It was one of Heidegger's cardinal mistakes not to have recognized this concern for understand-ing being through language and poetry in Renaissance humanism, a concern so congenial to his own philosophical project (Grassi 1983, 41).

Gadamer writes, "when the Greek idea of logic is penetrated by Christian theology, something new is born: the medium of language, in which the mediation of the incarnation event achieves its full truth. Christology prepares way for a new philosophy of man, which mediates in a new way between the mind of man in its finitude and the divine infinity" (Gadamer 2004, 428). Gadamer employs the incarnation to show that universal truths of human existence are indeed accessible to our minds through the mediation of language. On this basis, Gadamer reclaims self-knowledge and wisdom as the goals of humanistic education. He also reminds us, however, that because of the incarnation, the mediation of divine revelation through ontological structures is deeply rooted in Western, European thinking. In this way, the incarnation makes possible a synthesis of reason and faith, without thereby obviating the need for critical reasoning and interpretation. God's *kenosis* into being makes possible what theologians call a sacramental understanding of reality, in which worldliness, interpretation and historical-critical analysis of religion do not threaten the transcendence of God. Christology, in other words, allows Christian humanism to embrace a truly hermeneutical model of truth beyond secular or religious fundamentalisms. The belief that the wholly other God, truth Himself comes to us through the material world, that the eternal Word speaks to us through human words – this belief placed at the heart of Western humanism a unique love for words and interpretation and thus one of the best safeguards against bigotry and fundamentalism.

Conclusion

Our analysis of Europe's humanistic cultural ethos, and our brief examination of recent debates concerning the role of religion within democratic, constitutional societies were meant to show that without truly understanding the religious roots of our culture, we cannot really know, nor indeed begin to discuss adequately, who we are and what we ought to live for as a society. Above all, we have to eradicate every simplistic opposition of reason and faith. The history of humanism does not allow us, for example, to oppose a humanistic to a religious view of humanity. As we have seen, humanistic ideals grew on Christian soil, wherefore it is important that we recover the Christian humanistic tradition as a possible means for renewing our culture. Secularism is no help in this regard, because it is essentially parasitic, incapable of producing itself humane social values. Renewal of our humanistic cultural ethos will come only through a creative re-appropriation of our religious roots. Our ideals for being human and for becoming human derive from the biblical notion of our creation in the divine image, and on the specifically Christian view of the incarnation as the final interpretation of this image.

What does such a retrieval of Christian humanism look like? The Christian humanism of the German theologian Dietrich Bonhoeffer provides a good example. Bonhoeffer attributed the collapse of German culture and the general loss of human civilization to the occident's departure from the Christian ideal of humanity (Bonhoeffer 2010, 99). He argued that rebuilding Western culture after the war in

Germany required a spiritually vibrant and socially active Church, together with a strong secular government. Following the Augustinian model of politics, he ascribed to church and state different spheres of authority, but also argued that both authorities should be motivated by the same Christian humanist ethos, an ethos determined by the incarnation, death and resurrection of God in Christ, which signifies the reconciliation of the world to God, with the goal to bring to completion in all human beings the inherent image of God. Bonhoeffer retrieves the ancient Christian humanist notion that God became human in Christ so that we could achieve our full humanity, our god-likeness, through participation in God. And god-likeness, for Bonhoeffer, follows the kenotic example of the incarnation. Being a Christian necessarily is being humanistic because Christ's very being is a being for others. In one of his recent sermons, Pope Benedict states the same sentiment: "Christian existence is pro-existence, a being-there for another" (Benedikt 2011).[19] Becoming truly human should be the goal of every society and all politics. With this goal, Bonhoeffer recalls us to the ironically Christian origin of the word "secular," which was never meant to indicate a non-religious space but rather described two complementary spheres of public responsibility within a unified, divinely created reality shared by all citizens. Bonhoeffer divided this common sphere into divinely ordained responsibilities, such as government, family, work and culture. Each of these mandates enjoys relative autonomy, but all are meant to foster the free and responsible pursuit of our true humanity as embodied in the Christ event. The state itself cannot produce social values (Bonhoeffer 2010, 59), but ought to provide the political structures for ensuring the citizens' ability to pursue true humanity in freedom and responsibility. The church, however, proclaims and practices, but without any political or legal authority, the new humanity in Christ. This Christological centre ensures that religious and public self are not separated, but unified in the pursuit of our true humanity in all areas of life. The same Christological centre also enables social criticism and resistance against inhumane politics. Bonhoeffer's Christian humanism thus overcomes the still prevalent dualism of reason and faith, without, however, suggesting any form of theocracy.[20]

Time does not permit me to describe Bonhoeffer's Christian humanism in greater detail, and I will merely summarize three important points. First, Bonhoeffer regards the incarnation and Christian anthropology as the basis of Western culture. This religious foundation avoids the false dichotomy between religion and public life or between faith and reason.

Second, all areas of human life and knowledge are subservient to our becoming truly human. Third, Bonhoeffer ascribes to Christians the main role of rebuilding

---

[19] Stated in his homily during mass at the airfield Freiburg in Breisgau, Sunday, September 25, 2011.

[20] Bonhoeffer's Christian humanism is essentially an interpretive faith. Christian faith is not a static construct, and does not propagate timeless ethical principles that have to be "aped" without understanding application (Bonhoeffer 2010, 86). Rather, the central concern of the Christian faith is that Christ takes shape in church and society, so that the human ideal embodied in Him can manifest itself in concrete social and political practices through responsible action (Bonhoeffer 2010, 89).

culture. They constitute the soul and driving power behind the humanistic ethos, not through political or legal power but rather through the responsible practice of their faith. This Christian humanism is motivated by genuine participation in divine, transcendent realities. After all, as Bonhoeffer says, "who talks about a new world and a new humanity without hoping that he will participate in them" (Bonhoeffer 1984, 498–499)? Moreover, those who participate in Christ's new humanity renounce any desire for erecting God's kingdom on earth. Because God redeemed the world, not through asserting political power, but through identifying with humanity to the point of death, Christian humanism pursues a political realism rather than a revolutionary fanaticism. Christians should not expect the civil authorities to transform society. Renewal comes only as Christians live out their faith as those being shaped into Christlikeness (Bonhoeffer 2009, 294–295). In doing so, Christians should not think that they are called to construct some ideal society, but to imitate God's love for humanity through concrete actions. As Bonhoeffer once put it, "No one has the responsibility of turning the world into the kingdom of God, but only of taking the next necessary step that corresponds to God's becoming human in Christ" (Bonhoeffer 1996, 224–225).

References

Augustine, Saint. 1990. *Homilies on the Gospel of John 1–40*. The works of Saint Augustine: A translation for the 21st century, vol. 12, part 3. Trans. Edmund Hill. Hyde Park: New City Press.

Basil, Saint, the Great. 2005. *On the Human Condition*, Vladimir's Seminary Press "Popular Patristics" Series. Trans. Nonna Verna Harrison. Crestwood: St. Vladimir's Seminary Press.

Benedict XVI. 2007. *Gott und die Vernunft: Aufruf zum Dialog der Kulturen*. Augsburg: Sankt Ulrich Verlag.

Benedikt XVI. 2011. Eucharistiefeier. http://www.vatican.va/holy_father/benedict_xvi/homilies/2011/documents/hf_ben-xvi_hom_20110925_freiburg_ge.html. Accessed 13 May 2012.

Bonhoeffer, Dietrich. 1984. *1. Korinther 13:13. In Predigten – Auslegungen – Meditationen: 1925–1945, 2 v*. München: C. Kaiser.

Bonhoeffer, Dietrich. 1996. *Ethics. Dietrich Bonhoeffer works*, vol. 6. Minneapolis: Fortress Press.

Bonhoeffer, Dietrich. 2009. *Berlin: 1932–1933*, Dietrich Bonhoeffer works. Trans. Isabel Best and David Higgins. Minneapolis: Fortress Press.

Bonhoeffer, Dietrich. 2010. *Ethik. Dietrich Bonhoeffer Werke*. Gütersloh: Gütersloher Verlag.

Buck, August. 1987. *Humanismus: seine europäische Entwicklung in Dokumenten und Darstellungen*, Orbis academicus. Freiburg: Karl Alber.

Bulliet, Richard W. 2004. *The case for Islamo-Christian civilization*. New York: Columbia University Press.

Casanova, José. 2009a. *Europas Angst vor der Religion*, Berliner Reden zur Religionspolitik, 1st ed. Berlin: Berlin University Press.

Casanova, José. 2009b. The secular and secularism. *Social Research: An International Quarterly* 76(4): 1049–1066.

Cicero, Marcus Tullius. 1913. *Circero XXI: On duties*, The Loeb classical library, vol. 30. Cambridge, MA: Harvard University Press.

Dawson, Christopher. 2010. *The crisis of western education*, The works of Christopher Dawson. Washington, DC: Catholic University of America Press.

Dupré, Louis K. 2008. *Religion and the rise of modern culture*, Erasmus Institute books. Notre Dame: University of Notre Dame Press.

Chapter 5
The Search for the Meaning of Liberty from Christian Humanism: New Perspectives for the Twenty-First Century

Markus Krienke

Abstract Christian Humanism can provide an important contribution during this crisis of political and economic institutions based upon the ethical value of human liberty. As the only possible exit strategy, we need to rethink the original ethical implications of liberty, which are often confused with individualist or libertarian ideas on the one hand, or with collective and communitarian ideas on the other. Christian Humanism, as it is articulated in the most recent encyclical, *Caritas in Veritate*, provides an alternative conception: facilitating liberty means rebuilding society beginning from authentic human relationships. If we focus only upon the relationships of individuals, we are unable to escape from the libertarianism-communitarianism dichotomy. Such an impasse results even from an analysis of the major interpretations of the recent encyclical, which can be nominated "institutional reductionism" and "institutional overstrain". *Caritas in Veritate*, however, attempts to overcome this false dichotomy with the consideration of those more foundational relationships in which human liberty is articulated: those of the family and with the transcendent. Can our concept of liberty in society be rethought beginning from this ethical foundation implied in Christian humanism?

Keywords Liberalism • Anti-perfectionism • Civil society • Subsidiarity • Social market economy • Civil economy

Benedict XVI's pontificate, in light of his moral exhortations as well as his social teaching, can be read as an inspiration for a "new Christian Humanism": such a humanism is the Pope's response to the social challenges of the new century, characterized as challenges for liberty and thus as challenges for our social institutions based upon the fundamental value of liberty (Röpke 1950). From its very beginning, as well as during the era of globalization, Catholic Social Teaching was meant to contribute to the understanding and application of the meaning of liberty in this

M. Krienke (✉)
Theological Faculty of Lugano, Lugano, Switzerland
e-mail: krienke@rosmini.ch

© Springer Science+Business Media Dordrecht 2015
D. Melé, M. Schlag (eds.), *Humanism in Economics and Business*,
Issues in Business Ethics 43, DOI 10.1007/978-94-017-9704-7_5

69

context. In this paper, I will show that the "new humanism" of Benedict XVI creates the possibility of defining the idea of *moral liberty* or of *liberty in constitutive relationships* and thus liberty not only as a "right" but also as a "duty", regarded in the Catholic tradition as a structural element of social institutions. This specifically Catholic interpretation of social institutions is significantly different from a merely liberal or Protestant understanding.

In the opinion of the Pope, this dimension is fundamentally situated within a Trinitarian ontology and indeed, the entire encyclical *Caritas in veritate* (CV) can be read as a treatise on Trinitarian ontology. Thus, the core task of this paper is to elaborate which new dimensions for our concept of liberty can be extrapolated from this document: what are the institutional elements of a Christian personalism, or a new humanism, for the twenty-first century understanding of liberty? Methodically I will approach this question from the perspective of social order.

Without any doubt, one of the most important influences of the Catholic Social Teaching is found in the second half of the twentieth century in its synthesis with the ordoliberalism of the Freiburg school (Walter Eucken, Franz Böhm, Hans Grossmann-Dörth) and the liberal model of a Social Market Economy – "one of the most famous political and economic strategies of this century" (Rösch 2011). This strategy does not gamble with human dignity but creates the conditions for man's development as a free person (John Paul II 1991, 34f., 42; Benedict XVI 2009, 35). Its supporters consider this theory the only satisfying answer to the challenges of nineteenth century capitalism, the cause of the social question: from the beginning, the Social Market Economy recognizes that a "good" constitution of the economic sphere is only possible with a free market as the regulative model. Any other model inevitably destroys liberty and fails with regard to the unique social criterion of human dignity. Hence, Wilhelm Röpke has asserted: "What is liberalism? It is humanistic. This means that it begins with the presupposition that the nature of man is capable of good and that man is realized only in society, that his destination transcends his material existence, and that we owe respect to every single man as a man whose uniqueness forbids us to degrade him to a mere means. It is, thus, individualistic or, if you prefer, personalistic" (Röpke 1979, 19). Such a vision demands a system of rules that protects free competition against any monopolistic tendencies. The first defining characteristic of the Social Market Economy is that the State may influence the market rules but cannot interfere directly with the market in the manner of an economic actor: "What, therefore, should be the nature of state activity? The answer is that the state should influence the forms of economy, but not itself direct the economic process…. State planning of forms – Yes; state planning and control of the economic process – No! The essential thing is to recognize the difference between form and process, and to act accordingly" (Eucken 1951, 72). The second specific characteristic of the Social Market Economy is the insight that a free market works "well" only when combined with a system of social equity and fair partnership: without social security, the market would tend towards its own destruction. However, the state-organized system of social security must not contradict the freedom of market and thus the freedom of people. Hence, it can be realized only by interventions complying with the system and its rules rather than by State interference. The idea of the Social Market Economy follows the logic that the better market freedom works, the less need there will be of social assistance. However, this functioning presupposes a certain moral configuration of society, and the Christian humanism of *Caritas in veritate* focuses and reflects upon this moral configuration.

For this liberal interpretation of Catholic Social Teaching in regard to the market order, the major protagonists rely primarily upon the ordoliberals of the twentieth century (the so-called "liberalism of rules") and upon the liberal Catholic authors of the nineteenth and twentieth centuries. Today we find similar authors in Robert Sirico or Michael Novak in the U.S.A. or in Dario Antiseri and Flavio Felice in Italy (Sirico 1998; Novak 1981, 1993; Felice 2005; Antiseri et al. 2002).

Nonetheless, there are also other approaches within the discussion on Catholic social ethics. Communitarian positions criticize the liberal interpretation for empha-sizing individualism and underestimating the priority of the social dimension of the human person (Gutmann 1985). They attempt to demonstrate that the current crisis is the consequence of the "tragic victory" of liberalism at the end of the twentieth century, particularly after the fall of the Berlin Wall, and the increasing dynamics of globalized individualization and liberalization. They favor a skeptical attitude towards liberty. In their opinion, Catholic Social Teaching has always been opposed to the liberal tradition. Instead, they have proposed a "third way" beyond liberalism and communism. This position has a long tradition, having already characterized the solidaristic position of the turn of the nineteenth and twentieth centuries (Pesch 1902) and being well and alive today. But how can we reconcile this position not only with the undeniable liberal elements in the social encyclicals but also with the clear affirmation, since John XXIII, that Catholic Social Teaching "does *not* pro-pose a third way" (John Paul II 1988, 41)?

Thus, the contemporary discussion is framed by these two positions: on the one hand, the liberal current that relies primarily upon Protestant authors and a few lib-eral Catholic scholars, and on the other hand, the traditional Catholic interpretation, which is quite skeptical towards modern liberty. In my opinion, faced with this alternative reflecting the classical confrontation of capitalism and communism, we are dealing with the result of a serious reflection upon the situation of globalization as presented by *Caritas in veritate*: in responding to the challenge of globalization, it discloses a new position in order to establish a concept of liberty that can be authentically considered a Catholic position on liberty and the basis for a proposal for a new humanism in the twenty-first century. Benedict XVI, following an Augustinian orientation, relies upon a Trinitarian ontology, hence overcoming the modern dichotomy of liberalism-communitarianism. In order to understand the per-spective of the "new humanism" of *Caritas in veritate* – which understands "new" in the sense of a return to Christian origins, particularly to the Fathers – we need to understand that Benedict XVI does not focus upon a problem of too much liberty but a misunderstanding of what liberty means, or a certain lack of liberty. This "certain lack" concerns the *moral dimension* of liberty, which can be understood as the core concept of the encyclical. Against communitarian positions, this interpreta-tion underlines that in the perspective of Christian Humanism the present economic crisis is not the "victory" but the very "crisis" of the liberal concept of liberty. But against the liberal positions, the encyclical asserts that the answer is not to be found in a radicalization of the Protestant roots of the Social Market Economy. It is rather inspired by the idea that if Christian Humanism did not include liberty, and in reaction to the crisis negated liberty, then it would surrender to a most radical misunderstanding, and – most importantly – it would lose its force as a positive contribution to the overcoming of this crisis.

The Challenge of Globalization

The new situation in *Caritas in veritate* that requires a rethinking of the classical principles of Catholic Social Teaching, is the loss of State framework in the current era of globalization. The classical principles of the Catholic Social Teaching lose the institutional anchorage within which they had been developed in the twentieth century. In order to find new answers, Benedict XVI guides the discussion back to the fundamental inspirations of Christian Humanism.

The answer of the latest encyclical, coherent with a reconstruction of the social ethical argumentation of Joseph Ratzinger, is the integration of the model of the market economy with the dimensions of gift and forgiveness. This is not due to external coincidence but due to a systematic need. In this way, Pope Benedict XVI develops and integrates the social-liberal perspectives of *Centesimus annus*, characterized by an optimism of institutional liberty, with the dimension of individual morality (i.e., virtues). Gift and forgiveness, the first consequences of love, permeate the sphere of social institutions with the values of "real humanism" in a Christian perspective. But such a theological view of social thought causes a dilemma: if it is true that charity, as the Christian concretization of liberty, is the correct humanistic expression of the Christian faith, how can this dimension be combined with socio-institutional, and thus economic, ideas in social ethical thought? Although Benedict XVI tries to clarify the specifically Christian answer, we have to ask how this answer can be translated into a universal social ethical concept.

In my opinion, the key to the answer is to be found in two sentences of paragraph 37. I suggest approaching paragraph 37 in three interpretative steps: "[1] *Economic life* undoubtedly requires *contracts*, in order to regulate relations of exchange between goods of equivalent value. [2] But it also needs *just laws* and *forms of redistribution* governed by politics, [3] and what is more, it needs works redolent of the *spirit of gift*". In the first two steps, we find a summary of the two principles of the Social Market Economy: first, the catalytic structure of the market economy (a reinterpretation of Thomas Aquinas' *iustitia commutativa*), and second, the social dimension that cannot be realized by the state as economic actor but only by the state as the rule-setter, determining "just laws" and "forms of redistribution" (a reinterpretation of Aquinas' *iustitia legalis* and *iustitia distributiva*). The latter element must obviously not be interpreted as a type of assistentialism but as a statutory obligation of society towards every individual (Sirico 2001, 149, 153). Thus, these first two steps are the consequences of the fundamental negative and positive liberties of the person in his inalienable dignity: they realize *social justice*.

But, with the third step, Benedict XVI raises another question: what are the preconditions for this realization of liberty? Does the market economy have moral preconditions, as even many classic liberal scholars, such as Smith and von Hayek, do not deny? How can social justice, as *Quadragesimo anno* has already theorized, be integrated with social charity, particularly in the midst of recent challenges? The encyclical characterizes globalization as an extreme form of capitalism. In an article published only 2 months before the encyclical, Bockenforde – Ratzinger's and Habermas' primary reference in their 2004 discussion – called this form of capitalism "turbocapitalism" (Böckenförde 2011). Although we can exclude a possible influence of Böckenförde's article upon the encyclical, such a phrase expresses quite succinctly the fundamental problem of "self-referential individualism" as the propulsive power of capitalism, in which the "free market must of necessity be the only regulative principle" (Böckenförde 2011). Alternatively, Böckenförde does not suggest a return to a planned economy but points to a new social sphere between the individual and the State, which has not been considered by the classical dichotomy of liberalism and communitarianism: the society that realizes the value of solidarity. Since the ordoliberal system does not consider this sphere, its regulative instruments are considered insufficient tools against the current crisis. Therefore, the core problem of capitalism from a social ethical view is *not* the egoism of individuals as such – such egoism constitutes at the least a problem for individual virtues. But the real risk of anti-humanistic individualism is that it hinders the realization of the two principles of the Social Market Economy. The authors cited in Böckenförde's essay, Marx and Thomas Aquinas, indicate the direction in which he seeks to find an alternative model to capitalism: such an alternative should be based on solidarity and the common good. John Paul II, moreover, is called the "the most acute critic of capitalism after Karl Marx" (Böckenförde 2011). In my opinion, this essay confronts all of the risks in the famous "Böckenförde dilemma", according to which "the liberal, secularised state is nourished by presuppositions that it cannot itself guarentee. That is the great gamble it has made for liberty's sake" (Böckenförde 1991, 45). This theorem faces the risk of not confronting modernity and thus either denying modernity or dealing with it in a way that can hardly be harmonized with the liberal dimensions of the Catholic Social Teaching: indeed, for establishing social solidarity, Böckenförde – in an Hegelian tradition – rejects the first alternative and demands a strong State that defines the "common good".

In my opinion, the encyclical suggests an alternative solution: it does not reclaim any ground for the State but refers instead to the idea of the person and of its fundamental relational dimensions: this is the aim of its Trinitarian ontology. And there, the question of a humanistic dimension of civil society becomes virulent: for Ratzinger – as he has already pointed out in other statements – the presence of Christianity constitutes a vivid source of a type of relationship which is presupposed by the market economy but that cannot be achieved by the logic of economic order, because it is the consequence of the social-ontological dimension of human nature: "The Christian revelation of the unity of the human race presupposes a *metaphysical interpretation of the 'humanum' in which relationality is an essential element"* (Benedict XVI 2009, 55). The dimensions of gift and forgiveness are metaphysically collocated in a relational ontology offered by a Trinitarian ontology. In this context, relationship is as an essential aspect of human nature and not a mere accidental addition to the individual substance of a rational nature, as Boethius would have us think. The solidarity of giving and forgiving is the source of the renewal of the civil society. In this dimension of civil society, which is – as we have seen – the social dimension of moral liberty, the Pope finds the fundamental basis for the renewal of solidarity and subsidiarity as the basic normative elements of a society inspired by Christian Humanism. We must now elaborate how this approach can overcome the traditional contradiction between liberal and communitarian approaches, and therefore also the limitations of Böckenförde's theorem, in a new perspective of Christian Humanism.

Possible Misunderstandings of the Encyclical's Position

To find an answer to this question, we need to analyze the two major interpretations of the encyclical; this brings us to the conceptual background of the encyclical. The third dimension of the economic order in paragraph 37 can be interpreted as a synthesis of both major interpretations, which transcends their differences so as to converge in a specific Christian conviction. Confirmed by recent sociological and psychological studies, this conviction is the assertation that the *homo oconomicus-model*, characterizing the market economy in terms of an individualist rationality, is unable to reflect the nature of human action in its entirety. Human beings do not act purely as *homo oeconomicus* but also according to the dimensions of human, interpersonal relationships, as seen in gift and forgiveness. Consequently, we cannot say that the economic dimension is simply added to the reality of interpersonal life (Zamagni 2007, 55f.; Felice 2001, 21f.). Therefore, the third step is not a mere addition but a real paradigm shift in Catholic Social Teaching. In fact, both approaches intend to realize the Trinitarian ontology required by the encyclical (Zamagni 2007, 59). The most significant element of the new paradigm is the recovery of the dimension of civil society, transcending the individual-State dichotomy. In other words, both major interpretations argue that charity consists in regaining the dimension of civil society, often limited (in the Hegelian tradition) to a sphere of rational self-interests and thus a sort of "market place" that requires the State as the guarantor of social justice and common good. Now the question of the institutional dimensions opened by the encyclical arises. In this regard, the two major interpretations differ characteristically: while Flavio Felice reads the document from a Social Market Economy point of view, Stefano Zamagni re-proposes a model of the civil economy in order to face current challenges. These two authors represent the two primary European interpretations of the encyclical, which only meet within the Italian forum. For this reason, it is important to present this discussion to a broader international audience.

Institutional Reductionism

For Flavio Felice, the encyclical's position is not substantially different from a classic liberal point of view (Felice 2010, 28–33). He finds the moral dimension already present not only in Smith and von Hayek but primarily in the fathers of the Social Market Economy themselves, e.g. Müller-Armack and especially Wilhelm Röpke (Felice 2010, 13). He emphasizes the importance of the individual position in opposition to State assistentialism: the "social" aspect of the market economy does not consist in mired State interventions but in guaranteeing equal access to the market (Felice 2010, 33). The liberal rights protected by the State and its order are the most important instruments in defending individual liberty and achieving well-being for all. According to Dario Antiseri, the "liberal Catholic defends the market economy, because it generates, first of all, the greatest prosperity for the greatest number of persons and, generally, for everyone" (Antiseri 2007, 35). This is not an individualist utilitarianism, which the liberal Catholic approach would immediately reject. It rather shows the correspondence between the liberal Catholic tradition and liberal scholars; e.g. Hayek expressly points to a "true individualism", positively underlining the importance of the moral relational values of individuals against every form of "false individualism", which in the end identify society with a heap of individual grains of sand (Hayek 1947). Furthermore, this "false individualism" would lead directly to collectivism and totalitarianism since they require fragile and unrelated individuals. Applying a Christian lens to this approach, Röpke speaks of the necessary "spiritual and moral bond" of society as an indispensable condition for the market economy, a condition "beyond supply and demand" (Röpke 1958). In this sense, the liberal approach does not necessarily negate either the moral dimension or the importance of family and spontaneous associations at the level of civil society (Hayek 1947). But since markets are morally neutral, it is equally impossible to directly insert the moral perspective therein (Felice 2011, 213): for the liberal approach, the dimension of gift in *Caritas in veritate* is, and remains, an experience beyond the market – a dimension already recognized by Adam Smith.

Analyzing this position, we can trace this approach to the Protestant individualist tradition: it does not deny the moral dimension, but it transforms it into an individual duty. We can find this doctrine philosophically elaborated in Kant and also at the basis of Smith and of Röpke. For Röpke, moral values are realized not in and through social institutions – least of all through the market – but in the individual sphere by the morally elite of society. The social dimension is not characterized by a certain system of ethics, because economic and financial logic dominate this level (Felice 2010, 280). It is emblematic that both Röpke and the libertarian Friedman emphasize the importance of family not as a social institution, but exclusively in its individual-moral dimension (Röpke 2006, 146). If for Novak moral discipline creates success, it is the same success that inevitably corrodes moral discipline (Novak 1982): in other words, the liberal system entrusts its presuppositions to individual morality. Otherwise, the system would lead to its own decline.

Another important dimension of the liberal interpretation is the constitutive anti-perfectionism of Catholic Social Teaching (Felice 2011). Without any doubt, we are dealing here with a central dimension of Catholic social thought: due to the limitation of human nature by the reality of sin, no social system can reach perfection. All attempts to realize such perfection inevitably lead to totalitarianism and the sacrifice of individual persons. But the way in which Felice and other modern liberal Catholic scholars seek to identify this topic with the liberal Protestant tradition is significant: they read *Caritas in veritate* and *Centesimus annus* in the light of Röpke (Felice 2010, 39) and *The Federalist Papers* (Felice 2001, 27), and not the other way round. Consequently, the open nature of social systems, particularly the economic system, is the greatest ethical affirmation that this liberal Protestant approach can express. The moral dimension of Christian Humanism is left to be individually realized by the morally elite (Röpke 1958, 192; Goldschmidt 2009). This individualist morality, left to human nature characterized by sin, leads to moral pessimism. Since Felice's idea is quite close to Röpke's, we also need to consider the consequences of Röpke's approach for Felice's suggestion. Its primary characteristic is that it does not theorize an institutional realization of morality. I would like to call this approach "*institutional reductionism*". Although this liberal concept, upon which Felice and Röpke rely, is not opposed to Christianity (Röpke 1979, 18), it still operates within a very limited area of Christian social ethics.

Institutional Overstrain

For Stefano Zamagni, the position of the encyclical cannot be situated within the classical liberal tradition, and even less among liberal Catholic scholars, because the real aim of Catholic Social Teaching would be a radical change of the classical liberal approach to the economy: "the certainly less than marginal profit offered to us by *Caritas in veritate* consists in defining a position in favor of that conception of market typical of the tradition of the civil economics, according to which the experience of human society occurs within a normal economic life and not perhaps outside or beside it, somehow suggesting a dichotomy within the social order" (Zamagni 2009, 18). Scola follows the same argument when he affirms "the importance, also technical, of that which is referred to as 'economic logic' (CV 32, 36), or altruism. Without it, the market cannot function well (CV n. 35)" (Scola 2011, 231). In contrast to the liberal position, Zamagni and other scholars interpret the dimensions of gift and charity in the third step of paragraph 37 as somehow to be implemented within the marketplace itself: thus *homo oeconomicus* is substituted by *homo ethicus* (Zamagni 1995, XVII). In consequence of this interpretation, they also tend to consider the redistributive dimension of the second step as an affirmation of the necessity of welfare (Zamagni 2009, 88). Despite this clear contrast, however, they do agree with the anti-statism of the liberal interpretation. For Zamagni, welfare must not be funded by the State, but by a new market order, supporting not only profit-oriented companies but also non-profit businesses. This new paradigm, caused by the transforming power of gift, charity and altruism, has to create the conditions under which such non-profit businesses can exist. How can this be achieved? Zamagni sees only one way: referring and leading the economy back to its social basis, and thus reintegrating interpersonal relations therein. In this light, the encyclical examines not only the interpersonal relationships of human beings, but it also aims at re-valuing civil society (Zamagni 2008; Bruni 2008).

The reason for this approach is that without the constitutive dimension of charity for the economic order, *Caritas in veritate* would not add anything to the *status questionis* of *Centesimus annus*. In this context, Scola cites Guardini: "The Trinity teaches that everything, precisely everything could be, and in its highest grade should be, common" (Scola 2011, 231). This approach – like the liberal interpretation – reclaims the principle of subsidiarity in a communitarian dimension (Scola 2011, 232). As we can immediately see, these scholars, by valuing the Trinitarian ontology necessitated by the encyclical, try to avoid any individualist reduction of the human being that would lead to a consequent institutional reduction of the charity approach. Man is not to be understood as an individual, and *homo oeconomicus* is replaced by *homo reciprocans*. As a consequence, the dimensions regarding gift, charity and altruism, which *institutional reductionism* had placed in a dimension outside of, or better as subservient to, the market have now become a dimension within the market. The market itself must realize the dimension of gift: therefore Zamagni refers to the classical approaches of civil economics that founded the economy not upon the individual and his intentional actions, but upon reciprocity, including the constitutive dimensions of altruism and liberty. This approach obviously utilizes the same anthropological reasoning (personalism) of the representatives of *institutional reductionism*. But Zamagni, instead of reducing the moral dimension to the individual sphere, extends it to the social dimension. This brings a strong communitarian dimension into the social sphere. Consequently, the concept of the "common good" is the primary characteristic of this approach. This is problematic insofar as the moral dimension is hence to be realized not only by individuals but also by the social order; such a method tends to overburden the subject with its moral expectations. Therefore, I would like to call this approach "*institutional overstrain*".

But are these two positions – the institutional reductionism of social justice and the institutional overstrain of the common good – really incompatible? Beyond their differences, we can also find some agreement within their anti-state and anti-perfectionistic argumentation as well as the re-evaluation of civil society. This is due to the fact that both approaches go back to the Trinitarian idea of charity as it applied to the question of the economic order in paragraph 37 of *Caritas in veritate*. While the liberal approach interprets the Trinitarian perspective as a moral condition for the functioning of the Social Market Economy, the civil economy approach understands it as the inner and central dimension of the necessarily new interpretation of the market economy itself.

Confronting the difficulty of reconciling these different concepts by pointing to an inner coherence, we have to remember the encyclical's admonition that "[t]he Church does not have technical solutions to offer" (Benedict XVI 2009, 9). This means that whenever social ethical argumentation arrives at a contradiction, the discussion has to return to the anthropological foundation, beginning once more from such a basis: the aim of Catholic Social Teaching is not to present a "third system" but to find the right anthropological and institutional presuppositions for the "technical discourse". Thus, the recent discussion between the *institutional reduction* approach and the *institutional overstrain* approach brings us back to the initial question about the new Christian humanism in the Trinitarian perspective of the encyclical and its institutional consequences, particularly for the economic order. By means a Trinitarian ontology, we can constructively confront the current social challenges within a perspective that overcomes the sphere of contingent logic – the reason for the contradiction between the two systems analyzed.

Reconsidering the Perspective of Caritas in veritate

Within the Trinitarian perspective, the encyclical does not provide any solution to the antagonism of these two interpretations, because it does not correspond to the task of an encyclical to resolve systematic-technical problems but to open up possibilities of reflection and further development. It does not resolve the social challenge on the institutional level, and so it avoids a decision between *institutional reductionism* and *institutional overstrain*. While on the one hand, it does underline the ordoliberal approach and confirm the approach of *Centesimus annus*, on the other hand, it does not leave any doubt about the fact that the institutional approach is insufficient and that we need to elaborate strategies of reform for traditional institutions within the dimensions of gift, charity and altruism, thus with the elements of a new individual ethics. In order to avoid systematic incompatibilities and contradictions of a purely institutional approach, Benedict XVI suggests and favors an individualist approach to the virtues. In other words, the alternative between institutional reductionism and institutional overstrain is declared insurmountable. A solution can only be found by redirecting the discussion to the individual ethical dimension. The strategy of *Caritas in veritate* therefore seems to focus upon the reinforcement of Christian humanism in order to newly inspire society and its order. In such a perspective, the "relationship" underlined by the Trinitarian ontology of *Caritas in veritate* results in a mere individual concept and instructs the individual as to the best use of his liberty as employer, employee or consumer.

This perspective finds systematic support in Max Scheler: reflecting upon the manner in which an individualist moral approach can produce systematic results, Scheler views the economic system as a consequence of the anthropological commitments of society (Scheler 1979). Catholic Social Teaching would not have to suggest a "third system", but form the anthropological convictions of the society, influencing the social system in this way.

Böckenförde's theorem also provides certain arguments for the individualist moral approach: according to Böckenförde, the market cannot establish itself without moral predispositions. Thus, the dimension of gift has to be restituted to the public (not State or institutional) sphere (Böckenförde 2011).

But such an answer, which only divides the individual from the institutional dimension, and demands greater morality, is unsatisfying. Zamagni does well to criticize such a model based upon the polarity of the State and the individual, identifying the first with public interest and the common good, and the latter with private interests (Zamagni 2007, 22). But the Trinitarian approach of the encyclical itself is not reducible to such a dichotomy. In order to better understand the institutional consequences of the charity and gift approach of the encyclical, it seems worthy to defer to a forgotten thinker. Protagonist of a liberal Catholic approach already in nineteenth century Europe and thus too progressive for his time, he is only recently beginning to be appreciated in Catholic social thought.

The Perspective of Antonio Rosmini

The analysis of the ideas of Antonio Rosmini, who more than a century and a half ago reflected upon this dilemma in his monumental *Philosophy of Right*, can help us to discover a dimension that the current discussion has not yet considered (Rosmini 1993–1996). Avoiding both *institutional reductionism* and *institutional overstrain*, his strategy, contrary to the individualist Protestant tradition of modernity, would allow the social moral dimension of man to be brought into the social discourse and thus transfer the relational aspect of Christian humanism – which according to the encyclical is the centre of the Trinitarian ontology in social ethical thought – to the sphere of social institutions. Contrary to an approach that eliminates the individual dimension in the civil sphere and overburdens the individual with communitarian expectations, such a strategy would maintain the liberal constitutional foundational order that guarantees fundamental liberties to individual and intentional action. Furthermore, this dimension would institutionalize gift and altruism which, for both approaches remain simply and merely individualistic.

Rosmini's *Philosophy of Right* distinguishes, therefore, between individual and social rights (Krienke 2011). Individual rights are fundamental for the human being and hence found the individual consequences of his personalist approach. In regard to social rights, he develops the theory of the "three societies": man does not exist merely as an individual but his development requires social relations. These social relations are not at the arbitrary disposition of the individual. Although the individual can dispose of them to some extent, for Rosmini it is a fact that beyond their ontological foundation, their concrete realization in liberty is a constitutive aspect of human perfection. Arguing against perfectionism in the political system, Rosmini underlines that the *individual* tendency to perfection can be thought together with liberty and limitation of human nature.

For Rosmini, man realizes his perfection in two ways, in his nature and in his personality, through two relationships which precede the civil relationship. The perfection of nature takes place within the family and constitutes the natural relationship of the "domestic society"; the perfection of personality takes place in the "supernatural family", the religious community or "theocratic society", constituted by the transcendental relationship. Moreover, these two fundamental relationships of nature and of personality, ontologically founded, have to be constitutionally realized on the social level: the family and the religious community are the essential elements for a subsidiary structure of society. Therefore Rosmini nominates them the original societies, with which civil society is related only in a subsidiary way. In these original societies, the dimensions of gift and forgiveness are realized, and this realization is not a duty of the State or of the general public, but of individuals.

The social institutions of the family and religious communities which, founded upon the ontological dimensions of human nature and personality, are beyond the arbitrary decisions of individuals and, which are the ontological *a priori* for the concrete realization of human liberty, are the consequences of the reality of the person (i.e. personalism). Their concrete humanistic dimension is found in: (1) the perfection of the individual nature, and therefore the liberty of individuals which only act through individual, intentional actions, and (2) the non-arbitrary structure of the relationship aspect of human nature, which is essentially a mutual relationship, thus directed towards another person (matrimony, children) and to the transcendent (God). This shows why for Rosmini family and religious community are the constitutive elements avoiding the institutional reductionism of social order to the mere individual dimension as well as institutional overstrain, both of which reference an unilateral interpretation of subsidiarity. In the institutional sphere, realized by the systemization of fundamental social rights, the individual and the social spheres are reconciled. Thus, the social right in Rosmini can be considered as model for the realization of *Cartias in veritate*'s indications for the social ethical order in twenty-first century, reconciling solidarity and subsidiarity as anticipated by Benedict XVI (2009) 58. The State needs institutions that allow and facilitate the development of those social competences that transfer the dimensions of gift and forgiveness into reality. This is only possible if the State does not claim to produce these relational realities itself but leaves their development to the social sphere. The social sphere has to be systematically thought and constitutionally realized according to the fundamental ontological relations of the individual persons, not as a replacement of the State. In his idea of "social rights", Rosmini responds perfectly to this challenge. For this reason, Rosmini can contribute essential and unique ideas to our current discussion.

Civil society, in regard to the two original and fundamental societies of family and religious community, is subsidiary and does not derive directly from the dignity of human nature. Because of this nature, human beings need to live in family and transcendent relationships. Therefore, Rosmini characterizes society as necessary but not essential. Society must "only" provide the conditions that are required by man in order to reach his destiny-perfection. As we can see, the dimension of "right" for Rosmini does not suffer from an individualist reduction, but it is the realization of the moral liberty of man through relationships. However, the social dimension still does not possess an essential function for human nature. Rosmini avoids the idea by which the civil sphere, with its determinations of "common good" and public associations, infringes upon individual liberty. He thus presents an alternative system to institutional reductionism and to institutional overstrain.

This relational perspective makes possible the definition of social ethics by which the "common good" of the institutional sphere of society is a relational dimension (Donati 2008): it is reducible neither to the individual, nor to a dimension of common wealth, nor to the communitarian definition of the public sphere. On the contrary, this relational definition makes the common good the principle by which social ethics can consider anew the basic institutions of civil society: it makes clear that human rights cannot be understood as belonging merely to an individual. Every right means a relationship, and therefore for Rosmini, the most universal perspective of the human relationship is the global, including all of humanity. Since this relationship lacks a concrete, visible dimension, unlike the religious community, the family or the State which represent particular relationships, for Rosmini, it is in the visible Christian community that the universality of human dignity as a relational category is affirmed. In other words, the religious dimension is the necessary concrete reality that can culturally represent the irreducible worth of human dignity. This is the same argument which Ratzinger and Habermas emphasize in their dialogue at Munich in 2004 (Habermas and Ratzinger 2005), when they reflect on the fact that now, for "postmodernity", religion is no longer to be considered as a risk for the development of "social pathologies" but must be integrated with human reason, which in the twentieth century has given many signs of its own "pathologies" with respect to the consideration of human dignity.

Rosmini calls for a constitution that aims neither at realizing mere individual liberty nor sacrifices liberty to the social dimension of common good, "according to *social justice*" – he desires the construction of a society, not a State (Rosmini 2007). Rosmini's approach is important since it anticipates the central Trinitarian perspective of social ethics found in this most recent encyclical: society can guarantee fundamental and equal rights for all men as human beings. While the State introduces relationships of power and subordination, the idea of society, for Rosmini, realizes the civil dimension in which humanity facilitates relationships between people who are aware of their liberty and irreducible dignity. Consequently, the State cannot define what is "right", because *man* is "right". Rosmini concludes that the State possesses only the privilege and the duty of defining the "modality of rights" (Rosmini 1993–1996, II, 1615). This modality of rights must respect individual human dignity and the subsidiary order of the three societies: religious community – family – civil society. This is how Rosmini realizes the "institutional way of charity", emphasized by Benedict XVI and claimed, although not successfully articulated, by Felice (2010, 264f.), In contrast to his institutional reductionism, the Rosminian answer does not create first a system for the economy and then society, but first delineates society and then the judicial framework for the economy. In this way, Rosmini answers Zamagni's question: "how is it possible that relationships based on honesty, which are typical of primary networks – like those that emerge naturally within the family and small groups – can be built up into wide economic structures – in other words, how can you pass from interpersonal trust to institutional trust?" (Zamagni 2007, 64).

Within his structure of three societies, Rosmini establishes the social spheres where the indispensable dimensions of gift and forgiveness are realized. We have to ask if this discussion about the institutional foundation of society, which Rosmini also considers the judicial framework of economy, has to be specified for the economic sphere. In this regard, Zamagni has developed an interesting idea which we can elaborate more fully by means of the Rosminian position: when facing today's economic challenges, are we not forced to consider the corporate world no longer as a private matter but also as a constitutional one? We have to ask this question because, as Zamagni and others notice, the individualist and competitive approach of the Social Market Economy does not suit the corporate world. If we consider companies, in the line of Zamagni, as a genuine realization of personal relationships, then individual liberties could be saved while at the same time the foundational function of companies for the development of man and solidarity, and thus also for society, would be recognized. However, unlike Zamagni, we would have to specify with Rosmini that the company could never be a genuine society founded in human nature and ordered to its perfection, like the family and the Church, and therefore the interpersonal relationships within the company can only be personal relationships and never relationships founded upon the ontological structure of the human being. In this way, the Rosminian distinction gives us the possibility of distinguishing the different aspects more clearly than Zamagni does: while for Zamagni the formation of relationships in companies aims at producing gift and forgiveness, charity and altruism, for Rosmini, it is impossible to achieve these aspects in a company. These dimensions result from the family and transcendental relationships. However, the subsidiary relationships of social reality between persons aware of their dignity and genuine rights must be realized in the enterprise.

This is the consequence of the strictly personal-ontological and not social Rosminian concept of subsidiary (considering that the social dimension is not eliminated but joined in the same person). Man essentially realizes himself in his personal relations with his family and with the transcendent. Such relationships must be protected according to natural law. They produce fundamental human obligations in the social sphere (besides duties of individual morality) which, for Rosmini, are *not* reducible to the individualist rational logic of *homo oeconomicus*. It is rather the dimension of reciprocity, similar to that mentioned by Zamagni, while excluding gift and forgiveness. Man has his most genuine and natural duties within the familiar and the religious relationships; in society and in the corporate world, man has the reciprocal obligations of rights and recognition. Otherwise, this type of social thought would lead to competition between the family, the religious and the professional spheres. We need to be aware that the individual, in a corporate relationship, has to discover not only moral values and social relations, but also has to be protected. In this regard, the company is a social configuration belonging more fully to the sphere of society than to that of personality in the ontological sphere. In this aspect, the Rosminian solution is nearly identical with the conclusions drawn by Crivelli, who founded the corporate reality, in contrast to *homo oeconomicus* individualism, upon interpersonal reciprocity (Crivelli 2002, 28f.). However, this reciprocity can be found in the social sphere as long as it does not merge, as Crivelli underlines, with altruism, i.e. with gift and forgiveness. Indeed, Felice also mentions the dimension of the "we-rationality" in society (Felice 2001, 39–42) that overcomes the mere "self-rationality" of the mere *homo-oeconomicus* individualism.

By considering the personalist approach of Antonio Rosmini, with the distinction between the individual and the sphere of social rights, we have obtained a social ethical model that seems to be adapted to proposal of *Caritas in veritate*. Furthermore, this distinction helps us to fulfill a double task: the sphere of gift and forgiveness, while not a mere personal dimension, is still being protected by the social sphere, and the distinction between the individual and the social sphere is still maintained. When the first task is left unfinished, the system runs the risk of the liberal approach, similar to the Protestant approach; when the second is left unfinished, the system runs the risk of the civil economy model. Rosmini considered the social order to be a constitutional order of rights. Since man is the realization ("subsistent") of human rights, he is able to transform Christian humanism into principles of the social order. The economy belongs to this social order. From this point of view, we can reconcile the two models we analyzed above while avoiding their errors: the integration of the social dimension into the market, instead of the integration of the market into the social sphere (Zamagni 2007, 144), and the situating of the social dimension "outside of" the market (Zamagni 2007, 144).

Conclusions

As we have seen, Christian Humanism is neither a mere moral concept nor a political slogan, neither a romantic vision nor an unreachable illusion. Its original place in society is within the constitutional order. Only by means of personalist rights can the individual and the social dimensions of the person be reconciled without the loss of personal liberty. This can be summarily articulated in the following conclusions:

1. Within a Trinitarian perspective, the dimensions of gift and forgiveness as the authentic expressions of Christian Humanism do not contradict the liberal logic of the Social Market Economy, insofar as they strengthen the liberal dimension of man in the social order (subsidiarity) and his social relationships (solidarity). Thus, in the perspective of globalization, the Christian Humanism of Benedict XVI supports the liberal system of the Social Market Economy.
2. Christian Humanism is beneficial for the social order, not directly, but by recognizing personal liberty and the principles of subsidiarity and solidarity as constitutive principles of social justice. Since this liberty has not only an individualist but also a social dimension, Christian Humanism transfers the Trinitarian perspective into a liberal social order, through the reciprocal implications of individual and social rights and their personal moral significance.
3. This argument is indicated by the encyclical which – according to the principles of Catholic Social Teaching – does not elaborate specific arguments within the constitutional perspective, because this would establish a social model. In this way, Benedict XVI finishes with the sphere of the individual moral dimension of the virtue approach. This approach could be – if it was not open to constitutional integration – contemporaneously an individualist reduction and an individual

overstrain of the moral perspective. However, the encyclical does not close this argument but it leaves it open. When Felice, on the one hand, and Zamagni, on the other, try to "close" this openness of the encyclical by their systematic social approach, transferring the individual approach to the social sphere, they run the risks of institutional reductionism and institutional overstrain. In fact, they try to formulate two different approaches in their attempt to interpret the encyclical: first, the integration of the Trinitarian approach of the encyclical within the liberal approach (institutional reductionism) and second, the approach of the civil economy (institutional overstrain). However, neither Felice nor Zamagni follow a consequent personalist perspective, which reproduces this individualist sphere of Trinitarian ontology within a social-institutional approach. The synthesis of individual and social rights in Rosmini, together with his idea of the "three societies", realizes this specific need. Hence, Antonio Rosmini is able to avoid the two unilateral interpretations of Felice and Zamagni and transform the admonition of the encyclical into a social approach in order to realize a new humanism as the fundamental value and basis of the Christian social message.

References

Antiseri, Dario. 2007. *La "via aurea" del cattolicesimo liberale*. Soveria Mannelli: Rubbettino.
Antiseri, Dario, Michael Novak, and Robert Sirico. 2002. *Cattolicesimo, liberalismo, globalizzazione*. Soveria Mannelli: Rubbettino.
Benedict XVI. 2009. Encyclical *Caritas in Veritate*. *Acta Apostolicae Sedis* 101: 641–709 (abbreviation: CV).
Böckenförde, Ernst-Wolfgang. 1991. The Rise of the State as a Process of Secularisation. In *State, Society and Liberty. Studies in Political Theory and Constitutional Law*, 26–46. New York/Oxford: Berg.
Böckenförde, Ernst-Wolfgang. 2011. Woran der Kapitalismus krankt. In *Wirtschaft, Politik, Verfassungsgericht*, 64–71. Berlin: Suhrkamp.
Bruni, Luigino. 2008. The economy of communion. In *Pursuing the common good: How solidarity and subsidiarity can work together*, The Pontifical Academy of Social Sciences. Acta, vol. 14, ed. Margaret S. Archer and P. Donati, 527–534. Vatican City: The Pontifical Academy of Social Sciences.
Crivelli, Luca. 2002. Quando l'*homo oeconomicus* diventa reciprocano. In *Economia come impegno civile. Relazionalità, ben-essere ed Economia di Comunione*, ed. Luigino Bruni and Vittorio Pelligra, 21–43. Roma: Città Nuova.
Donati, Pierpaolo. 2008. Discovering the relational character of the common good. In *Pursuing the common good: How solidarity and subsidiarity can work together*, ed. Margaret S. Archer and P. Donati, 659–683. Vatican City: The Pontificial Academy of social sciences.
Eucken, Walter. 1951. *Unser Zeitalter der Mißerfolge. Fünf Vorträge zur Wirtschaftspolitik*. Tübingen: Mohr.
Felice, Flavio. 2001. Introduzione. Dottrina sociale e dottrina economica a confronto. In *Sirico, Robert. Il personalismo economico e la società libera*, ed. Flavio Felice, 9–42. Soveria Mannelli: Rubbettino.
Felice, Flavio. 2005. *Prospettiva "neocon". Capitalismo, democrazia, valori nel mondo unipolare*, La politica, vol. 69. Soveria Mannelli: Rubbettino.
Felice, Flavio. 2010. *Persona, impresa e mercato. L'economia sociale di mercato nella prospettiva del pensiero sociale cattolico*. Vatican City: Lateran University Press.

Felice, Flavio. 2011. L'economia sociale di mercato di Benedetto XVI. In *Agli Amici della Verità e della Carità. Contesti, Letture e Discussioni dell'Enciclica Caritas in veritate di Benedetto XVI*, ed. Giuseppe Franco, 211–216. Soveria Mannelli: Rubbettino.

Goldschmidt, Nils. 2009. *Liberalismus als Kulturideal. Wilhelm Röpke und die kulturelle Ökonomik.* Freiburg: Institut für Allgemeine Wirtschaftsforschung.

Gutmann, Amy. 1985. Critics of liberalism. *Philosophy & Public Affairs* 14: 308–322.

Habermas, Jürgen, and Joseph Ratzinger. 2005. *Dialektik der Säkularisierung. Über Vernunft und Religion*, 3rd ed. Freiburg: Herder.

Hayek, Friedrich August von. 1947. Individualism: True and false. In *Individualism and economic order (a collection of essays originally published by the author between the 1930s and 1940s)*, 1–32. Chicago: The University of Chicago Press.

John Paul II. 1988. Encyclical Sollicitudo Rei Socialis [1987]. *Acta Apostolicae Sedis* 80: 513–586 (abbreviation: SRS).

John Paul II. 1991. Encyclical *Centesimus Annus. Acta Apostolicae Sedis* 83: 793–867 (abbreviation: CA).

Krienke, Markus. 2011. La libertà della società. *Libertas* 1: 13–16. http://www.libertates.com/wordpress/wp-content/uploads/2012/09/libertas_01.pdf. Accessed 1 Oct 2011.

Novak, Michael. 1981. The economic system: The evangelical basis of a social market economy. *The Review of Politics* 43: 355–380.

Novak, Michael. 1982. *The spirit of democratic capitalism.* New York: Simon & Schuster.

Novak, Michael. 1993. *The catholic ethic and the spirit of capitalism.* New York: Free Press.

Pesch, Heinrich. 1902. Solidarismus. *Stimmen aus Maria-Laach* 63: 38–60, 307–324.

Röpke, Wilhelm. 1950. *The social crisis of our time.* Chicago: The University of Chicago Press.

Röpke, Wilhelm. 1958. *Jenseits von Angebot und Nachfrage.* Stuttgart: Rentsch.

Röpke, Wilhelm. 1979. *Maß und Mitte*, 2nd ed. Bern: Haupt.

Röpke, Wilhelm. 2006. La statizzazione dell'uomo. In *Il Vangelo non è socialista. Scritti su etica cristiana e libertà economica (1959–1965)*, ed. Carlo Lottieri, 143–154. Soveria Mannelli: Rubbettino.

Rösch, Michael. 2011. The German social market economy and its transformations. In Zentrum für Datenverarbeitung an der Universität Tübingen. http://tiss.zdv.uni-tuebingen.de/webroot/sp/spsba01_W98_1/germany1b.htm. Accessed 1 Oct 2011.

Rosmini, Antonio. 1993–1996. *The philosophy of right [1844].* Durham: Denis Cleary and Terence Watson.

Rosmini, Antonio. 2007. *The constitution under social justice [1841–1843].* Plymouth/Lexington: Alberto Mingardi.

Scheler, Max. 1979. *Die Zukunft des Kapitalismus. Tod und Fortleben. Zum Phänomen des Tragischen.* München: Manfred S. Frings.

Scola, Angelo. 2011. *Welfare* nel quadro della *Caritas in veritate.* In *Agli Amici della Verità e della Carità. Contesti, Letture e Discussioni dell'Enciclica Caritas in veritate di Benedetto XVI*, ed. Giuseppe Franco, 229–234. Soveria Mannelli: Rubbettino.

Sirico, Robert. 1998. The late-scholastic and Austrian link to modern Catholic economic thought. *Journal of Markets & Morality* 1: 122–129.

Sirico, Robert. 2001. The Pope and the free economy. In *Il personalismo economico e la società libera*, ed. Flavio Felice, 125–158. Soveria Mannelli: Rubbettino.

Zamagni, Stefano. 1995. Introduction. In *The economics of altruism*, xv–xxii. Aldershot/Vermont: Elgar.

Zamagni, Stefano. 2007. *L'economia del bene comune.* Roma: Città Nuova.

Zamagni, Stefano. 2008. Reciprocity, civil economy, common good. In *Pursuing the common good: How solidarity and subsidiarity can work together*, The Pontifical Academy of Social Sciences. Acta, vol. 14, ed. Margaret S. Archer and P. Donati, 467–502. Vatican City: The Pontifical Academy of Social Sciences.

Zamagni, Stefano. 2009. Fraternità, dono, reciprocità nella *Caritas in veritate.* In *Amore e verità. Commento e guida alla lettura dell'Enciclica Caritas in veritate di Benedetto XVI*, ed. Simona Beretta et al., 71–103. Milano: Paoline.

Part II
Catholic Humanism and Economic Activity

Chapter 6
Does Christian Humanism Make Sense in Economics?

Miguel A. Martínez-Echevarria

Abstract The aim of this chapter is to reflect and provide a tentative answer to the question posited in the title. The first section provides a brief summary of the origin of that "humanism" typical of Modernity. The second section attempts to demonstrate the intrinsically individualistic and atheistic dimension entailed in this Modernist vision of man. In the third part, which can be considered the nucleus of this chapter, we present an exposition of how, from the basic characteristics of this "humanistic" individualism, a new and revolutionary vision of the economy emerged – a vision now paradigmatic but still fraught with perhaps fatal ambiguities and difficulties. This vision can be seen as an "anthropological inversion" which drove the humanism of the Enlightenment. The last part, and by way of conclusion, provides some suggestions as to how, from a Christian conception of man, it might be possible to advance a more realistic and practical view of the economy.

Keywords Humanism • Individualism • Atheistic and theistic humanism • Economic thought • Anthropological inversion

Though initially I had reservations, I decided to accept the title suggested by the editors since it has grown on me as a convenient summation of the tensions between Christianity and the individualism at the root of modern economics, tensions that make it difficult to reconcile the two through such an ambiguous term as "humanism" – for they do not share a common concept of the "human". Indeed, it is precisely the difference in their understanding of man that raises the question as to whether it even makes sense to discuss Christianity as humanism in connection with economics, as though the former could be grafted onto the latter while the latter remains what it is. It is this tension that I wish to elaborate upon and make clear over the course of this paper.

With all due respect to opinions to the contrary, opinions that I recognize have been powerfully developed as well, I am not particularly fond of the phrase "Christian humanism" – for it can, in a way, be viewed as something of contradiction.

M.A. Martínez-Echevarria (✉)
School of Economics, University of Navarra, Pamplona, Spain
e-mail: mamechevarria@gmail.com

© Springer Science+Business Media Dordrecht 2015
D. Melé, M. Schlag (eds.), *Humanism in Economics and Business*,
Issues in Business Ethics 43, DOI 10.1007/978-94-017-9704-7_6

89

In fact, in my opinion, the origin of humanism is connected with an individualist anthropology to which the Christian vision of man cannot be reduced without violence to its essential character. The partisans of what we may call "Christian liberalism", especially among some North American Catholics, are engaged in precisely such an attempt: to make this "humanist" individualism compatible with the radically social character of openness toward and gift of the other that is an essential element of Christian life. The result, stated with all brevity, is something akin to the following: an attempt to join a utilitarian and self-interested explanation of human social relations as an autonomously self-regulating and optimal system to the Christian call for works of service to others wherein the justice and morality of human behavior is a critical condition for the achievement of a truly functioning economy that serves the community. I hope that over the course of this paper I can explain with greater clarity the reasons for my reservations concerning any such project.

In any case, I think that there has been frequent abuse of the term "humanism" and this to the point that the very term has become rather, even utterly, ambiguous. Thus, when it is necessary to use it, there is no remedy but to add several qualifications in order to explain its sense and meaning with regard to the "human." It is quite indicative that "humanism" seems to require that "Christian" be added to it in recognition that there is something in its essence that needs such correction, qualification or explanation.

On the other hand, neither am I particularly fond of using the expression "economy" without qualification given the contemporary supposition that it refers to a truly neutral or objective science, valid always and in all places, studying a set of abstractly isolatable and universalized but very determinate behavioral rules and their cumulative consequences as though they were far more than regularities of a certain time and place and people. Economy has not always been understood as it has today and neither is the contemporary view the only way of understanding it. From my point of view, there are as many economies as possible human communities, which nevertheless do not prevent us from being able to detect a certain conjunction of understandings that arise more from common and consistent contemporary practices than from a pure and theoretically a priori body of knowledge.

Today, in contrast, talk of "economics" is essentially the same as referring to so-called "neo-classical" economics, which – for many – has come to constitute the paradigm of economic science par excellence. As we will see, this focus on neo-classical economics as paradigmatic arises as a consequence of a "humanism" fostered by what is commonly referred to in philosophy as "Enlightenment." That is to say, by the idea of man painted out of his context, as simply individual, the individual man taken as a strange and timeless being, disentangled from all community and all tradition, with pretensions to being and having sufficient ground for his thought and action in himself alone – without a world and without a social world that offers him the perspectives and practices through which he engages in the world. In such an idealized conception, human action is viewed as the problem of externally coordinating independent and static, universalized individuals and is studied from the distance of a-historical and supposedly sterilized objectivity. Both of these emphases, however, require man to be capable of being taken as a given datum, constituted autonomously and without reference to the context in which he always already exists or the motives that actually constitute his behavior. Meanwhile, both of these emphases betray their own supposed abstraction and objectivity by insisting on a singularly determinate economic motive and "rationality" that is quite contrary to human experience.

The development of this work has the following structure. In the first section, I will offer a brief summary of the origin of the particular "humanism" typical of Modernity. In the second section, I will attempt to demonstrate the intrinsically individualist and atheist dimension entailed in this Modern vision of man. In the third part, which I consider to be the nucleus of my presentation, I will give an exposition of how, from the basic characteristics of this "humanist" individualism, a new and revolutionary vision of the economy emerged – a vision now paradigmatic but still fraught with perhaps fatal ambiguities and difficulties. This vision was, as I see it, implicit in the "anthropological inversion" which drove the humanism of Enlightenment. In the last part, and by way of conclusion, I give some suggestions as to how, from a Christian conception of man, it might be possible to advance a more realistic and practical view of the economy.

Humanity and Humanism

It is useful, at the outset, to distinguish between the human and "humanism." It is well to recall that in many cases, although not always, nor necessarily, such "isms" can bring with them an excessive simplification of a reality that is much richer and more complex. Thus, while by the first I understand the search for the truly human, viewed from a Christian perspective as essentially a limited indetermination that is constitutive of its very openness to and potential for variation as well as for completion – ultimately through the gift of self-gift, by the second I understand a somewhat biased position that attempts to defend an a priori and reductionist conception of man as autonomously given and invariant.

Since the time of Plato it has been evident that it is not so easy to understand man, to grasp where the soul and body coincide, where the individual and the communal, the transcendent and the immanent, the temporal and the eternal. The Christian vision of man makes it still more difficult by positing within man an opening toward unexpected horizons, which confer upon man a dignity hitherto unsuspected by ancient philosophy. With the revelation of the mystery of Christ, God made man and united by so much to all humanity, there remained the necessity of grasping the meaning of this interaction and connection between divine and human, between grace and nature, that remains hidden both in the life of all men and each one them individually.

For Aristotle, the properly human was the *logos*, the capacity of man to know and communicate. In this sense, he defined man as the only animal with language at his disposal (*Politics* 1252b 10). From this it followed that man also developed money, or what amounts to the same, that he gives value to things, he humanizes them by situating them as a sensible expression of the ties that unite and maintain a community wherein need is communicated. Thus money in a sense – as much as law and language – serves as the expression of social ties created by communal use and common practices of production, exchange and distribution formative of daily communal life. It was thus clear – to Aristotle (1984) – that man was properly and radically political and social by nature (*Politics* 1253a 9). This essentially political or social character shows itself in his capacity to develop his character in and through the continual pursuit of the common good, the development of which *is* both through its constant renewal of shared traditions and its renovation – that is to say, in a word, through its renaissance.

For this reason, whoever tried to live in solitary isolation demonstrated that he believed himself either a god or a beast. That is, to live in isolation suggests that one either believes oneself to be self-sufficient in capacity for human perfection or that one always already possesses the fullness thereof. In other words, either one believes society is of no use to one's own human development or one believes that no development is possible or necessary and that the brutish life of the barbarian is an adequate expression of human nature. The *logos*, that divine spark that permits man to escape submersion in nature, the radical ambiguity of man's nature as dependent upon tradition and community for his development, was – then – for Aristotle, proper to man, it was that which distinguished him as much from the animals as from the gods.

Although there was much depth in the anthropological insights of Aristotle, it was St. Augustine, a Christian thinker, who would truly illuminate these depths. As Levering (2013) points out not only was this divine spark proper to man as the creature whose nature stretches out beyond what might otherwise be a static and enclosed cosmos wherein he merely and infrequently approximated to earthly human perfection, but man *is* as capable of receiving grace. Through this gift, it is not so much man that advances solely on his own strength toward the apotheosis of the merely human as that man receives advancement toward a true divinization and unexpected completion through the grace which enhances his natural abilities and – in fact – brings him to himself, a pursuit in which he would otherwise falter and fail. Paradoxically, this kind of transcendence of humanity not only divinizes man's spiritual nature in a way, but also gives special importance to the temporal dimension of man – this is why the memory and will then appear as so essential in grasping the human *logos*. Memory and will are the temporal insofar as human development *qua* development requires the maintenance of both a past renewed and a projection into the future.

This *logos* was thus articulated in its three basic dimensions: memory, stretching back, in search of the sources and the origin of life; understanding, which attends to the present; and the will, that projects the past and present toward an end not yet reached. The three dimensions lean on and need each other. Human action is not possible without the understanding that judges and decides. Yet for this it needs memory to bring the past to bear upon the present, otherwise there can be no such thing as human understanding or human desire, which would otherwise be erased at every moment and live in the blissful ignorance and brutish instinct of the beast, determined with respect to particular objects. Not unlike the human hand's eminent versatility on account its indeterminate utility compared to animal organs devoted to very unique purposes, the human mind and human desire *are* precisely as partially indeterminate plasticity insofar as their natural objects are universal abstractions, truth in general and the good in general, that await judgments to specify this truth and this good in accordance with experience and education. The conjunction of past and present, or what is the same, memory and understanding, make it possible for the will to then project into the future the truth it has received and judged and the good it has recollected as a good and thus to act accordingly. If men choose that which seems "good" or "best" on account of an abstract principle drawn to good-ness in general on the basis of truth-judgment similarly related to men's innate submission to what is apparently true to them, this is truly an abstract rule of behav-ior and is only determined in and through a prior judgment of experience, training or education. Men's "rationality" is constituted by tradition by its very nature inas-much as it relies upon the "known" and "desired" in every new encounter with the knowable and desirable. Nor can these be said to have been given to him simply by personal experience independent of his historical and social context – his tradition and his action, then, are more than his own. His rationality is determined only through this inter-relatedness with his past and his communal character.

According to this explanation, it could be said that, for Saint Augustine, tradition is itself proper to man, throughout history the reception and submission of a divine gift of development and triumphal achievement is enveloped in human work. It is a work that each generation receives from the past and hands over to the future, giving unity – in a way – to the actions of all men: a common labor, a common project. Thus there is, through the gift of grace, both the divine and the human within every tradition insofar as what is received is both the creative action of God who is always present, a grace pouring itself out in a maintenance and assistance that is at the same time incorporated into the results of the free action of the men who have preceded us and responded to that grace. Within every tradition, then, the divine and human are coincident – and not necessarily in the sense of a simple linear historical pro-gression familiar to the modern mind, for therein are both what is always good and pure as well as what can be good or bad. Tradition, therefore, is constituted as the dynamic pillar of history in the realization of God's creative plan, counting on the collaboration of free men. This combination of human and divine is beautifully summed up in the famous phrase Augustine: "God who created you without you, will not save you without you."

Implicit in this is the two-fold character of tradition, both reception and renova-tion. No tradition is possible without community and without authority. It is the preservation of both that sustains the life of a tradition. That which is received and that which is handed on is not something purely individual, but a common good and a common work, increased or diminished by those who have preceded us in the maintenance of the tradition and by we who perpetuate it. Thus understood, an essential element of tradition is language, the communitarian dimension of which is evident, but above all there is also a requisite commitment to living in accordance with the profound sense of one's tradition, for it is the reception of the past that permits the discovery for oneself of that which deserves to be retained and passed on with veneration.

A tradition, then, is not something dead and inert – the stale and externally inheritance of a bygone age – but something that advances at every stage with the articulation given it by the present, which deepen its understanding through reasoning. This deepening permits the discovery of harmony between the gift of inherited vision and the recognition of the sense of rectitude of life of those that came before us. An articulation that is essentially social and common. To live in a tradition is not only to conserve it, but to make possible the invention of that which until then, although present, had remained hidden; in part because it had not yet met the "opportune time" – the time in which the life of one generation, relating its inheritance to the present, encounters the necessity of elaborating on what they discover through their experience by relating it to the broader human experience which they have received and will hand on to their descendants.

This action of integration into the community, the community of an entire tradition wherein one generation relates itself to another as much as one man relates his own experience to his community, is the participation of men in common action and thought both in origin and contribution. It is this participation that nourishes individual life, that opens up the possibility of making a beginning, not from a void but from an inheritance, and the possibility of carrying out one's own proper action in transforming that inheritance, giving expression to one's own peculiar mode of unrepeatable being. It is this integration that makes possible the particular contribution of all to the history of humanity. Only when thus viewed, is it discovered that time forms a whole. Only when thus understood, with a sense of the unity of action of all men, is the proper character of the whole tradition manifest in all its plenitude as the profound gift of liberty. For through tradition, human action is not trapped within the infinite repetition of a monotonously indistinct and undeveloped bestial origin but is offered the opportunity to take up and advance the inheritance he has received, in such a way as to weave his individuality into the tradition, which makes his very distinction possible.

Tradition in this sense, and liberty with it, then, presupposes the recognition of authority, of a prior wisdom that orients us, extending from time immemorial, that does not proceed from the will of the present, from men, an "unwritten law" which gives foundation and sense to human knowledge. This same mysterious and originative wisdom, that for Christians is the Creative and Salvific Word of God, wants to depend on human liberty and human *logos*, on the possibility and necessity that each man should think for himself and not be limited to passively and physiologically receiving and transmitting, as the animals that are limited to transmitting the same genetic code. Man's nature was liberated from the mindless submission and repetition of the bestial for the sake of going beyond the closed world of natural potential in order to become himself most truly – but this is both the possibility and necessity of tradition.

It may seem a paradoxical result that for a man to think for himself, it is indispensable that he live within a tradition, that he be possessed of a certain venerable authority through which he maintains communion with all other men. Yet thinking, just as much as speaking a language, is a radically communal action. A tradition makes possible the content with which a man engages, and through his activity maintains itself and is renovated only if each one of its members is capable of judging, for themselves, what he has received. Only once he rejects or accepts the received, for better or worse, can he become aware of the profound significance of his own tradition (Pieper 2000).

If in each tradition there were no authority that in some way or another transmitted the sacred, the judgment that each man must bring to bear upon an inheritance in his encounter with the world would be impossible. There could be no question of giving new life to that tradition and discovering the sense of one's own life within it. No man can proceed to a judgment of all tradition from outside of all of them, for he always already exists under some type of authority that helps him judge. Without partaking in some tradition, it is impossible to advance the humanity of man – indeed, an absolutely self-referential language, a word outside of *all* indices and meaning, a thought unrelated to *all* human thought, would be absolute madness stripped of all structure, logic and significance, an impossible nothing. Yet even madness generally retains some slender and tenuous thread of connection to the world that it once knew.

All tradition, then, requires a subject to be within a linguistic community and practice that makes communication possible, a human mode of living and thinking. This, of course, in no way implies suppressing the unrepeatable singularity of each individual. Quite the contrary, in fact, if human nature is universal and indeterminate potency for determination with respect to truth and goodness, that nature is in not so much individualized as person a priori as it is the ontological condition for the possibility of such individuality, its history and tradition make possible and affirms its singular identity. Relation, limit and definition belong together with identity. Without tradition and community it would not be possible for each man to make a contribution from his interior in the exercise of the liberty that he has been conceded and whereby he transforms his inheritance. Said another way, person, community and tradition are modes of referring themselves to that which constitutes the essence of the human.

Theistic and Atheistic Perspectives

Theism and Humanism

Before the profundity of Christian anthropology, wherein the divine and the human labor together, coincide and separate, wherein the good is taken together with the presence of evil in history, evil that Christians refer to as original sin and human failure, it is easy to fall into excessive emphasis on either of the two dimensions that are articulated within it: the divine or the human.

It was toward the end of the Middle-Ages that a tendency toward a more pessimistic anthropology arose (Gillespie 2008; Gregory 2012; Taylor 2007). Offering a poor interpretation of the reality of original sin no longer understood as related to the optimistic receptivity of an failing but possible human response to divine grace, human dignity was excessively divided from its capacity for grace and viewed in isolation as though its truest glory was to work alone and not in its capacity for cooperation, first praised for its independent capacity, then deprecated to the extreme for its persistent and consistent corruption – doubts were sown about human liberty as a natural reality. Through a false pietism that gave all honors to a randomized grace, late-Scholasticism began to deform the sense of tradition by devoting all their attention and tribute to the external, totalizing and despotic action of God as the singular protagonist in the development of human salvation and history and, in the end, were left with a God that, more than omnipotent, was presented as arbitrary.

It was then, in the fifteenth century, that humanism emerged as a reaction to this tendency to obscure the important feature of Christian anthropology that is human liberty and to proceed under a very deformed vision of God's totalizing action within history.

We have already had occasion to see how tradition stretches both backward towards the origin of authority as well as forward toward the end of history. For man to be situated outside of this time horizon, where his vision could take in the whole in some immediate and intuitive fashion, is simply impossible. This makes it very important that a divine authority situated beyond time and history be the base and fundament of tradition. For while thus always united with human authority, with socially practiced wisdom, tradition guides man as a venerable revelation that is bound to the inexhaustibility of its sacred origin and to the promise of a future depth in understanding that revelation. It is this faith and veneration that allow men to develop for themselves, to pursue the deepening of their inheritance. Without faith, as much human as divine, without some religious attitude that in some way or another makes reference to the mystery of Creation, or at least to the origin of time, tradition loses its sense and becomes deformed. In fact, without some faith, again as much in the human as in the divine together, tradition tends to dissolve into rootless social convention or into a call for its abolition in favor of direct and unmediated access to truth. In the case of the former, tradition becomes nothing more than an ancient imposition, the groundless inheritance of mediated social babble; in the case of the latter, it tends to convert itself into a demand for the intuitive presence of circumscribable and finished truth unmediated by tradition and with a body of permanently defined limits that exclude all other experience and intention.

It is therefore convenient to distinguish between traditions, that have to do with faith and human authority, and the Tradition, that has to do with the faith and divine authority. And it is precisely in this interplay of the human with the divine, of the contingent and the necessary, by means of memory, intelligence and will, where human action with divine guidance and aid makes possible the fullness of human life. Stated in Christian terms, tradition and life of man can only be properly conceived and maintained as the joint action of nature and grace, of God and men.

This opening of human life to the mystery of Authority makes tradition something uncontrollable as far as man in concerned, for he can never advance, from inside history, to a perfect dominion over his own life and to a position outside his temporal vision – to a vision that would make possible the achievement of a finished order of society and a finished, perfected Truth. To men belong truths, not in the sense of the untrue, but in the sense that they are always limited to some degree – and some far more than others. Within the whole tradition there is a continuous tension stretching toward the fullness of being that, like the horizon, is always displaced with the very same rhythm that one advances toward it. This relation to Being manifests itself, among many other ways, in the continuous and interminable debate over the sense and finality of the tradition, or what is the same, over the life of man.

In the face of this tension between the divine and the human, found united within tradition, it is important to attend to two extreme positions: theologism and humanism. While in some respect opposed, these extremities both attempt to resolve the complexity of divine and human inter-relation in acting together through a simplistic and hasty reduction of the complexity of the mystery of human action on one side or the other.

Thus understood, theologism, on the one hand, attribute all that happens to the direct and immediate intervention of the Divine will. It denies the capacity of human intelligence to judge the authority of all tradition and posits, in an inseparable way, the divine overwhelming of the human. There is here a problematic overlapping that in no way can be broken or distinguished and that already makes the profound and full sense of tradition as joint action or cooperation impossible. Human will and human understanding are, for theologism, mere apparent conduits of Divinity. For it often happens that, exalted by a misled pietism, thinking to aggrandize divinity, such theologism tends to denigrate human dignity. They consider man essentially corrupt, incapable of any natural opening or access to God. They fail to realize that such a depreciation of the creature also depreciates the Creator – for their Creator is thereby proclaimed incapable of any true creation inseparable from his own action to the very extent that his creation is incapable of action. It is a stillborn creation and an impotent Creator. Thus their anthropological pessimism is inextricably bound to a pessimistic theology.

For those guilty of theologism, the authority of tradition is understood as exclusively sacred, utterly unmixed with the human. They are thus led to place limits on human liberty in the investigation of any necessary distinction between the human and the divine, a distinction that underlies the true authority of the whole tradition: namely, that it is not simply and radically the inexplicable and irrational action of an unknown God. That is to say, the practical result of theologism is the imposition of an oppressive clerical authoritarianism that does not distinguish between the human and the divine, between the religious and the political, between reason and faith, and which is prohibitive of any inquiry into the arbitrary demands of God.

While thus destroying the sense and rationality of their own tradition, theologism also denies the possibility of any diversity of traditions and communities. For when tradition is truly understood, such a diversity of traditions is not only possible but also necessary and beneficial, offering a wealth of expressions and experiences that contribute to discourse. Yet the radically imposed and groundless tradition of theologism precludes the acceptance of any other contribution. In this way, tradition is disfigured and becomes ideology, made into a "dead tradition" that perishes under the "weight" of an immovable past and impedes its renovation by suffocating the orientation toward future development that is proper to true tradition.

As indicated, in reaction to such theologism, there emerges an equally radical humanism that assigns the entire force of history to purely human action. This too ends by making any true sense of tradition thoroughly unsustainable. It is a perspective that, while it does not necessarily exclude divine action, according to Blondel (1997), it nevertheless considers divine action extrinsic and essentially alien to human action. Humanism, then, posits a sphere of "purely human action" that only admits of human authority, totally detached or separated from any divine authority. Divine action, if admitted, comes only as an intervention that violently imposes itself on natural agency or randomly alters its initial conditions and inexplicably adds to its outcomes. Such Divine action is inexplicable from the point of view of the natural and strictly human. Thus, for humanism, only the human and the purely natural make any rational sense. Moreover, no such Divine action or revelation is relevant for the normal course of human affairs and human knowledge is, and must be, based purely upon its own resources.

The problem is that, as authority is a type of knowledge, for there to be a purely human authority, this knowledge must either be innately rooted or immediately intuited and firmly grounded in each man – for any other knowledge would be a received knowledge that presupposes a tradition and thus some type of alien authority. That is to say, the authority for each man can only be his own "reason" and method and the authority of tradition is thus found to be, ultimately, rootless and imaginary. This suggests the early modern concept of "reason" as rooted in an innate knowledge, separated from the memory and the will, from all past and all future, a reason that contemplates reality from an objectivity supposedly outside of the world, that contemplates "from nowhere". It would be from this idea that humanism would ultimately derive its vision of man as an individual, as enclosed within the self, without any potential opening to the world through tradition and community as formative of his human action, as independent of that world and possessed of an a priori "rationality" through which he manipulates and dominates nature and his own destiny – but does so without reasons derived from a world to which he no longer belongs.

In the case of theologism, then, men remain detached, atomized, each in direct dependence on an unknown and terrifying, arbitrary God. In the case of humanism, men are also decoupled in order to depend on the no less unknown and terrifying, arbitrary individual that he is himself, with no guide.

Both theologism and humanism are attitudes that only really make sense within a Christian anthropology, where they structure the problem of the relation between nature and grace, between God and men. Together they frame an eschatological tension that is not as easy as both extremes pretend. In fact, on the level of pure theory, where a fundamental and continuous relation between two co-operating powers is difficult to imagine in abstraction, the difficulty is the constant danger whereby extremity of abstract distinction becomes absolute separation in practice. The Augustinian vision of man as member of two cities, the celestial and terrestrial, is a vision that confronts this double dimension of the proper authority of all true human action and human tradition as something that resolves itself really only in the plane of practice since in abstraction it is only the possibility of co-operation that is posited while in reality it is only living fidelity to the profound sense of cooperation that constitutes it.

Outside of the Christian tradition, both humanism and theologism are not so easily distinguished with equal clarity. Thus when speaking, for example, of Roman-Stoic humanism, we are speaking of a humanism which is, in reality, nothing more than a Renaissance reinterpretation and which is in fact as much or more Christian than it is Roman. For no doubt, while the best of the Romans professed the ideal of an excellent life, yet in no way did the Stoics enter into the discussion of the kind of eschatological tension of which we have been speaking. This because their God or gods were no more capable of a truly pervasive Providence than Plato's demiurge or Aristotle's unmoved mover; their gods neither created nor ever truly controlled the cosmos and the fates of men. For the ancients, then, the principle of history was not free human response but simply an ineradicable chaos present in the cosmos that gave rise to tragic fatalism and the worship of fortune. Their "humanism" was merely the rise and fall of aristocratic men in harmonious resignation to a closed natural world without even the slightest tension with the divine gift of grace. For the Romans, the divine was absent or at least utterly indifferent and there could be no question of the relation between grace and nature as there was no gift of grace. Nor could there be any question of nature stretching beyond itself into anything like historical advance. Nor, for that matter, was there any real question of tradition in the sense of development and deepening of an original gift of wisdom – the cosmos ran its cyclical course and no movement broke the circular bounds or moved mankind forward, the future was the return of the origin on a purely temporal level of infinite repetition.

The genesis of what we refer to as humanism has, then, its ultimate roots in two historical facts that are both essentially Christian: the Renaissance that developed principally in the south of Europe; and Protestantism, that emerged in the north and center of Europe. In both cases, their essential character is determined by their response to the essentially Christian question of the relation between grace and nature. Or, more precisely, both are characterized by their positing an increasing unrelated-ness between grace and nature. This insofar as even within the bounds of adherence to the medieval axiom, "graces does not destroy but perfects nature," the relationship between the two can admit of greater or lesser degrees of essential co-operation and, in the end, their cooperation may not be essential to the natural in any sense other than a passive potential for an otherwise inhuman action. If the Renaissance proclaimed the activity of man, the Reformation proclaimed the passivity of man – this to the point, ultimately, of breaking the medieval axiom so that Divine action does violence to nature.

Yet this was obviously not the initial intent. The first reformers were not secular agents protesting against the theologistic authoritarianism of Rome so much as religious men striving against the impure humanity that had contaminated Rome. They aspired to a "purification" of Rome precisely as the corrupt impurity of tradition, rejecting tradition in a theologistic way and arriving at an understanding of tradition and authority that ultimately extended itself to influence the nascent sovereign states of the fifteenth century as they sought to uproot and discard long-standing customs and traditions en route to a purified and standardized nation-state. Their aim was to free Christianity of all that was human and fallen, to retain only a divine authority that they believed themselves to encounter directly, without mediation, in Scripture, where they were convinced they would find, in all its purity, the immediate Word of God. In their minds, they had to dismantle all that they judged to be human contamination in order to arrive, ultimately, and very much after the failure of successive reform efforts, at the principle of "sola scriptura", the only and unalterable Tradition and Authority.

In so doing, they were not aware that writing, like all language, is inseparable from tradition and community, inseparable from subjects that make it possible and give it life, in this case subjects originally tied, through tradition, to the community of the first Christians. Along this road, neglecting the communal and traditional character of language even in the writing and selection of Scripture, they did not hesitate to proclaim a novel message, a radically inhuman message: the total separation of grace and natural liberty.

The position of the Italian Renaissance was much more intricate. They did not deny the theologist thesis that man had been corrupted with respect to moral goodness and virtue, but they refused to admit that this corruption affected the capacity of human reason to achieve success in the secular affairs of the city. The success or failure of such strictly human affairs was independent of the Divine and, therefore, of the fullness of human development through grace; it could be achieved through a more moderate, purely human effort. Influenced by a Christian spiritualism of more Platonic origin, they were convinced that the affairs of civic life had nothing to do with the grace and salvation of men. In line with this attitude, they then came to establish a rupture between the realm of "purely human" activities, human "business" and secular administrative affairs, activities that pointed toward purely human ends and the realm of "purely supernatural" activities, activities related to grace and supernatural ends that had nothing to do with human nature's immediate and natural ends. This is not to fully repudiate the possibility of co-operating grace and nature, but it is to move that co-operation to the margins of their interaction. If there were such supernatural realities, they were more akin to extrinsic additions to human nature and not constantly interacting and conjoined developments thereof.

If the business of the city could be brought to completion and effectively run with nothing but the light of reason, this opened the possibility of an absolute liberty detached from grace, the very inverse, though equally inhuman, of the Lutheran view of grace without liberty. For the Renaissance, grace came to be something extrinsic and superfluous for living a fully human life. This was the origin and genesis of the concept of "pure human nature", a key element in the construction of the individualism of enlightened humanism.

For a Renaissance man such as Galileo, it was only through mathematical language, conceived as the activity most proper to human reason, the analysis of the intuited and pure mathematical language of reality, that knowledge of the present was possible, an abstract knowledge detached from all tradition (Gilson 2004). As Galileo himself recognized, he was thus inclined toward a Platonic tradition in place of the Scholastic Aristotelian tradition. Certainly, physical reality is outside of tradition, insofar as it lacks time or its time is its own and is distinct from that of any human tradition. Yet theoretical physics is itself a tradition and a language rather than a direct and immediate confrontation with physical reality, its knowledge is not detached from reality but united to it through a community of practitioners in a physical theory that stretches from Archimedes up through Galileo himself. To mistake the advance of this tradition with a sudden confrontation with physical reality in its absolute and own-most purity is to maintain that reason is closed upon itself, independent of tradition and community and has either suddenly discovered its innate possession of abstract theoretical knowledge or encountered its power of intuition of the same in such a way that human knowledge vaunts itself beyond reasoning into possession of a direct and finished truth about physical reality. Either way, such a mistake is to thereby impede the advance of an improved knowledge of this reality.

Thus, while the Protestants, for their part, with the supreme authority that Luther claimed to find disincarnated and in all purity in "sola Scripture", insisted that the Christian faith could live without the community of lived experience and tradition which transmits the historical experience and content of the encounter with God made flesh. The Renaissance, for its part, refused to take into account that no human knowledge, from politics to mathematics, is accessible to human reason simply outside of time. All human knowledge is only possible mediated through tradition as through a community of practitioners who, rightly and wrongly, give life to a tradition wherein they articulate the fruition of human wisdom's engagement with divine wisdom's inexhaustible presence as the former is constructed and transmitted through all and to all as an unfinished intellectual labor that can and must remain open to new horizons.

In both cases, at least in their origins, they were not reacting against the Tradition, which they considered unalterable and true, but against the deformation of Tradition by human traditions. They do not seem to have been aware that both dimensions, divine and human, are essential parts of a whole tradition. Within the whole tradition they live together, both the true and the false, both authority and reason, in a way that all are ambiguously incomplete. Access to this Truth, with a capital T, is possible only mediated through bounded instantiation or humanization. This, of course, brings the risk of its disfiguration, obscurity and extreme incompleteness, but this is the price that has to be paid for its revelation to limited understanding and human liberty. It is openness to and acceptance of the gift of such partial glimpses that constitutes and maintains the development of the rational and the free in man.

The development of all tradition, therefore, is fed through rational debate, not simply through theoretical systems of doctrines that may close themselves off to each other and cut off reason to its own future development. However, above all, tradition is developed through practical wisdom, the encounter with and experience of the world that approximates to the true sense and orientation of tradition. In this way, reason is a discourse possessed of a depth that has no end within history. Only from within this ongoing debate does it become apparent that there is an essential paradox to rationality: that a tradition must change in order to remain the same. In order to maintain itself and remain faithful to its origin and destiny, a tradition must deepen itself and ever strive to go beyond itself. No less paradoxical is the fact that a debate can only be rational under the auspices of an authority that places limits on those debates, not in the sense that it impedes or obstructs them, but in the sense that – as the inherited vision or grounds for alternative visions – its vision channels them, giving rise to the concrete and determinate questions through which it encounters new solutions or confronts the necessity of new ways of addressing problems that cannot be resolved on the basis of existing patterns of thought. It is through these critical encounters that traditions are vivified and sustained.

In all tradition, there is both the human as well as the anti-human, human failing, that which frees together with that which brings alienation and misunderstanding. There is, then, precisely in the very notion of a tradition as development, a principle of disorder that refers to its origin and that principle, in Christian language, is called original sin. It is the very reason why man cannot save himself from sin without the help of grace, without the immersion of God within history through the assumption of a human nature.

Atheistic Individualism and Humanism

In the effort to be rid of the frustrating impurity of tradition, and its corruption, and to vaunt themselves beyond original sin and the present human condition, both Protestantism and the Renaissance ended in human authority. This was true whether that authority took the form of clerical authoritarianism devolving into atomistic democratization of dogma until religion was a merely private affair or whether by starting out immediately from the premise of the purely human they pursued the attempt to ground knowledge on the mind as the only source of authority. What they left standing was their basic principle: the individualist conception of man. That is, the conception of the individual, not as someone whose identity can only be defined through his integration into a community and a tradition, through which he is integrated into nature, but as an individual who derives his identity from his consciousness alone.

In the end, this proved to be a consciousness merely enclosed in an empty interior. For as such an individual has no relation with the past nor projects himself toward a future, he thinks as though situated in a void. The individual, thus conceived, is converted into a strange a-temporal being, a species of phantasm that floats in the middle of the nothing, and whose only identity has its base in self-consciousness. It is, then, the original and through itself content of this consciousness that becomes all important. Yet, as we shall see, this content is and was found to be elusive.

The difficulty is that individualism proves to be, by definition, atheist and a-social, negating the tradition and the community as essential to man, making impossible all real and fundamental relations both between men and, through them, between men and God. This is to say that while, as we have said, all tradition implies faith, as much in human as divine authority, and implies them in an inseparable way, it therefore also implies that without community with men and with God, and without the human development to which they lead and to which man is led through them, it is in fact impossible to speak of any humanity in humanism and any knowledge that can be truly understood as given except that which is merely taken as given – convenient assumptions.

In order to grasp this impossibility, we need only look at the idea of man as individual and the corresponding philosophical project aimed at obtaining self-grounded knowledge. It is a project that only admits the beginning on the basis of the validity of "clear and distinct" ideas; that is, ideas defined in such a way that they are both so fully known that their content must be exhausted in the gaze that fixes them and so distinctly known that their content can have no origin apart from an absolutely unmediated intuition of that which is thus known as distinct. Or, what amounts to the same, they must be separable from their original context and culture; they must be universal and abstract, unmixed with the polluting influence of varying and singular experience. In this way, both the individual mind as well as things-perceived become abstract representations in a mind. The mind itself is represented as universal and abstract, sufficient in itself for knowledge and completely distinct from body in its anteriority to all community and tradition. Mind is conceived as capable of determining with full precision and exhaustible determination that in which all things consist. Here there is no rational encounter with the world that intervenes between the abstract and universal as it processes toward determinate and concrete – only the suddenness of pure unmediated intuition or the internal and purely logical development of innate ideas can attempt to save such a mind from the emptiness of its own abstraction.

Now, the difficulty is that if the human mind cannot advance to these original and originative ideas by means of tradition and access to nature, then they can only be innate to the mind. In which case, as Descartes argued, the innate ideas are only grounded through trust in the benevolence of God who guarantees that these ideas correspond with a reality that is "out there" and with which there is otherwise no way of connecting. Thus the autonomous individual mind is incapable of religion that derives from integration in and access to the world in which he exists. The individual remains incapable of relating himself to Nature, with men and with God. There is no way of giving a real ground for these relations and they can only be the result of an a priori content of the mind, a belief or worse, a pure fantasy.

When thus placed outside of all tradition and suspended above nature, human action becomes impossible. Human action is something that can no longer be understood – for on account of the chasm between a man devoid of content and the world which he cannot reach, there is no explanation of how the world can induce an individual to act who is, by definition, a passionless and solitary mind. An individualist reason situated outside the vital dynamic of the human cannot in any way explain or give sense to action. As Hume saw very well, this type of reason can only be passively opposed to or slave to passions that move it or cross it with the violence of alien force.

Moreover, for such a disembodied mind, human action can only be contemplated from the outside, from a theoretical and abstract focus. It is not understood from the interior, for the very passions, motives and contextual relations which constitute the life of man are not the life of the disembodied mind. The mind has, supposedly, a rationality all its own. It is a rationality that is somehow prior to, distinct from and unchanging in its relation to the various ends which men evidently pursue. Intentions, therefore, are not from the mind's rationality, which now only serves those impenetrable intentions merely as a form of calculation. Motives, then, are obscurely violent in their relation to the mind and can only be known a posteriori on the basis of revealed preferences and generalized only on the basis of patterns of exterior action. That is, with no motive originating within him as a human being in connection with the use of his reason, and no interior psychological introspection permissible since motives are a priori and opaque, the individual and his rationality are thereby converted into a mathematical problem of "optimal decisions" in relation to curiously impenetrable and intransigent motive sets. This is precisely the base and fundament of modern economic theory: an individual with a set of pre-determined utility preferences and no rationality but maximization in relation to that utility; that is, there are no real rational human motives but merely a cold rationality, dependent only on the quality of his information for the achievement of his particular state of satiety.

Thereafter, supposing external and a-temporal consequences of these same actions perfectly known a priori through logic, modern economic analysis tries to decide which of these consequences offers the individual greater advantage. The difficulty resides in the fact that, in this schema, there is no human life. To be sure, there is abstract logic, but not any real human life and therefore no real basis for deciding human advantage. In fact, there is nothing here for economics to decide that is not already somehow implicit in its suppositions.

For as we have already said, there is no such thing as individualist human action, action autonomously brought about through an isolated individual without any mediation; for action presupposes a community that projects itself in time, with values and reasons, and it cannot be reduced to perfectly foreseeable consequences on the basis of an abstract logic that, precisely as such, does not and cannot take into account the variety of concrete ends and strategies that a community entails. In fact, the very precision which is sought by economics is only achieved through reductionist assumptions, the conditions of the model. True human action is that which is integrated into that vital and rational dynamic that we call tradition, with its plethora of motives, rationalities and strategies united within the limits and identity of common practice. These limits constitute the ground for relative stability and expectation, and cannot be determined or foreseen on the basis of an a priori deductive logic unless human action is reduced by supposition to a homogenous mass of persons single-minded in their maximizing agency and in possession of a homogenous quantity of qualitatively identical information. In its effort to obtain purity, economics has posited a conception of human agency that is, in fact, no agency at all, but merely a passivity in the face of its own prior determination to maximization in connection with given information. The constitution of a true moral agent, however, is possible only where someone can give a reason for his actions in the face of others. For this, the individual must be part of a community.

Without tradition, without community, without authority, there is no possibility for virtue. There is only the chaotic exercise of predetermined paths without sense or finality. In short, there is only violence. This is something that Thomas Hobbes clearly saw in his account of the radical individualism of his "state of nature." For Hobbes, the only thing that can bring order to the chaos of the war of all against all is the imposition of an extreme "authority." Such authority, however, is nothing but the extreme violence of the "super-individual", with a monopoly on an impressive coercive force, the very origin of the modern State and the conception of a power without authority or tradition.

The Modern Economy as an Anthropological Inversion

In the Aristotelian conception (*Politics* Book 1), economy was the activity proper to a community, set within and subordinated to its values – more concretely, it was the activity proper to the family, as its proper name, *oikos*, household, indicates. As such it was oriented toward the achievement of the common good. In this way, property, accumulation, production and distribution, the essence of the economy, were subordinated to the prudence and life of each family. Moreover, with the appearance of cities, the economy did not become detached from community, for it remained linked to political prudence and the common life of the city. This in a way that the exchanges between families were made to conform to "just prices", that is to say, those prices that conformed to the true common good of all families and the achievement of the good life.

In this sense the city-market was, for Aristotle (*Politics* 1253a 14), a more ample form of having all things in common through exchange; it was, in theory, simple equitable exchange constituting a type of common use among all the families. This was, for Aristotle, only possible within the community called the city. For only in the city – and without annulling the autonomy of the economies of the families – is it possible to practice the good life; that is, it is only possible to exercise the full extent of the moral and intellectual virtues within a broader community wherein men may participate in civic life. The proper value or price of things is the manifestation of the unified pursuit of the common good of the city wherein prices express the true needs of society with respect to ordered living. Without such general justice, general rectitude, the expression of the life of the city and the form of society ordained to having the good life in common, true value is not possible, nor are the exchanges through which value is properly expressed possible without some basic level of community. This explains why, for Aristotle, language and money were both expressions of the common need, in such a way that their proper ordination to the common good vividly expressed the justice and unity of each city. Tradition, authority, value, justice, all these are communal determinations that are prior to and constitutive of human action on the individual level. Only on the basis of that prior determination is anything like need, justice, price and exchange value conceivable.

Modern individualism, on the other hand, denies the existence of the community as prior to the individual. Whether this community is the family or the city, modernity insists that each individual can and does act in isolation, without mediation or formation, as if others neither existed nor influenced their action. This produces what we have called an "anthropological inversion" in which the individual becomes anterior to all community rather than the reverse.

The problem that this poses is how to explain the origin of society. For without a natural community into which he is born, the isolated individual must enter into social relations from a position of anteriority such that those relations take on the character of purely formal arrangements. This has the aggravating consequence that in the modern sense, one is not truly speaking of a community sharing a life, but of a sort of deliberate a priori "rational" coordination on the plane of virtual action such that each individual proposes to himself, inside his mind, the optimal arrangement but no unity is truly found there. Thus a problem that corresponds to this is the concrete question: how can a situation where a multitude of isolated individual rationalities, by definition seeking to maximize their satisfaction but nevertheless closed off from each other, give rise to a static situation as a simple consequence of "decisions" that would somehow be compatible between themselves and "optimal" for all?

Among individuals, in the modern sense, there are only external relations or relations of power. There is no possibility of justice, in the classical sense of a common life as the common good. Yet a type of "justice" must be imposed upon these external relations, so that there may be some semblance of social order – which though lacking similarity to that communal and Aristotelian sense of justice, may nevertheless offer at least the appearance of harmony. This has the aggravating consequence that such a "species of justice" can only be commutative in the sense of an equilibrium through which no individual diminishes his initial possession. Such equilibrium obscures and neglects the original sense of justice, offering instead only a relative stabilization of mutual isolation as a corrupted form of "community." This is the "optimal" for "society" based on the "anthropological inversion."

For, absolutely speaking, the aim of commutative justice is only possible in a political community, where it would be possible for men to pursue the development of that virtue proper to their common, vivifying, good life. That which moderns call market exchange and equilibrium are simply not such, they are instead simply mechanical equilibriums between forces that fight amongst themselves, their apparent harmony in "equilibrium" is merely the tension of their firm resolution to further maximize whenever possible.

It is very significant that from the eighteenth century onward, the concept of the "just price," which had hitherto made sense only within a community and within a tradition, was transformed into the term "equilibrium price"—which refers to the fight between antagonistic forces—just at the same time that the notion of the common good transformed into the word "common-wealth." To speak of a "just price" is a way of making it clear that its origin resides in the virtues of the men that form the community, in their justice or rectitude, while to speak of equilibrium price is to give expression to the fact that there is no real possibility of virtue. For there is no common life that forms the aim of the community as the good life and men might as well live in isolation with regard to their virtue since all they are is automated information processors set together to form a mechanism that attempts to supplant human action.

For Modernity, the economy is the static result of a mechanical process and is externally composed of many isolated individuals that are predisposed by a rational calculus, and are moved by a "will to power", by the incessant desire to increase their possession of the external. All modern economic theory is reduced to demonstrating mathematically that this process can lead to a mechanical equilibrium.

Newton, who had also attempted to explain the order of the universe on the basis of individuals or atoms, had encountered a similar problem: how to move from such isolation to an interaction of predictable form? Or, to put it another way: how is it possible to give a mathematical or rational explanation of the order of the universe on the basis of physical laws? This brought him to posit an external factor mediating the behavior of all of things, a universal gravitational force, whose existence seemed evident to him, but could never be more than a functional hypothesis.

In the construction of modern economic theory, there is a similar hypothesis: the incessant desire of all men to enrich themselves without end, driving them onwards to rational "optimization" and "stability" between themselves; something that for Aristotle constituted the vice of *pleonexia* and that Nietzsche translated with the significant name of *Mehrundmerwollhaben*.

For Modernity, the economy leaves off being a practical wisdom and transforms itself into a "social physics," a pure working theory, an abstract knowledge of mechanism. It's objective consists in studying the epistemological conditions under which the mental interaction of "rational" individuals that are moved by an incessant desire for gain does not generate chaos, but achieves a situation of equilibrium, in which all have the maximum compatible with the conditions of the game.

Yet without community, without tradition, the initial conditions can only be inexplicable, considered "given" or exogenous to the model and unrelated to any true sense of justice. The economy presents itself, then, as an abstract rationality separated from the individual and his good, from the formation of his tastes and preferences in relation to his community, from the particular sense and evaluation which he gives to property and accumulation, to production and, of course, to money.

The nucleus of the modern economy is not constituted by the family, or by the city. Neither can a market be properly said to exist, for there is merely a conjunction of virtual price assignations, realized in abstraction, in a "void" of real human relations, where all that is important is the resultant assignation. From the formal point of view, it is treated as a mathematical problem where, from a conjunction of "goods" that are taken as "given" or "produced", and from a conjunction of individuals that are also taken as "given", the attempt is made to determine some correspondence between both conjunctions at a point where there will be equilibrium, in the sense that nobody can continue improving their insatiable desire to have more without reducing the aggregate total of their satiation.

The principle objective of modern economics was political, this also in a new sense: to justify a "society" wherein the interaction of individuals who act as if the others do not exist, can give rise, not merely to mechanical equilibrium and not chaos, but to a constrained optimal society.

The modern economy, then, is a mechanical and static system, incapable of explaining the genesis of value. Value is presupposed and then determined. On account of this, from the beginning it has encountered the so called "paradox of value": why does water, which is so useful for human life, have so little value and, on the other hand, gold, which has such low utility for human life, have such great value? It is a paradox that is impossible to resolve from the closed rationality of the modern individual – for value is only possible on the basis of a previous gift of life and nature, an essential element of mystery that is hidden in the tradition and the community and totally absent in modern economics. Instead, quantities valued are simply posited a priori, on the basis of desires without a context, with little to no attention given to their relation to each other, to the men who are subjects of the passions and desires so important to the interplay and transformation of value that occurs within a community over time.

Now is not the time to treat in detail the repeated attempts of modern economics to search for some type of artificial solution for the mediation between individuals, suffice it to say that the search has constituted the history of economic theory for the last two centuries. Only in the last 40 years has there begun to be some recognition, and only among some economists, that such an attempt is not possible on the basis of orthodox assumptions. Some have seen what had been argued almost 100 years earlier by some philosophers, giving rise to a new attitude, invading philosophy of science, an attitude characterized by a morally skeptical or nihilist individualism, a movement that is called "post-modernity."

The distinguishing feature of Postmodernity is its skepticism in the face of the possibility of constructing something that substitutes for what appears to them as otherwise empty traditions and façade communities. It is an attitude that has everything to do with the persistence of an individualist conception of man. That individualism is now treated as compatible with a relaxation of epistemological principle of clarity and distinction as well as a relaxation of the autonomy of the individual – who instead of being independent of tradition is now utterly at the mercy of tradition and community, not possessing anything that is proper to himself. Instead of commanding history, he is submerged in it without light or guidance. In this way, Postmodernity has accentuated the problem of its own legitimacy, employing the terminology of Blumenberg (1983).

Among economists, the first that belong to Postmodernity, are Keynes, under the influence of Wittgenstein, and Schumpeter, under the influence of Weber and

Nietzsche (Coates 1996). Both, without leaving aside individualism, opposed the rationalist optimism of those that still trusted blindly in the principle of "laissez faire" and believed in the harmony of equilibrium. This brought them to an ambiguous attitude with respect to the capacity of "modern reason" to give rise to a political regime of "individual liberties" other than the simple myths of the Enlightenment Project.

In confrontation with Keynes and Schumpeter there is the Neo-modern reaction of economists such as Hayek and Lucas. These have tried, in some way, to reconstitute the old and tired Enlightenment Project. In a different way, they have tried to continue pursuing the development and elaboration of a new means of "rational mediation" that makes it clear to all both the manner in which and the extent to which they are mutually conditioned. At stake in all these novel efforts to rebuild human relations on the basis of atomistic individualism is the individual himself – his isolation, his abstraction, his discursive existence.

How to Humanize the Economy?

It is, then, necessary to be very precise when it comes to speaking of humanism, for as we have seen, it brings, through its own historical genesis, a germ of individualism and atheism. It brings the advocacy of a system whose stability is predicated upon the exclusion of the necessity of grace and a common good for men; that is, in humanism, the communal character of human life is viewed as something extrinsic to its stability and harmony, it is an addition that is not required by a closed system of equilibrating forces, balanced by the gravitational pull of a single motive. It is a view from which, as recent history has shown, it is not so easy to liberate oneself.

I have the impression, an impression that could be wrong, that on many occasions the expression "Christian humanism" has come to be an attempt to introduce a certain partial correction to humanism, on the part of both confessions, both Catholic and Protestant. It is a correction that pretends that there is not an essential incompatibility between modern individualism and the supposition of a supernatural end for man. It is a correction that presumes that this latter, a supernatural end for man, can be simply added to the human and understood as simply extrinsic to the completion of human nature and society, which can – on its own – arrive at a stable and fulfilling system. Yet it is only in the person of Christ, in the hypostatic union, that the fullness of man can be brought to completion. In this sense, for me, to humanize and Christianize are the same thing – whereas humanism is to refuse the necessity of Christianity.

I think it urgent and necessary to overcome the tragic and bitter inheritance of the individualistic anthropology of Modernity. For this reason, we must begin by curing the lamentable blindness, induced by centuries of Enlightenment that impedes a vision of all the dimensions of the real. We cannot go on insisting that only the fomentation of envy and greed can constitute a truly human society.

What is needed is to undo the anthropological inversion that gave place to modern economic theory. To clarify, through well-founded rational arguments, why it is that without tradition and community, there is no way of understanding human action, and how, in consequence, the individualist inversion makes it very difficult to understand the complexity of economic activity in all its unfinished dynamism. Only through this process of rediscovering the internal dynamic of human action will we recover the double and intrinsic dimension of gift and communality. This implies seeing action from the interior of the agent, for the road that leads to an opening toward others passes through the interior of each agent. At every moment it is even more necessary to develop a new education in action, action oriented toward interiorization, which is only possible on the plane of practice. The indispensable condition for each man's capacity to convert himself into an individual singular and unrepeatable, into someone that has a profound experience of the liberty, is only possible within a tradition and community into which they integrate themselves and through which they articulate themselves.

To bring forward this eminently practical focus, it is necessary that there be true communities, normally small: families and businesses, where human contact between interiors is possible, true communication between men, from which springs the energy and cooperation that makes a viable human society possible.

The unsaid of our postmodern society in crisis is that it is based only upon the loneliness implanted by centuries of theoretical and practical individualism, an isolation that eliminates the possibility of loving and being loved and the true harmony of a common life that flourishes on the basis of such an "exchange."

In this sense, it is highly suggestive that, on the plane of economic activity, it has been precisely through the recent study of what really happens in the workplace where the last 40 years have begun to see with some clarity that there are – in fact – many rationalities and many possible rationalities, complex strategies and alternative ends and horizons through which man can organize his economic life in accordance with something other than a simple and abstract principle of incessant gain. It has become apparent that these rationalities relate to each other and create varying dynamics amongst themselves. Moreover, it is now seen that it is in and through this network of communities that relate themselves continuously, that the abilities, needs and capacities arise that make possible, not only the genesis of value, but also more importantly: the possibility of a life of full humanity, of service and gift to others in the arena of material requirements.

We have begun to be aware that each business is a different community, with its own tradition in that, to each one of its members, it offers the possibility of the development of their own proper and unrepeatable singularity.

References

Aristotle. 1984. *The complete works of Aristotle. The revised Oxford translation*, ed. Johanatan Barnes. Princeton: Princeton University Press.
Blondel, Maurice. 1997. *Historia y Dogma*. Madrid: Ediciones Cristiandad.
Blumenberg, Hans. 1983. *The legitimacy of the modern age*. Trans. Robert M. Wallace. Cambridge, MA: MIT Press.

Coates, John. 1996. *The claims of common sense. Moore, Wittgenstein, Keynes and the social science*. Cambridge, UK: Cambridge University Press.

Gillespie, Michel A. 2008. *The theological origins of modernity*. Chicago: Chicago University Press.

Gilson, Etienne. 2004. *La unidad de la experiencia filosófica*. Madrid: Rialp. Original in English: 1947. *The unity of philosophical experience*. New York: Charles Scribner's Sons.

Gregory, Brad S. 2012. *The unintended reformation: how a religious revolution secularized society*. Cambridge, MA: Harvard University Press.

Levering, Matthew. 2013. *The theology of Agustine: An introductory guide to his most importants works*. Grand Rapids: Baker Academic Publishers.

Pieper, Josef. 2000. *Obras*, Escritos sobre el concepto de filosofía, vol. 3. Madrid: Ediciones Encuentro. Original in German. 1995. Werke: Schiften sum Philosophiebegriff. Hamburg: Felix Meiner Verlag.

Taylor, Charles. 2007. *A secular age*. Cambridge, MA: The Belknap Press of Harvard University Press.

Chapter 7
Three Keys Concepts of Catholic Humanism for Economic Activity: Human Dignity, Human Rights and Integral Human Development

Domènec Melé

Abstract Understanding Catholic Humanism and its consequences in economics and business entails discussing three key concepts of this humanism with great ethical relevance: human dignity, human rights and integral human development. The chapter presents the Catholic position on these concepts and discusses their foundation. This foundation, based on a combination of faith and reason, harmonically intertwined, entails a comprehensive view of the human being. Being open to transcendence gives a profound meaning to the ultimate questions of human life and makes a valuable proposition for economics and business.

Keywords Human dignity • Human rights • Human development reports • Integral human development

Understanding Christian Humanism and its consequences in economics and business entails knowing both its main contents and its foundation. In this chapter we try to show that Catholic Humanism, i.e., Christian Humanism (CH) inspired by Catholic Social Teaching (CST), entails three powerful key concepts, which in turn become a solid base for further developments and contents.

The first key element regards the enormous consideration and respect of CH for the human being, regardless of gender, religion, ideology, race or ethnic group to which one belongs or the stage of life an individual is in. This is expressed by the notion of *human dignity*, or excellence, which is inherent to every single human individual. A second key element is that all humans are endowed with innate rights – usually termed *human rights.* The third basic element is *human development*, with is understood in an integrative sense of two interrelated aspects. The first regards

D. Melé (✉)
IESE Business School, University of Navarra, Barcelona, Spain
e-mail: mele@iese.edu

© Springer Science+Business Media Dordrecht 2015
D. Melé, M. Schlag (eds.), *Humanism in Economics and Business*,
Issues in Business Ethics 43, DOI 10.1007/978-94-017-9704-7_7

personal human development, embracing the whole person. The second refers to the human development of every human being worldwide.

These concepts, as with all the Christian tradition, find their foundation in both faith and reason, which are closely related. This is particularly true for Thomas Aquinas, who understands the human being, and the whole world in the light of both reason and faith. He put great importance on reason and maintained that faith helps reason toward a deeper understanding, and in turn reason can contribute to a better understanding of divine Revelation (Aquinas 1981, I, 1, 8 ad 2). This episte-mological approach is also emphasized in papal encyclical-letters – essential documents of CST. One of these –*Fides et ratio* (FR)[1] written by John Paul II in 1998 – specifically presents the essential relationship between faith and reason. In line with Aquinas, John Paul II affirms: "faith builds upon and perfects reason. Illuminated by faith, reason is set free from the fragility and limitations" (FR 43); faith and reason strengthen each other (FR 73).[2]

Following this approach, this chapter analyses these previously mentioned concepts – human dignity, human rights and integral human development – drawing from significant documents of CST, and in contrast with other approaches.[3] It also presents an overview of the implications of the requirements of these concepts in some current socio-economic and business ethics issues. The first and second sections develop the foundations and contents of human dignity and human rights respectively. It is also argued that the recognition and respect for both human dignity and innate human rights in CH converge with other philosophical positions and with well-known international declarations of human rights. The third section outlines how human development is understood within CST, showing some convergences and divergences from other ways of understanding development. It concludes by pointing out some practical consequences for economics and business.

Human Dignity, a Crucial Reference

The Notion of Human Dignity

The word 'dignity', from Latin *dignitas*, refers to the quality of being worthy or honorable; it also signifies excellence. For Romans dignity meant a certain honorable status which imposed on others an obligation of recognition and respect (Balsdon 1960).

---

[1] This and other CST documents are presented here in abbreviations with two letters –such as FR– followed by a number which correspond to the numeration of official documents (www.vatican. va). See a full list of these abbreviations at the beginning of this book, also in the references at the end of this chapter.

[2] Pope Francis (2013) has also emphasized the link between faith and reason (LF, 32–36).

[3] Within the limited space available, we only aim to present a brief comparison to some other approaches that differ from CST. Basically we aim to present an overview of the Catholic position.

In our current context, *human dignity* means the consideration that every human is constitutively worthy of esteem, respect and honor. It has been defined as "a kind of intrinsic worth that belongs equally to all human beings as such, constituted by certain intrinsically valuable aspects of being human" (Gewirth 1992, 12). In practical terms, human dignity requires treating others and even oneself with respect and consideration. Human dignity has been proposed as a basic social principle (Schlag 2013), which allows building of a decent society (Margalit 1998).

The notion of dignity has a long history (Rosen 2012). The modern notion of human dignity is generally associated with the moral philosophy of Immanuel Kant (1724–1804) and his second formulation of the Categorical Imperative: "Act in such a way that you treat humanity, whether in your own person or in the person of any other, never merely as a means to an end" (1993/1785, 30). Kant distinguishes between things that should not be discussed in terms of value, and those which have dignity. Things have value, persons have dignity. He argues that every human being is endowed with dignity by being a moral agent – a being who is capable of acting with reference to right and wrong – and with an end in him or herself (1993/1785, Chap. 2). Kant therefore understands human dignity as a rational finding, independent of any religious faith, and places this concept at the heart of his ethical and political theory.

The content of *human dignity* is not, however, a Kantian invention. Several scholars (Ullmann 1967; Morris 1972; Hanning 1977; Bynum 1980; Gurevick 1994) have shown that in the twelfth century, and perhaps before, the individual was especially emphasized. We can clearly find the notion of human dignity in the fifteenth and sixteenth century in Europe. Human dignity was stressed by the Italian philosopher and scholar Pico della Mirandola in the celebrated public discourse *Oration on the Dignity of Man* (2012).

We can go even further by pointing out that the understanding of human dignity, which attributes every human being an intrinsic value regardless of their individual merits, race, religion, and of their social position has its roots in the Judeo-Christian tradition. We will try to show this next, with special emphasis on Catholic tradition.

Human Dignity in the Bible and Early Christian Writers

A crucial reference to human dignity appears at the beginning of the Bible, in the context of the Creation. The entire relation of the creation shows a particular love of God for human beings, by presenting a clear distinction between humans and non-rational animals, granting humans dominion over the Earth, and placing them in the garden of Eden to cultivate it. The human being is directly created by God (The Holy Bible 1966, *Gen* 1:26–27; 2:7) and what is more "God created humankind in his image, in the image of God he created them; male and female he created them." Thus, men and women are images of God on Earth. This shows the intrinsic value or dignity of every human being, which does not depend on personal qualities or merits, nor on legal mandate or social status.

The image of God finds a particular expression in human rationality as a distinctive category from other animals, and this is present in one Psalm: "Be not like a horse or a mule, without understanding" (*Ps* 31:9). In another Psalm there is a reflection on the greatness of the human being with: "what are human beings that you are mindful of them, mortals that you care for them? Yet you have made them a little lower than God, and crowned them with glory and honor" (*Ps* 8:4–5).

In the New Testament, human dignity is especially stressed by the fact that Jesus Christ being eternally the Son of God became man in the womb of the Virgin Mary (*Jn* 1; *Lk* 1: 26–38)[4] and for the universal Redemption of all human individuals from their sins, wrought by Jesus Christ. This grants human beings a great dignity. In addition, humans are called to become children of God[5] and to seek a close intimacy or 'communion' with God. According to the interpretation of the Catholic Church, this latter provides the human being with the highest dignity (Second Vatican Council 1965, *Gaudium et Spes*, #19). Such dignity is universal, since according to the New Testament, Redemption is universal and is addressed to all humankind: God "desires everyone to be saved and to come to the knowledge of the truth" (*1 Tim* 2:4).

Human dignity is also expressed in the New Testament in other ways. The commandment to love one's neighbor is especially worthy of note: "You shall love your neighbor as yourself" (*Mt* 19:19; cf. *Mk* 12:31). "In this commandment" –John Paul II (1993) wrote– "we find a precise expression of *the singular dignity of the human person*" (VS, 13).

Early Christian writers, termed the Fathers of the Church, expressed human dignity in different manners, at least implicitly. This is the case, for instance, of Pope Gregory the Great in his *Homilies on the Gospels* (2009: 8th Homily, 2) He came to consider that the angels now revere human nature as being superior to theirs, and praise humans for having accepted the King of Heaven, the God-Man. St. Augustine is particularly eloquent in his monumental work the *City of God* (1887, published originally in the early fifth century). He repeatedly mentions the dignity of man (II, 29; VI, 5, and others), or the dignity of the rational soul (VIII, 15), and the call to everybody to an everlasting dignity (III, 17). He emphasizes that God endowed humans with a nature that placed them between angels and beasts (XII, 21).

---

[4] This is a central point of Christian faith, known as the Incarnation of the Second Divine Person of the Holy Trinity. Regarding this, St. Paul wrote "when the fullness of time had come, God sent his Son, born of a woman, born under the law" (*Gal* 4:4). It was "in order to redeem those who were under the law, so that we might receive adoption as children" (*Gal* 4:5). Thus, Jesus Christ became the Mediator between God and humankind: "For there is one God; there is also one mediator between God and humankind, Christ Jesus, himself human, who gave himself as a ransom for all—this was attested at the right time" (*Gal* 4:5–6).

[5] Being children of God means being one with Christ and participating deeply in the divine life. Thus, humans might become sharers in divine nature (*2 Pet* 1:4) and call to increase such participation in the divine life forever: "we are God's children now; what we will be has not yet been revealed" (*1 Jn* 3:2).

Human Dignity: From the Middle Ages to the Renaissance

In the thirteenth century, Thomas Aquinas developed the notion of person, which was already used in Christian theology in the fourth and fifth centuries A.D. He accepted the definition of person introduced by the philosopher Boethius, in the sixth century, as "a subsistent individual of a rational nature".[6] Person, in short, means "a rational subject".

According to Aquinas, talking of 'person' is talking of 'high dignity' (1981, I, 29, 3, 2), and "because subsistence in a rational nature is of high dignity, therefore every individual of the rational nature is called a 'person'" (Ibid.). More explicitly, he affirms that "person signifies what is most perfect in all nature" of and, as applies only to the rational nature, this latter is endowed with dignity (1981, I, 29, 3).

It was in the Renaissance period, with the rise of humanists such as Pico della Mirandola –mentioned above–, when *human dignity* acquired special consistency. He argued (2012) that God fixed the nature of all other things but left man alone to determine his own nature. It is this freedom of choice and the responsibilities attached to it that constitute the dignity of the human being. The old Roman concept of *dignitas,* which Romans exclusively applied to very important persons with suitability, worthiness, rank, status, position, standing, esteem, honor and the like (Balsdon 1960), was now applied to every human being.

Dignity in Modern Catholic Social Teaching

Pope Leo XIII (Pope between 1878 and 1903), generally considered the initiator of modern Catholic Social Teaching, had great concern for human dignity and human rights. In his Encyclical Letter *Rerum Novarum* (1891), he condemned the working conditions, under which some employees had to suffer, as "repugnant to their dignity as human beings" (RN 36), adding that "[n]o man may with impunity outrage that human dignity which God Himself treats with great reverence" (RN 40). On the positive side, he encouraged everyone "to respect in every man his dignity as a person ennobled by Christian character" (RN 20).

Since Leo XIII, papal documents have insisted on human dignity. This was the case of Pius XI (1922–1939), who strongly defended (QA) such a dignity, particularly in the labor context.

Pope Pius XII (1939–1956), intensified the importance of human dignity and John XXIII (1956–1963), made human dignity a central concept in his teaching, particularly in his two social Encyclical Letters: *Mater et Magistra* (1961), where he emphasized the "sacred dignity of the individual" (MM 220), and *Pacem in terris*

---

[6] In Latin, *Naturæ rationalis individua substantia*. This definition appears in Boethius' work *De persona et duabus naturis* (c. II; mentioned by Aquinas 1981, I, 29, 1 and 3).

(1963), where he invited us to define "the scope of a just freedom within which individual citizens may live lives worthy of their human dignity" (PT 104).

The Second Vatican Council (1963–1965) again mentioned human dignity several times and presented human dignity as a key value, along with brotherhood and freedom (GS 39). At the same time it welcomed the fact that human dignity had given rise in many parts of the world to attempts to bring about a politico-juridical order which would give better protection to the rights of the person in public life (GS 73).

In more recent Catholic Church documents, human dignity continues to be strongly emphasized. In his Encyclical *Centesimus annus* (1991), Pope John Paul II (1978–2005) affirmed:

> …in a certain sense, the guiding principle (…) of all of the Church's social doctrine, is a *correct view of the human person* and of his unique value, inasmuch as 'man … is the only creature on earth which God willed for itself.' (GS 24) God has imprinted his own image and likeness on man (cf. Gen 1:26), conferring upon him an incomparable dignity. (CA 11)

John Paul II (1988) regretted the influence of some ideologies in obscuring the awareness of a human dignity common to all, and encouraged us "*to rediscover and make others rediscover the inviolable dignity of every human person,*" and added that this "makes up an essential task, in a certain sense, the central and unifying task of the service which the Church, and the lay faithful in her, are called to render to the human family" (CL 37; always italics in the original unless the contrary is indicated). He also emphasized the fruitful activity of millions of people spurred by the social Magisterium of the Church as forming a great movement for "*the defence of the human person* and the safeguarding of human dignity" (CA 3). On his part, Pope Benedict XVI (2005–2013) presented (2009a) human dignity as a central value (CV 15) and proposed "the inviolable dignity of the human person and the transcendent value of natural moral norms." as a moral normative guideline (CV 45).[7]

Human Dignity: Contrasting Christian Humanism and Other Approaches

According to Mattson and Clark "Western philosophers and theologians have arrived at a more-or-less shared understanding of human specialness, imparting dignity" (2011, 306). This seems correct and, to some extent, it may even be accepted beyond Western civilization, as we will see below.

As noted above, Kant has been extremely influential in the modern philosophical foundation of human dignity and in the above-mentioned second formulation of the Categorical Imperative, essential for Kantian ethics. This formulation entails

---

[7] A good synthesis of the Church's teachings on human dignity can be found in the *Catechism of the Catholic Church* (2003 nn. 1934, 1997, 1700ff) and in the *Compendium of the Social Doctrine of the Church* (CSDC), published by the PCJP (2004, Chap. 3).

"respect" for persons and the idea that treating human beings as mere instruments with no value beyond this is ethically unacceptable. Respect for persons, without any distinction of who they are is also crucial for Christian Humanism (e.g., CL 37).

John Paul II does not challenge Kant's argument that the reason for human dignity is that a person is a moral agent, with free will, and consequently, persons are an end in themselves, but extends the case by saying "the person is not at all a 'thing' or an 'object' to be used, but primarily a responsible 'subject', one endowed with conscience and freedom, called to live responsibly in society and history, and oriented towards spiritual and religious values" (CL 5).

The Kantian rational foundation of human dignity is reinforced by other philosophical positions, such as those held by Aristotle and Thomas Aquinas, who considered that the human being has been endowed with a spiritual and immortal soul. This is a position also defended by CST (GS 14, CCC 1703).

CH shares the consideration and respect for human dignity with other religions and international declarations of human rights. With Judaism, in both the Torah and Talmudic tradition, human dignity is central (Sicker 2001).

Regarding Islam, human dignity is not a well-defined concept. Nevertheless, some modern interpretations of Islam find in this faith a foundation for human dignity. Thus, the *Universal Islamic Declaration of Human Rights* (1981) stated that "Islam gave to mankind an ideal code of human rights fourteen centuries ago. These rights aim at conferring honor and dignity on mankind and eliminating exploitation, oppression and injustice". Similarly, the *Cairo Declaration on Human Rights in Islam*, states: "All men are equal in terms of basic human dignity (...) The true religion is the guarantee for enhancing such dignity along the path to human integrity (1990, art. 1).

In Chinese wisdom traditions the concept of human dignity does not exist as an innate feature. For the Confucian ethic, dignity is acquired by having good intentions, acting honorably, being sensitive to changes in human dynamics, calculating self-interest, and reciprocating in the right way at the right time. However, according to Koehn and Leung (2008), despite these differences, analysis of concrete practical cases suggests that it is possible to devise courses of actions that honor both types of dignity: innate and acquired.

Human dignity is also central in international declarations or covenants of human rights, starting with the Universal Declaration of Human Rights (UDHR) (1948). According to Arieli (2002, 1), the human dignity of every human being is "the cornerstone and the foundation on which the United Nations sought to reconstruct the future international order of mankind and of public life in general."

The UDHR recognizes the "inherent dignity and the equal and inalienable rights of all members of the human family" (Preamble). This expression is repeated in two other important documents, to which many countries have adhered: the International Covenant on Economic, Social and Cultural Rights (1966a) and in the International Covenant on Civil and Political Rights (1966b). In contrast to CST, the justification of UN Declarations is more pragmatic than philosophical or theological. These documents see the recognition of such inherent dignity, equality and rights as "the foundation of freedom, justice and peace in the world" (UDHR, Preamble).

Human Rights, an Essential Requirement of Justice

The Notion of "Human Rights"

Human rights are moral rights possessed by a person who is entitled to own, perform or demand something. Thus, human rights are independent of any human authority and previous to their promulgation by means of civil law. However, human rights are often recognized as fundamental legal rights too, and even included in the constitutions of many countries. As Sepúlveda et al. affirm, human rights are "commonly understood as inalienable fundamental rights to which a person is inherently entitled simply because she or he is a human being" (2004, 3). A right creates a duty of justice for someone else or a group of people to respect or satisfy the right, since justice, according to an old definition coming from the Roman Jurist Ulpian's is "the perpetual and constant will to render to each one his right" (mentioned by Aquinas 1981, II-II, 58).

The correspondence between right and other people's duty entails "a reciprocal moral relationship that binds them all together" (Williams 2005, 9). Some authors hold that human dignity is the basis of human rights, while others think of human dignity independently of human rights. However, currently "the link between human rights and human dignity is increasingly seen as normative rather than accidental" (Donnelly 2009, 83).

The notion of 'human rights' is relatively recent, even more so than human dignity. In the intellectual history of human rights the British philosopher John Locke (1632–1704) is often mentioned as the pioneer in developing the concept of "natural rights". According to Locke, property, life, liberty and the right to happiness are natural rights of all individuals. They are seen as self-evident and derived from divinity, since human beings are creatures of God. Natural rights are innate and therefore do not rely on any law of the state nor are privative of any particular group.

In political and legal terms, it is generally considered that the first record of human rights is *The Twelve Articles* (1525) establishing the peasants' demands to the Swabian League during the German Peasants' War. These articles, which contain several religious connotations, demand specific rights for peasant communities.

In 1689, the *Bill of Rights* was proposed in England, limiting the powers of the crown and setting out an array of rights of individuals and of Parliament, and which, to great extent reflected the ideas of John Locke, which had become quite popular.

In the eighteenth century in the United States several key rights were introduced in *The United States Declaration of Independence*, the constitution of the United States. In Europe, during the French Revolution the *Declaration of the Rights of Man and the Citizen* was proposed.

In all of these cases, the documents mentioned were the result of socio-political movements and a reaction against situations of oppression. This was the primary stimulus, but underlying it is the humanistic sense of human dignity and the demand for rights previous to any political concession.

Human rights are a core element of CH, the roots of which can be found in the Bible, early Christian writers, the great 'Doctors of the Church', particularly St Thomas Aquinas, and some authors in the sixteenth and the first half of the seventeenth centuries.

Human Rights, Implicit in the Bible

Human rights do not explicitly appear in the Holy Bible (1966). However, implicitly they can be found in the Ten Commandments, shared by the Jewish, Christian and Muslims with scant differences (Ali et al. 2000), since these obligations or commandments presuppose the existence of rights inherent in persons (Harrelson 1980). Thus, "You shall not kill" entails the right of life; "You shall not steal" supposes the right to own property; "You shall not commit adultery" entails the right to marry and to found a family on the basis of mutual faithfulness; "You shall not bear false witness against your neighbor" implies the right to a fair trial, and so on. As the *Catechism of the Catholic Church* affirms, the Ten Commandments "shed light on the essential duties, and so indirectly on the fundamental rights, inherent in the nature of the human person" (CCC 2070).

The prophets preached justice often related to what we now term human rights. Isaiah, for instance, rebukes rulers telling them: "Ah, you who make iniquitous decrees, who write oppressive statutes, to turn aside the needy from justice and to rob the poor of my people of their right, that widows may be your spoil, and that you may make the orphans your prey!" (10:1–2) Similarly, in the Ecclesiastes (5:8) we read: "If you see in a province the oppression of the poor and the violation of justice and right, do not be amazed at the matter; for the high official is watched by a higher, and there are yet higher ones over them." The prophets exhort the respect for each person's dignity and rights, paying special attention to those who are weaker or marginalized, such as the foreigner, the widow and the orphan (e.g., Zech 7:10).

Human Rights: Aquinas and the School of Salamanca

In the Medieval period theologians and canonists (experts on ecclesiastical law) emphasized justice, understood as the permanent and constant will to give each his or her right. This led them to consider duties toward God and to the supremacy of God in public life, laws and institutions. The acceptance of the primacy of God did not prevent them from recognizing the rights of every human being; on the contrary, this was the very basis of their position. Although individual human rights were not explicitly presented, indirectly they were recognized in the teaching of moral duties in dealing with others. Garcia López (1979) studied how human rights are present in the writings of Thomas Aquinas (1224–1274), probably the most important medieval theologian, and finds the following individual rights: life, physical integrity, wellbeing, private property, just trial, fame, and intimacy. Aquinas also recognized the right to participate in public life within certain limits and other rights related to the common good of society.

In the sixteenth century and the first half of the seventeenth a number of theologians, members of what is known as of the School of Salamanca (Spain), openly defended the existence of universal rights in the context of the discovery and the colonization of the New World. In opposition to some who denied that the Native Americans were real human beings or were endowed with inherent rights, they defended the innate dignity and rights of men and women based on the fact of being human.

Francisco de Victoria (1483–1546), a Dominican friar and professor in the University of Salamanca, provided a firm intellectual defense of the rights of the indigenous (Amerindians). He stated that Indians were not inferior beings at all, and they had the same rights as any human, including the right to own land and other property (Fazio 1998). Another champion of what now we term human rights was Bartolomé de las Casas (1484–1566), Bishop of Chiapas, Mexico. He was also an advocate for Amerindians, defending the position that they were free persons in the natural order and deserved the same treatment as others, according to Catholic theology. Both had a great influence in enacting new laws (*Leyes Nuevas de Indias*) which established that Indians were free human beings and put them under the direct protection of the Spanish Crown (Beuchot 1994).

Regarding slavery, on the part of the Papacy, in spite of some controversy, as was shown by Panzer (1996), Popes did condemn racial slavery and the slave trade of Native American as early as 1435. This author has also reviewed a number of papal documents in which such condemnation is made explicit.

Human Rights in Catholic Social Teaching

As noted, the Bible and the Christian tradition, at least implicitly, entail the existence of innate rights inherent in every human being. However, the Roman Catholic Church was not initially too enthusiastic about the rights and freedoms of man contained in the *Declaration of the Rights of Man and the Citizen* enacted within the historical context of the French Revolution. There was a climate of hostility to the Church and an intellectual context in which human autonomy was understood as placing one's own conscience as the supreme norm of morality. Human dignity and rights rather than being based on divine transcendence and supported by God's authority were founded on human autonomy. Popes Pius VI (1775–1799) and Gregory XVI (1831–1846) strongly opposed this view and Pope Pius IX (1846–1878) condemned an array of 'errors of liberalism' in a document known as the *Syllabus* (1864).

Some years later, his successor, Pope Leo XIII reflected on the importance of human freedom, underscoring the supremacy of truth over freedom. He wrote: "to all matter of opinion which God leaves to man's free discussion, full liberty of thought and of speech is naturally within the right of everyone; for such liberty never leads men to suppress the truth, but often to discover it and make it known" (1888, #23). However, precisely for the sake of the truth, Leo XIII energetically defended the natural rights of the human being, especially in the context of labor abuses. Leo stood up for the rights of the people especially the poor and weaker (RN 20) and did not hesitate to demand the "natural rights of man" (RN 51–53) and to defend those rights that citizens are entitled to as human beings (RN 39).

Pius XI (1857–1939) reiterated the teachings of Leo XIII by proclaiming the rights of man against various types of totalitarianism of his days (Nazism, Communism and Fascism), as well as against religious persecution in Mexico, and highlighted the legitimacy of civic defense of human rights. Pius XII (1939–1956) stressed the position of defense of the rights of man, which are presented as closely related to human dignity and democracy. It was this Pope who, from the early 1940s, sought to restore moral and inalienable rights and to develop a doctrinal statement in favor of their recognition (1940, #26). He defended human rights supported by natural right, and ultimately by God's law (1948) and maintained that to "safeguard the inviolable rights of the human person and to facilitate the fulfillment of their duties, shall be duty of every public authority" (1941, #15).

It was during Pius XII's pontificate when the United Nations Universal Declaration of the Human Rights (UDHR) was approved in 1948. This Declaration was welcomed by Pius XII's successor, Pope John XXIII (1956–1963), although with some reservations:

> We are, of course, aware that some of the points in the declaration did not meet with unqualified approval in some quarters; and there was justification for this. Nevertheless, We think the document should be considered a step in the right direction, an approach toward the establishment of a juridical and political ordering of the world community. It is a solemn recognition of the personal dignity of every human being; an assertion of everyone's right to be free to seek out the truth, to follow moral principles, discharge the duties imposed by justice, and lead a fully human life. It also recognized other rights connected with these. (PT 144)

The Second Vatican Council (1962–1965) did not mention human rights declarations but alluded to them indirectly (GS 73, 75) and talked about the necessity of a political-legal order to protect the rights of man and by considering institutions for public life (GS 74). After the Second Vatican Council, there have been numerous interventions in favor of human rights by Popes Paul VI (1963–1978) and John Paul II (1978–2005) (see a partial compilation of texts in Filibeck 1994). Benedict XVI (2005–2013) has also insisted on the importance of fighting for the promotion and respect for human rights[8], and so are doing pope Francis (2013, nn. 64, 65, 67, 190, and others) who, besides, has remembered that "again and again, the Church has acted as a mediator in finding solutions to problems affecting peace, social harmony, the land, the defence of life, human and civil rights, and so forth" (EG 65).

Pope John XXIII published the Encyclical-Letter *Pacem in Terris* in 1963, a crucial document of CST in which human rights are central.

---

[8] Two addresses of Benedict XVI are particularly worthy of note regarding human rights. One to the General Assembly of the United Nations (2008) and another to the Pontifical Academy of Social Sciences (2009b).

Foundations of Human Rights

Pacem in terris, as the whole of CST, emphasizes the inextricable link between rights and duties, all applying to one and the same person (PT 28). It makes it clear by giving some examples of the link between rights and duties: "the right to live involves the duty to preserve one's life; the right to a decent standard of living, the duty to live in a becoming fashion; the right to be free to seek out the truth, the duty to devote oneself to an ever deeper and wider search for it" (PT 29). In other words, we humans have personal moral duties to perform in accordance with moral law, and such duties require that others respect the corresponding rights which make possible the compliance of these duties. Thus, moral duties, which provide justification for human rights, are based on natural moral law, which according to Thomas Aquinas (1981, I–II, q. 94) is rationally discovered from human tendencies. And "every basic human right draws its authoritative force from the natural law, which confers it and attaches to it its respective duty" (PT 30). Human rights give rise to recognizing and respecting those rights and therefore the corresponding duty in other people (PT 28, 30). This position is closely related to those who proposed human needs as a foundation for human rights (e.g., Adler 1970, 137–154; Donnelly 1985).

The foundation of rights on duties has been recurrent in CST. In 2003, John Paul II made a call for "a renewed reflection on how *rights presuppose duties, if they are not to become mere licence*", warning of the current paradox that while some appeal to rights, arbitrary and non-essential in nature, some elementary and basic rights remain unacknowledged and are violated in much of the world. The latter can include lack of food, drinkable water, basic instruction and elementary health care. Six years later, his successor Benedict XVI insisted that when individual rights are detached from a framework of duties which grants them their full meaning, such rights can run wild, leading to an escalation of demands which is effectively unlimited and indiscriminate. "Duties –he affirmed– set a limit on rights because they point to the anthropological and ethical framework of which rights are a part, in this way ensuring that they do not become license" (CV 43).

CH defends personal freedom with responsibility, and the respect and protection of human rights, including those relevant in business. Within the economic and business context, Benedict XVI stated that "among those who sometimes fail to respect the human rights of workers are large multinational companies as well as local producers" (CV 22). The defense of the human rights is firm, argued on the basis of their transcendent foundation. The risk we face is that of human rights being ignored "either because they are robbed of their transcendent foundation or because personal freedom is not acknowledged" (CV 56).

This emphasis on duties and on the ethical and transcendental foundation of human rights, characteristic of CH as proposed by CST, contrasts with other positions in which rights are presented with no ethical foundation, only as a matter of fact; or others in which rights prevail over duties, or personal duties remain as a subjective matter on which nothing can be said in the public arena. This leads to claim rights, while ignoring duties (PT 30).

The contrast is even greater regarding the foundation of human rights. Some theories derive human rights from certain social contract or as a, more or less, universal consensus. From this perspective the principal function of human rights would be to protect and promote certain essential human interests. This is one influential theory on human rights, nowadays (Fagan 2005). CST finds such a position problematic: "if the only basis of human rights is to be found in the deliberations of an assembly of citizens, those rights can be changed at any time, and so the duty to respect and pursue them fades from the common consciousness. Governments and international bodies can then lose sight of the objectivity and "inviolability" of rights. When this happens, the authentic development of peoples is endangered" (CV 43).

According to CST, human rights are universal (PT 132; GS 26) and original – they do not depend on will and political power (PT 28, GS 65). They are fundamental (GS 65), because they are at the base of any human relationship. They are also inalienable and inviolable (Pius XI 1937) and "the protection and promotion of the inviolable rights of man ranks among the essential duties of government" (Second Vatican Council 1965, *Dignitatis humanae*, 6). Their roots are in human nature and ultimately in God, author of this nature. Thus, human rights are sacred because they respond to God's plan. It is God the Creator who provides the ultimate support to human rights as inviolable. This has been a constant teaching of the Church since Leo XIII. This Pope, talking about the right of workers, stated: "for it is not man's own rights which are here in question, but the rights of God, the most sacred and inviolable of rights" (RN 40).

Whether or not human rights are accepted with this transcendental foundation, nowadays there is a wide recognition of the international declarations of human rights, which has contributed to the fact that human rights have generally become commonly accepted both ethically and legally worldwide. However, some countries – or to be more precise their governments – object that human rights are a product of Western culture. Sometimes this may be only an excuse to violate human rights by some dictatorial governments, but it is true that the elaboration of human rights began in the West, as did the notion of human dignity. As we have tried to show, both concepts came from the Judeo-Christian tradition, but the recognition of human dignity and innate rights are becoming a patrimony of humanity.

Human rights are not a matter of cultural imperialism. Their contents are transcultural and universal since they are based on the common condition of being human. As Mary Ann Glendon wrote, "If relativism and imperialism were the only choice, the prospect for the Declaration's vision of human rights would be bleak indeed. Fortunately that is not the case. Much confusion has been created in current debates by two assumptions that would have been foreign within the framework of the Declaration. Today both critics and supporters of universal rights tend to take for granted that the Declaration mandates a single approved model of human rights of the entire world. Both also tend to assume that the only alternative would be to accept that all rights are relative to the circumstances of time and place" (2002, 229–230).

We can conclude by saying that human rights together with human dignity are a point of encounter between the doctrine of the Church and contemporary society (Benedict XVI 2009b).

Development for the Whole Person and for All Persons

In Old French, *desveloper* (to develop) means "unwrap, unfurl, unveil". The etymology of "development" comes from this word, with a meaning close to "unfolding" and with special reference to matters regarding property. It has been applied with the sense of "bringing out the latent possibilities", for instance, making improvements on new lands, by cultivation, and the erection of buildings, and so on.[9] Extending the notion of development to humans, some talk of "human development", denoting unfolding human capabilities, improvement as a human being; and even flourishing or human excellence.

The UN Notion of "Human Development"

Development of one's own capabilities is presented by the UDHR as closely related with human rights. This Declaration states that it is essential to promote the development of friendly relations between nations (Preamble) and mentions that every human being is entitled to his or her realization; it also stresses the necessity of economic, social and cultural rights "indispensable for his dignity and the free development of his personality" (art. 22). Furthermore, "education shall be directed to the full development of the human personality" (art. 26). The UDHR also posits the necessity of the community for full development of one's personality and, related to this, the duties of each one toward his or her community (art. 29).

The notion of "Human Development" became popular through the United Nations. For a long time most people had talked of "development" only in a material and economic sense. Thus, development has been almost synonymous of economic growth, generally measured in terms of national income. The term "human development" was introduced in the late 1980s by the United Nations Development Programme (UNDP) and the elaboration and subsequent publication of annual Human Development Reports (HDRs) from 1990. One of the main components of these reports is the Human Development Index (HDI), which covers three basic variables: life expectancy, education and incomes. These HDRs were devised and launched by Pakistani economist Mahbub ul Haq with the aim of shifting the focus from national income accounting to peoples' well-being. The Nobel laureate Amartya Sen (1999) provided the underlying conceptual framework for HDI.

---

[9] cf. Online Etymology Dictionary, voices "develop" and "development": www.etymonline.com/index.php?allowed_in_frame=0&search=develop&searchmode=none

In these reports, human development is understood as a process of enlarging the range of choices in all areas of human endeavor and for every human being.

Nowadays, HDRs are globally recognized as a crucial aid in measuring, monitoring, and managing human development. They allow policy-makers to analyze diverse challenges that poor people and poor countries face, rather than imposing a rigid economic rationality with a set of policy prescriptions. Although this vision of human development is highly oversimplified, this index and the reports on human development extend the scope of development and have become useful to convince the public, academics, and policy-makers that they can and should evaluate development in terms of improvements in human well-being, and not only through economic growth. This is why the notion of "human development" has become popular worldwide.

The notion of "human development" is not at all strange to the Christian Humanism tradition. On the contrary it is one of its key core concepts, as we try to show in this section. However, the understanding of human development in CH is wider than that presented in the HDRs and is, by no means, reduced to a process of enlarging choices.

Human Development in Catholic Humanism

Sacred Scripture and early Christian writers call the person to a progressive identification with Christ and this includes developing oneself in his or her humanity by acquiring virtues to flourish as a human being. Concern for the poor and for people's needs in order to improve their living conditions is also to be found in the oldest Christian tradition.

The wish for human development is very much present in modern Catholic social teaching. John XXIII encouraged the attainment of a degree of economic development that enables citizens to live in conditions more in keeping with their human dignity (PT 122). Pope Paul VI (1967) wrote the encyclical-letter *Populorum Progressio* (PP) specifically devoted to the development of people. In this document, the Pope started by remembering the deep interest and concern for the progressive development of peoples of his predecessors and the Second Vatican Council (cf. PP, introductory words). Paul VI did not use term "human development", but the concept is there. Furthermore, he mentioned "development" 52 times in this encyclical, often without any adjective, by making clear that the development he spoke about "cannot be restricted to economic growth alone" (PP 14). He added that development "to be authentic, (it) must be well rounded; it must foster the development of each man and of the whole man" (PP 14). At the same time, he encouraged a "collaboration that contributes greatly to the common development of mankind and allows the individual to find fulfillment" (PP 84).

This human development includes both "the whole person and every person" and, since Paul VI, has been called "integral human development". The importance of integral human development was repeated by John Paul II (1990, #42), and

Benedict XVI extended this concept in his encyclical *Caritas in veritate* (2009a) stating that "the truth of development consists in its completeness: if it does not involve the whole man and every man, it is not true development" (CV 18, cf. CV 8). Pope Francis, insists on the "the integral promotion of each human being" (EG 182) and on "the integral development of all" (EG 240).

These twofold aspects of integral human development mentioned above – the whole person and every person – invite us to analyze them separately, although keeping in mind that they go together, since, as we discuss below, contributing to the development of another contributes to one's own development.

The development of the whole person entails every single dimension of the human being (PP 14, CV 11). However, the spiritual dimension is paramount, because of the spiritual nature of humans. Spiritual growth is, therefore, an essential part of human development, although this also must include material progress, since man is unity of body and soul (CV 76). Personal development is made by good acts of freedom, which develop virtues with the subsequent human flourishing. This is a finding of reason, as the ancient Greek philosopher Aristotle (1925) suggested. Freedom is essential for this spiritual progress but it is not enough. "Fidelity to man requires *fidelity to the truth*, which alone is the *guarantee of freedom* (cf. Jn 8:32) and of *the possibility of integral human development*" (CV 9).

The development of every person concerns groups of people, starting with the family, the very core of society, and it extends to the whole of humankind. It also includes material means and conditions of freedom, education and culture for the spiritual development of people. In many countries and places there is poverty, in both material and cultural terms, and a lack of freedom and justice. This challenges individuals, societies, governmental and non-governmental institutions, national and international organizations.

Social structures may play a great role in such development. However, as CST makes clear, each individual remains the principal agent of his or her own success or failure, whatever the circumstances might be (PP 15). In Benedict XVI's words, "*integral human development presupposes the responsible freedom* of the individual and of peoples; no structure can guarantee this development over and above human responsibility" (CV 17).

Human Development as a Transcendental Calling

CST sees the development of each person as a calling or vocation. Even more, "integral human development is primarily a vocation" (CV 11). Within us, we can discover certain aptitudes and abilities in germinal form. Some are generic to all human beings, such as the capacity for acquiring rational knowledge and for entering in communion with other persons, while others are particular talents. We are called to flourish as a human being and to employ our talents usefully. This calling, although in a different manner, extends also to social groups, such as families and peoples. Responding to this innate vocation to development entails a sense of duty, which is actually a radical ethical obligation.

Regarding the calling to personal development, CST distinguishes between two planes: one natural, focused on achieving human fulfillment, or perfection as a human being, and another, supernatural, which regards a full communion with Christ, and requires divine help. Both of these include a transcendent vocation. In the natural plane there is a response to the calling from God the Creator, which we find in our nature, although when God is eclipsed, our ability to recognize the natural order decreases. The supernatural plane regards the Christian vocation. It includes both the natural plane and the supernatural plane (CV 18).

The vocation to development is therefore not a matter of choice, although one can respond in different ways. Benedict XVI emphasized, that "the vocation to development on the part of individuals and peoples is not based simply on human choice, but is an intrinsic part of a plan that is prior to us and constitutes for all of us a duty to be freely accepted" (CV, 52).

Recognizing *development as a vocation* has relevant consequences. First, the discovery of such a vocation is something which transcends us and leads us to understand that "Someone" higher than me is calling me. CST defends the position that development derives from a transcendent call (CV 16). Paul VI openly stated: "In God's plan, every man is born to seek self-fulfillment, for every human life is called to some task by God" (PP 15). In developing one's own seminal qualities through formal education of personal effort, "the individual works his way toward the goal set for him by the Creator" (Ibid.).

A second consequence is that the vocation to development is incapable, on its own, of supplying its ultimate meaning. Vocation gives human life its true meaning (CV 16, PP 42). This leads one to affirm, that "there is no true humanism but that which is open to the Absolute", and is conscious of the meaning to life provided by the vocation to development (Ibid.)

A third consequence of seeing development as a vocation is the *central place of love (charity) within human development* (CV 19). Considering the development of the whole person, love, in the Christian sense of *agape* is at the core of all virtues (Melé 2012), and growing in love –not any love but love in truth– is growing as a human being. Based on the Gospel (Lk 17:37), *Gaudium et spes*, states that man "cannot fully find himself except through a sincere gift of himself" (GS 24). Regarding the development of people, love –or also, if you prefer, brotherhood or sense of solidarity– is also essential: Underdevelopment is an important cause of the lack of brotherhood among individuals and peoples (PP 66). Benedict XVI added a truth we realize every day: "As society becomes ever more globalized, it makes us neighbors but does not make us brothers" (CV 19).

Achieving Human Development

Human development inspired by CST converges with other approaches, but goes beyond most of them. It is fully in agreement with what UDHR says about the right to develop one's personality, and mentions "humanity's right to development" as well as the role of institutions to foster this end (CV 11). The contribution of the individual to the community to favor the development of others is also considered by CST, which stresses the importance of contributing to the common good (CV 7), understood as the "sum of those conditions of social life which allow social groups and their individual members relatively thorough and ready access to their own fulfillment" (GS 26).

However, above all, CST insists on achieving a full development, as well as a good society, which is much more than a question of rights and duties and building efficient institutions. It is rather a matter of virtuous relationships. Benedict XVI affirms, using the Augustinian term *earthly city* that this "is promoted not merely by relationships of rights and duties, but to an even greater and more fundamental extent by relationships of gratuitousness, mercy and communion" (CV 6). More explicitly, he adds: "*Development is impossible without upright men and women, without financiers and politicians whose consciences are finely attuned to the requirements of the common good*" (CV 71).

Another point of agreement with United Nations is that development cannot be reduced to economic development. By no means does CH accept the separation of the human from economic development. At the beginning of 1960s, within the CH tradition, Lebret wrote: "We cannot allow economics to be separated from human realities, nor development from the civilization in which it takes place. What counts for us is man – each individual man, each human group, and humanity as a whole" (1961, 28). Paul VI echoed these words (PP 14) as did his successors John Paul II (SRS 8–9), and Benedict XVI (CV 21).

CST not only makes clear, that development cannot be restricted to economic growth alone, but also underlines that all development entails a moral dimension (SRS, 34), and, as noted above, development, to be authentic, must be well-rounded by fostering the development of each person and of the whole person (PP 14). When rationality is limited to technical or economic evaluations rejecting the rational consideration of the human being as a whole it becomes irrational: "because it implies a decisive rejection of meaning and value" (CV, 74). Since economic or instrumental rationality is not the whole of human rationality, Benedict XVI (2009) advocated *broadening the scope of reason* (CV 33) which not only includes technical and economic evaluations but the consideration of the whole person and a full meaning of development.

Another point of agreement of CST with the UN notion of Human Development is the concern for rescuing people from hunger, deprivation, endemic diseases and illiteracy, but furthermore CST has an "articulate vision of development" (CV 21) which includes defending an active participation, on equal terms, in the international economic process, the development of educated societies marked by solidarity, and the consolidation of democratic regimes capable of ensuring freedom and peace.

When CST affirms that authentic human development should permit the transition from less than human conditions to truly human ones (cf. PP 20), it not too far from the idea of "human development" proposed by Amartya Sen (1999) and others, that has already been mentioned above. However, the notion of integral human development proposed by CST presents a substantive difference from the ideas of Amartya Sen. Sen sees development as freedom and liberty and advocates a comprehensive view which includes the expansion of human capabilities, understood as aspects and possibilities of action and identity. Thus, development is seen as improving capabilities and, therefore, making choices possible. This leads people to live in accordance with what they prefer. According to Sen, pursuing one's own capabilities requires both resources and the ability to use them (skills) in order to make capabilities real. Consequently, development is about removing the obstacles to freedom, such as illiteracy, ill health, lack of access to resources, or lack of civil and political freedoms.

As noted above, CST presents freedom as being very important as a condition for development, and stands for the necessity to remove external obstacles, but insists that this is not sufficient. Freedom requires responsibility of individuals and of peoples.

Social and political structures can foster development, but no structure can guarantee this development over and above human responsibility. Obstacles and forms of conditioning hold up development, but each individual is the main agent of his or her personal development. In other words, freedoms are necessary but not sufficient. Integral human development requires acting virtuously to flourish as a human being. This is a personal task rather than a matter of public policies. However education and culture, which are not completely independent of politics, can have an influence on a responsible use of freedom.

Practical Implications

In this chapter we have tried to show three core concepts of CH –human dignity, human rights and integral human development–, based on both reason and faith and following Catholic social teaching. All of these can serve as a base of further developments and offer relevant ethical requirements for economics and business.

Respect for human dignity entails the ethical requirement of treating people as ends, and not as mere instruments: "In virtue of a personal dignity the human being is *always a value as an individual,* and as such demands being considered and treated as a person and never, on the contrary, considered and treated as an object to be used, or as a means, or as a thing" (CL 37). In business, persons are central, and people must never be regarded merely as resources for production or as consumers to obtain gains. This entails a *fair treatment* to everybody and a positive attitude toward *diversity.* All persons deserve respect, independently on their race, sex, religion, ideology, age or sexual orientation. Unfair discriminations in selection and promotion of personnel based on criteria alien to the job requirements are not acceptable.

As concerns work in organizations, it should be considered that work itself can have a greater or lesser objective value, but all work should be judged by the measure of dignity given to the person who carries it out. Thus, John Paul II (1981)

: "work is in the first place 'for the worker' and not the worker 'for work'" (LE 6). In this line of thought CST proposed the priority of labor over capital by considering that labor is the cause of production; while the means of production (capital), are only mere instruments or tools (LE 12).

The recognition and respect for human rights entails practical requirements for economic activity, particularly regarding labor. CST emphasizes, that *labor rights*, which flow from work "are part of the broader context of those fundamental rights of the person" (LE 16). Among these rights, which determine the correct relationship between worker and employer, CST mentions the right to a just wage, understood as that sufficient to support the worker and his or her family, and associated social benefits; the right to a working environment and to manufacturing processes which are not harmful to the workers' physical health or to their moral integrity; the right of workers to form unions or other associations to secure their rights to fair wages and working conditions; the *right to rest, first of all* a regular weekly rest comprising at least Sunday, and also a longer period of rest (vacations), the right to a pension and to insurance for old age and in case of accidents at work (LE 19–20).

Integral human development also has practical implications for business and the economy. As noted, development cannot be reduced to economic progress. CH suggests a deep meaning to development, avoiding a materialistic view, which reduces development to wealth accumulation. Development should be oriented to the service of people. CST emphasizes, that "in the economic and social realms, too, the dignity and complete vocation of the human person and the welfare of society as a whole are to be respected and promoted" (GS 63). And from here, a fundamental criterion emerges: "man is the source, the center, and the purpose of all economic and social life" (Ibid.).

Consequently, business should be oriented to people, to their development. "The fundamental finality of this production is not the mere increase of products nor profit or control but rather the service of man, and indeed of the whole man with regard for the full range of his material needs and the demands of his intellectual, moral, spiritual, and religious life; this applies to every man whatsoever and to every group of men, of every race and of every part of the world" (GS 64).

The development of the whole person requires organizing work in such a way that workers can share in the responsibility and creativity of the very work process, and can feel that they are working for themselves, instead of feeling like 'cogs' in a huge machine moved from above (LE 15). Integral Human development leads one to consider how making decisions favor or erode such development and how organizational structures can have an influence on fostering or preventing human development.

The development of all people leads to be concern with alleviation of poverty, fair international trading and being sensitive with the limitations of laws and in their application in some countries, and a firm attitude in fighting against corruption.

Responsibility in the application of these concepts requires practical wisdom and the prudent judgment of one's own conscience. Responsibility in economic activity, as in every human action, entails being aware not only of actions committed but also of omissions of what is due and possible through negligence or recklessness, willingness to cooperate in doing good and to avoid cooperation in wrongdoing, and fostering a positive influence on others' good behavior and, of course, avoiding the contrary.

It is worth noting that responsibility could be indirect (see CCC 1934–1937). This would be the case of a *supply chain* in which the final producer does not respect human dignity and basic human rights (e.g., working conditions in "sweatshops"). A company – or any other agent – bears responsibility for cooperation in wrongdoing if these unacceptable ethical conditions are foreseeable and the company or agent has the possibility of preventing them.

Considering the core concepts discussed in this chapter we can affirm that Catholic humanism has much in common with some current proposals of business ethics, especially those which emphasize human dignity and rights. However, business ethics approaches frequently only focus on ethical issues involving unacceptability or dilemmas which require certain deliberation but rarely consider the contribution of business to human development. An important difference of Christian humanism is the centrality of some specific virtues, such as charity, humility, willingness to forgive, and others. Furthermore, Catholic humanism provides reasons and motivation for respecting the dignity and innate rights of person and for promoting people's development.

Another difference regards the foundations of the concepts under consideration. God not only strongly supports human dignity and innate rights, He also gives full meaning to the vocation for development. This reference to God is so important that Pope Paul VI stated that humanism without God is, in a certain sense, inhuman: "True humanism points the way toward God and acknowledges the task to which we are called, the task which offers us the real meaning of human life" (PP 42).

On his part, Benedict XVI affirms, that "openness to God makes us open towards our brothers and sisters and towards an understanding of life as a joyful task to be accomplished in a spirit of solidarity." The rejection of God, on the contrary, is a great obstacle to development today (CV 78). Some atheistic "humanisms", as Henri de Lubac (1949) pointed out, end up being inhuman by degrading the human person: "closed off from God, they will end up being directed against man. A humanism closed off from other realities becomes inhuman" (1949, 7; Cf PP 42). Similarly, Benedict XVI defends the position that "true humanism points the way toward God and acknowledges the task to which we are called, the task which offers us the real meaning of human life" and remarks upon the importance of a transcendental humanism (CV 18) facing other visions in which God is denied, or at least, is presented –using the well-known Grotius' dictum– *etsi Deus non daretur* (if God does not exist). The exclusion of God is a risk of becoming equally oblivious to human values and subordinating humans to ideologies, interests or power.

References

Adler, Mortimer J. 1970. *The time of our lives: The ethics of common sense*. New York: Fordham University Press.
Ali, Abbas J., Robert C. Camp, and Manton Gibbs. 2000. The ten commandments perspective on power and authority in organizations. *Journal of Business Ethics* 26(Part 2): 351–361.
Aquinas, Thomas. 1981[1273]. *The summa theologica*. London: Burns Oates and Washbourne.

Arieli, Yehoshua. 2002. On the necessary and sufficient conditions for the emergence of the doctrine of the dignity of man and his rights. In *The concept of human dignity in human rights discourse*, ed. D. Kretzmer and E. Klein, 1–17. The Hague: Kluwer Law International.

Aristotle. 1925. *The nicomachean ethics*. Oxford/New York: Oxford University Press.

Augustine of Hippo. 1887 (Published originally early 5th century). *City of God*. Trans. Marcus Dods. From Nicene and Post-Nicene Fathers, First Series, vol. 2, ed. Philip Schaff. Buffalo: Christian Literature Publishing Co. Revised and edited for New Advent by Kevin Knight: http://www.newadvent.org/fathers/1201.htm. Accessed 16 July 2013.

Balsdon, J.P.V.D. 1960. Auctoritas dignitas, otium. *The Classical Quarterly* 10: 43–50.

Benedict XVI. 2008. Address to general assembly of the United Nations Organization, Apr 18. http://www.vatican.va/holy_father/benedict_xvi/speeches/2008/april/documents/hf_ben-xvi_spe_20080418_un-visit_en.html

Benedict XVI. 2009a. Encyclical-letter 'Caritas in veritate'. http://www.vatican.va/holy_father/benedict_xvi/encyclicals/documents/hf_ben-xvi_enc_20090629_caritas-in-veritate_en.html. Abbreviation: CV.

Benedict XVI. 2009b. Address to the 15th plenary session of the pontifical academy of social sciences, May 4. www.vatican.va/holy_father/benedict_xvi/speeches/2009/may/documents/hf_ben-xvi_spe_20090504_social-sciences_en.html

Beuchot, M. 1994. *Los fundamentos de los derechos humanos en Bartolomé de las Casas*. Madrid: Anthropos.

Bible, the Holy. 1966. *New revised standard version (Catholic edition)*. Princeton: Scepter.

Bynum, C.W. 1980. Did the twelfth century discover the individual? *Journal of the Ecclesiastical History* 31: 1–17.

Cairo Declaration on Human Rights in Islam. 1990. http://www1.umn.edu/humanrts/instree/cairo-declaration.html

Catholic Church. 2003. *Catechism of the Catholic Church*. London: Random House. Available in: www.vatican.va/archive/ENG0015/_INDEX.HTM. Abbreviation: CCC.

de Lubac, H. 1949. *The drama of atheistic humanism*. London: Sheed and Ward.

Donnelly, Jack. 1985. *The concept of human rights*. London: Croom Helm.

Donnelly, Jack. 2009. Human dignity and human rights. www.udhr60.ch/report/donnelly-HumanDignity_0609.pdf

Fagan, Andrew. 2005. Human rights. The internet encyclopedia of philosophy. www.iep.utm.edu/hum-rts/

Fazio, M. 1998. *Francisco de Vitoria. Cristianismo y Modernidad*. Ciudad Argentina: Buenos Aires.

Filibeck, Giorgio. 1994. *Human rights in the teaching of the Church: From John XIII to John Paul II*. Vatican City: Libreria Editrice Vaticana.

Francis. 2013. Apostolic Exhortation *Evangelii Gaudium*. Available at: http://w2.vatican.va/content/francesco/en/apost_exhortations/documents/papa-francesco_esortazione-ap_20131124_evangelii-gaudium.html.

García-López, J. 1979. *Los Derechos humanos en Santo Tomás de Aquino* (Human Rights according to Thomas Aquinas). Pamplona: Eunsa.

Gewirth, Alan. 1992. Human dignity as the basis of rights. In *The constitution of rights: Human dignity and American values*, ed. M.J. Meyer and W.A. Parent, 10–28. Ithaca: Cornell University Press.

Glendon, Mary Ann. 2002. *A world made new: Eleanor Roosevelt and the universal declaration of human rights*. New York: Random House.

Gregory the Great. 2009. *Forty Gospel homilies*. Priscataway: Gorgias Press.

Gurevick, A.J. 1994. *La nascita dell'individuo nell'Europa medievale*. Roma/Bari: Laterza.

Hanning, C.W. 1977. *The individual in the twelfth-century romance*. New Haven: Yale University Press.

Harrelson, W.J. 1980. *The ten commandments and human rights*. Philadelphia: Fortress Press.

John XXIII. 1961. Encyclical-letter 'Mater et Magistra'. www.vatican.va/holy_father/john_xxiii/encyclicals/documents/hf_j-xxiii_enc_15051961_mater_en.html. Abbreviation: MM.

John XXIII. 1963. Encyclical-letter 'Pacen in terris'. www.vatican.va/holy_father/john_xxiii/encyclicals/documents/hf_j-xxiii_enc_11041963_pacem_en.html. Abbreviation: PT.

John Paul II. 1981. Encyclical-letter 'Laborem execerns'. www.vatican.va/holy_father/john_paul_ii/encyclicals/documents/hf_jp-ii_enc_14091981_laborem-exercens_en.html. Abbreviation: LE.

John Paul II. 1988. Apostolic exhortation 'Christifideles Laici'. www.vatican.va/holy_father/john_paul_ii/apost_exhortations/documents/hf_jp-ii_exh_30121988_christifideles-laici_en.html. Abbreviation: CL.

John Paul II. 1990. Encyclical-letter 'Redemptoris Missio'. www.vatican.va/holy_father/john_paul_ii/encyclicals/documents/hf_jp-ii_enc_07121990_redemptoris-missio_en.html#-1Z. Abbreviation: RM.

John Paul II. 1991. Letter encyclical 'Centesimus annus'. www.vatican.va/edocs/ENG0214/_INDEX.HTM. Abbreviation: CA.

John Paul II. 1993. Encyclical-letter 'Veriatis splendor'. www.vatican.va/holy_father/john_paul_ii/encyclicals/documents/hf_jp-ii_enc_06081993_veritatis-splendor_en.html. Abbreviation: VS.

John Paul II. 1998. Letter-encyclical 'Fides et ratio'. www.vatican.va/holy_father/john_paul_ii/encyclicals/documents/hf_jp-ii_enc_14091998_fides-et-ratio_en.html. Abbreviation: FR.

Kant, Immanuel. 1993/1785. *Grounding for the metaphysics of morals*. Indianapolis: Hackett.

Koehn, Daryl, and Alicia Leung. 2008. Dignity in western versus in Chinese cultures. Theoretical overview and practical illustrations. *Business & Society Review* 113(4): 477–504.

Lebret, J.-L. 1961. *Dynamique concrète du développement*. Economie et Humanisme. Les Editions Ouvrières, París.

Leo XIII. 1888. Encyclical-letter 'Libertas'. www.vatican.va/holy_father/leo_xiii/encyclicals/documents/hf_l-xiii_enc_20061888_libertas_en.html. Abbreviation: LP.

Leo XIII. 1891. Encyclical-letter 'Rerum Novarum'. www.vatican.va/holy_father/leo_xiii/encyclicals/documents/hf_l-xiii_enc_15051891_rerum-novarum_en.html. Abbreviation: RN.

Melé, D. 2012. The Christian Notion of Αγάπη (agápē): Towards a More Complete View of Business Ethics. In *Leadership through the Classics. Learning Management and Leadership from Ancient East and West Philosophy*, ed. G.P. Prastacos, F. Wang, and K.E. Soderquist, 79–91. Heidelberg, Germany: (Springer.

Margalit, Avishai. 1998. *The decent society*. Boston: Harvard University Press.

Mattson, David J., and Susan G. Clark. 2011. Human dignity in concept and practice. *Policy Sciences* 44: 303–319.

Morris, C. 1972. *The discovery of the individual (1050–1200)*. London: SPCK.

Paul VI. 1967. Encyclical-letter 'Populorum Progressio'. www.vatican.va/holy_father/paul_vi/encyclicals/documents/hf_p-vi_enc_26031967_populorum_en.html. Abbreviation: PP.

Panzer, J.S. 1996. *The Popes and slavery*. Staten Island: Saint Pauls/Alba House.

PCJP (Pontifical Council for Justice and Peace). 2004. Compendium of the social doctrine of the Church. Città del Vaticano Libreria Editrice Vaticana. Also available in www.vatican.va/roman_curia/pontifical_councils/justpeace/documents/rc_pc_justpeace_doc_20060526_compendio-dott-soc_en.html

Pico Della Mirandola, Giovanni. 2012. In *Oration on the dignity of man. A new translation and commentary*, ed. Francesco Borghesi, Michael Papio, and Massimo Riva. Cambridge: Cambridge University Press.

Pius XI. 1931. Encyclical-letter 'Quadragesimo anno'. www.vatican.va/holy_father/pius_xi/encyclicals/documents/hf_p-xi_enc_19310515_quadragesimo-anno_en.html

Pius XI. 1937. Encyclical-letter 'Mit Brennender Sorge'. www.vatican.va/holy_father/pius_xi/encyclicals/documents/hf_p-xi_enc_14031937_mit-brennender-sorge_en.html

Pius XII. 1940. Speech, Dec 24. www.vatican.va/holy_father/pius_xii/speeches/1940/documents/hf_p-xii_spe_19401224_venerabili-fratelli_sp.html (in Spanish).

Pius XII. 1941. Speech 'La Solemnità', June 1. http://www.vatican.va/holy_father/pius_xii/speeches/1941/documents/hf_p-xii_spe_19410601_radiomessage-pentecost_sp.html

Pius XII. 1948. Speech, Nov 7. www.vatican.va/holy_father/pius_xii/speeches/1948/documents/
    hf_p-xii_spe_19481111_nous-sommes_it.html (in Italian).
Rosen, Michael. 2012. *Human dignity: Its history and meaning*. Boston: Harvard University Press.
Schlag, Martin. 2013. *La Dignità dell'Uomo come Principio Sociale. Il Contributo della Fede
    Cristiana alla Stato Secolare*. Rome: Edusc.
Second Vatican Council. 1965. 'Dignitatis Humanae', and 'Gaudium et Spes'. www.vatican.va/
    archive/hist_councils/ii_vatican_council/index.htm
Sen, Amartya. 1999. *Development as freedom*. Oxford: Oxford University Press.
Sepúlveda, Magdalena, Theo Van Banning, Gudrún Gudmundsdóttir, Christine Chamoun, and
    Willem J.M. Van Genugten. 2004. *Human rights reference handbook Ciudad Colon*. Costa
    Rica: University of Peace.
Sicker, Martin. 2001. *The political culture of Judaism*. Westport: Praeger.
Ullmann, W. 1967. *The individual and society in the middle ages*. London: Methuen.
United Nations. 1948. Universal declaration of human rights. www.un.org/en/documents/udhr
United Nations. 1966a. International Covenant on Economic, Social and Cultural Rights. www.
    ohchr.org/EN/ProfessionalInterest/Pages/CESCR.aspx
United Nations. 1966b. International Covenant on Civil and Political Rights. https://treaties.
    un.org/doc/Publication/UNTS/Volume%20999/volume-999-I-14668-English.pdf
Universal Islamic Declaration of Human Rights. 1981. www.alhewar.com/ISLAMDECL.html
Williams, Thomas D. 2005. *Who is my neighbor?: Personalism and the foundations of human
    rights*. Washington, DC: Catholic University of America Press.

Chapter 8
Christian Humanism: The Ethical Basis of the German Model of Social Market Economy

Arnd Küppers

Abstract This chapter examines Ralf Dahrendorf's thesis that Catholic Social Teaching and Ordoliberalism are incompatible and that thus far the idea of a Social Market Economy is an accidental, historical compromise without future in the world of globalization. The background to this thesis is the presupposition that the Christian value of solidarity and the free-market-concept of Neoliberalism are antagonistic. It is argued that Christian personalism is not only part of the tradition of Catholic Social Teaching, but also part of the tradition of Ordoliberalism. Thus there are significant similarities in the moral foundation of both theories. Nevertheless there are differences in the conclusions that the two theories draw from this common principle. Dahrendorf is right in so far as he says that the Social Market Economy is composed of different elements. But he is mistaken in his belief that these elements are incompatible. The paper outlines the main-differences between Ordoliberal theory and the Social Doctrine of the Church. The thesis of the paper is, in contrast to Dahrendorf, that in the synthesis of the Social Market Economy both theories complement each other. A second thesis is that the Christian elements in the concept of the Social Market Economy are still essential.

Keywords Ordoliberalism • Social market economy • Catholic social teaching • Liberalism

In 2004 Lord Ralf Dahrendorf pointed out that when a German speaks about the Social Market Economy (*Soziale Marktwirtschaft*), "he means Ludwig Erhard plus Catholic Social Teaching," a "program of incompatibilities, that shaped the early Christian Democratic Union and Christian Social Union and shapes them in some way until now" (Dahrendorf 2004, 13). Of course, this statement was meant in a critical way: Dahrendorf meant that the Germans, who had tried to link the principle

A. Küppers (✉)
Catholic Centre for Social Sciences of the German Episcopal Conference,
Mönchengladbach, Germany
e-mail: a.kueppers@ksz.de

© Springer Science+Business Media Dordrecht 2015   137
D. Melé, M. Schlag (eds.), *Humanism in Economics and Business*,
Issues in Business Ethics 43, DOI 10.1007/978-94-017-9704-7_8

of a free market (Ludwig Erhard) with the principle of solidarity (Catholic Social Teaching) in their concept of a Social Market Economy, had created a socio-economic system that in the face of globalization can no longer be competitive.

The paper does not discuss this thesis of Dahrendorf but will focus on its presuppositions, namely the assertion that in the concept of a Social Market Economy the principle of solidarity as a Christian value and virtue came from the Catholic Social Teaching and that this stood from the beginning in contradiction to the free-market-principle that was held by Ludwig Erhard and his fellow-Ordoliberals in the Freiburg School of Economics, such as Walter Eucken, Franz Böhm and other economists (e.g. Wilhelm Röpke and Alexander Rüstow).

This assertion ignores completely the historical circumstances that led these Ordoliberal thinkers to their firm conviction that a free economic (and political) system needs a constitutional order, the rules of which hold the competitors in the market within certain limits, which guarantee the maintenance of a free and fair competition. The Ordoliberals saw how the Republic of Weimar failed not only for political but also for socio-economic reasons such as the concentration of market power in the hands of a few cartels and the existence of a thicket of *clientelism*, which destroyed the system of fair competition. And during the Second World War they were already thinking forward to an economic order that would avoid such mistakes in the future.

The Historical Roots of Ordoliberalism: Christian Values and Resistance to the Nazis

Even in Germany it is no longer well-known that most of the Ordoliberal economists were active members of the political resistance against Hitler and his murderous followers during the Nazi Dictatorship (Goldschmidt 2005a). And it is even less well-known that the resistance of the Ordoliberals was founded on Christian faith. Walter Eucken, the head of the Freiburg School of Economics, and other important Ordoliberals were members of the "Confessing Church" (*Bekennende Kirche*), which fought within the German Protestant Church against the "German Christians" (*Deutsche Christen*), who collaborated with the Nazi regime. Eucken and Böhm were members of a conspiratorial group of the resistance in Freiburg (Freiburger Kreis) which in 1943 drew up a government program for the time after the defeat of the Nazis on behalf of Dietrich Bonhoeffer – one of the leading theologians of the Confessing Church (executed in April 1945). This government program also included a section on the social and economic order, which included the basic ideas which Eucken and the others developed in their publications after Second World War.

Like Catholic Social Teaching the memorandum of the Freiburg economists and resistance members takes its starting point from the theological tenet that God created man in His image. From this article of faith man receives an inalienable dignity. And as in Catholic Social Teaching, Eucken and his colleagues are of the opinion that the economic system – like all social institutions – must stand in the service of people, or as John XXIII formulates the basic principle of the Church's Social Teaching in his Encyclical *Mater et Magistra*: "individual human beings are the foundation, the cause and the end of every social institution" (MM 219). Following this fundamental conviction, the Freiburg memorandum unfolds a personalistic and humanistic outline of a socio-economic order at the centre of which stands the human person and his or her inalienable rights, including his or her social rights. Thus the memorandum emphasizes both the personal responsibility of each individual and solidarity in the social community. It is an interesting detail in this context that Joseph Cardinal Höffner, one of the thinkers at the forefront of Catholic Social Teaching in Germany after Second World War, wrote a doctoral thesis in economics under the supervision of Walter Eucken (Höffner 1941; see also Goldschmidt and Nothelle-Wildfeuer 2010).

Dahrendorf is mistaken if he believes that the Christian influences came only from Catholic Social teaching. There are genuine and fundamental Christian elements in the early Ordoliberal theory itself. Since most of the first generation of Ordoliberals were committed Protestants, these Christian elements were first and foremost of Protestant, not of Catholic origin. That is one of the reasons that some German Catholic ethicists after Second World War, e.g. Oswald von Nell-Breuning (1955/1960) and Edgar Nawroth (1961), were very distrustful of Ordoliberalism and had reservations about the Social Market Economy.

Paleo-liberalism, Neoliberalism and Catholic Social Teaching

It is due to Joseph Cardinal Höffner and his studies that the Catholic view of Ordoliberalism and Social Market Economy changed. Höffner pointed out, that while there remained differences between Neoliberalism and Catholic Social Teaching, possibilities exist for a fruitful and productive dialogue between the two theories (Höffner 1959/2006). Höffner distinguishes between "old Liberalism" or "Paleo-Liberalism" (Rüstow) on the one hand and "Neoliberalism" on the other. He says that the Neoliberals have understood and corrected the worst failures of the old Liberalism, first and foremost the danger that pure *laissez-faire* capitalism leads to the dominance of monopolies. In Ordoliberalism the central insight is that fair competition is not the natural, inevitable consequence of economic freedom, so the central task of economic policymakers is to set up legal frameworks to ensure a fair, performance-based competition (*Leistungswettbewerb*). Monopolies, cartels and price-fixing must be forbidden, so that that the system of free prices can work. For Walter Eucken this is the fundamental principle of the economic constitution (Eucken 1952/2004, 254).

The necessity of an extensive economic order with a strong legal framework is also stressed by Pope John Paul II in his Encyclical Letter *Centesimus annus* in 1991. Here the Pope considers the question of whether or not the Church can give its approval to capitalism. The Holy Father answers: "If by 'capitalism' it is meant an economic system which recognizes the fundamental and positive role of business, the market, private property and the resulting responsibility for the means of production, as well as free human creativity in the economic sector, then the answer is certainly in the affirmative". On the other hand, John Paul writes: "if by 'capitalism' it is meant a system in which freedom in the economic sector is not circumscribed within a strong juridical framework which places it at the service of human freedom in its totality, and which sees it as a particular aspect of that freedom, the core of which is ethical and religious, then the reply is certainly negative" (Centesimus annus 42). This distinction between a *laissez-faire*-economy and an economic order with a juridical framework is astonishingly similar to the central convictions of the Ordoliberals. Lothar Roos has even written that with *Centesimus annus* the Social Doctrine of the Church had adopted the theory of Social Market Economy (Roos 1991). Nils Goldschmidt explicitly speaks about a closeness of Pope John Paul's social thoughts to Ordoliberal theory (Goldschmidt 2005b).

Free Competition: A Useful Instrument, But Not a Regulatory Principle of the Economy

In 1959 Höffner's main-point of criticism against the Neoliberals is that most of them are of the conviction that the guarantee of performance-based competition is on the whole sufficient to realize a good social order. Through use of the words of Pope Pius XI he stresses that "free competition, while justified and certainly useful provided it is kept within certain limits, clearly cannot direct economic life" (Quadragesimo anno 88). The understanding of the market-mechanism as the regulatory principle of the economy is the central point in the controversy between Catholic ethicists and neoliberals in the early years of the Federal Republic of Germany, and still even in 1985, as Archbishop of Cologne, Cardinal Höffner renewed this critique on the occasion of his opening address during the autumn-assembly of the German Bishops' Conference: the "market-mechanism is unable to act as the regulative principle underlying economic affairs. The economy is not an automation, but cultural process which takes place in accordance with the proper and regulatory wishes of mankind" (Höffner 1985, 25).

Catholic Social Teaching still states that the market, if it is really regulated by a legal system to provide fair competition, is an important instrument for attaining important objectives of social justice, but it is not the one and only instrument (Compendium of the Social Doctrine of the Church 347). The market is a necessary precondition, but not an adequate precondition to achieve the goal of social justice. Höffner 1985: "Disposition over private property, market mechanisms and striving for economic success must be complemented by the social aims of economic activities. The market economy is also capable of and in need of steering. The urgent tasks which now arise in connection with the objectives of economic activity and the common good cannot be mastered simply by market and price mechanisms: the wide distribution of wealth, the continuous growth of the economy undisturbed by cyclical crises; overcoming unemployment; environmental protection requirements and so forth" (Höffner 1985, 25). Daniel Finn (1998) lists four points, which are important for Pope John Paul II as supplements to the free-market-principle in economy: (1) a legal framework to regulate the economic life in regard of the common good; (2) the supply of all people, also the poor with the basic goods and services; (3) the promotion of common morality; (4) the promotion of private and voluntary initiatives in civil society.

Pope Benedict XVI strongly underlined the importance of the latter aspect in his Encyclical Letter *Caritas in Veritate* in 2009. He complained that in the past "unfortunately, too much confidence was placed in [...] institutions, as if they were able to deliver the desired objective automatically. In reality," he pointed out, "institutions by themselves are not enough, because integral human development is primarily a vocation, and therefore it involves a free assumption of responsibility in solidarity on the part of everyone" (CV 11). So he believes that in addition to the "logic of exchange" (the logic of the market) and the "logic of public obligation" (the logic of the State and of politics) there is the necessity of a "logic of unconditional gift", represented by voluntary initiatives from private persons, entrepreneurs and associations. This idea is inspired by Stefano Zamagni and Luigino Brunis' concept of Civil Economy (Bruni and Zamagni 2007), which shows some similarities to the theory of the Social Market Economy but also has significant differences from it.

Ethics in Ordoliberal Theory

If we ask what the Ordoliberal position is in this *whole* complexity we have to realize first of all, that there are remarkable differences among the neoliberal theorists. Not every Neoliberal completely trusts in the invisible hand of the market. Of all the Neoliberals perhaps Friedrich August von Hayek trusts most in the market and free competition. Hayek also refuses completely the term of social justice and says that this idea is not compatible with a free society. His conviction is that the people have to choose: freedom *or* justice, *tertium non datur* (Hayek 1978). But neither does Hayek have a technical, rationalistic understanding of the economy, based on an instrumental sense of reason. On the contrary, he is an intransigent adversary of rationalism, and he has often stressed the significance of history and culture, even of religion, for the development of a free society (Hayek 1996).

The cultural and religious pre-assumptions of freedom and free societies are the great theme of Wilhelm Röpke, who wrote a whole book about it: *Jenseits von Angebot und Nachfrage* ("Beyond Supply and Demand"). Röpke formulates the ideal of an "economic humanism", which means an economic order which respects and promotes the dignity of human life. Although a professed Protestant Röpke was very interested in Catholic Social Teaching. He found many of his own convictions in *Quadragesimo anno*. Already in 1955 he wrote an article on *Ethics and Economic Life*:

> And thus even the prosaic world of business affairs draws on the ethical resources with which it stands or falls and which hold greater importance than the whole gamut of economic laws and principles. It is not the market nor competition nor the interplay between supply and demand which create these reserves. In fact, they consume them and must draw reserves from areas beyond the market. Nor can they be replaced by any manual of political economy. Qualities such as self-discipline, a sense of justice, honesty, fairness, chivalry, moderation, public spirit, respect of human dignity, reliable ethical standards – all these are things which people must already possess when they enter the market. They are the indispensable mainstays affording protection against degeneration. The institutions which endow them with these qualities are the family, the Church, genuine communities, and traditions. People must also grow up in conditions which favour such convictions and concepts, conditions peculiar to a natural system which promotes genuine communities, respects traditions and looks after individuals. (Röpke 1955/1982, 374f.)

In contrast to Hayek, Eucken writes, that "the intention of social justice cannot be taken seriously enough" (Eucken 1952/2004, 315), but he is also convinced that social justice should be realized first and foremost by installing a system of performance-based competition, and also writes about the necessity of an extensive economic order with elements of social policy.

Alexander von Rüstow on the other hand has developed a certain concept of social policy, which he calls "vital policy" (*Vitalpolitik*). Vital policy would complement the institutional order of the market. The intention of vital policy is to make a humane life possible for every man and woman in all fields of society, in the family, in the job. Rüstow points out that from the neoliberal point of view the vital policy is the most important and that the market is only a means to an end (Rüstow 1961). Nevertheless vital policy is in Rüstow's theory part of economic policy, and so in his opinion it should also be regulated by the Ordoliberal principles of e.g. market-conformity and subsidiarity.

Obviously Rüstow's standpoint is quite similar to Catholic Social Doctrine: the market is not the measure and the goal of the economic order. Human dignity is higher than market itself. So it is no wonder that Höffner adopted Rüstow's considerations about vital policy in one of his own essays about social policy (Höffner 1953/2006). Höffner believes that Rüstow's approach could help to develop the system of social security from a paternalistic concept to a model that strengthens the forces and promotes the individual efforts of those in need. Before many others Höffner saw that an overgenerous welfare state has negative effectives on the will and the strength of people to help themselves, as Pope John Paul II stresses in his encyclical letter *Centesimus annus*:

> In recent years the range of such intervention has vastly expanded, to the point of creating a new type of State, the so-called "Welfare State". This has happened in some countries in order to respond better to many needs and demands, by remedying forms of poverty and deprivation unworthy of the human person. However, excesses and abuses, especially in recent years, have provoked very harsh criticisms of the Welfare State, dubbed the "Social Assistance State". Malfunctions and defects in the Social Assistance State are the result of an inadequate understanding of the tasks proper to the State. Here again *the principle of subsidiarity* must be respected: a community of a higher order should not interfere in the

internal life of a community of a lower order, depriving the latter of its functions, but rather should support it in case of need and help to coordinate its activity with the activities of the rest of society, always with a view to the common good. By intervening directly and depriving society of its responsibility, the Social Assistance State leads to a loss of human energies and an inordinate increase of public agencies, which are dominated more by bureaucratic ways of thinking than by concern for serving their clients, and which are accompanied by an enormous increase in spending. (CA 48)

Both Ordoliberalism and Catholic Social teaching had great influence in German politics after Second World War, both in the foundation of the Social Market Economy and in the creation of its institutions. Therefore Dahrendorf is right that the Social Market Economy is composed of different elements. But these elements are not incompatible, they complement each other. The managing of the financial crisis in recent years has shown that in a globalized world the Social Market Economy can compete with other economic systems and orders.

Cultural Foundations of the Concept of Social Market Economy

My thesis is that the Christian elements of the concept of Social Market Economy are not only accidental, but rather are essential. The connection of a competitive economy with the principle of solidarity is not just an instrumental, technical judgement, but a value-based judgment, founded upon the metaphysical and moral traditions of European culture, which include a certain concept of man. This concept of man is personally as well as socially oriented. It is rooted in the ancient humanist and Christian tradition of Western culture.

Precisely: the concept of the Social Market Economy is founded substantially upon the Western ideas of personality and justice, and solidarity. The idea of personality was historically derived from the ancient Greek moral philosophy, the Roman theory of civil law and the Biblical faith that man is created in God's image (Nemo 2005). The dignity of the human person is stressed ultimately in Christianity by the faith that God Himself has become man in Jesus Christ.

> Since human nature as He assumed it was not annulled, by that very fact it has been raised up to a divine dignity in our respect too. For by His incarnation the Son of God has united Himself in some fashion with every man. He worked with human hands, He thought with a human mind, acted by human choice and loved with a human heart. Born of the Virgin Mary, He has truly been made one of us, like us in all things except sin. As an innocent lamb He merited for us life by the free shedding of His own blood. In Him God reconciled us to Himself and among ourselves; from bondage to the devil and sin He delivered us, so that each one of us can say with the Apostle: The Son of God "loved me and gave Himself up for me" (Gal. 2:20). By suffering for us He not only provided us with an example for our imitation, He blazed a trail, and if we follow it, life and death are made holy and take on a new meaning. (GS 22)

The ideas of justice and solidarity are of the same origin: already in Greco-Roman philosophy justice was one of the cardinal virtues and solidarity known as a term in civil law. The fundamental idea of the Greco-Roman concept of justice, however, is retribution (*do ut des*). The term "solidarity" refers in Roman civil law to the case of joint debt, which is the constellation that each of several debtors is obliged to render the total performance (*solidum*), but the creditor is entitled to one performance only. The Christian understanding of justice and solidarity is very different from these juridical readings.

The eldest known definition of justice is: *suum cuique*. This definition must be filled with specific contents: one has to determine what the *suum* of someone is to say what justice means in regard of him. For the Christians the *suum* of every man and woman is his/her personality and dignity. From this derives the meaning of the language of Christian personalism and personalistic ethics. So in the Christian concept of justice and solidarity the starting point is personality, and so first and foremost the dignity of every human being. And in this way the Christian commandment of compassion colors the interpretation and reformulation of the ideas of justice and solidarity. To be more precise: solidarity, understood as reciprocal responsibility of each member of social community, becomes from the Christian point of view part of the concept of justice. So the Christian claim of justice is not fulfilled if everyone gets what is legally owed to him (*do ut des*), but if everyone gets what is necessary to live a dignified life as a respected member of the social community.

The humanist, Christian concept of man, which is both personally and socially oriented, is still the best starting point for a policy which seeks to realize social justice in a free society. Personalistic anthropology and ethics help us avoid unbalanced policies, the failures of either a rough individualism or an enslaving collectivism.

In their Pastoral Letter *Economic Justice for All* (1986), the bishops of the USA used the term "justice as participation" to renew the specific Christian understanding of justice in regard to modern, developed society. From this point of view social justice claims that everyone should get not only the abstracts right, but also the real possibility of participating in the central political, economic and cultural fields of the community's life. According to the idea of participative justice everyone in society has the right to benefit from the prosperity of the community, just as everyone has, on the other hand, the duty to cooperate with his fellow-citizens to increase this prosperity. This concept of participative justice differs significantly from the traditional understanding of social justice as distributive justice in the welfare state, which is, by the way, the object of Hayek's critique. Thus the concept of justice as participation offers also an innovative perspective in the debate about the reform of the system of social security.

Without a vital awareness of its cultural dimension – as outlined above – the idea of the Social Market Economy loses its moral foundation. Based on these insights, knowledge about the historical and ethical foundation of the Social Market Economy in Germany can also enrich the debate about Pope Benedict's demand for "a true world political authority" in *Caritas in Veritate*. He intends by this "the establishment of a greater degree of international ordering, marked by subsidiarity, for the management of globalization" (Caritas in Veritate 67). It is quite easy to find suitable links between this demand and similar considerations in the tradition of the

Social Market Economy and its idea of regulatory policy according to Eucken. It is a big challenge to try to realize the goal of social justice in a free society, and it is an even bigger challenge to realize social justice in a globalized world. The constitution of a global institutional order is the one and only realistic perspective in which to achieve this goal. This global institutional order must be based on consensus about basic constitutional and legal rules with regard to the order of political, economy and social life. The necessary condition of such consensus is a basic agreement about the concept of man. In 2004 at the Catholic Academy of Bavaria, on occasion of his famous dialogue with the German philosopher Jürgen Habermas, the then Cardinal Ratzinger stressed that such an agreement about the concept of man and a consent about basic social rules will only be achieved as a result of an intercultural dialogue. Jürgen Habermas is an unsuspicious witness that the church can take part as a self-confident participant in such an intercultural dialogue in the modern world. In an interview in 1999 he, who calls himself a "methodological atheist", pointed out:

> For the normative self-understanding of modernity, Christianity has functioned as more than just a precursor or catalyst. Universalistic egalitarianism, from which sprang the ideals of freedom and a collective life in solidarity, the autonomous conduct of life and emancipation, the individual morality of conscience, human rights and democracy, is the direct legacy of the Judaic ethic of justice and the Christian ethic of love. This legacy, substantially unchanged, has been the object of a continual critical reappropriation and reinterpretation. Up to this very day there is no alternative to it. And in light of the current challenges of a post-national constellation, we must draw sustenance now, as in the past, from this substance. Everything else is idle postmodern talk. (Habermas 2002, 149)

References

Benedict XVI. 2009. Encyclical-letter 'Caritas in Veritate', on Integral human development in charity and truth. www.vatican.va

Bruni, Luigino, and Stefano Zamagni. 2007. *Civil economy: Efficiency, equity, public happiness.* Bern: Peter Lang.

Dahrendorf, Ralf. 2004. *Wie sozial kann die Soziale Marktwirtschaft noch sein?* Ludwig- Erhard-Lecture, vol. 3. Berlin: Initiative Neue Soziale Marktwirtschaft.

Eucken, Walter. 1952/2004. *Grundsätze der Wirtschaftspolitik,* ed. Edith Eucken and K. Paul Hensel. Tübingen: Mohr Siebeck.

Finn, Daniel. 1998. John Paul II and the moral ecology of markets. *Theological Studies* 59: 662–679.

Goldschmidt, Nils (ed.). 2005a. *Wirtschaft, Politik und Freiheit. Freiburger Wirtschafts-wissenschaftler und der Widerstand,* Untersuchungen zur Ordnungstheorie und Ordnungspolitik, vol. 48. Tübingen: Mohr Siebeck.

Goldschmidt, Nils. 2005b. *Der Brückenschlag zum Markt.* Das wirtschaftspolitische Erbe von Papst Johannes Paul II, Frankfurter Allgemeine Zeitung 16. 15 Apr 2005.

Goldschmidt, Nils, and Ursula Nothelle-Wildfeuer. 2010. *Freiburger Schule und Christliche Gesellschaftslehre. Joseph Kardinal Höffner und die Ordnung von Wirtschaft und Gesellschaft,* Untersuchungen zur Ordnungstheorie und Ordnungspolitik, vol. 59. Tübingen: Mohr Siebeck.

Habermas, Jürgen. 2002. *Religion and rationality. Essays on reason, God, and modernity.* ed. Eduardo Mendieta. Cambridge, MA: MIT Press.

Hayek, Friedrich August von. 1978. *Law, legislation and liberty,* The mirage of social justice, vol. II. Chicago: University of Chicago Press.

Hayek, Friedrich August von. 1996. *Die verhängnisvolle Anmaßung. Die Irrtümer des Sozialismus.* Tübingen: Mohr.

Höffner, Joseph. 1941. *Wirtschaftsethik und Monopole im fünfzehnten und sechzehnten Jahrhundert,* Freiburger Staatswissenschaftliche Schriften, vol. 2. Jena: G. Fischer.

Höffner, Joseph. 1953/2006. Soziale Sicherheit und Eigenverantwortung. Der personale Faktor in der Sozialpolitik. In *Joseph Höffner (1906–1987). Soziallehre und Sozialpolitik,* ed. Karl Gabriel and Hermann-Josef Große Kracht, 139–155. Paderborn: Schöningh.

Höffner, Joseph. 1959/2006. Neoliberalismus und Christliche Soziallehre. In *Joseph Höffner (1906–1987). Soziallehre und Sozialpolitik,* ed. Karl Gabriel and Hermann-Josef Große Kracht, 187–195. Paderborn: Schöningh.

Höffner, Joseph. 1985. Wirtschaftsordnung und Wirtschaftsethik. Richtlinien der katholischen Soziallehre, Eröffnungsreferat des Kardinals Joseph Höffner bei der Herbstvollversammlung der Deutschen Bischofskonferenz, 23 September 1985 (translation into English by Obiora F. Ike, Edited by Ordo Socialis, Cologne 2005).

In der Stunde Null. Die Denkschrift des Freiburger Bonhoeffer-Kreises (1943/1994). In *Die protestantischen Wurzeln der Sozialen Marktwirtschaft. Ein Quellenband,* ed. Günter Brakelmann and Traugott Jähnichen, 341–362. Gütersloh: Gütersloher Verlagshaus.

John XXIII. 1961. Encyclical-letter 'Mater et Magistra' on Christianity and social progress. www.vatican.va

John Paul II. 1991. Encyclical-letter 'Centesimus annus' on the hundredth anniversary of Rerum Novarum. www.vatican.va

National Conference of US Catholic Bishops. 1986. Economic justice for all, a Pastoral letter on Catholic social teaching and the US economy, Washington, DC. http://www.usccb.org/upload/economic_justice_for_all.pdf

Nawroth, Edgar. 1961. *Die Sozial- und Wirtschaftsphilosophie des Neoliberalismus.* Kerle: Heidelberg.

Nell-Breuning, Oswald von. 1955/1960. Neoliberalismus und Katholische Soziallehre. In *Wirtschaft und Gesellschaft heute,* Zeitfragen 1955–1959, vol. II, ed. Oswald von Nell-Breuning, 81–98. Freiburg i.Br.: Herder.

Nemo, Philippe. 2005. *Was ist der Westen? Die Genese der abendländischen Zivilisation,* Untersuchungen zur Ordnungstheorie und Ordnungspolitik, vol. 49. Tübingen: Mohr Siebeck.

Pius XI. 1931. Encyclical-letter 'Quadragesimo anno' on reconstruction of the social order. www.vatican.va

Pontifical Council for Justice and Peace. 2004. Compendium of the social doctrine of the Church. www.vatican.va

Roos, Lothar. 1991. *Centesimus annus. Botschaft und Echo,* Kirche und Gesellschaft, vol. 182. Köln: Bachem.

Röpke, Wilhelm. 1955/1982. Ethics and economic life. In *Standard texts on the social market economy,* ed. Wolfgang Stützel et al., 367–376. Stuttgart/New York: Fischer.

Röpke, Wilhelm. 1979. *Jenseits von Angebot und Nachfrage,* 5th ed. Bern: Haupt.

Rüstow, Alexander von. 1961. Paläoliberalismus, Kommunismus und Neoliberalismus. In *Wirtschaft, Gesellschaft und Kultur Festgabe für Alfred Müller-Armack,* ed. Franz Geiß and Fritz W. Meyer, 61–70. Berlin: Duncker & Humblot.

Second Vatican Council. 1965. Pastoral constitution 'Gaudium et Spes', on the Church in the modern world, promulgated by Pope Paul VI. www.vatican.va

Chapter 9
Italian *Economia Aziendale* as a Model Inspired by Catholic Humanism

Ericka Costa and Tommaso Ramus

Abstract The ongoing global economic and financial crisis has exposed the risks of considering market and business organizations only as instruments for creating economic wealth while disregarding their role in ethics and values. Christian Humanism based on Catholic Social Teaching (CST) could provide a useful contribution in a rethinking of the role of values in business organizations and markets because CST proposes an anthropological view that involves thinking of the marketplace as a community of persons with the aim of participating in the Common Good (CG) of society. In the light of the CST tradition, this article investigates the thinking of some of the historical scholars of the Italian *Economia Aziendale* (EA), by focusing on the concept of *azienda*, in order to reinterpret the role of business organizations in society in a more humanistic way. By linking CST and EA, the dichotomy between for-profit and not-for-profit organizations and the stereotype of the so-called business amorality that has, for a long time, driven business managers can be transcended. The conclusions imply a forward-looking application of the ethical concepts embedded in the Italian science of EA.

Keywords *azienda* • Catholic social thought • Common good • *Economia aziendale* • For-profit and not-for-profit organizations

In the neoclassical economic paradigm the human being is considered a rational agent whose aim is to maximize his self-interest or utility function. This approach also defines firms and corporations as "black boxes" that are part of the economic system with the unique purpose of profit maximization. In this sense a firm's only responsibility lies in using resources and engaging in activities to increase profit without deception or fraud (Friedman 1970). According to this theory the manager

E. Costa (✉)
Department of Economics and Management, University of Trento, Trento, Italy
e-mail: ericka.costa@unitn.it

T. Ramus
Catolica Lisbon School of Business and Economics,
Catholic University of Portugal, Lisbon, Portugal

© Springer Science+Business Media Dordrecht 2015
D. Melé, M. Schlag (eds.), *Humanism in Economics and Business*,
Issues in Business Ethics 43, DOI 10.1007/978-94-017-9704-7_9

is seen as an agent for those who hold the company's property rights (Jensen 2001), the firm is considered an instrument for economic efficiency (Coase 1937) and disregards any specific role for ethics or links between economic and ethical consequences and values.

The neoclassical approach that has characterized Anglo-American public policy since the 1970s has hindered governments' ability to reduce corporate abuses and has highlighted *short-termism* (Phillips 2006) which could be considered one of the most important causes of the current economic and financial crisis (Treviño and Nelson 2011). Many academics, politicians and practitioners agree that at the core of this crisis lies a lack of values (Clark 2009; Doran and Natale 2011) and underline the need to reconsider the role of management in business organizations (Melé 2009b).

An important contribution to rethinking the role of economic activities and the market in general is offered by Pope Benedict's Encyclical Letter *Caritas in Veritate* (2009). For the first time a Papal Encyclical adopted an economic rationale to support its ethical arguments thus giving policy insights based on economic reasoning rather than on exogenous theological teaching or natural law arguments (Grassl and Habisch 2011).

In particular CV goes beyond the idea that the aim of a business is mere profit maximization and points out that "the economic sphere [...] is part and parcel of human activity and precisely because it is human it must be structured and governed in an ethical manner" (p. 35). This approach surmounts the dichotomy between for-profit and not-for-profit organizations and the stereotype of so-called business amorality (Solomon 1999; Freeman 1994) and contributes to the business ethics field underpinned by Catholic Social Teaching (CST).

The literature on business ethics based on CST is quite recent (Garriga and Melé 2004) but the corpus has increased in the last decade (Abela 2001; Alford and Naugthon 2001; Melé 2003, 2005; Naughton and Cornwall 2006; Guitián 2009).

In light of the CST tradition this paper adds to the business ethics discussion by providing a link between the Common Good (CG) principle and the traditional Italian managerial theory – the so-called *Economia Aziendale (EA)*[1] – founded by Gino Zappa (1879–1960).

CG refers to "the overall condition of life in society that allows the different groups and their members to achieve their own perfection more fully and more easily" (Second Vatican Council 1965). As suggested by Melé "the concept of the 'common good' appears when considering the social dimension of human beings. People belonging to a community are united by common goals and share goods by the fact of belonging to the community" (2009a, 235). Therefore as a community of persons embedded in a social community (Sison and Fontrodona 2008) business organizations should not only maximize organizational efficiency but also consider their role and duties as members of society (Sandelands 2009; Guitián 2009; Asslaender 2011).

---

[1] Arguments that support the choice not to translate the term *Economia Aziendale (EA)* can be found in works by several Italian authors (Zan 1994; Dagnino and Quattrone 2006).

By reinterpreting *EA* through the lens of CST and in particular the CG principle this paper aims at pointing out the possible contribution that this theory could provide to business ethics discussion and to rethinking the role of business organizations in society. Moreover the paper sheds light on the ephemeral dichotomy between for-profit and not-for-profit organizations.

Ethics and Business in Catholic Social Thought Through the Lens of the Common Good Principle

Modern CST is a body of doctrine based on the four principles of (i) the centrality of the human being (ii) the common good (iii) subsidiarity and (iv) solidarity (Barrera 2000).

In the last decade a series of documents have been issued including the Papal Encyclical Letters to develop and update CST and provide a rich and comprehensive source of guidance on social and economic subjects with broadly acceptable theoretical foundations (Guitián 2009). Thus the CST perspective has been increasingly adopted in business ethics research (Abela 2001; Alford and Naugthon 2002; Melé 2005, 2009a; Naughton and Cornwall 2006; Naughton and Laczniak 1993).

In line with this perspective Pope John Paul II's Encyclical Letter *Centesimus Annus* (1991, CA, hereafter) maintains that firms should not be considered only as a collective of individuals but also as communities of persons who in various ways are endeavoring to satisfy their basic needs and who form a particular group at the service of the whole of society (CA 35). As suggested by Abela (2001) this statement points out that business organizations are complex anthropocentric entities with a threefold purpose: (i) profit (ii) service to society and (iii) satisfaction of basic human needs by providing decent work. In this context profit has a legitimate role in every business organization and "it is only equal to the other aspects of the purpose of the firm" (Abela 2001, 111).

This approach promotes a holistic and humanistic vision of life and business based on the centrality of the human being. In this view human beings find their fulfillment in relationships on an individual and a collective level (Melé 2009a, b). When the social dimension of human beings is considered CG surfaces because people in a particular community are linked by common goals and should strive to contribute and improve their community.

By adopting the CG concept it is possible to understand the role of ethics in defining the responsibilities of business organizations in society and the way in which they should be managed. In the context of a firm the internal CG thus refers to the production of goods and services in which human beings participate through their work while the external CG refers to the efficient production of goods and services that meet the real needs of society (Sison and Fontrodona 2008).

Accordingly CST points out that business organizations, being part of human activities, cannot be guided only by self-interest and by profit maximization purposes. This approach does not discuss profit per se but instead criticizes when the concept of *profit* is used not as a means to develop the CG but as an instrument for purely selfish interests because in organizations and in the marketplace space needs to be made for commercial logic as well as for friendship gifts and love (Argandoña 2012).

Given these premises business enterprises might have multiple purposes because they should create not only wealth for shareholders but also value for a broader range of stakeholders and for local and global communities in general (Alford and Naugthon 2002). Moreover every business enterprise should serve the CG of society by collaborating with the State and other private actors to address social questions through a true sense of solidarity and by respecting the subsidiary principle.

Following this approach the Encyclical Letter *Caritas in Veritate* (2009, CV hereafter) points out that the classical dichotomy between for-profit and not-for-profit organizations should be overcome because both of them could work together to create a more civilized market and to satisfy human needs. Since the role of business organizations in society might be better understood from a perspective of shifting or sharing in values and competences between for-profit and not-for-profit organizations Pope Benedict XVI suggested a cross fertilization between these – a reciprocal encounter – and thus more attentiveness to ways of civilizing the economy (CV 41).

In conclusion CST questions business ethics and the economic discussion regarding the role of enterprises in society and the needs they should satisfy. Useful indications for dealing with this discussion may be found in *EA* because it considers the *azienda* as a social sub-system with an ethical basis whose *raison d'être* is to satisfy human needs (Zappa 1927) through its contribution to the CG of society (Masini 1974). Given these assumptions *EA* contributes to narrowing the gap between for-profit and not-for-profit organizations because *EA* considers profit as an instrument that allows the *azienda* to satisfy the well-being of all the persons directly and indirectly involved in its activity (Onida 1971).

The Common Good Approach in the Italian *Economia Aziendale*

Economia Aziendale (*EA*) is the Italian management theory that studies the economics of economic units which are called *aziende*.[2] Conventionally the birth of this science is attributed to the opening speech of Gino Zappa for the Academic Year 1926–1927 at the University of Venice. During the same period the first management theories were being developed in the USA (e.g. Taylorism and Fordism and Elton Mayo's Human Relation School) (Dagnino and Quattrone 2006) and in some European countries (for a review see Zambon 1996; Mattessich 2003).

---

[2] The above note also applies to *azienda* but this term can be loosely translated as 'firm' (for more details see Viganò 1998, 382).

Zappa's proposal is considered a milestone of contemporary *EA* (Dagnino and Quattrone 2006; Zan 1994; Viganò and Mattessich 2007) because he superseded traditional accounting, political and general economic studies and created a new holistic science that has the "potential to bring together multiple disciplines in a unitary study of the economic unit" (Viganò 1998, 381).

EA rejects the reductionist separation between business and ethics in which the only purpose of an economic organization should be efficiency and profit maximization (Albach and Bloch 2000) because according to *EA* every business organization (*azienda*) is an "economic coordination in action which is set up and run to satisfy human needs" (Zappa 1927, 30).[3] *EA* is thus *person-centered* since it puts the satisfaction of human being at the core of business goals and includes not only wealth creation but also the advancement of the human condition from a political moral and religious point of view (D'Ippolito 1964). In this perspective the human being is not driven solely by utilitarian motives but rather is characterized by altruism, solidarity and cooperation (Zappa 1962; Masini 1960). In this framework *EA* conceived the *azienda* as a place of cooperation and not only of economic exchanges between different actors in it. The *azienda* is not merely an instrument for production or consumption or the sum of individual interests governed by contractual arrangements but is an institution that tends to pursue the CG of its members and serve the broader CG of society (Zappa 1962; Masini 1960).

In summary *EA* can be described as follows:

1. It requires that profit has an instrumental character because the accumulation of economic wealth should not be considered the *raison d'être* of the business organization even if it is profit-oriented, but solely as a means for pursuing the organization's purposes (Masini 1960; Ferrero 1968);
2. It refers to the CG of the members of all business organizations that indirectly serve the CG of the society (Masini 1960);
3. It covers all forms of economic organization for-profit organizations, not-for profit organizations and those which are publicly-owned (Flower 1996); indeed it refers to the broader concept of *azienda* that could not be conceived of only as a profit-maximizing organization.

In the field of business ethics Signori and Rusconi (2009) and Argandoña and Von Weltzien Hoivik (2009) acknowledge the importance of *EA* by linking it respectively to Stakeholder Management Theory (SMT) and Corporate Social Responsibility (CSR).[4]

Following on from these studies this chapter shows the link between *EA* and the CG principle and rejects the dichotomy between for-profit and not-for-profit organizations as suggested in the last Encyclical Letter.

---

[3] Original text in English by Signori and Rusconi (2009).

[4] Numerous books and articles have been published on the relationship between business and ethics (e.g. Rusconi and Dorigatti 2005) at the national level.

The azienda

Since Zappa's speech of 1927 many scholars have offered contributions to enrich the definition of *azienda* and to further develop his theory (e.g. Onida 1971; Masini 1974; Ferrero 1968; Ceccherelli 1964). According to Ferrero (1968, 5–6) it is possible to divide these studies into three categories with respect to the definition of the main characteristics of the *azienda*. These categories are as follows:

1. The unitary approach which considers the *azienda* an open and dynamic subsystem with an economic objective to promote the human well-being of the major shareholders as well as the individuals who cooperate in the business (Zappa 1927; Amaduzzi 1963; Ceccherelli 1964; Onida 1954).
2. The long-term approach where the *azienda* is defined as "a long term durable institution" (Zappa 1956, 34) and "not a mishap in the economic cycle or a set of events intended to be extinguished in the short term" (Zappa et al. 1964, 2).
3. The social order approach that investigates the social function of the *azienda* and the so-called *socialità* requirement which implies that every *azienda* should contribute to the CG of society (Zappa 1962; Onida 1971; Masini 1960, 1974).

The unitary approach is based on the vision of the *azienda* as an economic and unitary institution and stresses two aspects: *istituto* (Dagnino and Quattrone 2006) and *system* (Signori and Rusconi 2009). In this view the *azienda* is seen as "an economic institution intended to last for an indefinite length of time and which, with the aim of meeting human needs, manages the production, procurement or consumption of resources in continuous coordination" (Zappa 1956, 37).[5] As an institute the *azienda* is (i) an *abstract* concept that refers strictly to the economic objective of an organization (Zappa 1956); (ii) *autonomous* because it is different from the sum of the single elements of which it is composed but is rather a "freestanding organic system" (Rossi 1964); and (iii) it finds its *institutional aim* "in the needs it helps to satisfy" (Zappa 1956, 46). Given these features the notion of *istituto* is related to all types of organizations: for-profit, publicly owned and not-for-profit organizations.

The long-term approach emerges in the second definition of *azienda* provided by Zappa (1956) in which he stresses the capacity of the *azienda* to be durable, or to survive over time in order to satisfy human needs by linking the social and human dimensions with monetary and economic aspects (Amaduzzi 1963). To be durable an *azienda* must respect the requirement of *economicità* namely the ability to achieve not only a short-term return on investment but mainly long-term economic sustainability related to "the durable existence and the fitting development of the *azienda*" (Onida 1971, 105 our translation). Therefore in this approach managers have to reject decisions that might favor short-term profit in order to guarantee the economic long-term sustainability of the *azienda* (Amaduzzi 1991).

Finally the social order approach considers not only the economic dimension of the *azienda* but also its multiple social qualities called *socialità*. Indeed *socialità*

---

[5] Original text in English by Signori and Rusconi (2009).

refer to the promptness of the *azienda* to act for the CG within itself and for society in general (Zappa 1962; Onida 1971; Masini 1960). Signori and Rusconi (2009) suggest that *EA* provides two dimensions of the CG concept: the first is more *internal* and applies to the common interest of the participants in the *azienda* whereas the second is more *external* and refers to the *azienda* as a system of relationships with other organizations and envisages the role that it covers in society. The CG is therefore the good of the participants in the *azienda* and the good of society because the *azienda* is a sub-system embedded in a much broader sphere. These two types of CG are however not simply the sum of particular interests or the sum of the value produced by each organization in society; rather they refer to a greater universal "convenience and advantage" (Zappa 1956, 42).

In terms of internal CG *EA* asserts that "in an *azienda* it is possible to harmoniously synthesize the individuals' interest in order to guarantee the common good over and above self-interest" (Zappa 1956, 38 our translation).

The external CG implies that the *azienda* carries out a social function because of its role in society and the more the *azienda* concurs to enhance the CG the better it is administered. A well-managed *azienda* is not only able to create economic wealth for shareholders and investors but also participates in the CG of society by providing services and goods in harmony with higher moral needs (Onida 1971).

By jointly considering the unitary long-term and social order approaches the *raison d'être* of the *azienda* can be correctly interpreted as *to satisfy human needs through participating in the CG*. Indeed, being a social and anthropocentric institution, the *azienda* should have social and human centered purposes and it would be incorrect to consider profit as its only goal (Ferrero 1968):

> even if the *azienda* has to work in the market in accordance to the *economicità* requirement its non-ephemeral long term sustainability requires attention to multiple dynamically combined objectives (salaries dividends and financing by corporate saving) and not just to profit maximization as the single objective function. (Onida 1971, 91 our translation)

EA stresses the ethical role of the *azienda* because as a social institution it enhances well-being, favors the development of the human being as a community of persons and encourages the attainment of human goals – all of which are essentially ethically-based. Thus the concrete behavior of the *azienda* is underpinned by these values, and, as a result, is based on ethics (Onida 1971, 43–44).

The Role of Business Organizations in Society: The Link Between the Italian *Economia Aziendale* and the CST

The aim of this discussion is to link the *EA* thought with CST and in particular with the CG principle in order to better interpret the profound changes regarding the role of organizations in society as called for in *Caritas in Veritate* (Grassl and Habisch 2011).

In particular given the two previously mentioned dimensions of the internal and external CG of business organizations (Signori and Rusconi 2009) the paper proposes insights regarding (i) how business organizations should prioritize different stakeholders' claims; (ii) the duty of the business to produce "wealth for all of society not just for the owners but also for the other subjects involved in their activity" (CSDC 338) and (iii) the need for a shift in competence between for-profit and not-for-profit organizations (CV 41).

Internal Common Good and Ethical Management of the Firm

In keeping with CST the understanding of the firm as a community of persons with a social role could contribute in demonstrating that a business organization is more than a mere nexus of contractual relationships owned by shareholders as assessed by the methodological individualism of neoclassical economics (Fontrodona and Sison 2006; Ferreira Vasconcelos 2010).

In this sense the Encyclical Letter *Caritas in Veritate* gives some important insights because it clearly calls for managerial practices that consider not only shareholders' interests but also "assume responsibility for all other stakeholders who contribute to the life of the business: the workers the clients the suppliers of various elements of productions the community of reference" (CV 40).

Benedict XVI understanding of stakeholders' claims and needs differs from the interpretation of stakeholders given by Freeman (Evan and Freeman 1988; Freeman and Phillips 2002; Freeman et al. 2007) and from the predominance of stakeholders' theorists (for a review see Phillips et al. 2003). In fact most of these approaches derive from a reductionist and contractual view of human beings that considers the role of business organizations as satisfying the interests of different groups (Sison 2007) in a way that cannot be accepted from a CST perspective (Alford and Naugthon 2001; Melé 2005, 2009c). CST tradition in fact purports that members of business organizations are not merely self-interested individuals but human beings with a moral orientation and ethical preferences which could in turn reinforce the members' capacity to cooperate with a sense of service and sometimes gratuity altruism and reciprocity (Zamagni 2008; Melé 2009c). For these reasons from the CST point of view the stakeholders' needs could be better understood by referring to the CG concept (Alford 2006) which indeed could be a possible normative basis of the stakeholder theory (Argandoña 1998; Phillips et al. 2003; Signori and Rusconi 2009).

The internal CG of a business is by definition not in contrary to the true personal aims of the organizational stakeholders and with their real flourishing, which is the purpose of any social institution. From a managerial point of view "the fundamental orientation to the common good does not exclude managerial concern for the legitimate interests of stakeholders" (Melé 2009a, 239) but does underline that the various stakeholders engaged in the organization have the duty to subordinate their personal claims to the organization's CG (Argandoña 1998).

EA may provide some insights into understanding the manner in which the CG concept could be concretely adopted as an ethical foundation to manage stakeholders' needs. In fact a contribution by Signori and Rusconi (2009) clearly highlighted the existing link between the vision of the *azienda* as an ethically oriented social sub-system with the aim of satisfying human needs (Onida 1954) and normative stakeholder theory based on the CG concept. The systemic and dynamic view of the *azienda* could be considered a prelude to the stakeholder concept because the need for cooperation to guarantee the survival of the *azienda* as well as a "synthesis of the individuals' interest for the common good beyond particular interest" (Zappa 1956, 38) seems to suggest a normative core to the stakeholder theory based on the CG. This approach further implies a reformulation of the maximization concept that should be linked to a complex system of well-being involving not only economic, but also social, cultural and relational dimensions.

The Multiple Purposes of the azienda and Its Contribution to the Societal Common Good

Linking the theoretical framework of *EA* with CST could help in better understanding the final purpose of business organizations – serving the CG of society – and the resulting managerial implications.

With reference to the purpose of business organizations it is worth mentioning that *EA* has never considered profit maximization as the sole purpose of economic activity but as a "powerful stimulus" (Ferrero 1968, 28) and a non-exhaustive though fundamental condition pertaining to the long-term survival of the *azienda* (Onida 1971).

The same considerations are emphasized by CST and by the business ethics research streams grounded in it. The instrumental role of profit and its link with other purposes are fundamental concepts in John Paul II's *Centesimus Annus*. In this Letter profit is clearly understood as one, but not the only, indicator of good business acumen because the purpose of a firm is not simply to make a profit but to serve the basic needs of the people involved in the business and of the society in which the firm works (CA 35).

Moreover, CST business ethics researchers (Abela 2001; Alford and Naugthon 2001) have pointed out that business organizations as part of society should contribute to the CG by pursuing multiple purposes: "offering goods or services creating and distributing economic value added work performed within the company organizational culture and leadership creating channels of investment and providing continuity to the company itself" (Melé 2002, 197–198).

Like CST, *EA* also suggests that the function of every business organization is not reducible to a single dominant goal but is always a synthesis of multiple integrated purposes (Coda 1983, 1988). By incorporating the profit-seeking objective within other ethically-oriented ones a business organization may be able to achieve

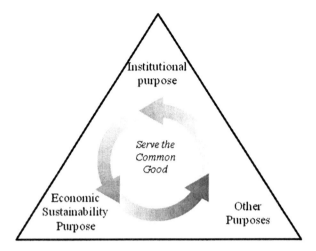

Fig. 9.1 Multiple purposes of the *azienda*

its true *raison d'être* which is to satisfy the well-being of the individuals involved in the organization's activity (Onida 1971) and to serve the societal CG i.e. to contribute to the "social and economic growth and development of the country in a harmonious and integrated way" (Coda 1983, 34 our translation).

By reinterpreting the *EA*'s scholarly managerial insights through the lens of CST we propose an understanding of the purposes of business organizations based on a threefold function that identifies (i) the institutional purpose (ii) the economic and sustainability purpose and (iii) the 'other purposes' (Fig. 9.1).

First, the institutional purpose is defined as the sum of the "interests of those the *azienda* has been set up for" (Coda 1983, 29) and it differs from the sum of the particular purposes of the stakeholders directly or indirectly involved in the activity.

Second, the economic and sustainability purpose is related to the ability to create wealth as an instrument to be durable in the long term to maintain the competiveness of the *azienda* and to guarantee its economic and financial stability to trade over time.

Finally, the 'other purposes' are not residual objectives but refer to the ability of the *azienda* to provide dignified working conditions to answer customers' needs to offer genuine goods and services to treat suppliers and competitors fairly and to avoid negative impacts on the environment and on society in general.

These purposes may not in practice be separated or individually considered, but rather integrated within a cooperative perspective because none can be perceived per se as the *raison d'être* of the firm. Instead they are means that together contribute to real *raison d'être* of every type of business organization: promoting the well-being of human beings through participation in the CG of society.

Blurring the Boundaries Between For-Profit and Not-For-Profit Organizations: The Unitary View of the azienda

The unitarian and anthropocentric understanding of business organizations as proposed by *EA* and reinterpreted in this paper could be fruitful in comprehending the existing differences and similarities between for-profit and not-for-profit organizations.

Given that the *raison d'être* of every firm is to satisfy human needs through a contribution to the societal CG and that this aim is satisfied when the 'institutional purpose', 'economic sustainability purpose' and the 'other purposes' are jointly achieved it follows that the main difference between for-profit and not-for-profit organizations lies in their institutional purposes. The 'economic and sustainability purpose' does not differ between a for-profit organization and a not-for-profit because both should maintain financial conditions in order to survive over time. In addition they should respect customers, workers, societal and environmental demands, thus achieving their so-called 'other purposes'. For-profit and not-for-profit organizations differ mainly because of their different institutional purposes: a for-profit organization refers to the creation of added economic value for the owners and investors while a not-for-profit relates to the creation of social value to benefit a particular target group and the community.

This interpretation of the purposes of business organizations enables us to narrow the ephemeral dichotomy between for-profit and not-for-profit organizations. Indeed the *raison d'être* of any organization (whatever the institutional purpose) is to promote the growth of human well-being through participating in the CG of the society. This *raison d'être* should therefore be embedded in the mission of the firm and should be concretely applied in the organization's strategic objectives policies and activities.

To serve the CG of society organizations should pursue the 'institutional', the 'economic and sustainability' and the 'other' purposes at the same time. On the one hand wealth creation for shareholders as well as for all other stakeholders is only one purpose of a for-profit firm. On the other social value creation as defined in the institutional purpose does not suffice to guarantee that not-for-profit organizations are able to contribute to the CG of society.

A for-profit organization aiming to maximize its 'institutional purpose' by neglecting the 'other purposes' and the 'economic and sustainability purpose' might destroy the business's internal and external CG because the organization seriously risks interpreting its *raison d'être* in a reductionist way.

Conversely a not-for-profit organization that is too focused on its socially-oriented institutional purpose could also risk undermining its capacity to contribute to the CG of society for at least two reasons. First a not-for-profit organization might address social weaknesses at the expense of its long-term economic sustainability. Second a socially-oriented institutional purpose does not guarantee per se that a not-for-profit organization would be responsible toward all its stakeholders and society as a whole. The strength of the social purpose and its orientation toward a specific target group or social weakness could lead not-for-profit organizations to treat other stakeholders in an unethical manner (Bouckaert and Vandenhove 1998; Fassin 2009) thus not providing the conditions that would allow each member of the organization to flourish as human beings (Cornelius et al. 2008).

This interpretation of the purposes of business organizations blurs the boundaries between for-profit and not-for-profit organizations and may help in better comprehending the Papal call for "cross-fertilization" and "shift in competence" between them (CV 40).

On the one hand for-profit firms should learn from not-for-profit organizations to include social and environmental claims in their economic thinking and strategy and should introduce skills and technology to produce and measure social value as well as economic wealth. Moreover, just as not-for-profit organizations define their mission and activities based on moral values (Cornelius et al. 2008), for-profit firms should base their managerial practices not only on profit maximization but also on broader moral considerations by introducing social responsibility as a core business strategy based on ethical requirements and not on self-interested ones.

On the other hand not-for-profit organizations should learn from the for-profit world to efficiently manage financial resources in order to address social weakness while maintaining financial sustainability. Adopting practices such as human and production management in order to consolidate the business's sustainable growth could be helpful for not-for-profit organizations not only to support their institutional purpose but also to concretely participate in the CG thus fulfilling their *raison d'être*.

Conclusion

This chapter shows that the *EA* seems to be fully consistent with the CST tradition understanding of business organizations, albeit implicitly. Both are grounded in an ontological understanding of enterprises as communities of persons whose aims are to serve the CG of society and to contribute to the flourishing of the human being. Therefore by virtue of the intellectual heritage of those scholars who theorized *EA* and by linking their thought with the normative understanding of business organizations proposed by CST and in particular by the Encyclical *Caritas in Veritate* this paper offers insights into how to transfer the notion of the CG to the managerial level.

According to CST and *EA* business organizations have a duty to serve the CG of society by virtue of producing useful goods and services. Economic efficiency cannot be the ultimate and unique goal of a business organization because in addition to this objective there is another which is equally important but of higher importance: contributing to social usefulness (CSDC 348).

In this sense it seems that *EA* can probably offer some useful insights for applying these assumptions at the managerial level. According to *EA* firms could be seen as a community of persons with the purpose of serving the CG of society through a threefold purpose: the institutional the economic and the so-called other purposes. This threefold function might be used as a compass for managing business organizations and for taking into account all the responsibilities firms have as members of society. Following CST and applying its ethical principles, a well-managed business organization should (i) fulfill its purposes ('institutional' 'economic sustainability' and 'other'); (ii) achieve internal CG i.e. enable everyone involved in the organizational activity to flourish as a human being; (iii) serve the external CG; and (iv) achieve the business *raison d'être* i.e. to satisfy human needs.

In this sense *EA* could very well be able to provide a useful conceptual framework for managing business organizations coherently with CST and thus to contribute to the growing research stream adopting the Catholic perspective to deal with business-related issues (Alford and Naugthon 2001, 2002; Melé 2002, 2005; Grassl and Habisch 2011; Asslaender 2011).[6]

References

Abela, Andrew V. 2001. Profit and more: Catholic social teaching and the purpose of the firm. *Journal of Business Ethics* 31(2): 107–116.

Albach, Horst, and Brian Bloch. 2000. Management as a science: Emerging trends in economic and management theory. *Journal of Management History* 6(3): 138–157.

Alford, Helen J. 2006. Stakeholder theory. In: Proceedings of the VI international conference on Catholic Church social thinking and manager education The Good Company. Catholic Social Thought and Corporate Social Responsibility in Dialogue, Rome, 5–7 Oct.

Alford, Helen J., and Michael J. Naugthon. 2001. *Managing as if faith mattered. Christian social principles in the modern organization.* Notre Dame: Notre Dame University Press.

Alford, Helen J., and Michael J. Naugthon. 2002. Beyond the shareholder model of the firm: Working toward the common good of a business. In *Rethinking the purpose of business. Interdisciplinary essays from the Catholic social tradition*, ed. S.A. Cortright and M. Naugthon, 27–47. Notre Dame: Notre Dame University Press.

Amaduzzi, Aldo. 1963. *L'azienda nel suo sistema e nell'ordine delle sue rilevazioni*, 2nd ed. Torino: Unione Tipografica – Editrice Torinese.

Amaduzzi, Antonio. 1991. *Istituzioni di economia aziendale*. Bari: Cacucci Editore.

Argandoña, Antonio. 1998. The stakeholder theory and the common good. *Journal of Business Ethics* 17(9–10): 1093–1102.

Argandoña, Antonio. 2012. The 'Logic of Gift' in the business enterprise. In *Human development in business. Values and humanistic management in the in the encyclical "Caritas in Veritate"*, ed. D. Melé and C. Dierksmeier, 198–216. New York: Palgrave MacMillan.

Argandoña, Antonio, and Heidi Von Weltzien Hoivik. 2009. Corporate social responsibility: One size does not fit all. Collecting evidence from Europe. *Journal of Business Ethics* 89: 221–234.

---

[6]A previous version was published by the authors, E. Costa, E., and T. Ramus, in 2012, under the title 'The Italian *Economia Aziendale* and Catholic Social Teaching: How to Apply the Common Good Principle at the Managerial Level' in the *Journal of Business Ethics* (Springer) 106(1), 103–116. With permission.

Asslaender, Michael. 2011. Corporate social responsibility as subsidiary co-responsibility: A macro-economic perspective. *Journal of Business Ethics* 99(1): 115–128.

Barrera, Albino. 2000. Social principles as a framework for ethical analysis (with an application to the Tobin tax). *Journal of Business Ethics* 23(4): 377–388.

Bouckaert, Luk, and Jan Vandenhove. 1998. Business ethics and the management of non-profit institutions. *Journal of Business Ethics* 17(9–10): 1073–1081.

Ceccherelli, Alberto. 1964. *Problemi di economia aziendale*. Pisa: Colombo Cursi Editore.

Clark, Charles M.A. 2009. A Christian perspective of the current economic crisis. *The American Economist* 53(1): 16–27.

Coase, Ronald H. 1937. The nature of the firm. *Economica* 4(16): 386–405.

Coda, Vittorio. 1983. *Appunti di Economia Aziendale*. Venezia: Libreria Editrice Cafoscarina.

Coda, Vittorio. 1988. *L'orientamento strategico dell'impresa*. Torino: Unione Tipografica – Editrice Torinese.

Cornelius, Nelarine, Mathew Todres, Shaheena Janjuha-Jivraj, Adrian Woods, and James Wallace. 2008. Corporate social responsibility and the social enterprise. *Journal of Business Ethics* 81(2): 355–371.

D'Ippolito, Teodoro. 1964. *Istituzioni di amministrazione aziendale*. Palermo-Roma: Bbaco srl Editore.

Dagnino, Giovanni B., and Paolo Quattrone. 2006. Comparing institutionalisms. Gino Zappa and John R. Commons' accounts of "institution" as a groundwork for a constructive view. *Journal of Management History* 12(1): 36–52.

Doran, Caroline J., and Samuel M. Natale. 2011. ἐμπάθεια (Empatheia) and Caritas: The role of religion in fair trade consumption. *Journal of Business Ethics* 98(1): 1–15.

Evan, William M., and Robert E. Freeman. 1988. A stakeholder theory of the modern corporation: Kantian capitalism. In *Ethical theory and business*, ed. T. Beauchamp and N. Bowie, 75–93. Englewood Cliffs: Prentice Hall.

Fassin, Yves. 2009. Inconsistencies in activists' behaviours and the ethics of NGOs. *Journal of Business Ethics* 90(4): 503–521.

Ferreira Vasconcelos, Anselmo. 2010. Spiritual development in organizations: A religious-based approach. *Journal of Business Ethics* 93(4): 607–622.

Ferrero, Giovanni. 1968. *Istituzioni di economia d'azienda*. Milano: Dott. A. Giuffrè Editore.

Flower, J. 1996. Schmalenbach, Zappa and Limperg: The 'accounting heroes' of continental Europe. In *Essay in accounting thought: A tribute to W.T. Baxter*, ed. I. Lapsley, 173–192. Glasgow: The Institute of Chartered Accountants in Scotland.

Fontrodona, Joan, and Alejo J.G. Sison. 2006. The nature of the firm agency theory and share-holder theory: A critique from philosophical anthropology. *Journal of Business Ethics* 66(1): 33–42.

Freeman, R. Edward. 1994. The politics of stakeholder theory: Some future directions. *Business Ethics Quarterly* 4(4): 409–429.

Freeman, R. Edward, and Robert A. Phillips. 2002. Stakeholder theory: A libertarian defence. *Business Ethics Quarterly* 12(3): 331–349.

Freeman, R. Edward, Kirsten Martin, and Bidhan Parmar. 2007. Stakeholder capitalism. *Journal of Business Ethics* 74(4): 303–314.

Friedman, Milton. 1970. The social responsibility of business is to increase its profits. *New York Times Magazine*, September 13, 32–33, 122, 126.

Garriga, Elisabet, and Domènec Melé. 2004. Corporate social responsibility theories: Mapping the territory. *Journal of Business Ethics* 53(1–2): 51–71.

Grassl, Wolfgang, and André Habisch. 2011. Ethics and economics: Towards a new humanistic synthesis for business. *Journal of Business Ethics* 99(1): 37–49.

Guitián, Gregorio. 2009. Conciliating work and family: A Catholic social teaching perspective. *Journal of Business Ethics* 88(3): 513–524.

Jensen, Michael C. 2001. Value maximization stakeholder theory and the corporate objective function. *Eur Financ Manag* 7(3): 297–317.

Masini, Carlo. 1960. *L'organizzazione del lavoro nell'impresa. Volume Primo*. Milano: Dott. A. Giuffrè Editore.

Masini, Carlo. 1974. *Lavoro e Risparmio*. Torino: Unione Tipografica – Editrice Torinese.

Mattessich, Richard. 2003. Accounting research and researchers of the nineteenth century and the beginning of the twentieth century: An international survey of authors ideas and publications. *Accounting Business and Financial History* 13(2): 125–170.

Melé, Domènec. 2002. *Not only stakeholder interests. The firm oriented toward the common good.* Notre Dame: University of Notre Dame Press.

Melé, Domènec. 2003. The challenge of humanistic management. *Journal of Business Ethics* 44(1): 77–88.

Melé, Domènec. 2005. Exploring the principle of subsidiarity in organizational forms. *Journal of Business Ethics* 60(3): 293–305.

Melé, Domènec. 2009a. Integrating personalism into virtue-based business ethics: The personalist and the common good principles. *Journal of Business Ethics* 88(1): 227–244.

Melé, Domènec. 2009b. Editorial introduction: Toward a more humanistic management. *Journal of Business Ethics* 88(3): 413–416.

Melé, Domènec. 2009c. The view and purpose of the firm in Freeman's stakeholder theory. *Philos Manag* 8(3): 3–13.

Naughton, Michael J., and Jeffrey R. Cornwall. 2006. The virtue of courage in entrepreneurship: Engaging the Catholic social tradition and the life-cycle of business. *Business Ethics Quarterly* 16(1): 69–93.

Naughton, Michael J., and Gene R. Laczniak. 1993. A theological context of work from the Catholic social encyclical tradition. *Journal of Business Ethics* 12(12): 981–994.

Onida, Pietro. 1954. *L'azienda. Primi principi di gestione e di organizzazione*. Milano: Dott. A. Giuffrè Editore.

Onida, Pietro. 1971. *Economia d'azienda*, 3rd ed. Torino: Unione Tipografica – Editrice Torinese.

Phillips, Kevin. 2006. *American theocracy: The peril and politics of radical religion oil and borrowed money to the 21st century*. New York: Viking.

Phillips, Robert, Robert E. Freeman, and Andrew C. Wicks. 2003. What stakeholder theory is not. *Business Ethics Quarterly* 13(4): 479–502.

Pope Benedictus XVI. 2009. Encyclical letter 'Caritas in Veritate – Love in Truth'. Libreria Editrice Vaticana.

Pope John Paul II. 1991. Encyclical letter 'Centesimus Annus'. Libreria Editrice Vaticana.

Rossi, Napoleone. 1964. *L'economia di azienda e i suoi strumenti di indagine*. Torino: Unione Tipografica – Editrice Torinese.

Rusconi, Gianfranco, and Michele Dorigatti (eds.). 2005. *Etica d'impresa*. Milano: Franco Angeli.

Sandelands, Lloyd. 2009. The business of business is the human person: Lessons from the Catholic social tradition. *Journal of Business Ethics* 85(1): 93–101.

Second Vatican Council. 1965. 'Gaudium et spes' *Acta Apostolicae Sedis* 58.

Signori, Silvana, and Gianfranco Rusconi. 2009. Ethical thinking in traditional Italian *Economia Aziendale* and the stakeholder management theory: The search for possible interactions. *Journal of Business Ethics* 89: 303–318.

Sison Alejo, J.G. 2007. Toward a common good theory of the firm: The Tasubinsa case. *Journal of Business Ethics* 74(4): 471–480.

Sison Alejo, J.G., and Joan Fontrodona. 2008. The common good of the firm in the Aristotelian-Thomistic tradition. Presented at the seminar humanizing the firm and the management profession Barcelona IESE Business School, June 30–July 2. Barcelona.

Solomon, Robert C. 1999. *A better way to think about business: How personal integrity leads to corporate success*. New York: Oxford University Press.

Treviño, Linda K., and Katherine A. Nelson. 2011. *Managing business ethics. Straight talk about how to do it right*, vol. 5. New York: Wiley.

Viganò, Enrico. 1998. Accounting and business economics traditions in Italy. *The European Accounting Review* 7(3): 381–403.

Viganò, Enrico, and Richard Mattessich. 2007. Accounting research in Italy: Second half of the 20th century. *Rev Account Finance* 6(1): 24–41.

Zamagni, Stefano. 2008. L'etica cattolica e lo spirito del capitalismo. Working paper AICCON 49. http://www.aiccon.it/working_paper.cfm.

Zambon, Stefano. 1996. Accounting and business economics traditions: A missing European connection? *The European Accounting Review* 5(3): 401–411.

Zan, Luca. 1994. Towards a history of accounting histories: Perspectives from the Italian tradition. *Eur Account Rev* 3(2): 255–307.

Zappa, Gino. 1927. Tendenze nuove negli studi di ragioneria. Opening Speech of the Academic Year 1926–1927, University of Venice.

Zappa, Gino. 1956. *Le produzioni nell'economia delle imprese. Tomo primo.* Milano: Dott. A. Giuffrè Editore.

Zappa, Gino. 1962. *L'economia delle aziende di consumo.* Milano: Dott. A. Giuffrè Editore.

Zappa, Gino, Lino Azzini, and Giuseppe Cudini. 1964. *Ragioneria generale.* Milano: Dott. A. Giuffrè Editore.

Part III
Catholic Humanism in Business

Chapter 10
The Business of Business Is the Human Person

Lloyd E. Sandelands

Abstract I describe an ethic for business administration based on the social tradition of the Catholic Church. I find that much current thinking about business falters for its conceit of truth. Abstractions such as the shareholder-value model contain truth – namely, that business is an economic enterprise to manage for the wealth of its owners. But, as in all abstractions, this truth comes at the expense of falsehood – namely, that persons are assets to deploy on behalf of owners. This last is "wrong" in both senses of the word – it is factually wrong in that persons are far more than business assets, they are supernatural beings, children of God; and it is morally wrong in that it is an injustice to treat them as the former when they are the latter. I draw upon the social tradition of the Catholic Church to recognize that the business of business is not business, but is instead the human person. Following Church teachings, I describe a person-centered ethic of business based upon eight social principles that both correct and enlarge the shareholder-centered ethic of much current business thinking. I discuss implications of this person-centered ethic for business administration.

Keywords Business ethics • Shareholder-value model • Catholic social teaching • Human person • Person-centered ethics • Business management

In the broad terms that most of us speak in most of the time, it is almost too easy to criticize business. Viewed in the abstract, as an instrument of commerce rather than as human persons making lives for themselves, business is an off-putting affair. According to the "shareholder-value model" that dominates thinking about business in universities today and now sets the agenda for business in the wider culture, a business is a financial entity composed of resources, including employees who are "human resources" (capital costs, factors of production), to be used to maximize the wealth of its owners (Jensen and Meckling 1976). This idea of business as an instrument of capital makes for a narrow and dismal idea of the human person who

L.E. Sandelands (✉)
Stephen M. Ross School of Business Administration, University of Michigan,
Ann Arbor, MI, USA
e-mail: lsandel@umich.edu

© Springer Science+Business Media Dordrecht 2015   165
D. Melé, M. Schlag (eds.), *Humanism in Economics and Business*,
Issues in Business Ethics 43, DOI 10.1007/978-94-017-9704-7_10

becomes a sort of slave – a wage-salve to be precise. Proclaimed today by students of economics and finance, this idea of business was anticipated and encapsulated years ago by Alfred Sloan, architect and executive of the General Motors Corporation, who opined that: "The business of business is business." This cool pragmatism has been taken by many to be the cardinal virtue of business. "It's nothing personal," we say, "it's just business." Business has become the conscienceless idea of "never mind." Never mind the plight of workers – they are their own contractors, free to come and go as they please. Never mind the common good of society – that is for government to decide. And never mind "corporate social responsibility" – that's just a "guilt trip" to coerce regrets business cannot have.[1] Viewed in the abstract, as an instrument of economic interest, business is an ambivalent proposition at best.

Certainly business is no ambivalence in the literary imagination. In the caricature drawn by writers, business is the pretense that life is economics. Business is supposed to be a devil's bargain – wealth and amenity today for the soul in eternity. Its standard bearers are the likes of Charles Dickens' Scrooge (Dickens 2005), a man estranged from love and life by a hard and flinty avarice, and Sinclair Lewis' Babbitt (Lewis 1922), a man no less estranged from love and life by a soft and needy middle-class lifestyle. These figures of greed and vacuity are real. Today's Scrooges are the "Barbarians at the Gate" of Wall Street (Burrough and Helyar 1990) and the "Smartest Guys in the Room" on the power trading floor at the Enron Corporation (McLean and Elkind 2003). Today's Babbitts are denizens of the "Moral Mazes in the World of Corporate Managers" (Jackall 1988) and, more generally, of America's pervading "Culture of Narcissism" (Lasch 1979). Truth is no stranger to fiction.

A Bad Rap

Whatever their grain of truth, such easy charges against business are a bad rap. They are founded upon misleading abstractions. The shareholder-value model of business is just that, a model, not the reality. And of course literary imagination is just that, imagination, not the whole truth. Although real and worrisome, the evils that attend these abstractions are neither intrinsic nor universal. They are accidents of thinking that mistakes ideas about business with business itself. It is not business per se that gets us into trouble, but our thinking about business that gets us into trouble.

Our thinking about business falters for its conceit of truth. Abstractions such as the shareholder-value model contain truth – not least that business is an economic enterprise to manage for the wealth of its owners. But, as in all abstraction, this truth comes at the expense of falsehood – not least that persons are assets to deploy on behalf of owners. This last is "wrong" in both senses of the word – it is factually wrong in that persons are much more than material assets of a business, they are

---

[1] Of this last, the Nobel Prize winning economist Friedman (1970) notoriously declared, "the only social responsibility of business is to shareholders." To think otherwise is communism or is at least "taxation without representation."

supernatural beings, children of God; and it is morally wrong in that it is an injustice to treat them as the former when they are the latter.[2] This intrinsic hazard of abstraction is pointed in our thinking about ourselves. As is known to the Church, if not widely elsewhere, our self-understanding is fundamentally flawed (John Paul II 1998; *Fides et ratio*, FR hereafter). Whereas our reason abstracts from nature, our human being is not only of nature but also of God. Whereas we can think more or less truly about everything in nature, we cannot think truly about ourselves (see Sandelands 2007). Being above nature – literally being "super-natural" – we are beyond our own estimate.[3] Thus when we think about ourselves in the abstractions of business we do so at the risk of our essential truth; namely, that as special creations of God we are not of this world, but of His being. To keep hold of our human being we must reach beyond reason to God. We must accept in faith what. He has revealed about us. With Pope John Paul II we must see that "Revelation has set within history a point of reference which cannot be ignored if the mystery of human life is to be known" (FR 14). And more generally, again with the Pope, we must see that our self-understanding requires both faith and reason:

> Faith and reason are like two wings on which the human spirit rises to the contemplation of truth; and God has placed in the human heart a desire to know the truth—in a word, to know himself—so that, by knowing and loving God, men and women may also come to the fullness of truth about themselves (FR Initial blessing)

Looking to faith, we must find the reference points for understanding ourselves, the truths within which our abstractions about business can be put in proper context. And looking to faith, we must augment our thinking about such things as the shareholder-value model to acknowledge truths of the human person that originate outside the natural world of economics, in man's essential dignity in God.

The question therefore is not whether we should use God's gift of reason in thinking about business. The question is not even whether in doing so we should use a tool such as the shareholder-value model. Indeed, we must think every thought and use every tool to make the most of business as a means to our dominion of the earth that God created for us. Rather, the question is how we should use God's gift of reason in thinking about business. To what end should our reason be put? To rephrase the question in the terms of our old friend Alfred Sloan, what should be

---

[2] This point is being made with increasing frequency, especially by the many writings in the Catholic social tradition (e.g., Alford and Naughton 2002), and also by a few writings in the tradition of science (e.g., Ghoshal 2005).

[3] Because our being is beyond our powers of conception and reason, to know it we require a different knowledge, one that arises not from abstract reasoning, but from the trust and love of intimate personal relationships. This knowledge is connatural as opposed to rational. It is not of the mind alone but of the ensouled body as well. It originates not as a projection of abstract reasoning but as a bodily trust between mother and child. Thus, in "making a life" we come to a startling truth that we have "known all along" – that our business in the world rests not only upon the powers of reason given to us by God our Father, but also and more immediately upon the intimacy and trust we learned from our human mothers. The truth upon which all abstract truths are founded is personal and material. This is the truth of our mothers; an image of the first of all human truths, Jesus Christ. Our being in God is not abstract, but incarnate.

the business of business? This ethical question is answered distinctively and decisively by the Catholic Church in what in recent decades, and particularly during the Pontificate of John Paul II, has come to be called her *Social Tradition*. In what follows I draw upon this tradition to suggest that the business of business – its weight and glory – is the human person. With the Church, I describe the weight of business in terms of eight principles that honor the dignity of the person in God. And with Catholic theologian and business writer Novak (1996), I describe the glory of business in terms of three cardinal virtues of business that help bring the person to God. I conclude with a confirming word from one of our greatest students of business, Mary Parker Follett.

To Make a Living

The business of business is to know, not in the cold abstractions of shareholder-value and not in the harsh light of literary examination, but in the warm flesh-and-blood of our personal lives and in the revelatory light of faith. The ethic of business is revealed in the nearness of human work that is personal and material, not in the distance of reason that is abstract precisely in that it has detached itself from both. Business is a matter of heart.

Nearly everyone speaks of work as a means to "make a living." But what does this mean? Is this a figure of speech that means "to make a buck" (to invoke another figure of speech)? Or is this a declaration of something much greater; namely, "to make a life"? According to faith we make a life by incarnation – literally by embodying God. To live is to be in God in body and mind. To live is to be in Christ who is "The Word" and "The Way".

According to faith, the God of creation "spoke our being" in two ways – He named us His son, Adam, as the one in His image who shares in His power of naming and knowing; and He created us in love, as male and female in one flesh, as one who shares in His power to create life in love. Thus we incarnate God in two ways. We are a person, literally 'of son' to God. As such we are to answer and serve His will for us by following His commandments. And we are man and woman in one flesh, an embodiment of His creative will in love, especially in nuptial union from which we create new life. As such we are to extend His love in and through our love of others. Thus our human being is personal (a son-ship to God) and material (an embodiment of God).

In the person of Jesus Christ, carpenter of Bethlehem, we learn that one important arena in which we may incarnate God is work. Recounting the thought of Pope John Paul II in his encyclical on work, *Laborem Exercens* (LE) Calvez and Naughton explain:

> Because they have been made in God's image, all people have been given the command, which is both a right and a duty, to subdue the earth. He defines the expression "subdue the earth" as a human activity that discovers all the resources the earth provides so as to use

them for people to develop, not simply to maximize capital returns or to balance individual interests. It is only through work that people can tap the richness creation has to offer, and it is through organizations that this work is carried out most effectively. (2002, 10)

Thus we come into our humanity at work, and indeed everywhere else, when we come into the truth of our creation by God. As John Paul II described in a later encyclical about economic life, *Centesimus Annus* (1991, CA hereafter), without this realization we are lost to our own humanity:

> When man does not recognize in himself and in others the value and grandeur of the human person, he effectively deprives himself of the possibility of benefiting from his humanity and of entering into that relationship of solidarity and communion with others for which God created him. (CA 41)

With the idea of divine incarnation we know what it means to make a living. It is to make a life in God. This reverses the usual understanding of the relationship between man and work. Too often it is supposed that man is for work; that he is an instrument of shareholder interests; and that he is responsible to these interests. The truth is to the contrary, that work is for man; that man has the right to be in God in and through the circumstances of work; and that business has the responsibility to honor this right. In a word, business is responsible for the divine lives of those in its employ. In a sharper word, the business of business is the human person.

In allowing this much, and it is everything, we realize that business is not merely material and worldly; it is also spiritual and other-worldly. To serve its true purpose, the purpose that justifies its esteem in society, business must provide for the divine being of all whose lives it touches. This is something it cannot do if it reduces the person to an instrument of shareholder ambition.[4] Speaking to business on behalf of the human person, the Church reminds us that:

> Man cannot give himself to a purely human plan for reality, to an abstract ideal or to a false utopia. As a person, he can give himself to another person or to other persons, and ultimately to God, who is the author of his being and who alone can fully accept his gift. (CA 41)

Unfortunately, as Calvez and Naughton point out, too often business does not allow people the opportunity and room to "make a life" in this way, but to the contrary alienates them by treating them as means rather than as ends (2002, 10). As Pope John Paul II explains, "the concept of alienation needs to be led back to the Christian vision of reality, by recognizing in alienation a reversal of means and ends" (CA 35). What is more, in the idea of divine incarnation we better understand what it means to "make a buck." We make money to provide for ourselves and others so that we may fulfill our vocation in God. Odd though it may sound, it is more than a clever turn of phrase to say that the work is not for the money but that

---

[4] According to John Paul II, "if economic life is absolutized [for example to focus narrowly upon shareholder wealth] (…) the reason is to be found not so much in the economic system itself as in the fact that the entire socio-cultural system, by ignoring the ethical and religious dimension, has been weakened, and ends by limiting itself to the production of goods and services alone" (CA 39, the expression in brackets is mine).

the money is for the work. For it is indeed true that we do not work for bread alone. Sustained by bread we are able to fulfill one of our most important vocations, to be and grow in God through our work. The world of difference in this turn of phrase is captured nicely in a poem written by author Kurt Vonnegut in memory of his friend Joseph Heller:

> Joseph Heller, an important and funny writer now dead, and I were at a party given by a billionaire on Shelter Island.
>   I said, "Joe, how does it make you feel to know that our host only yesterday may have made more money than your novel 'Catch-22' has earned in its entire history?"
>   And Joe said,
>   "I've got something he can never have."
>   And I said, "What on earth could that be, Joe?"
>   And Joe said, "The knowledge that I've got enough."
>   Not bad! Rest in Peace![5]

The Weight and the Glory

Thus the business of business is not only or mainly to maximize shareholder wealth. It is more essentially to help persons make lives by creating conditions under which they can grow and develop in relationship to God. To be sure, it is a struggle for business to reconcile its worldly values for entrepreneurship and capital risk with its other-worldly values for life and being in God. As described by Pope John Paul II, business can and must not take a stand against making a profit, which is important and necessary for its well-being. Instead, business can and must take a stand for making human lives, which is in the end far more important and necessary for us all. The needful trick is to put the first value in the context of the second. According to John Paul:

> The Church acknowledges the legitimate *role of profit* as an indication that a business is functioning well. When a firm makes a profit, this means that productive factors have been properly employed and corresponding human needs have been duly satisfied. But profitability is not the only indicator of a firm's condition. It is possible for the financial accounts to be in order, and yet for the people — who make up the firm's most valuable asset — to be humiliated and their dignity offended. Besides being morally inadmissible, this will eventually have negative repercussions on the firm's economic efficiency. In fact, the purpose of a business firm is not simply to make a profit, but is to be found in its very existence as a *community of persons* who in various ways are endeavouring to satisfy their basic needs, and who form a particular group at the service of the whole of society. Profit is a regulator of the life of a business, but it is not the only one; *other human and moral factors* must also be considered which, in the long term, are at least equally important for the life of a business. (CA 35). (Italics in the original)

---

[5]Quoted by John C. Bogle in a commencement address to MBA graduates of the McDonough School of Business, Georgetown University, Washington, D.C. (18 May 2007).

As the business of business is to serve man, and the business of man is to serve God, the business of business is to serve God.[6] This is the weight and glory of business; its solemn responsibility and its noble virtue. And this is the work-order for business administration. I close this essay with a too brief survey of what the weight and glory of business might mean for those who would lead.

The Weight

Business is not alone in its obligation to honor man's being in God; it can and must look for help to the Church who embraces this obligation as her mission for the whole of humankind. This is not to suggest that business can pass its responsibility off to the Church (as a value the Church might take up on Sunday mornings, while business plies other values the rest of the week); to the contrary, it is to insist that business accept its responsibility in league with the Church. It is perhaps in business more than in any other activity that Christian conscience encounters the real world. And thus it is in business perhaps especially that man's being in God must be realized. On its path to salvation, business can find help in the Social Doctrine of the Church, which is her wisdom for man "as he is involved in a complex network of relationships within modern societies" (CA 55). According to Pope John Paul II: "[B]y its concern for man and by its interest in him and in the way he conducts himself in the world," the Church's social doctrine "belongs to the field of theology and particularly of moral theology. The theological dimension is needed both for interpreting and solving present day problems in human society" (CA 55).

Directed to the whole of man's life in society, this doctrine comprises a set of guidelines within which business can and must take its place within society. Only by fidelity to these guidelines can business meet its obligation to the person and to society. This is the weight of business.

The Church's social doctrine is a living body; its fundamental principles support each other in aid of man's personal and social destiny in God. To this end, while each principle is necessary, only the collection is sufficient as doctrine. And while each principle warrants an essay of its own, it must suffice in the pages remaining to this essay to lay them out as a group so to see in broad terms the Church's wisdom for business. As compiled in her *Compendium of the Social Doctrine of the Church* (CSDC 2004), these principles are:

Meaning and Unity

This first refers to the entire set, to insist the collection be appreciated in its "unity, interrelatedness, and articulation" (CSDC 71). This is to recognize that man's being in God is unitary and is to encourage and protect in all its aspects. Thus while

---

[6]This phrase and that of this section borrows from C.S. Lewis who penned a book of this title.

individual principles refer variously to the person, to society, and to relations between the two, it must not be forgotten that person and society define one another as parts of God's unitary creation. For business this means that its obligation to the person cannot be separated from its obligation to society. The business of business is man, both in person and in society.

The Principle of the Common Good

According to this principle: "A society that wishes and intends to remain at the service of the human being at every level is a society that has the common good – the good of all people and of the whole person – as its primary goal" (CSDC 2004, 73). For business this means that its economic activity take place within the limits of the moral order and more particularly within God's plan for humankind. The fundamental finality of production – according to *Gaudium et Spes* (1965, GS hereafter), an important document of the Vatican Council II– "is not the mere increase of products nor profit or control but rather the service of man, and indeed of the whole man with regard for the full range of his material needs and the demands of his intellectual, moral, spiritual, and religious life; this applies to every man whatsoever and to every group of men, of every race and of every part of the world" (GS 64, 37). By this principle, the good of self-interest, which is so enshrined in business thinking today, cannot be all, or even first. Individual goods, including that of shareholders, must find their place within the super-ordinate good of humankind.

The Universal Destination of Goods

This is the principle that each and every person "must have access to the level of well-being necessary for his full development" (CSDC 75). This is actually a two-handed principle: on one hand it confirms the necessity of private property as the ground upon which persons can make lives for themselves; on the other hand it recognizes that the earth and its resources are God's gift to all humankind for all to share and enjoy. Thus while this idea substantiates an absolute right to property and capital, this right is not unlimited but is instead constrained by the no less important and no less absolute right that the goods of God's gift to man be shared. For business, as Calvez and Naughton explain in describing the thought of Pope John Paul, this principle has clear meaning for its concepts of property and capital:

> Consequently, any idea of an absolute right to property and capital, expressed through formulas of shareholder wealth maximization, or any idea of a corporate body as merely a nexus of competing interests is rejected, because it denies the significance of this human vocation to work and impedes persons' development in and from their work. Nevertheless –he adds–, this principle of universal destination "does not delegitimize private property;

instead it broadens the understanding and management of private property to embrace its indispensable social function, to the advantage of the common good and in particular the good of society's weakest members." (Calvez and Naughton 2002, 10–11)

The Principle of Subsidiarity

According to this principle, "every social activity ought of its very nature to furnish help to the members of the body social, and never destroy and absorb them" (CSDC 81). For the social activity of business this means that "While the authority of the owner ought to be protected, no room can exist in…business for practices that deny the profound worth of the employees of the enterprise" (Calvez and Naughton 2002, 8). This principle thus opposes two tendencies of modern business, particularly in its most highly industrialized sectors. One is the tendency in manufacturing to treat worker as objects, as factors of production to manage like any other. This denies workers worth as autonomous and independent-minded subjects who take part in the creative will of God. The other is the tendency to treat workers as means to ends rather than as ends themselves. This equates the value of workers with what they produce rather than with who they are. To recognize workers as ends in themselves means that "…the entire process of productive work … must be adapted to the needs of the person and to his way of life, especially in respect to mothers of families, always with due regard for sex and age" (GS 67, 39). Among these needs are the material ones of personal and family sustenance, which means that workers must be paid not only a living wage, but for workers with families a family wage. Also among these needs are those of self-expression and self-development: "The opportunity … should be granted to workers to unfold their own abilities and personality through the performance of their work" (GS 67).

Participation

This principle provides for "activities by means of which the citizen, either as an individual or in association with others, whether directly or through representation, contributes to the cultural, economic, political, and social life of the civil community to which he belongs" (CSDC 83). This principle carries a strong message for business at odds with the emphasis today upon shareholder capitalism. According to the Church, in economic enterprises it is persons who are joined together, that is, free and independent human beings created in the image of God. Therefore, with attention to the functions of each – owners or employers, management or labor – and without doing harm to the necessary unity of management, the active sharing of all in the administration and profits of these enterprises in ways to be properly determined is to be promoted. Since more often, however, decisions concerning economic and social conditions, on which the future lot of the workers and of their children depends, are made not within the business itself but by institutions on a higher level, the workers themselves should have a share also in determining these conditions – in person or through freely elected delegates (GS 68, 39).

The Principle of Solidarity

This principle recognizes "the intrinsic social nature of the human person, the equality of all in dignity and rights, and the common path of individuals and peoples toward an evermore committed unity" (CSDC 84). In a word, there is a unity of unities to which all human enterprise must tend. For business this means acting on behalf of the whole of humankind by producing goods that are truly "goods," that add to rather than subtract from the life of persons and society. Questionable, therefore, are businesses that contribute to vice and dissipation (such as by fostering use of unhealthy drugs or pornography) or businesses that through aggressive advertising create empty or misplaced "needs" (such as by playing up insecurities about physical beauty or social status). For business this also means acting in cooperation with others, including its competition. Thus, competition in business is not, as some say, a Hobbesian "war of all against all" (Hobbes 1958), but instead a spirited play in which all are safe and secure, a "struggle for existence with a mellow denouement" (Durkheim 1933). Competitors are not prey to over-whelm by market power or predatory pricing, but are loyal adversaries to welcome as a test of one's mettle in the marketplace. Competition is not cooperation's opposite, but its sincerest form.

The Fundamental Values of Social Life

According to this principle, "all social values are inherent in the dignity of the human person, whose authentic development they foster. Essentially, these values are: truth, freedom, justice, love" (CSDC 88). There can be no human dignity – no human person and no human society – without these values, which every person and society must therefore uphold. For business these values must underlie every activity and relationship. It could hardly be otherwise as these values are written upon the human heart. In fact these values are presupposed by most abstract thinking about business, including particularly the shareholder-value model, which begins upon an assumption of "the market." As Nobel economist Arrow (1994) explains, modern economic theory rests upon an idea of the market that it cannot explain. This market, Arrow notes, rests upon such humane values as truth, freedom, justice, and love. Thus, behind the conduct called for by abstract theories of business is a mundane reality of fundamental values for human dignity called for by God and propounded in faith by the Church.

The Way of Love

This final principle finds in love the "highest and universal criterion of the whole of social ethics. Among all paths, even those sought and taken in order to respond to the ever new forms of current social questions, the 'more excellent way' is that marked out by love" (CSDC 91). True happiness "is not found in riches or well-being, in human fame or power, or in any human achievement … but in God alone, the source of every good and of all love" (Catechism of the Catholic Church 1995, #1723). This principle recognizes in the most general way possible what it is to be in God. As God is love, we are in God when we are in love. This love is a 'many splendored thing' that begins in God and extends to every human relation and to every corner of existence. Love is dynamism of division in unity and unity in division. In the moment of love comes the moment of play whereby people together create a social order. Play is the creative edge of love whereby come new divisions in unity and new unities in division.[7] And in the moment of play comes the moment of individuation whereby persons take their place in the life of the whole. Individuation is a fruit of play, the division in unity and unity in division that is the human person in society (Sandelands 2003). Thus love is the ground of all social life, including that of business of course.

The Glory

Although the weight of business is a heavy one, rarely carried well or far, and too often confirmed in the dropping, it is the glory of business and the lie in our too easy criticism of it. At its best, business is a glory of God. It is a noble calling to being in God that serves man's heart's desire.

Business glorifies God as it helps man to his incarnation; to his realization of God in becoming a person and to his embodiment of God in taking part in a union of male and female in one flesh. Far from the cold abstractions of the shareholder-value model, the glory of business is in the concrete doings of real people making real lives together. Among the voices for this glory is Catholic theologian Novak (1996) who insists upon an image of business as a vocation, as a conscious or unconscious calling of the human spirit to God. In business he finds three cardinal virtues in whose exercise man comes to be in God: creativity, building community, and practical realism. About the first, creativity, he writes:

> At the very heart of capitalism … is the creative habit of enterprise. Enterprise is, in its first moment, the inclination to notice, the habit if discerning, the tendency to discover what other people don't yet see. It is also the capacity to act on insight, so as to bring into reality things not before seen. It is the ability to foresee both the needs of others and the combinations of productive factors most adapted to satisfying those needs. This habit of intellect constitutes an important source of wealth in modern society. (Novak 1996, 120)

This virtue of creativity, which is the primary source of wealth and the engine of man's successful dominion of the earth, is man's imaging of God. By his creativity, man "participates from afar in the source of all knowledge, the Creator. Sharing in God's creativity … the principal resource of humans is their own inventiveness. Their intelligence enables them to discover the earth's productive potential…" (Novak 1996, 123).

---

[7] For an exposition of play in the making of human society, see Huizinga (1950).

About the second virtue, building community, Novak begins with the truism that capitalism is not about the individual, but is about "a creative form of community":

> In a word, businesspeople are constantly on all sides, involved in building community. Immediately at hand, in their own firm, they must build a community of work. A great deal depends on the level of creativity, teamwork, and high morale a firms' leaders can inspire. (Novak 1996, 126)

This virtue of building community, according to Novak, "throws a practical light" on a divine truth about the human person which faith affirms, a truth which again is a sign of man's imaging of God:

> That truth is this: the Creator made the human person to work in community and to cooperate freely with other persons, for the sake of other persons (italics in original) (Novak 1996, 127)

And finally, about the third virtue of business, practical realism, Novak traces a surprising connection between an alert and hard-nosed business practice and Providence. Comparing businesspeople to athletes and professional warriors, he notes in common a state of life given to peril which leads them to "be unusually aware of how many facets of reality are not under their control, how dependent they are on such factors, and the great difference between being smiled on – or frowned on – by Providence" (Novak 1996, 131). Whereas one might expect the practical realism of businesspeople to be far from faith, Novak finds in it an intimation of incarnation, of God in action. For this, many in business feel blessed – as if "God had shed His grace on thee" – so much so that "Those whose efforts to better the human community mark them as creators, made in the image of their Creator, develop a mental habit in which prayer seems to accord with the natural law itself – and even with the law of grace" (Novak 1996, 131–132).

Although founded upon the concrete actions of real persons in community, these virtues of business do not oppose the abstract value of making a profit or for that matter the use of rational techniques aimed at profit (such as those that might derive from the shareholder-value model). Quite the contrary, these virtues promote the value of making money, which can be seen as a secondary virtue and glory of business. These virtues are the context within which exigencies of profit can be interpreted and appreciated. In these virtues we see that business is not only or mainly an exercise of economic rationality, but is truly an art of divine reach. Indeed, in view of its complexity, its human dimensions, and its premium on intuition and judgment, business might well be the practical art par excellence. Within this art, economic rationality is a tool like any other; its value and good are not intrinsic but depend upon how it is used. When it helps bring man to God it is a tool to the good and there is virtue in its use. When it diverts man from God it is an instrument of sin and there is evil in its use. Business is the worldly art of using all available tools for the glory that is God.

A Final Word

At the essay's end we recall the needful marriage of reason and faith. The Church honors her mission by advocating for that divine revelation that sets the reference points within which business can reason its way to salvation. In her Pastoral Constitution of Vatican II, *Gaudium et Spes*, the Church states: "In the economic and social realms … the dignity and complete vocation of the human person and the welfare of society as a whole are to be respected and promoted. For man is the source, the center, and the purpose of all social life" (GS 63). These reference points of person and society are the ultimate purposes that have guided the most acute students of business administration. Here, in a word from perhaps the greatest of these, Mary Parker Follett, we come to a fitting end:

> The leader releases energy, unites energies, and all with the object not only of carrying out a purpose, but of creating further and larger purposes. And I do not mean here by larger purposes mergers or more branches; I speak of larger in the qualitative rather than the quantitative sense. I mean purposes which will include more of those fundamental values for which most of us agree we are really living. (1942, 168)[8,9]

References

Alford, Helen, and Michael J. Naughton. 2002. Beyond the shareholder model of the firm. In *Rethinking the purpose of the business*, ed. S.A. Cortright and M.J. Naughton. Notre Dame: University of Notre Dame.

Arrow, Kenneth. 1994. Methodological individualism and social knowledge. Boston: American Economic Association Papers and Proceedings, 1–9 May.

Burrough, Bryan, and John Helyar. 1990. *Barbarians at the gate*. New York: Harper and Row.

Calvez, Jean-Yves, and M.J. Naughton. 2002. Catholic social teaching and the purpose of the business organization. In *Rethinking the purpose of the business*, ed. S.A. Cortright and M.J. Naughton. Notre Dame: University of Notre Dame Press.

Catechism of the Catholic Church. 1995. New York: Doubleday. It is also available at http://www.vatican.va

Compendium of the Social Doctrine of the Church. 2004. Vatican City: Pontifical Council for Justice and Peace.

Dickens, Charles. 2005. *A Christmas Carol*. Clayton: Prestwick House.

Durkheim, Emile. 1933. *The division of labor in society*. New York: Macmillan.

Follett, Mary. 1942. Dynamic administration. In *The collected papers of Mary Parker Follett*, ed. H.C. Metcalf and L. Urwick. New York: Harper & Brothers.

---

[8] I would like to thank Jane Dutton, section editor Muel Kaptein, and the two anonymous reviewers at the *Journal of Business Ethics* for their constructive and detailed comments.

[9] This article was originally published as 'The Business of Business is the Human Person: Lessons from the Catholic Social Tradition', *Journal of Business Ethics*, (2009) 85:93–101. Reproduced with authorization.

Friedman, Milton. 1970. The social responsibility of business is to increase its profits. *New York Times Magazine*, September 13.

Ghoshal, Sumantra. 2005. Bad management theories are destroying good management practices. *Academy of Management Learning and Education* 4(1): 75–91.

Hobbes, Thomas. 1958. *Leviathan*. Indianapolis: Bobbs-Merrill.

Huizinga, Johan. 1950. *Homo ludens*. Boston: Beacon Press.

Jackall, Robert. 1988. *Moral mazes*. New York: Oxford University.

Jensen, Michael C., and William H. Meckling. 1976. Theory of the firm: Managerial behavior, agency costs, and ownership structure. *Journal of Financial Economics* 3(4): 305–360.

John Paul II. 1991. Encyclical letter *Centesimus Annus*. http://www.vatican.va

John Paul II. 1998. Encyclical letter *Fides et Ratio*. http://www.vatican.va

Lasch, Christopher. 1979. *The culture of narcissism*. New York: W.W. Norton.

Lewis, Sinclair. 1922. *Babbitt*. San Diego: Harcourt, Brace, Jovanovich.

McLean, Bethany, and Peter Elkind. 2003. *The smartest guys in the room*. New York: Penguin.

Novak, Michael. 1996. *Business as a calling*. New York: The Free Press.

Sandelands, Lloyd E. 2003. *Thinking about social life*. Lanham: University Press of America.

Sandelands, Lloyd E. 2007. *An anthropological defense of God*. New Brunswick: Transaction.

Vatican Council II. 1965. Pastoral constitution *Gaudium et Spes*. http://www.vatican.va

Chapter 11
Thinking Institutionally About Business: Seeing Its Nature as a Community of Persons and Its Purpose as the Common Good

Michael Naughton

Abstract We are increasingly facing in contemporary society significant debates over the nature and purpose of our institutions. In business, its purpose is often pitted between a shareholder maximization or stakeholder balance principle. This purpose discussion, however, too often fails to get to the underlying nature of the business institution itself, which entails how we understand who is in the business (individual vs. person) and its communal character (association vs. community). This essay describes the *nature* of a business on a continuum between an "association of individuals" and a "community of persons" and the various shadings in between. It is accepted as compelling that the nature of business is a "community of persons" and then lays out the principle of the common good as its purpose. Recognizing the various obstacles of the principle in relationship to business, we explain how the common good views the institutional goods that are particular to a business (good goods, good work, good wealth), and how these goods are ordered to human development (ordering principles, goods held in common, virtues).

Keywords Business institution • Common good • Community of persons • Human development • Nature of the firm • Stakeholder balance

Our fiercest debates these days center around conflicting claims on the nature and purpose of institutions, especially marriage/family, religion, education, healthcare, charities, the state and business. Yet, while we debate the nature and purpose of institutions, there is a general agreement that our institutions have morally and spiritually suffered over the years, which has increased the anti-institutional attitude of people, the increasing apathy among the general public for these institutions, and the general loss of confidence in their ability to serve the common good (see Heclo 2008; Brooks 2012). Nonetheless, institutions are the places where we exist.

M. Naughton (✉)
University of St. Thomas, Saint Paul, MN, USA
e-mail: mjnaughton@stthomas.edu

They give structure to the way we live our lives together and if we are to make a better world, we need an institutional path, a common way of thinking institutionally (Benedict XVI 2009a, CV 7)[1] about business in a way that promotes a humanistic philosophy for management. What is proposed in this paper is a way of thinking institutionally that explores the relationship between the nature of institutions as a community of persons and the common good as their purpose.[2] More specifically, this essay examines the integrated relationship between a community of persons and the common good as two critical terms to understand more clearly the nature and purpose of business.

The focus of the paper will be principally upon the institution of business, but as will become clear, we cannot speak of business as an isolated institution, but one that is in relation to other institutions.

Business has become a significant institution in the last one hundred years with the rise of the modern corporation and the growth of production and consumption world-wide. Its nature and purpose has been debated and with the recent financial crisis, the intensity of this debate has increased. In his contribution on understanding this crisis, Benedict XVI explained that a fundamental problem of our economic system "is the ethical deficit in economic structures. It has been understood that ethics is not something 'outside' the economy, but 'inside', and that the economy does not function if it does not include the ethical element" (Benedict XVI 2009b). The failure to develop an internal ethic that connects business to the common good has contributed to the public's loss of confidence in it (Edelman Trust Barometer 2012). It is hard to trust an institution when its owners and leaders seek only their private interest motivated by economic incentives and limited by the law, and where virtue is replaced by technique and relationships are supplanted by contracts. And it is increasingly difficult to respect an academic institution, particularly its elite business and law schools, that assume the nature of business is a collection of individuals seeking their own utility and its purpose is shareholder wealth maximization (West 2011).

---

[1] See list of Pontifical documents at the beginning of this work with the corresponding abbreviation symbol and bibliographical references.

[2] For the past 15 years, I have written several essays attempting to articulate the relationship of the firm to the common good and more recently to the notion of a community of persons. This attempt follows similar expressions within the Catholic social tradition. In 1931, Pius XI began to evaluate the meaning of the corporation explicitly and Pius XII devoted several essays to this question in the 1940s and 1950s, particularly in light of Germany's codetermination laws. This discussion continued with John XXIII in his encyclical *Mater et magister* (1961). Recently, John Paul II has used the phrase "community of persons" when speaking about the modern corporation and Benedict XVI has spoken of the logic of gift in relation to economic exchange. I started writing on this topic with Sr. Helen Alford O.P. where we argued that the common good provides a distinctive view of the corporation that is substantively different than the shareholder and stakeholder models (Alford and Naughton 2001, Chap. 2, 2002). I have also written with Jean Yves Calvez S.J., where we distinguish between a "society of shares" and a "community of persons" and how that distinction has worked its way through the Catholic social tradition (Calvez and Naughton 2002). This research continued in another publication (Naughton 2006). More recently in the Père Marquette Lecture I gave in 2011, I develop in greater detail what we mean by a community of persons (Naughton 2012).

If business and business education is to overcome this trust gap and develop an "internal ethic," it must address a *"profoundly new way of understanding the business enterprise."* (CV 40, emphasis in the original). Laws, markets, contracts, and incentives, while necessary for business, are not sufficient to overcome this ethical deficit. Something far more robust and deeply human is needed to define the good business should do. This internal ethic or good of business must address what has been advocated by the "humanistic management approach" articulated by the authors of this book, namely that the *nature* of business is a "community of persons" and its *purpose* is the "common good" (Melé 2003, 2012). These two claims are the focus of this paper.

First, the paper lays out that the *nature* of business is premised on how we see the person (anthropology) and how persons are related to each other (institutions). This is a highly debatable issue, and I frame this debate along a continuum between an *association of individuals* on one end and a *community of persons* on the other. Understanding the anthropological and social orientation of institutional life allows us to see more clearly that business is on a course toward one of two poles: either business moves on a trajectory that sees itself as a "community of persons" rooted in a transcendent and familial orientation and premised on a logic of gift, or it sees itself as an "association of individuals" that is largely disconnected from home and religion and only has legal, market and technological resources to draw from. This frame is helpful since it both confronts the first principles of what we mean by business—is it made up of individuals or persons and is it an association or a community—assumptions that are rarely addressed in business literature. While there is significant debate over the purpose of business (maximizing shareholder wealth, stakeholder balance, common good), often the real debate is on what the nature of business as an institution is.

Second, it is precisely on an understanding of the nature of business that one can then understand its purpose. The purpose of business and institutions in general is predicated upon how one views the institutional goods that are particularly theirs and how these goods are related to each other. Institutions, in order to have legitimacy in society, order life in such a way that creates conditions for people to develop. This is not debatable. What is debatable is what do we mean by "development" and what conditions will lead to this development.

This paper is an argument that business in its nature is a community of persons with the common good as its purpose. This particular position is premised on a view of institutional life that assumes a "human ecology" (CV 51). Business cannot be understood as an autonomous entity, but it is in an embedded reality influenced by the larger culture. When business is grounded in communities of persons such as families, religion, and education, as well as a healthy and non-corrupt state, it is more prone to order its work toward the common good properly understood. Chuck Denny, former CEO of ADC Communications, in pointing out the sources of the ethical and social responsibilities of business states the following: "Recall that business executives were raised in your neighborhood, attended your schools, populate your churches and may have married your siblings. . . . This suggests to me that the reformation of the business community begins where we all were formed; namely, in our homes, our schools and the cultural organizations that touch our youth.

This is an issue of the embedded values that shape and govern our lives and that help steer us through uncharted and dangerous waters" (Denny 2005). While Denny's point is more personal in tone, we need to see that the nature and purpose of business ought to be informed by and connected to cultural institutions such as the family, religion, and education. If businesses have shut off the influence of the larger culture, especially familial and religious culture, it will create a vacuum that will be filled by the law and monetary incentives. To avoid this vacuum effect, business needs to draw upon sources that have the capacity to create conditions to humanize the relationships among people in a competitive economic environment. Business and business ethics have been hesitant for the most part to think that the family and religion are such sources, but this paper will argue that they are irreplaceable sources for a humanistic based management.

Nature of a Business: An Association of Individuals *or* a Community of Persons?

It is important to note that when we speak of the term "business," "corporation," or "firm" we need to keep in mind its wide ranging expressions. There are millions of businesses world-wide providing a rich plurality of incarnations: cooperatives, multinational corporations, employee owned businesses, family businesses, social businesses, partnerships, sole-proprietorships, joint ventures with government, profit/non-profit collaborations, and so forth. With these wide ranging expressions of business, however, is there a way of thinking about businesses that provides an explanation of its nature as an institution? I propose there are two defining directions, two poles of sorts with a wide variety of variations in between, that one can take to this question: either business is moving toward an *association of individuals* or toward a *community of persons*. I believe these two poles of business are more foundational and more helpful than the typical description one finds in business literature between the shareholder and stakeholder models, which for the most part are working from the same anthropological and institutional basis. The two opposing directions proposed in this paper help us to see more clearly that our understanding of business derives from two different anthropological visions that can be described with the distinction between *individual* and *person*, or individualism vs. personalism. This anthropological continuum results in institutional implications for business found in either an *association* or in a *community*. While each set of terms are often used interchangeably in ordinary language, understanding their distinctions can provide the intellectual scaffolding on which we can then see the deeper reasons for competing notions of what a business is and how we understand its purpose.

Anthropology: Individual and Person

Jacques Maritain distinguishes within the human being two poles that he describes as an *individual* and a *person* (Maritain 1947, Chap. III). He argues that we are *individuals* by the fact that we are individuated deriving from matter, making each individual different from other individuals. As individuals, we have different bodies, personalities, dispositions, wants, tastes, etc. We intend particular interests motivated by particular appetites to achieve particular ends. Without such individual action, life would come to a halt.

When the human being is seen as *only* an individual, life is described in "individualistic" categories such as self-interests, emotive preferences, private decisions, utility choice maximization and the protection of mutual individual autonomies. Within this individual worldview, human interaction is seen as a series of negotiations with other self-interested individuals and when win/win outcomes are achieve, self-interests are called enlightened. This highly individualistic vision of the world sees the free-floating individual as "the essential moral unit" of deliberation (Brooks 2011). And while the individual can never be fully liberated from all social constraints, the greater the freedom to act without restraints from the norms of religion, custom and even family, the greater the possibility that the individual will serve as the essential engine of creativity that paradoxically creates the ability for societies to progress. This view of the individual has influenced neoclassical economics, which has had a large influence on modern business theory and practice.

For Maritain, we are individuals, but not *only* individuals. We are also *persons* and the real paradox is found not in individualism but a personalism where the person "cannot fully find himself except through a sincere gift of himself" (GS 24). While it is true that all people have interests and desires, they are not simply static given facts, but realities that are in motion and must be ordered. This ordering brings either decline or progress, community or detachment. What makes our interests and desires *good* is how they are ordered and related to others and the Other, which is the basis of our growth into persons (Maritain 1947). We grow as persons not through our shouts of autonomy or our calculations of self-interests—such shouts and calculations over a life time only make us lonely. We grow as persons through our relations, our bonds of communion, in service to others. Emmanuel Mounier explains that "the person is only growing in so far as he is continually purifying himself from the individual within him" (Mounier 1952, 19). Whereas, the "individual" is always drawing things into him or herself, the "person" is always expanding the chain of solidarity with others. Whereas the individual sees only parts in reference to his or her particular interests, the person situates and orders his or her particular interests to the common good. What this distinction between individual and person points to is that while we can be rich alone, we can't be happy alone (see Bruni and Uelmen 2006).[3]

Institution: Association and Community

The claim here thus far is that anthropology is the basis of institutions. Depending upon how one principally understands the individual/person distinction will orient one's understanding of an institution as either an *association* or a *community*.[4]

Premised on an individualistic account of the human, the firm as an "association of individuals" is an aggregate or collection of individuals who are largely motivated through self-interests and bonded by contracts to achieve particular goals. Such entities see no common action but only individual discrete exchanges on mutually agreed upon goals. It is largely an impersonal association where relationships are thin and fleeting and where true fulfillment is found outside of institutions not through them (Heclo 2008). Because of the thinness of human relationships, business as an association of individuals will usually be focused on limited goals such as survival, security, and financial success. The highest good of an association is usually the alignment of interests through contracts and incentives among the various stakeholders.

These exchanges of the firm as an association of individuals are largely viewed in a binary mindset that takes only *economic* (market) and *legal* (state) categories seriously. Influenced by a larger culture of liberalism that sees only individuals, an association of individuals discounts cultural influences such as family and religion as

---

[3] Put another way the person *sublates* the individual. This sublation is where a higher system (the person) can integrate elements of a lower system (individual), but a lower system cannot integrate elements of the higher. The person integrates the elements of the individual, but the individual cannot integrate elements of the person. Bernard Lonergan describes this sublation as a process of development: "What sublates goes beyond what is sublated, introduces something new and distinct, yet so far from interfering with the sublated or destroying it, on the contrary needs it, includes it, preserves all its proper features and properties, and carries them forward to a fuller realization within a richer context" (Longeran 1972, 241). If I look at my work as simply a job, for example, to gain money, my world view eliminates the vision to see my work as a profession and its social purpose or even as a vocation as the end of my work. But, if I see my work as part of my profession or vocation, of a social good calling me toward virtue, I can see my work in terms of money, but not only money. I see money as a means ordered toward an end that makes good use of money.

[4] This institutional distinction has many variations to it. Ferdinand Tönnies (2007) distinguishes between a *society* (*Gesellschaft*) and a *community* (*Gemeinschaft*). Philip Selznick (1957) distinguishes between an organization and institution. Louis Putterman (1988) speaks of the firm as either a commodity or association. Yves Simon (1951) distinguishes between partnership and community. In this essay, I have decided to use the distinction between association and community. While no one set of terms seems quite satisfactory, corporations tend to reflect the nature of an association rather than a society, and because we are trying to describe the moral character of a corporation, the word community does this better than institution or association.

sources of insight and meaning (see Friedman 1982; Mill 2002). In terms of economic exchanges dominated by a shareholder approach of the firm, individual actions within corporations are seen as bargained-for, voluntary exchanges or transactions, not relationships. In the corporate world of a market-oriented association of individuals, the firm is simply a nexus of discrete human actions described as transactions or exchanges with costs and benefits associated with them. The most sophisticated account of these exchanges is found within a school of thought called "transaction cost theory" which painstakingly takes into account the information, search, negotiation and re-negotiation, contracting and enforcement costs of transactions (Jensen and Meckling 1976; Williamson 1975; Alchian and Demsetz 1972). The firm is the aggregate of these exchanges with the goal to maximize the economic value of the firm. Within this view of the firm, incentives dominate the landscape of how behavior is understood.

In terms of the legal exchanges dominated by a stakeholder approach of the firm, business as an "association of individuals" is viewed as simply a bundle of contracts or a social contract that best achieves "the sum-total of individual well-beings" (see Zamagni 2005; see also Alford et al. 2006). The enterprise is seen as a zero sum game since when goods are shared they are diminished. Thus, a business is a place where the principle of equivalence and balance dominates the landscape, where exchanges are defined in terms of a *quid pro quo* and where contracts not human relationships establish a measure of (or substitute for) trust.

While the view of the corporation as an "association of individuals" is not without its own insight in terms of people's motivations, how incentives can be structured, procedures and processes to check and balance power, etc., it is simply one philosophical model of the corporation and, as we argue below, a morally thin one. Too many people come to regard businesses as mere exchanges having no capacity to unite them in any meaningful way beyond their individual interests nor, they come to understand, should they expect otherwise. These exchanges generate the unsettling sense of one being used and in return one using others at work. These results in the financialization of the firm, where its value is reduced to its price, and thus relationships with the firm's various stakeholders, employees, customers, suppliers, are reduced to economic exchanges.

While business as an association of individuals describes part of its reality, it nonetheless crowds out important dimensions of the firm (Melé 2012). Incentives and contracts may make people better off, but by themselves, "they will not relieve their lonesomeness" (Simon 1951, 65). They are not rich enough by themselves to be "inserted into a structure of common action" that binds people together in a meaningful way (Zamagni 2005). Because people are social beings, they not only want to be individual "mes" but a collective "we," a community of persons (Kurtzman 2010). This is not only a point of principle, but it is a practical reality of every business leader. A business is an organization of people who get together to achieve something as a community and not merely as individual parts. Business leaders are often challenged by getting a collective group of individuals to be and act as a common entity, a community. This is why "common or shared purpose," that is, goods that are held in common with each other, is so often discussed in management literature (see Bartlett and Ghoshal 1994). Getting from a "me" to a "we" or from an association of individuals to a community of persons is critical to both the economic success of a business and its fundamental meaning. While people can be motivated by legal sanctions and economic incentives for a period of time, they tend not to be good long-term motivators. They exhaust the human spirit after a while, which leads to their disordering tendencies. Organizational theorists utilizing social capital theory, for example, explain that legal and economic categories can get people to act in their own interests, but they are not robust enough to explain why employees will sacrifice their interest in going beyond their contractual duty to achieve the good of the firm (Sorenson 2013). In other words, the understanding of the firm as an "association of individuals" is not rich enough to capture the full spectrum of behaviors within firms as well as to identify good companies from disordered ones.

Continuum Graph

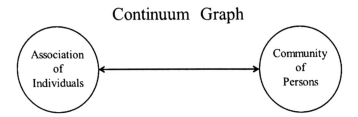

Just as the individual should grow into a person, an association of individuals should grow into a community of persons. This is why the continuum graph (above) is an important visual. Either firms by their actions, strategies, policies, practices are moving in a direction toward an association of individuals or toward a community of persons. Either the encounters they are having are exchanges motivated and ordered by contracts and incentives or they are relationships motivated and ordered by moral principles and virtues. Firms, like people, are always under construction. They are either growing or atrophying and often in the midst of the moment it is hard to tell, but over time the wise leader sees it.

Deeper Foundations to a Community of Persons

The Catholic social tradition has been one body of literature that has increasingly described the modern business corporation as a "community of persons." In 1991, John Paul II, in his Encyclical *Centesimus annus,* provided one of the most explicit definitions of business using the phrase "community of persons." He states that business cannot be "simply to make a profit, but is to be found in its very existence as a *community of persons* who in various ways are endeavoring to satisfy their basic needs, and who form a particular group at the service of the whole of society" (John Paul II, 1991, 35). While the phrase "community of persons" is not commonly used in business literature today, it actually gets to the root meaning of the words "company" (see Mintzberg 2009; Solomon 1994). The etymology of the word company derives from "companions," *cum*—with and *panis*—bread, breaking bread together (see PCJP 2012). This etymology clues us into a deeper meaning of the nature of business. The clue, however, directs us not to business itself but takes us deeper, to the place where we originally break bread together and where most people experience for the first time a community, namely in family and religion. When John Paul II states that business is "to be found in its very existence as a *community of persons*" (John Paul II, 1991, 35) he is pointing to the reality that there is something prior and primary to business that informs its nature and sense of community. Businesspeople are not born into a business but into a family. They are not baptized into a firm but a church. These institutions, family and religion, are "primary institutions" because they form the first and most meaningful relationships people should have—relationships with a mother, father, brother, sister, cousin, etc. They are primary because they define the principal place of our belonging and loyalty (Keating, unpublished). These institutions along with education form the first principles in one's life that ought to direct the activities of business. They "strengthen the social fabric, preventing society from becoming an anonymous and impersonal mass, as unfortunately often happens today" (CA 49).[5]

When family and religion are at their best, they do two very important things for business that an association of individuals cannot.[6] First, they limit economic activity.

---

[5] A distinction that both reveals and conceals these insights above come from the German sociologist, Ferdinand Tönnies, who popularized the distinction of a society or what I call above an association of individuals (*Gesellschaft*) and a community or what I call a community of persons (*Gemeinschaft*). He explains that communities form an "essential will" derived from blood relations, spatial relations and spiritual relations. Family, religion as well as small local towns are typically communities; whereas, societies or associations emerged by "will of choice" for common interests or to attain specific ends. Writing at the time of the industrialization and urbanization he saw the large corporation and the large city as societies unable to become communities (Tönnies 2007). What Tönnies' distinction reveals is that family and religions are at the heart of the realization of what a true community is. What it conceals, however, is that these communities have a social power to humanize and civilize business. For Tönnies, the modern corporation is largely unable to become a community of persons, and consequently is relegated to an "association of individuals" or what he would call a society, an impersonal artificial construct. Its very structure, he argued, prevented it from such a human form. Unlike Tönnies, however, the Catholic social tradition speaks about business as a "community of persons" that can have internal forms of solidarity so long as these forms are connected and informed by family and religion. The moral and spiritual center of community life is family and religion, which is why if business is not connected to this cultural center, it loses its identity by severing itself from the moral and spiritual resources that can make it a community of persons. As pointed out at the beginning of this paper, businesses are not monolithic institutions. They have the freedom to move in the direction of a community of persons, although a freedom that is challenged and constrained depending upon their structure, size, markets and regulatory environment.

[6] Of course not all families and religions are at their best. Actually disordered families and religions make for the most inhumane of businesses. They become cesspools of nepotism and cronyism. Religious zealots within business use their power to proselytize employees and suppliers disrespecting the fundamental right of religious liberty. These problems are of a higher order than what can be caused by an association of individuals.

Religion, especially the monotheistic religions of the West, does this through the Sabbath and other various religious practices and rituals. As Abraham Joshua Heschel puts it, the Sabbath tells us that production and consumption do not own or completely define us (Heschel 2000). Families also constrain economic activity when they are committed to the two fundamental goods of marriage, goods which have been influenced and supported by religion. The unity of the couple and its covenantal bonds takes time and commitment that cannot be violated by the demands of work, and the procreative good of children demands time for their formation and development.[7]

Second, family and religion order economic activity and inform it of its purpose by connecting business to the common good, which we will discuss in further detail in the next section. The family plays a foundational role in all institutions, since it is the first school of virtue where desires are matured, reason is formed, the will is shaped, and relationships are developed. This familial formation which serves as the fundamental cell of culture should influence business not to be another family but for business to be human places of production. Religion, when it has a mature social tradition, will speak of work and economic life not as a necessary evil, but as a vocation that fosters the growth of people. This is why true leadership "begins and finds its most important expression in the leadership of the primary institutions" (Keating, unpublished). They are the places where we see the inherent dignity of others, where we share goods in common, where we experience the importance of integral human development. And if we fail to see, share and experience such things in primary institutions, we will find it so much more difficult to develop such qualities in secondary institutions such as business.

This embedded relationship of business within family and religion is made more concrete by looking specifically at family and entrepreneurial firms. Family businesses in particular live at a crossroads of the economy and culture. In their study of family-run businesses, Aronoff and Ward provide a helpful distinction between

---

[7] The key insight here is that when the Catholic social tradition speaks about business as a "community of persons," the nature of this community does not come principally from the business itself, or from law or from markets. The notion of community must come from the larger culture and in particular family and religion. The foundation of community life is family and religion, which is why if business is not connected to this cultural center or worse violates it (corrupting goods and services, overworked careerists, etc.), it loses its identity by severing itself from the moral and spiritual resources that can make it a community of persons. It is also the reason why law and markets, while necessary to healthy businesses, are insufficient to fully explain the nature as well as purpose of business. This is not to say that a business is a family or a religion, nor is it to underestimate the important conditions of law and markets, but rather that its civilizing and humanizing character is dependent upon a familial and religious form. People who come from healthy familial structures and religious upbringing are more relational, more other focused and more giving. For example, social capital research shows that people committed to a faith tradition were more likely "to give money to charity, do volunteer work, help the homeless, donate blood, help a neighbor with housework, spend time with someone who was feeling depressed, offer a seat to a stranger or help someone find a job" (Sacks 2012). These relational contacts are formative for the kind of relationships people have in business with employees, customers, suppliers and investors. When relationships no longer have a familial or religious or spiritual form within business, instrumental rationality dominates, reducing relationships to utility and price.

functional versus fundamental values that helps us to see the relationship between culture and business (Aronoff and Ward 2001; Tapies and Ward 2008). They explain that non-family businesses often base themselves upon *functional* values such as profits, teamwork, innovation, creativity, industriousness, etc. These values are obviously important to running a business, but they don't touch the person in any profound fashion in relation to community, solidarity or the common good with the other, nor do they provide any kind of distinctive vision to the business itself. Family-run and entrepreneurial businesses are often informed by a richer understanding of principles that are more *fundamental* and that often connect to the deeper meaning of the person.[8] Families and entrepreneurs connect their existence as a business to their family. These values create stronger cultures since they often have "a more celebrated and preserved history" in which to draw upon to make sense of day-to-day practices and actions. Aronoff and Ward explain that "[f]amily firms emphasize collectivity more than individuality; family firms emphasize past and future orientation to time more than present orientation; family firms have a stronger belief in the 'natural goodness of man'" (Tapies and Ward 2008, 4). Their "familiness" create a deeper human reason for one's action, which is often the basis for a stronger organizational culture.

Many family businesses have drawn upon religious-based values as a guide to decision making. Companies such as Cadbury (Quaker), Kikkoman (Buddhist), Amway (Evangelical), Herman Miller (Calvinist), Service Master (Evangelical), Dayton Hudson (Presbyterian), Marriot (Mormon), Cummins Engine (Disciples of Christ), Reell Precision Manufacturing (Lutheran/Covenant), The Opus Group, C&A and Ouimet-Cordon Bleu Foods Inc. (Catholic) have referred to the influence of faith in their families and businesses (Murphy and Enderle 1995; Dana 2009; Cornwall and Naughton 2008; Naughton and Specht 2011). The founders and leaders of these companies were, and some still are, culturally embedded in a faith tradition. This familial and religious culture imbued them with a theological vision and moral orientation that informed their practical decisions. They saw their company not as an association of individuals, but as a community of persons, which humanized and civilized not only their own particular companies but the industries and communities in which they resided. This is not to say these are perfect companies without blemish. They are flawed, shortsighted and sinful like other companies, but what they have are correction mechanisms that allow them to transcend the company through the family's history and relationship to a belief system that can evaluate the behaviors of the company. This belief system usually entails a theology of creation that has a concept of sin that goes beyond the law and economic categories and a belief in forgiveness and the importance of reconciliation (see Naughton and Specht 2011).

---

[8]Various studies have indicated that family-owned businesses are more socially responsible than other kinds of business (see http://www.heraldextra.com/news/local/education/college/family-businesses-are-more-socially-responsible-study-shows/article_2aad6f26-4c0e-5daf-a5b0-189fe3a34f63.html). Accessed January 10, 2013.

While few of the companies described above may be fully conscious of their firms as a community of persons, the common good or their own religious tradition, they nonetheless are informed by a larger culture that played a significant role in how they viewed and structured their companies. They intuitively knew that the good of a corporation cannot be sustained through markets and law alone. Actually, they would be offended if some academic insinuated that their motives were only economic or legal. They are mindful of the constraints and opportunities of markets and laws, but as moral and faithful actors, they see that corporate life holds a high degree of discretion where moral and spiritual principles can operate. This is why for many of them, family and religion play a central forming role in the culture of the corporation.

Purpose of Business as the Common Good[9]

Assuming that business is a "community of persons," its *nature* arises out of the primary institutions of culture and in particular the family and religion. Thus, as a secondary institution, business' purpose is connected to the larger embedded culture from which it arises. The good that business does must be ordered by the principles and goods these primary institutions uphold. This is why business as a community of persons cannot describe its purpose in self-referential terms as found in the financial theory of the firm—maximization of shareholder wealth. Business is not simply about maximizing its own capital base. As a community of persons informed by familial and religious sources, its purpose should have an "integrative force" to connect the good of business as an institution to the good of the larger society and in particular to the primary institutions and the principles they hold (Sison and Fontrodona 2012, 239). Maximization of shareholder wealth is simply too weak of a force to connect the good of business to the good of society. In the Catholic social tradition, this integrative force is described in the principle of the common good, which reveals the paradoxical reality that if we fail to order our particular goods to a common life of desire and action our particular goods will lead to personal and institutional decline.

In Catholic social teaching, the common good has been described as "the sum total of social conditions which allow people, either as groups or as individuals, to reach their fulfillment more fully and more easily" (GS 1965, 26, see also MM, 65, PCJP 2005, 164). To unpack this description and to see its relevance for business, we need to focus on the two fundamental components of the common good: the *social conditions* that are usually necessary before persons can attain their proper

---

[9]The common good is different from what we call private or public goods. Private (or particular) goods are those things that are mine and not yours. Public goods are those things that are ours to use but not owned by anyone in particular, such as parks, roads, sidewalks, public beaches, clean air, etc. Both are very important to the common good, but they cannot capture what the common good means. The common good is attempting to explain the bonds of communion that comes about when my good is inextricably bonded to your good.

development of b...y About Business: Seeing Its Nature as a Community…

human fulfillment wh.

Michel 1987; Sison an...rson in relation to others, and the actual *attainment of* the common good (see gardener who nurtures the...lp us to get to the heart of the common good (see increases the seed's chances fo...a 2011). These two components are akin to a must grow (integral human devel...gh watering, tilling, and fertilizing, which business, family, school, or state can se... (social conditions), but it is the seed that it is the person who must make the choice ...ditions). In a similar way, institutions such as of institutions must see themselves as institut...lop for human development, but tions to foster the growth of people, but realizin...ders, in relation to others. Leaders people grow and develop. Understanding these two ..., those who create condi- importance of how business contributes to the common go...themselves cannot make move us to seeing the

Social Conditions: Three Institutional Goods of Business

What is behind the common good's description "the sum total of social conditions" is that it takes many institutions in good relationship with each other to foster the common good. One of the things we need to be clear about is that no one institution, including the state, can embody the fullness of the common good. We need a host of institutions, especially the family and religion, but also business, charities, educa- tion, health care, as well as the state. It does not take much to see that if a society does not have vibrant institutions the conditions for social living will suffer. Without a dynamic entrepreneurial economy, for example, societies stagnate. Countries, for example, "that do not have enough business activity tend to lose their best trained people to other countries because they cannot see a future for themselves or their families in their present situations" (PCJP 2012, 35). While business cannot create the "sum total of conditions," it is a necessary part of the totality.

A business, when it is operating well, creates three goods which positively con- tribute to the social conditions of society:

- *Good Goods*: making goods and services which are truly good and services which truly serve (Goodpaster 2011).
- *Good Work*: organizing work where employees develop their gifts and talents so as to serve the world, which in turn develops them.
- *Good Wealth*: creating sustainable wealth so that it can be distributed justly.

While each of these goods and their corresponding principles, policies and prac- tices deserve more description, the point is that these goods create the *conditions* for people to flourish in their connection to business (see PCJP 2012; see also Specht and Broholm 2009). When all three of these goods are present, business contributes positively to the social conditions that increase the probability that people will develop.[10]

---

[10] These three institutional goods map on to what Alasdair MacIntyre explains as three goods people want out of their work: "Most productive work is and cannot but be tedious, arduous, and fatiguing

Human Development

At the *heart* of the common good resides ..., or wealth, or policies, but the quality of relationships (the goods held ; on) established among people that brings forth the integral development ..e and of the whole person" (PCJP 2005, precisely defined as "the good of paradoxical reality that I cannot achieve my 165). The common good reveal your good in such a way that we develop community where each devel good except by ordering it to an integral way. This is why institutions are so important since they a places where these bonds of connection often take place. No human ins on, then, "can escape the issue of its own common good" if it is to foster th development of people (PCJP 2005, 165). Thomas Aquinas made this point er 700 years ago: "a man's will is not right in willing a particular good, unless ne refer it to the common as an end" (Aquinas 1947, I-II q. 19, a. 10, Reply). The common good is the principle that describes how we share goods in common that build up a business as a community of persons. Rather than seeing it as an extrinsic principle imposed upon business, we need to see the common good as it is understood in the Catholic social tradition—an intrinsic principle that describes the good that business does and how this good is related to the integral development of persons.

The common good helps us to understand that "social conditions" are necessary but insufficient to express the full good of what business does. Social conditions are necessary since it is simply more difficult to establish "communions" with others when, for example, poor products are made (violating good goods), jobs are designed bureaucratically and mindlessly (violating good work) or wages are sub-living (violating good wealth). Yet, social conditions must be ordered not only to one's self-interest but to a common life of goods shared among each other for the good of each in order to *participate* fully in the common good.

This is why one can have all three goods of business described above but still not develop in an integral way, which frustrates the fullness of the common good. William O'Brien, former CEO of Hanover Insurance, explained that even in workplaces where good products are produced, people are treated well by enlightened human resource practices, and wealth is created and distributed, people can still be disenchanted and "frustrated because their work lacks meaning for them" (O'Brien 2008, 104). Companies can have all the social conditions in place but still lack community and ultimately integral human development. Often this lack of meaning and development stems from the way these goods are ordered. A business leader can work toward balancing all the interests of its stakeholders and bring greater equality

---

much of the time. What makes it worthwhile to work and to work well is threefold: that the work that we do has a point and purpose, is productive of genuine goods [good goods]; that the work that we do is and is recognized to be *our* work, *our* contribution, in which we are given and take responsibility for doing it and for doing it well [good work]; and that we are rewarded for doing it in a way that enables us to achieve the goods of family and community [good wealth]" (MacIntyre 2011, 323).

in exchanges, but still fail to build community and develop as a leader. This stagnation can result from workplaces that are full of leaders and owners who are self-interested maximizers who instrumentalize relationships, entitled and careerist employees concerned only about their interests, and customers who reduce all relationships to a price. Shareholders, employees and customers can have all the rights in the world and still be wrong, especially when their particular interests are ordered only to their own particular gain.

O'Brien concludes that to move out of this place that lacks integral human development, we have to move to virtue, especially the virtue of love, since only love has the capacity to build an authentic community of persons. As a practitioner, O'Brien recognizes that one often chokes on the words of virtue and love in the corporate environment, but if we are concerned about integral human development, we cannot grow as persons within business without the virtues. As Benedict XVI put it, "[t]he more we strive to secure a common good corresponding to the real needs of our neighbours, the more effectively we love them" (CV 7). Thus, any description of the common good must entail an understanding of virtue and especially love.

In order for the three goods of business to contribute to the common good's task to integral human development, they have to be *rightly ordered* by businesspeople in a way that the goods are shared not only materially but also morally and spiritually, which is at the heart of virtue. This proper ordering of business' institutional goods entails two important realities, which reflect the nature of virtue: *properly ordered goods* and *relational goods*.

Properly Ordered Goods: First, as indicated above, there is not one good or so-called "bottom line" to business but rather all three of these goods are important to defining what we mean by a successful business. As a community of persons, business sees itself not as a uni-dimensional enterprise reduced to shareholder wealth maximization, but as a multi-dimensional one where a proper ordering of the multiple goods are shared in common with multiple stakeholders (Kennedy 2006). These three goods, however, are in constant tension with each other. Because of these tensions, they are prone to become disordered, which is why they demand virtuous leaders who can manage these tensions, especially in difficult times, and discern true from apparent goods. We need to recognize, nonetheless, that tensions within business and the challenges they generate are natural. Frank Schwinn, president of Schwinn Bikes in the 1950s, is supposedly said: "Being in trouble and being in business is the same thing. The day you're out of trouble is the day you're out of business." Tensions and the troubles they generate are unavoidable in business.

While tensions are natural within a business, they become fixations when businesspeople lose sight of the importance of one of the other two goods. The most common fixation within business centers over the *goods of wealth*. Without revenue, profits, efficient methods of operations, etc. businesses die. Yet, like a health crazed person who is obsessed with health and thus has lost sight of relationships with others, a business becomes disordered and even pathological if it lives only for profits. When the profit of a firm becomes its end and purpose, alienation gradually seeps in because there has been a "reversal of means and ends" (CA 41). Profit is a means, not an end, and when it becomes an end it denies over time authentic relationships among customers, employees, shareholders, and the larger community. Profit as an end is too small of a good to bind people together. While it makes for a good servant, it is a poor master. (PCJP 2012). The goods of wealth are in service to the kinds of goods and services it produces and the kinds of work it provides for its employees.

Good companies often make this ordering explicit in their founding documents such as mission, vision and value statements. Reell, a small global manufacturing company headquartered in St. Paul explains the character of profit as a means in their founders' welcoming message to new employees: "We do not define profits as the purpose of the company, but we do recognize that reasonable profitability is necessary to continue in business and to reach our full potential. We see profits in much the same way that you could view food in your personal life. You probably do not define food or eating as the purpose of your life, but recognize that it is essential to maintain your health and strength so you can realize your real purpose." Other companies such Johnson & Johnson does this in its Credo Statement pointing out that while shareholders deserve reasonable returns on their investments, these returns are in service to their customers, employees and the larger community.[11]

Relational Goods: Second, when these three goods are present and properly ordered to each other, they are more likely to have the capacity to create bonds of communion among those who participate in the business. The common good impels people to create social conditions, but in order for these conditions to attain human development, the goods that are shared in common must connect people with each other not only instrumentally but also morally and spiritually. This moral ordering does not negate their own instrumental benefits, but such benefits are not the last word. Instrumental goods tend to have an *arithmetic* quality about them.[12] When I can see my instrumental benefits are adding up in a situation, I see my situation positively, but at each point I am adding the credits and debits in terms of the sum total situation.

---

[11] Business is always prone to profit or shareholder fixation, but it is not the only fixation in business. For example, in a market economy one is constantly tempted to favor the customer over the employee, which is why consumerism is a serious problem in today's economy. In a world of consumerism, the highest good in the economy is the choice of the consumer, not the nature of the choice. Not only does such consumerism legitimize pornography, drugs, violent video games, tobacco, gambling, excessive alcohol consumption (so long as you have a sober driver), etc. but it also justifies and promotes all sorts of practices which place burdens on workers. For example, reverse auctioning, imposing excessive costs reductions, shifting all risks to suppliers, demanding work 24/7, etc. all of which exhaust employees for the benefit of consumers. Pius XI explained that "[i]t is a scandal when dead matter comes forth from the factory ennobled, while men there are corrupted and degraded." The grandeur of one's work should not only lead to improved products and services, but should also develop the worker. When NASA put a man on the moon, for example, the workload of its engineers, scientists and managers was so overwhelming for some that marriages were broken, children were alienated, and their health were compromised. One should not justify such conditions of work that would lead to familial disintegration. What does it matter that you gained the whole world or the moon at least, but lose your family, children, health and soul.

[12] The following insight comes from a conversation with Zamagni at a Uniapac event in Paris, France, December 7, 2012.

The common good, on the other hand, has a multiplying mentality. When people order things for the good of others (moral rationality), they bestow on one another "'communications' or signs aimed at producing 'communions'" (Simon 1951, 64). These communions are expressed through virtues that bond people together. They begin to establish relationships that are real communions and not merely contracts or mutually self-serving exchanges. These relationships generate trust, loyalty, patience, the ability to sacrifice, etc. that allow people to do greater things which each other. They create multiplying effects that are not easily measurable or predictable. When someone is treated with justice, for example, he or she is more prone to respond in justice, and when two people are treating each other justly they are creating relationships that foster a real community of persons. All the virtues work in a similar manner: love, loyalty, trust, patience, and so forth. These communions do not happen automatically; nor are they usually perfectly reciprocal, but they are the substance of good institutions (Boswell 1990).[13] Because we are social by nature, we cannot become good unless we share with others the goods we have that create such bonds of community. This sharing with others creates relationships, since when we see our particular goods are inextricably linked with the good of others, we order these goods not only for ourselves, but for the good of the other.

In business, these goods that are shared in common, these bonds of communion are the metaphorical threads that make up a strong chord to connect the various stakeholders—employee and employer, customer and producer, supplier and customer, etc. They make the difference between good and poor morale within a company. They are the basis of whether there is trust or not in a business relationship. And they create relationships that are not simply reducible to a price or wage, even though prices and wages are important realities in the relationship.

These relationships are not easily measurable so they get little play in business academic scholarship, since so many journals have made it their mantra "if it can't be measured, it does not exist." Yet, these bonds of connection, what Peter Maurin called "the art of human contacts," (Maurin 1984, 94) can be experientially found in practices that come naturally and free such as the warmth of a greeting, the concern for the other, the handshake of agreement, the time for the conversation, the sacrifice for the other, the lack of gossip. These bonds of communions are also fostered in policies and structures that promote the good of the other—just wages, layoffs as a last alternative, fair prices, common ownership, reasonable payment schedules, etc. As stated above, these policies and practices do not guarantee these bonds of communions, but when they are joined by people of virtue their combination are a powerful force of binding people together that leads to their integral human development.

---

[13] In Martin Buber's language, between the 'I' and the 'Thou' is a moral reality that cannot be exhausted in contracts or self-interests. It is the place where the social development of each of us takes place, where we begin to experience the deep profound truth of interdependence, not in a merely physical way or where we see 'others' as an instruments of utility, but an interdependence that sees the other as part of a community of work for the common good.

For example, can wages or compensation create a communion between employee and employer that foster the common good? When we think of a wage in light of the common good, we need to see it as a relationship and not simply as a monetary exchange. Managers will often describe wages as an instrumental activity that attracts, rewards, retains, and motivates employees who best achieve the instrumental goals of the company (increase productivity and efficiency, raise customer satisfaction and retention, maximize shareholder wealth). This instrumental value of pay, while important and necessary to any compensation system, can cloud and even crowd out the insight from the common good, namely that *work can never be reduced to the pay given, a price, that is, the wage given can never fully account for the labor done, precisely because work is always more than its economic output or instrumental value.* (Pieper 1963, Emphasis is our) While markets and contracts are important to a wage relationship, the common good tells us that there is *more* to be accounted for. If, for example, a market wage contractually agreed upon was a sub-living wage, a just wage would demand responsibilities of both the employee and employer to find effective and sustainable means to make it a living wage. Justice comes from the Latin *ius* which means "right," that is, the just person is in *right relation* to others, or in the words of Aquinas is "well disposed towards another" (Aquinas 1947, II-II q. 58, a. 12). It is simply difficult to have a "right relationship" when people are paid sub-living wages. Compensation, then, is no mere exchange, but an opportunity for employees and employers in corporate life to create a community of persons in the distribution of goods. When employees see employers concerned about their well-being by working toward a just wage, not only are the social conditions of a just wage established, but the relationship, the good shared in common between employer and employee, is strengthened. The common good is not only the wage itself, but the relationship that is generated between the employer and employee through the wage. Another way of putting this is to see that work as an aspect of human existence is "incompletely commodified" (Kaveny 2002, 111–27). While one's work is exchanged for money and can be commodified by the price given for it, work is at the same time a relationship that participates in the good of justice that is not diminished when shared. The relationship is not only how the pie is divided, but what kind of bonds of communion is created to foster a community of persons.

Conclusion

This paper has been an exercise to "think institutionally" about business in a way that promotes a humanistic philosophy for management informed by Christian Humanism and more specifically by the Catholic social tradition. The first claim is that to do this, we need to connect business to other cultural institutions such as the family, religion and education. This connection has an embedded relationship and highlights the underlying anthropological presuppositions that are held when people speak of business. At the heart of my argument is that business as a community of persons is embedded in a culture of communities, and that if the nature and purpose of business is to have a robust internal ethic that helps people to integrally develop, it needs to be embedded in the best of the cultural community that it comes out of. Without these deeper roots, business will increasingly find it difficult to integrate its self-understanding with the larger good of the culture.

Further research needs to be fostered to strengthen the nature and purpose of business and in particular connecting the community of persons to the common good. This type of work can more clearly expose and examine the underlying anthropological principles operating in peoples understanding of business. While such theoretical inquiries are helpful, what is more necessary are case studies and practices and policies, which explicate the relationship between action and principle. As John Paul II put it, "Today more than ever the Church is aware that her social message will gain credibility more immediately from the *witness of actions* than as a result of its internal logic and consistency" (John Paul II, 1991, 57). A business can only be an authentic community of persons when it *serves* those outside itself (good goods), which then serves as the basis for *developing* those within the business (good work) in a way that is financially sustainable (good wealth). But these realities have to be seen in the flesh and not only thought in the abstract.

References

Alchian, Arman A., and Harold Demsetz. 1972. Production, information costs, and economic organization. *American Economic Review* 62: 777–795.

Alford, Helen, and Michael Naughton. 2001. *Managing as if faith mattered: Christian social principles in the modern corporation*. Notre Dame: Notre Dame University Press.

Alford, Helen, and Michael Naughton. 2002. The common good and the purpose of business: A critique of the financial theory of the firm. In *Rethinking the purpose of business: Interdisciplinary essays from the Catholic social tradition*, ed. Steven A. Cortright and Michael Naughton, 27–47. Notre Dame: University of Notre Dame Press.

Alford, Helen, Barbara Sena, and Yuliya Shcherbinina. 2006. Philosophical underpinnings and basic concepts for a dialogue between CST and CSR, Position paper. http://www.stthomas.edu/cathstudies/cst/conferences/thegoodcompany/Papers/00POSITION.Paper.Fou.pdf. Accessed 8 Jan 2013.

Aquinas, Thomas. 1947. *Summa Theologica*. New York: Benziger Brothers.

Aronoff, Craig E., and John L. Ward. 2001. *Family business values*. Marietta: Family Enterprise Publishers.

Bartlett, Christopher, and Sumantra Ghoshal. 1994. Changing the role of top management: Beyond systems to people. *Harvard Business Review* 72: 79–88.

Benedict XVI. 2009a. Encyclical letter caritas in veritate. http://www.vatican.va/holy_father/benedict_xvi/encyclicals/documents/hf_ben-xvi_enc_20090629_caritas-in-veritate_en.html. Accessed 10 Jan 2013.

Benedict XVI. 2009b. Interview of the Holy Father Benedict XVI during the flight to Africa, Journey of the Holy Father Benedict XVI to Cameroon and Angola March 17–23, 2009. http://www.vatican.va/holy_father/benedict_xvi/speeches/2009/march/documents/hf_ben-xvi_spe_20090317_africa-interview_en.html. Accessed 10 Jan 2013.

Boswell, Jonathan. 1990. *Community and the economy*. New York: Routledge.

Brooks, David. 2011. If it feels right. *The New York Times*, September 12. http://www.nytimes.com/2011/09/13/opinion/if-it-feels-right.html. Accessed 21 Dec 2011.

Brooks, David. 2012. Why our Elites Stink. *The New York Times,* July 12. http://www.nytimes.com/2012/07/13/opinion/brooks-why-our-elites-stink.html?_r=0. Accessed 7 Jan 2013.

Bruni, Luigino, and Amy J. Uelmen. 2006. Religious values and corporate decision making: The economy of communion project. *Fordham Journal of Corporate and Financial Law* 11: 645–680.

Calvez, Jean-Yves, and Michael J. Naughton. 2002. Catholic social thinking and the purpose of the business organization: A developing tradition. In *Rethinking the purpose of business: Interdisciplinary essays from the Catholic social tradition,* ed. Steve A. Cortright and Michael Naughton, 3–19. Notre Dame: University of Notre Dame Press.

Cornwall, Jeffrey, and Michael J. Naughton. 2008. *Bringing your business to life.* Ventura: Regal.

Dana, Leo P. 2009. Religion as an explanatory variable for entrepreneurship. *Entrepreneurship and Innovation* 10: 87–99.

Denny, Charles. 2005. Better leadership begins at home. *Minneapolis Star Tribune,* January 2.

Edelman Trust Barometer. 2012. http://trust.edelman.com/. Accessed 12 Jan 2013.

Friedman, Milton. 1982. *Capitalism and freedom.* Chicago: University of Chicago Press.

Goodpaster, Kenneth E. 2011. Goods that are truly good and services that truly serve: Reflections on caritas in veritate. *Journal of Business Ethics* 100(S1): 9–16.

Heclo, Hugo. 2008. *On thinking institutionally.* Boulder: Paradigm Publishers.

Heschel, Abraham. 2000. The Sabbath. In *Working: Its meaning and its limits,* ed. Gilbert C. Meilaender, 261–267. Notre Dame: University of Notre Dame Press.

Jensen, Michael C., and William H. Meckling. 1976. Theory of the firm: Managerial behavior, agency costs and ownership structure. *Journal of Financial Economics* 3: 305–360.

John XXIII. 1961. Encyclical letter *Mater et magistra* http://www.vatican.va/holy_father/john_xxiii/encyclicals/documents/hf_j-xxiii_enc_15051961_mater_en.html. Accessed 17 June 2013.

John Paul II. 1991. Encyclical letter *Centesimus annus.* http://www.vatican.va/holy_father/john_paul_ii/encyclicals/documents/hf_jp-ii_enc_01051991_centesimus-annus_en.html. Accessed 17 June 2013.

Kaveny, Cathleen. 2002. Living the fullness of ordinary time: A theological critique of the instrumentalization of time in professional life. In *Work as key to the social question.* Vatican City: Libreria Editrice Vaticana.

Keating, Michael. The nature and purpose of institutions. (unpublished)

Kennedy, Robert. 2006. *The good that business does.* Grand Rapids: Acton Institute.

Kurtzman, Joel. 2010. Common purpose: Getting from me to we. DVS from *Standford Executive Briefings.* http://www.kantola.com/Joel-Kurtzman-PDPD-366-S.aspx. Accessed 7 Jan 2013.

Lonergan, Bernard. 1972. *Method in theology.* New York: Herder and Herder.

MacIntyre, Alasdair. 2011. How Aristotelianism can become revolutionary: Ethics, resistance and Utopia. In *Virtue and politics,* ed. Blackledge Paul and Knigh Kelvin. Notre Dame: University of Notre Dame Press.

Maritain, Jacques. 1947. *The person and the common good.* New York: Charles Scribner and Sons.

Maurin, Peter. 1984. *Easy essays.* Chicago: Franciscan Herald Press.

Melé, Domènec. 2003. The challenge of humanistic management. *Journal of Business Ethics* 44(1): 77–89.

Melé, Domènec. 2012. The firm as a "Community of Persons": A pillar of humanistic business ethos. *Journal of Business Ethics* 106(1): 89–101.

Michel, Virgil. 1987. *The Social question.* St. Cloud: Parker Printing Company.

Mill, John S. 2002. *On liberty.* New York: Dover Publications.

Mintzberg, Henry. 2009. Rebuilding companies as communities. *Harvard Business Review* 87(4): 1–5.

Mounier, Emmanuel. 1952. *Personalism.* Notre Dame: University of Notre Dame Press.

Murphy, Patrick E. and Georges Enderle. 1995. Managerial ethical leadership: Examples do matter. *Business Ethics Quarterly* 5:115–126.

Naughton, Michael J. 2006. The corporation as a community of work: Understanding the firm within the catholic social tradition. *Ave Maria Law Review* 4: 33–75. http://www.stthomas.edu/cathstudies/cst/Naughtonarticles/AveMaria2006.pdf. Accessed 17 June 2013.

Naughton, Michael J. 2012. *The logic of gift: Rethinking business as a community of persons (The Père Marquette Lecture in Theology)*. Milwaukee: Marquette University Press.

Naughton, Michael J., and David Specht. 2011. *Leading wisely in difficult times: Three cases of faith and business*. New York: Paulist Press.

O'Brien, William J. 2008. *Character at work*. New York: Paulist Press.

Pieper, Josef. 1963. *Leisure, The basis of culture*. New York: Random House.

Pontifical Council for Justice and Peace (PCJP). 2005. *Compendium of the social doctrine of the Church*. Washington, DC: USCCB Communications.

Pontifical Council for Justice and Peace (PCJP). 2012. Vocation of the Business Leader: A Reflection. http://www.stthomas.edu/cathstudies/cst/VocationBusinessLead/VocationTurksonRemar/VocationBk3rdEdition.pdf. Accessed 10 Jan 2012.

Putterman, Louis. 1988. The firm as association versus the firm as commodity. *Economics and Philosophy* 4: 243–266.

Sacks, Jonathan. 2012. The moral animal. *New York Times*, December 23.

Selznick, Philip. 1957. *Leadership in administration*. New York: Harper & Row.

Simon, Yves R. 1951. *Philosophy of democratic government*. Chicago: The University of Chicago Press.

Sison, Alejo J.G., and Joan Fontrodona. 2011. The common good of business. Addressing a challenge posed by *Caritas in Veritate*. *Journal of Business Ethics* 100: 99–107.

Sison, Alejo J.G., and Joan Fontrodona. 2012. The common good of the firm in the Aristotelian-Thomistic tradition. *Business Ethics Quarterly* 22(2): 211–246.

Solomon, Robert. 1994. The corporation as community: A reply to Ed Hartman. *Business Ethics Quarterly* 4: 276ff.

Sorenson, R.L. 2013. How moral and social values become embedded in family firms. *Journal of Management, Spirituality, and Religions* 10(2): 116–137.

Specht, David, and Richard Broholm. 2009. Three-fold model of organizational life. http://www.seeingthingswhole.org/uploads/Watermark-Three-Fold-Individual_439175.pdf. Accessed 10 Jan 2013.

Tapies, Josep, and John L. Ward (eds.). 2008. *Family values and value creation: The fostering of enduring values within family-owned businesses*. New York: Palgrave Macmillan.

Tönnies, Ferdinand. 2007. *Community and society*. New Brunswick: Transaction Publishers.

West, Darrell. 2011. *The purpose of the corporation in business and law school curricula*. Washington, DC: Brookings Institute.

Williamson, Oliver E. 1975. *Markets and hierarchies: Analysis and antitrust implications*. New York: The Free Press.

Zamagni, Stefano. 2005. What CST can contribute to CSR. http://www.stthomas.edu/cathstudies/cst/conferences/thegoodcompany/Finalpapers/Zamagni%2005.10.06%2011..pdf. Accessed 19 Dec 2011.

Chapter 12
Why Is a Catholic Manager Different?

Antonio Argandoña

Abstract A Catholic is a person who, beyond any way of life or moral or spiritual practices, follows Christ in accordance with the teaching of the Catholic Church. Catholic theology shows how this influences the life of the Christian. Even in today's secularized society, the Christian is seen as a person with a distinctive view of life and goals. Yet when we see the Christian, and more specifically the Catholic, as an entrepreneur or manager – i.e., engaged in the task of creating and managing companies – his outward activity seems no different from that of other, non-Christian entrepreneurs. The purpose of this chapter is to understand what makes the Catholic who works as an entrepreneur different, in order to try to answer the questions we may ask ourselves about the advantages and disadvantages of being a Catholic. We argue that religion provides to managers a wider view of business and helps them to understand reasons for ethical behavior. At the same time, it gives him or her spiritual and ascetical means for good behavior.

Keywords Business • Catholic • Christian • Company • Entrepreneur • Firm • Manager • Work

Given its role in satisfying consumers' needs, creating value for those who take part in it, ensuring that scarce resources are used efficiently, promoting innovation, developing nations, fostering social cohesion and furthering the common good, the business firm is a very important institution. At the same time, it is subject to criticism, including in Christian circles, even to the point where business culture is condemned as "a realm of evil and idolatry, a realm that must be destroyed, rather than changed") (van Wensveen Siker 1989, 884).

An institution such as the firm cannot be indifferent to religion, especially not to the Christian religion. In fact, the Catholic Church has a great appreciation for the persons and tasks of businesspeople. "In the Gospel, Jesus tells us: 'From everyone who has been given much, much will be demanded; and from the one who has been

A. Argandoña (✉)
IESE Business School, University of Navarra, Barcelona, Spain
e-mail: argandona@iese.edu

© Springer Science+Business Media Dordrecht 2015   201
D. Melé, M. Schlag (eds.), *Humanism in Economics and Business*,
Issues in Business Ethics 43, DOI 10.1007/978-94-017-9704-7_12

entrusted with much, much more will be asked' (Lk 12:48). Businesspeople have been given great resources and the Lord asks them to do great things" (Pontifical Council for Justice and Peace – PCJP 2011, no. 1). What concerns us here is to consider how Catholicism today views the person who promotes or manages a private firm in a capitalist economy. In this chapter we aim to help find answers to questions such as: Is there such a thing as a "Catholic entrepreneur" or manager? Is, or should be, a Catholic entrepreneur different in any way from other entrepreneurs? What do religious convictions add to the task of the entrepreneur? Do they make an entrepreneur "better" in any way?

As the rest of this book, the present chapter is addressed to a wide audience. First and foremost, to help Catholic entrepreneurs and managers reflect on how their faith may help them in their work (PCJP 2011, no. 5). In other words, it is written for the convinced. Even so, it may also be very useful for non-Christians and for scholars of economics, management, business ethics and related matters, to whom it may offer ideas in two directions. First, is the Catholic manager at a disadvantage to the manager who is not a Catholic? And second, can the Christian view of the manager's task help us understand what constitutes a management that is both efficient and respectful of human values?

It is not my intention to carry out a sociological study of who the Catholic entrepreneur is or how he acts, nor an analysis of the situation facing Christian businesspeople in society today. Indeed, the image of Catholics reflected in these pages may seem far removed from that of the flesh-and-blood men and women, with all their accomplishments and mistakes, who labor to take their companies forward. And yet I have not attempted to depict the "ideal type" (Weber 1949) of the Catholic manager, because in the Catholic religion the distance between the ideal and the reality is not a major problem, as Catholicism starts from the fact that man[1] is a fallen creature, but also from the certainty that he is called to perfection, that he has the means to achieve it and that if he really wants to he will achieve it, though not in this life. Christianity, in accordance with Catholic faith, is an optimistic and, at the same time, realistic religion because the distance between what "ought to be" and what "is" can always be overcome – with the help of God.

In what follows I shall try to explain, first, what distinguishes a Catholic; second, how this differentiating factor is projected in the task of the entrepreneur or manager through work; and lastly, in what sense it is true to say that the Catholic manager is "different", or acts or should act "differently", from the non-Catholic businessperson, ending with the conclusions.

Before we continue, there are four points I must make clear. First, I use the terms "company" and "firm" as synonymous with any activity aimed at the production of goods or services to satisfy needs, using an organizational form that tends to be privately owned and for profit, but without excluding other institutions (third sector, community purpose, etc.) or other forms of organization or management (nonprofits, cooperatives, NGOs, state-owned enterprises, etc.), because there are certain

---

[1] In this paper I use the word "man" to mean man and woman, as it appears in many documents of the Catholic Church, without giving it any sexist meaning.

common features in the management of all these activities, at least insofar as they all must be managed so as to achieve economic efficiency – though not only economic efficiency.

Second, I take the terms "entrepreneur", "manager" and "businessperson" as equivalents. Obviously, they are not,[2] but the main concern here is the person whose job is to create or manage business activities.

Third, I identify "Christian" with "Catholic". This does not imply a lesser respect for other Christian confessions; it is simply a way of limiting the scope of the discussion, although some of my statements naturally also apply to other confessions.[3]

Lastly, I back my arguments up with quotations from the official documents of the Catholic Church. I realize that there may be private interpretations of theologians, philosophers or economists and I will draw on them occasionally; but it is not my intention to analyze differing views on the subject at hand. Again, this does not imply a lesser respect for these private views.[4] Furthermore, I have retained the actual terms used in the documents I have consulted, without attempting to "translate" a language which for many people nowadays is difficult to understand.[5]

The Christian

The *Catechism of the Catholic Church* (CCC)[6] contains no precise definition of what it means to be a Christian. In any case, the "identity" of the Christian cannot be defined as unique. In other words, there is no single list of characteristics that define unequivocally what being a Christian consists of: as a creature created in the image and likeness of God, who is infinitely wise, full of perfections and omnipotent, each person will partially reflect these perfections to a greater or lesser degree.

---

[2] For an approximation to the Christian view of the entrepreneur, see Alford and Naughton (2001), Cornwall and Naughton (2003), Cortright and Naughton (2002), Novak (1981). On business as a vocation, see Chamberlain (2004), Clark (2004), Garvey (2004), Novak (1996), PCJP (2011), and Sirico (2000).

[3] In particular, I do not discuss Weber's (1992) argument about Calvinist ethics and the vocation of the entrepreneur, nor the question of whether the task of the entrepreneur is a "vocation".

[4] As the reader will verify, in many aspects of my interpretation of what distinguishes the Christian, especially as regards the theology of work, I am indebted to Saint Josemaría Escrivá, although I must emphasize that my statements on these matters are not to be attributed to him. In Argandoña (2004b, 2011) I discuss some of his ideas about work and the education of the manager.

[5] It is possible that this work should have engaged in dialogue with some of the sociological, political, ideological and moral trends prevailing in today's society, such as individualism, hedonism, relativism or materialism, as these currents influence the interpretation of what it is to be a Christian today, what is good or evil, or how a person should behave. I have not tried to do this, as it would have diverted me from my main concern. Yet their influence is not to be underestimated.

[6] This and other abbreviations of official documents of the Catholic Church used in this chapter are listed at the beginning of the book.

There are many ways of being a Christian, although they all have some traits in common (Orlandis 1998).

We shall assume that the traits of the Christian man are known:

- he is a created being (i.e., he does not give himself his ultimate end, but finds it); he is a unity of body and soul;
- he therefore has a spiritual side (with rationality – not only instrumental but also directive rationality – and will);
- he has a (limited, but real) capacity to seek and find the truth and do good; he is endowed with conscience (i.e., he does not give himself the moral rules);
- he is free (with a freedom oriented to an end); historical (i.e., he becomes over time);
- relational ("unless he relates himself to others he can neither live nor develop his potential", GS 12);
- open to transcendence;
- capable of perfection;
- endowed with dignity (which is inherent, not given or earned);
- called to an eternal life;
- wounded by sin ("he often does what he would not, and fails to do what he would", GS 10); and
- "[h]e can transcend his immediate interest and still remain bound to it" (CA 25), and so on.

Insofar as this list is more realistic than, say, that of *homo oeconomicus*, it may help to understand whether the Christian view of man has anything to add to that of neoclassical economics, for example (Argandoña 2012).

To start with, we can say that a Christian is a person who "knows" something about God, namely that God exists, that he (God) created the world and that he created him, that he (God) has his own plans for the world, for humankind and for each person, and that he does not wash his hands of these realities. This knowledge of God is based on reason (CCC 36) and, above all, on faith, which is "a gift of God" (CCC 153), but also "an authentically human act [so that] trusting in God and cleaving to the truths he has revealed is contrary neither to human freedom nor to human reason" (CCC 154).

This faith in God leads to "a personal adherence of man to God" (CCC 150); adherence to a Person, not to an idea; only afterwards does there appear a "free assent to the whole truth that God has revealed" (CCC 150), to a creed. The Christian counts on the action of God because natural means, including human capabilities and limitations, are important but not decisive. And if God intervenes in the life of men, the dichotomies between good and evil, matter and spirit, etc., are not decisive: Good is always more fertile than evil, it "overflows" (Polo 1996a).

How can man adhere to God if "[n]o one has ever seen God" (Jn 1:18)? Because God has taken the initiative: "In times past, God spoke in partial and various ways to our ancestors through the prophets; in these last days, he spoke to us through a son" (Heb 1:1–2). "For a Christian, believing in God cannot be separated from believing in the One he sent (…). We can believe in Jesus Christ because He is himself God, the Word made flesh" (CCC 151). "Belief in the true incarnation of the Son of God is the distinctive sign of Christian faith" (CCC 463).[7]

A Christian is therefore a person who "has encountered" Jesus or, rather, who "encounters Jesus every day". "Being Christian is not the result of an ethical choice or a lofty idea, but the encounter with an event, a person, which gives life a new horizon and a decisive direction" (DCE 1). It is not, of course, a physical encounter, but nor is it an imagination or a dream. The Christian encounters Christ when he understands, through faith that God exists and that he (God) is present in the life of the Christian and acts in him. And "Christ (…) fully reveals man to man himself and makes his supreme calling clear." (GS 22) That is to say, when the Christian "encounters" Christ, he comes to know things about himself that go beyond the natural knowledge he has of what is human; for example, that he has been created "in the image and likeness" of God (Gen 1:26), i.e., that there is something divine in him; therefore, that he "is capable of self-knowledge, of self-possession and of freely giving himself and entering into communion with other persons" (CCC 357); and that he has been created by love, because he is "the only creature on earth which God willed for itself" (GS 24).

In this way he discovers that he is "called to share, by knowledge and love, in God's own life" (CCC 356). At the same time as he lives his life like other men, the Christian "reproduces" the life of Christ; his works are now, in some way, works of Christ (this takes place through grace, which "is a participation in the life of God": CCC 1997). The Christian thus becomes the adoptive son of God; he experiences an "invasion" of God in his life (Polo 1996a). This does not mean that he is capable of doing superhuman things, such as walking on water or predicting the future, but that his existence is not limited to its own order of perfection. In other words, the Christian is not limited to living his own life, but also lives the life of God, who is acting in all that he does.

This "invasion" of God respects man's freedom, for "God has willed that man remain 'under the control of his own decisions' (Sir 15:14), so that he can seek his Creator spontaneously" (GS 17). Accordingly, "God's free initiative demands man's free response" (CCC 2002). The Christian must therefore strive to live in a way that is consistent with the life of Christ, who now lives and acts in him. Accordingly, there are certain behaviors that are incompatible with being a son of God, because they entail a rejection of the possibility of living the life of Christ: that is sin.

Being a Christian thus implies following a certain ethics – a set of rules or commandments – and living certain virtues. But that is not enough to define the Christian, because many non-Christians do the same. Being a Christian is not mainly a way of

---

[7]And "one cannot believe in Jesus Christ without having a part in his Spirit. It is the Holy Spirit that reveals to men who Jesus is" (CCC 152). Faith in the Trinity of God is a central point of Christianity. In fact, the relationship of the Christian with God starts in Baptism "in the name of the Father, and of the Son and of the Holy Spirit" (CCC 1272).

life. "The first calling of the Christian is to follow Jesus" (CCC 2253) and to behave like a son of God.[8] And that is achieved through love. Once again, the initiative comes from God, who "first loved us" (1 Jn 4:19) and who, in loving man, "also calls him to love, the fundamental and innate vocation of every human being" (CCC 1604). There are two dimensions to this; namely, "You shall love the Lord, your God", and "You shall love your neighbor as yourself" (Mt 22: 37–40). That is why Christ makes love the sign of the Christian: "This is how all will know that you are my disciples, if you have love for one another" (Jn 13: 35). A Christian, therefore, is a person who loves God and others.

Love is not a vague feeling; it is recognized in works. But love is also "an extraordinary force which leads people to opt for courageous and generous engagement in the field of justice and peace (...) a force that has its origin in God" (CV 1). The experience of the encounter with Christ contributes not only inspiration but also capacities for action, provided by the sacraments and the others means available to Christians.

A Christian's encounter with Christ is not an intellectual encounter or the result of study, personal reflection or an inner illumination. Man is a social being who receives life through other people, learns from other people and develops with other people. Christian faith and practice come to him in the same way, i.e., through belonging to the Church. "No one can believe alone, just as no one can live alone. You have not given yourself faith as you have not given yourself life" (CCC 166). "It is in the Church (...) that the Christian fulfills his vocation. From the Church he receives the Word of God containing the teachings of 'the law of Christ' (Ga 6:2)" (CCC 2030). From the Church he receives the grace of the sacraments that sustain him in the 'way'. From the Church he learns the example of holiness" (CCC 2030). Christianity is learned, developed and made concrete in a community of persons, which is not a mere human organization, because Christ dwells in his Church, thus making it possible for men of all ages to encounter him.

This encounter with Christ in order to take part in his life clearly allows degrees. But the goal is excellence, or holiness: "[A]ll the faithful of Christ, of whatever rank or status, are called to the fullness of the Christian life and to the perfection of charity" (LG 40).

All the above is a necessarily partial and very poor explanation of what it is to be a Christian. Now we must apply it to the task of the manager. To do that we need an intermediate step, which we find in work.

---

[8] From the above it is not to be concluded that the practice of the Christian life is unimportant. On the contrary, the virtues and the practices of piety are the Christian's way of encountering Christ, of recognizing him and advancing in the identification with Christ. The important thing, though, is not the practices but the intention – the love – with which they are carried out.

The Christian Who Works

"[W]ork is a fundamental dimension of man's existence on earth" (LE 4). Man, "as the 'image of God' (...) is a person, that is to say, a subjective being capable of acting in a planned and rational way, capable of deciding about himself, and with a tendency to self-realization. As a person, man is therefore the subject of work" (LE 6). We saw earlier that God has plans for man, whom he calls to a filial relationship with him. And those plans include work. As we read in the first biblical stories of creation, God took man "and settled him in the Garden of Eden [the world], to cultivate and care for it" (Gen 2:15), i.e., to work.

Through work man achieves external results that are necessary for his life and development: work produces goods to satisfy needs, develops nature, giving rise to technology (LE 5), and so on. It also brings about internal results – knowledge, capabilities and values that the agent acquires and that perfect him – because "the primordial value of labor stems from man himself, its author and its beneficiary" (CCC 2428). Lastly, there are other results, which are projected onto other men: the satisfaction of other people's needs, contributions to the well-being of society, the development of other people's knowledge and capabilities, and so on. Work is thus something "positive and creative, educational and meritorious" (LE 11). This can be applied to all workers, however, not just Christian workers[9]: the right and duty to work and so to achieve human survival and perfection is demanded of every man.

The Christian, however, knows by faith that God has put him in the world to dominate it (Gen 2:15). Here man receives from God, through his ancestors, the gift of the world (LE 12) and, with it, "a mandate to subject to himself the earth" (GS 34), which constitutes the core of his vocation, which he exercises through work. In work, also, there occurs that encounter of man with Christ, who came to the world to redeem it, also through work. Thus, "[b]y enduring the toil of work in union with Christ (...), man in a way collaborates with the Son of God for the redemption of humanity" (LE 27). "Work, all work, bears witness to the dignity of man, to his dominion over creation. It is an opportunity to develop one's personality. It is a bond of union with others, the way to support one's family, a means of aiding in the improvement of the society in which we live and in the progress of all humanity. For a Christian these horizons extend and grow wider. For work is a participation in the creative work of God. When he created man and blessed him, he said: 'Be fruitful, multiply, fill the earth, and conquer it. Be masters of the fish of the sea, the birds of heaven and all living animals on the earth' (Gen 1:28). And, moreover, since Christ took it into his hands, work has become for us a redeemed and redemptive reality. Not only is it the background of man's life, it is a means and path of holiness. It is something to be sanctified and something which sanctifies" (Escrivá de Balaguer 1974, no. 47).

---

[9]There are also negative views of work – as the cause of alienation, for example, or as a punishment or curse, etc. However, these views do not belong to the core of the Christian tradition, at least not without proper qualification.

The Christian, like other men and women, makes his decisions regarding the scope and content of his work based on his preferences, capabilities, history and environment. All these situations are, in principle, good, because "God saw that [the world] was good" (Gen 1:10, 12, 18, 21, 25, 31). Clearly, this is not to say that everything in this world is good; the important thing is that evil is not what defines the world. Obviously, like any other honest person, the Christian will exclude activities and decisions that are immoral, i.e., that may degrade him as a person.[10] That is not something specifically Christian, either, because there is no reason why moral criteria should be any different for a Christian.[11] Moreover, there are no reasons why a Christian should not know and do everything that other people know and do. The fact that work is done in a Christian way does not guarantee nor hinder human success. Needless to say, he cannot use immoral means: that is not a restriction, however, but strength, assuming the aim is not to achieve an external result at any cost but to achieve also the integral human development of the person and the good of others.[12]

The Christian will have also the same motivations as the non-Christian, including the pursuit of an income, the satisfaction of doing a job well or of acquiring new knowledge and capabilities; and both may act seeking the good of others – doing their best, for example, to provide a good service to a customer or to help a colleague perform a task. But if work also has a (religious) significance, this gives the Christian additional motives to do it, because "men are not deterred by the Christian message from building up the world, or impelled to neglect the welfare of their fellows, but (...) they are rather more stringently bound to do these very things" (GS 34). "We would therefore be on the wrong path if we were to disregard temporal affairs, for Our Lord awaits us there as well. (...) But we shall not attain our goal if we do not strive to finish our work well; if we do not sustain the effort we put in when we began our work with human and supernatural zeal; if we do not carry out our work as well as the best do and, if possible, (...) better than the best, because we will use all the honest human means as well as the supernatural ones which are required in order to offer Our Lord a perfect job of work, finished like filigree and pleasing in every way" (Escrivá de Balaguer 1981, no. 63).

Yet there is more. Although the Christian has no advantage when it comes to natural knowledge, he knows "something more" from the Christian Revelation (faith). The world is the work of God, there is an eschatological reality beyond this world, and God acts on Earth through the work of his children: reality is "something more" than what a person who does not have faith is capable of seeing. "The Kingdom of God, being in the world without being of the world, throws light on the order of human society, while the power of grace penetrates that order and gives it

---

[10] "The moral rule tells us not only 'don't do this because it is bad', but also 'don't do what is bad because doing it makes you bad'" (Polo 1996b, 87).

[11] This obviously cannot be said of all ethical conceptions. The relevant point here, though, is that applying moral criteria to work-related decisions is not something that is distinctive of Christianity.

[12] And to believe that the Christian must devote a large part of his time to spiritual activities or part of his income to charitable activities is simply a false conception of what it is to be Christian.

life" (CA 25). That is to say, the Christian cannot use that enlightenment to make better technical decisions, but he can use it to make better moral decisions. Let's see how that is possible.

If they share the same natural anthropology, a Christian and a non-Christian may have the same knowledge of what is good for man. Therefore, the list of moral "duties" prepared by each may be the same, because "both for the Christian and for the non-believer the same standards of human perfection apply, because both have the *same* human nature and live in the *same* world and the same society" (Rhonheimer 1987, 923; emphasis in the original). But that is true only for a list of abstract moral "duties". In practice, the moral agent must consider these moral rules not only as theoretical knowledge but as "factually *possible* contents" (Rhonheimer 1987, 925; emphasis in the original), derived from "experiences and judgments about the possibilities of realizing" what is good (Rhonheimer 1987, 926). If the agent considers those duties to be not possible for him, they will cease to be duties.

The Christian and the non-Christian will therefore formulate different judgments about the practical possibility of performing those duties, because "the believer must possess a knowledge of what is human different from that of the non-believer" (Rhonheimer 1987, 929). Indeed, the Christian knows, through faith, things that the non-believer cannot know by natural means, such as original sin and inherited guilt (which go beyond the practical experience we may all have of the failings of humanity) and the redemption wrought by Christ. "With respect to what is human, 'salvation' means liberation from the – evident – human incapacity to fully meet the demands of what is human (…). Yet Christian revelation also teaches us that the will of God consists of ordering and integrating human perfection in divine perfection, or holiness (…) and that, therefore, there is no human perfection *outside* that perfection that is more than human, in accordance with the salvific divine will, which can *only* be known through revelation. [Revelation] also teaches us that to receive salvation and so achieve *human* perfection, there must be personal conversion, the mercy of God and His forgiveness, as well as saving grace. It teaches us something that is not at all obvious, namely, that suffering injustice, hunger, poverty, persecution and humiliation is not opposed to true human realization or 'happiness' (…) It reveals to us the meaning and dignity of suffering and ultimately makes us the promise that the last and definitive intervention of God in history will renew and perfect the face of the earth" (Rhonheimer 1987, 929–930; emphasis in the original).

The non-believer cannot know all this, so that "the moral demands in the sphere of what is human, accessible to every man, in many cases exceed the moral capacity of man in his fallen state and in need of redemption" (Rhonheimer 1987, 931). As Rhonheimer (2001) explains, doing good often has negative consequences, which may lead to the conclusion that a morality "of the possible" is more human. An example would be when the "evils" of an unwanted pregnancy or of a failed marriage are weighed against the "goods" of unconditional respect for life or fidelity in marriage. In such cases, faced with the rift between what "must" be done and what "can" be done without suffering those undesirable consequences, a non-Christian morality may end up identifying what "must be done" with "the best that can be done". The root of the problem lays not so much in the identification of what is good for man, but in the practical judgment about whether that good can be realized. And here the difference between the point of view of the Christian and that of the non-Christian will be decisive, because the practical judgment of the Christian, who has grace, will be different.

The conclusions to be drawn from this are, it seems to me, very relevant to the subject of this chapter. "The credibility, clarity and appeal of the Christian message [are founded] not on the demonstration of new or higher motivations for knowable and realizable moral demands for all men but on showing a path to overcome the divide, which is painful to any man of good will, between his (rational and autonomous) moral knowledge of the good and duty and his moral capacity" (Rhonheimer 1987, 932). "A non-Christian *ethos* will reduce what is Christianly obligatory to what is humanly possible and so will only incompletely detect the true possibilities of human action" (Rhonheimer 1987, 936).

"This does not mean that the moral demands of the pure human being are accessible only to the believer (…) It means that, because of the disjunction between duty and ability, this knowledge is obscured, and that whole societies may be without it (…) This means that precisely Christian morality implies the true humanism (…) compared with the various forms of non-Christian humanism, the only true humanism in the full sense is the *specifically Christian* humanism" (Rhonheimer 1987, 933; emphasis in the original). Benedict XVI is, in a way, more radical: "A humanism which excludes God is an inhuman humanism" (CV 78).

In short, the Christian has, in his work, access to the same means, criteria and aids as the non-Christian. As is the case for other men and women, the purpose of his work is to achieve material and spiritual results, i.e., to satisfy needs, improve his standard of living, develop human knowledge and capabilities, serve others and society as a whole, and so on. For the Christian, however, there is a further dimension, in that man is called to a life in God, which begins in this world (through adherence to God's plan and also through work) and will continue afterwards.[13] Based on what we have said so far, there is no work that is improper for a Christian, provided it is carried out in a way that is compatible with the encounter with God.

The Catholic Who Creates or Manages a Company

Business has sometimes been condemned as an unacceptable activity for a Catholic, perhaps under the influence of various ideologies (Marxism, for example), or because certain motivations and vices found in business activity are incompatible with a Christian life. We shall not argue with these views here, but we shall appeal

---

[13] The Christian may also benefit from other aids, such as spiritual guidance and counsel; but the non-Christian also has access to such aids.

to a criterion of authority: according to John Paul II, "[a] person who produces something other than for his own use generally does so in order that others may use it (…). It is precisely the ability to foresee both the needs of others and the combinations of productive factors most adapted to satisfying those needs that constitutes another important source of wealth in modern society. Besides, many goods cannot be adequately produced through the work of an isolated individual; they require the cooperation of many people in working towards a common goal. Organizing such a productive effort, planning its duration in time, making sure that it corresponds in a positive way to the demands which it must satisfy, and taking the necessary risks [which are the tasks of a manager] — all this too is a source of wealth in today's society. In this way, the role of disciplined and creative human work and, as an essential part of that work, initiative and entrepreneurial ability becomes increasingly evident and decisive. (…) Indeed, besides the earth, man's principal resource is man himself. His intelligence enables him to discover the earth's productive potential and the many different ways in which human needs can be satisfied. It is his disciplined work in close collaboration with others that makes possible the creation of ever more extensive working communities which can be relied upon to transform man's natural and human environments" (CA 32; cf. PCJP 2011, no. 2–3).

This long paragraph develops the arguments given earlier for the work of Christians in the world: business enterprise, like other human activities, is good and the social function of the entrepreneur deserves recognition. This is not to say that there are not particular businesses (such as drug trafficking or prostitution), or particular ways of conducting economic activity (e.g., based on fraud, deception, exploitation or corruption), that are incompatible with the encounter of the entrepreneur with Christ – as there are in other professions. On this basis, the manager may develop the human quality of his activity for the satisfaction of his own and other people's needs, for his own personal development and that of those who work with him, and for the common good. But this will be a challenge for both the Christian and the non-Christian manager.

However, the work of the businessperson also has a new dimension for the Christian lay people whose "special task" it is "to order and to throw light upon these affairs in such a way that they may come into being and then continually increase according to Christ to the praise of the Creator and the Redeemer" (LG 31). Its goal therefore goes beyond the mere satisfaction of human needs, wealth creation and human and social development, because "[t]he initiative of lay Christians is necessary especially when the matter involves discovering or inventing the means for permeating social, political, and economic realities with the demands of Christian doctrine and life" (CCC 899). It also provides additional motivations for working hard and well, because "[t]he knowledge that by means of work man shares in the work of creation constitutes the most profound motive for undertaking it" (LE 25). In any case, the profession of the manager should be integrated with the other dimensions of his personal and social life, in order to avoid "the split between the faith which many profess and their daily lives", a risk that the Second Vatican Council calls as "one of the more serious errors of our age" (GS 43, cf. PCJP 2011, no. 10).[14]

Conclusions

Who is a Christian businessperson? He is a person who creates, develops or manages a company oriented toward the satisfaction of human needs (the needs of customers, owners, managers, employees and suppliers) as well as toward the human, professional and economic development of these people through the production of goods and services. The firm is not intrinsically a cause of harm although, like all human activities, it may have defects, perhaps many defects, but, again like all human work and like man himself, it is redeemable.

A Christian is a man or woman who believes in God, who comes to that knowledge of God through Jesus Christ, and who adheres to him: God is not indifferent to him, just as he is not indifferent to God. He knows that God acts and has plans for him, and he seeks to collaborate in those plans. Created in the image of God and constituted as an adoptive son of God, he seeks to imitate Jesus Christ, reproducing the life of Christ in his own life. This means loving God and others. And as love has no limit, the Christian knows that he is called to excellence, i.e., to holiness. He also knows that he is a member of the Church, the community of men and women created by Jesus. The encounter of the Christian with God takes place in the Church; in it he finds faith and the means to live as a Christian. The encounter of the Christian with God consists of knowing what God wants of him and trying to do it, following certain moral rules, although the decisive thing is not the code of ethics but the quest for Jesus ("Lord, what will you have me do?", Acts 9:6).

The life of a human being revolves largely around work, which is not a punishment or a curse but an expression of the dignity of man as an image of God. Through work man changes the world by producing goods to satisfy his own and others' needs; develops himself by acquiring knowledge, capabilities and virtues; and serves others. Work is a quintessentially social activity. All men work, but Christians add the dimensions that derive from being Christians, that is to say, they adhere to

---

[14] PCJP (2011) in an important source of ideas and suggestions on how to put into practice the demands of the manager's Christian vocation, "practicing ethical social principles while conducting the normal rhythms of the business world. This entails seeing clearly the situation, judging with principles that foster the integral development of people, and acting in a way which implements these principles in light of one's unique circumstances and in a manner consistent with the teaching of the Faith" (PCJP 2011, no. 14). The first dimension, *seeing*, means to examine the "signs of the times" (GS 4, 11, 44; cf. PCJP 2011, no. 15–26), something connatural with the activity of the managers. The second one, *judging*, is exercised through the application of the principles of the Catholic Social Teaching (PCJP 2011, 27–59. The third dimension, *acting*, means that the businesspeople should take aspirations into practice, being "witnesses of action" (PCJP 2011, no. 60; cf. 60–80).

Christ and encounter Him in their task; seek to accomplish the will of God in their task; manifest their love of God and others; know that they are contributing to important things, such as the continuation of creation and the redemption of humanity; try to serve others, because they see in them not only people but children of God; and try to bear witness to their faith (CCC 2044).

There is no such thing as the Christian entrepreneur or manager; there is the Christian whose job is to create or manage companies. He is expected to do what every entrepreneur must do, with the same resources. What does his being a Christian add to his task as a manager? The same as being a Christian adds to the task of any worker. He is subject to no additional restriction; he can know and do the same as any other entrepreneur. If anything is prohibited to him, it is not because he is a Christian but because he is a person, and immoral behavior would degrade him as a person. However, his religion helps him understand the reason for these restrictions, and gives him spiritual and ascetic means to behave as he should.

Yet the Christian entrepreneur knows that he is in a "business" that goes beyond profit, efficiency, human promotion or social progress. It is the "business" of God, who has charged him with continuing the task of creation and redemption, from a privileged place – the firm – which is a key institution for the material, human and spiritual advancement of persons and peoples. This gives the Christian entrepreneur a new, broader view of his task. God thus asks him to overcome "a basic feeling of weariness that obstructs the spirit in the face of ideals, so that it considers them unachievable (…), [and] a certain dullness (…) that is blind to the content of things and contents itself with superficial formalities, without going deeper" (Polo 1996a, 273). In a word, the manager needs "someone to teach him to raise his sights and strive faithfully to keep his sights high" (Polo 1996a, 277). That is what being a Christian adds to the entrepreneur.

> Entrepreneurs, managers, and all who work in business, should be encouraged to recognize their work as a true vocation and to respond to God's call in the spirit of true disciples. In doing so, they engage in the noble task of serving their brothers and sisters and of building up the Kingdom of God. This message has the aim of providing inspiration and encouragement to business leaders, calling them to ever deepen their faithfulness at work. (PCJP 2011, no. 87)[15]

References

Alford, Helen, and Michael J. Naughton. 2001. *Managing as if faith mattered: Christian social principles in the modern organization.* Indianapolis: University of Notre Dame Press.
Argandoña, Antonio. 1995. *El empresario cristiano y su función en la construcción de la sociedad. In El empresario: Razones para la esperanza.* Valencia: Instituto Social Empresarial.

---

[15] This paper is part of the work of the "la Caixa" Chair of Corporate Social Responsibility and Corporate Governance at IESE. I have dealt with this subject in Argandoña (1995, 2004a, 2007), although with different approaches from the one attempted here.

Argandoña, Antonio. 2004a. What does being a Catholic add to a business vocation? IESE Occasional Paper 04/5-E.

Argandoña, Antonio. 2004b. El trabajo según las enseñanzas de San Josemaría Escrivá. Una reflexión desde la perspectiva de las actuales corrientes económicas y sociológicas. In *Trabajo y espíritu*, ed. Juan Jesús Borobia, Miguel Lluch, José Ignacio Murillo, and Eduardo Terrassa, 301–330. Pamplona: Eunsa.

Argandoña, Antonio. 2007. La identidad cristiana del directivo de empresa. In *Identidad cristiana. Coloquios universitarios*, ed. Antonio Aranda, 383–404. Pamplona: Eunsa.

Argandoña, Antonio. 2011. Josemaría Escrivá de Balaguer y la misión del IESE en el mundo de la empresa. *Scripta et Documenta* 5: 131–162.

Argandoña, Antonio. 2012. The theory of the firm and Catholic Social Teaching. Presented to the conference Renewing mission and identity in Catholic business education, Dayton, 18–20 June.

Chamberlain, Gary L. 2004. The evolution of business as a Christian calling. *The Review of Business* 25: 27–36.

Clark, Charles M.A. 2004. Bringing realism to management education: Contributions from Catholic social thought. *The Review of Business* 25: 6–14.

Cornwall, Jeffrey R., and Michael J. Naughton. 2003. Who is the good entrepreneur? An exploration within the Catholic social tradition. *Journal of Business Ethics* 44: 61–75.

Cortright, Steven A., and Michael J. Naughton (eds.). 2002. *Rethinking the purpose of business: Interdisciplinary essays within the Catholic social tradition*. Indianapolis: University of Notre Dame Press.

Escrivá de Balaguer, Josemaría. 1974. *Christ is passing by*. London: Scepter.

Escrivá de Balaguer, Josemaría. 1981. *Friends of God*. New York: Scepter.

Garvey, George E. 2004. Business as a vocation: Implications for Catholic legal education. *The Review of Business* 25: 37–44.

Novak, Michael. 1981. A theology of the corporation. In *The corporation. A theological inquiry*, ed. Michael Novak and John W. Cooper, 203–224. Washington, DC: American Enterprise Institute for Public Policy Research.

Novak, Michael. 1996. *Business as a calling: Work and the examined life*. New York: Free Press.

Orlandis, José. 1998. *Qué es ser católico*. Pamplona: Eunsa.

Polo, Leonardo. 1996a. Acerca de la plenitud. In *Sobre la existencia cristiana*, 271–288. Pamplona: Eunsa.

Polo, Leonardo. 1996b. *Ética. Hacia una versión moderna de los temas clásicos*. Madrid: Unión Editorial.

Pontifical Council for Justice and Peace – PCJP. 2011. *Vocation of the business leader. A reflection*. Vatican City: PCJP.

Rhonheimer, Martin. 1987. Moral cristiana y desarrollo humano. Sobre la existencia de una moral de lo humano específicamente cristiana. In *La misión del laico en la Iglesia y en el mundo. VIII Simposio Internacional de Teología de la Universidad de Navarra*, ed. Augusto Sarmiento, Tomás Rincón, Jose María Yanguas, and Antonio Quirós, 919–938. Pamplona: Eunsa.

Rhonheimer, Martin. 2001. Is Christian morality reasonable? On the difference between secular and Christian humanism. *Annales Theologici* 15: 529–549.

Sirico, Robert A. 2000. The entrepreneurial vocation. *Journal of Markets and Morality* 3: 1–21.

van Wensveen Siker, Louke. 1989. Christ and business: A typology for Christian business ethics. *Journal of Business Ethics* 8: 883–888.

Weber, Max. 1949. Objectivity in social science and social policy. In *The methodology of the social sciences*. New York: Free Press (original 1904).

Weber, Max. 1992. *The protestant ethic and the spirit of capitalism*. London: Routledge (original 1904–05).

Chapter 13
Business and Management Practices Influenced by Catholic Humanism: Three Case Studies

Geert Demuijnck, Kemi Ogunyemi, and Elena Lasida

Abstract This chapter presents three cases studies which show how Catholic Humanism can be a source of inspiration in managing business. The first case study deals with a medium size company, the owner-manager of which has a solid Catholic education and a great sense of integrity and discipline. This company has high quality policies and practices in treatment of people, acting with justice, care and promoting the development of managers and employees. The second case study focuses on a small company that is organized according to the principles of the 'economy of communion'. In this case, Christian humanism adopts particular characteristics of the Catholic *Focolare* movement. This is not merely reflected in particular management and business practices, but it pervades the company, as well as all of its internal and external relations. The third case relates how a retail company, created by a Catholic family, has grown rapidly to become a multinational corporation. During this process the influence of Christian humanism on business practices has evolved and become more indirect, but undeniably, the company has fostered a corporate culture of responsible business.

Keywords Catholic humanism • Focolare movement • Management • SMEs

G. Demuijnck (✉)
EDHEC Business School, Roubaix, France
e-mail: geert.demuijnck@edhec.edu

K. Ogunyemi
Lagos Business School, Pan-Atlantic University, Lagos, Nigeria

E. Lasida
Institut Catholique, Paris, France

© Springer Science+Business Media Dordrecht 2015   215
D. Melé, M. Schlag (eds.), *Humanism in Economics and Business*,
Issues in Business Ethics 43, DOI 10.1007/978-94-017-9704-7_13

Introductory Note

This chapter aims to show how Christian-Catholic humanism can be a source of inspiration for business and its management, although in different manners. It is organized in three parts, and presents three case studies of enterprises that have developed business and management practices inspired by such humanism.

How Catholic Humanism Pervades Management at *Kadick Integrated Limited*

The first case study[1] is Kadick Integrated Limited, a services company selling tele-communications products in Nigeria which had a turnover of approximately USD45 million in 2013. A significant part of the business is situated in Warri, Delta State, Nigeria – the hometown of the owners. It began as a business experiment in 2000 in an army barracks in Lagos, when the founder, a soldier, was considering a change of career. He was an educated Catholic and strongly believed in discipline and integrity. Currently the owners of the company have top management positions; the founder is the Project Director and the other owner is the Managing Director. The company was incorporated in 2002, and in 2005 they started a connect store as a franchise from Mobile Telephone Network (MTN) – a leading telecommunications service provider of South African origin. The business direction now is retail, focusing on providing airtime and data services to their customers. They also have a dealership, smart shops, and one more connect store. The current staff strength is 137 employees in the three company locations – Lagos, Warri and Oshogbo. This figure also includes some implants[2] working at MTN service centres – a few in Ibadan; one in Enugu, and a few more in Matori in Lagos.

Catholic humanism, including the human values common in many humanistic approaches, permeates the company. This includes the centrality of the person within the organization (Sandelands 2009), respect for human dignity and rights and people development (Melé 2015, i.e. Chap. 7, in this volume), the understanding of work (Naughton and Laczniak 1993; Tablan 2013), the consideration of the business organization as a community of persons (Melé 2012; Naugthon 2015, i.e. Chap. 11, in this volume), and the way people are treated within the organization. The latter entails not only avoiding negative aspects, such as maltreatment or indifference toward people, but practising and promoting positive aspects – dealing with people with justice and care and promoting their development (Melé 2014).

---

[1] Written by Kemi Ogunyemi from several sources of information: from semi-structured in-depth interviews with relevant managers and employees of the company and from archival data (corporate statements and other significant documents of the firm such as policies, minutes of meetings, and exit interviews). These have been complemented by her personal observation over a period of about 4 days.

[2] Terminology used to describe staff of trade partners who work in MTN service centres.

The company ethos at Kadick is focused on developing people and, in addition to the intrinsic value of this, the owner-managers see the survival of the business as depending on the people who pass through it and believe that developing them is a way for the business to contribute to society.

To meet their goal of impacting the thinking and orientation of the people in the area by developing them, the company employs many local people and introduces them into the Kadick culture. According to a member of staff in Warri, "if you do well, you get rewarded, if you do badly, you get sanctioned. But the expectation is that you become a better person by passing through". The induction process covers various aspects of basic human development – decorum, eating habits, dressing. In the words of a manager, " 'bush' people come and they experience a transformation". The company has a collection of photographs of some employees showing how they looked when they were first employed and then 3–4 months down the line – after the induction process.

There are no traces of the typical signs of maltreatment such as bullying, sexual harassment, insults, and so on. Only once, an employee wanted to leave because he felt bullied; when this was revealed, he "was counselled out of the decision" and he is now a happy staff member again. Instead, there is much evidence of *respect for people*.

Every month employees have a meeting to organise end-of-the-week recreational activities termed TGIF (meaning 'Thank God; it's Friday!'). This is coordinated by staff in turns, including the security man or the office attendant, to emphasize "that all staff are equal as human beings and that the higher placed ones should respect the others." A secondary purpose is to encourage people "to be able to talk to their colleagues on topics of their own choosing". They are prompted not to focus on work-related topics, thus the topics are usually related to life and family.

Transparency is something that top management practice and foster among their people. They maintain an "open office" since they believe that "an uninformed employee will not add value" and so "shared services staff have access to all bank details and assets". This transparency cuts across many dimensions: "budgets (are) proposed by the owners and defended; and everyone agrees"; "different branches are signatories to their own accounts"; "there are four signatories for each account – two staff and the two directors; this creates ownership".

The organizational chart of the company is available and clear for every level – organisation, branches, units; there are clear job descriptions for every staff position and there is "a chance to say when you can deliver on the job; no force"; targets are "realistic and within reason; you have discretion as to how to do your job"; policies are clear and have recently been compiled into a staff handbook.

The fairness of *remuneration*, on which Catholic social teaching insists, seems to be the norm for Kadick. Salaries in the company are "competitive in the telecoms distribution industry" and are paid on time. In addition, the company always pays for documented overtime.

A small but significant detail is that the researcher attended interviews for the selection of new employees in which a very clear explanation of the role was given. The interviews were conducted with cordiality and respect for the applicants.

When a disciplinary committee looks at cases, the owners do not vote "so as not to influence the others' views". For a recent problem in the phone shop, regarding the dismissal of a man who had previously received "three warnings for performance issues, with metrics that were very clear to all", a "5-people committee" was set up.

Regarding *performance appraisal*, a query normally follows "any 5 % discrepancy between self-appraisal and supervisor" so that any unfairness in the appraisal system can be detected. According to an intermediate manager, "there is an appraisal system and it is fair. The goals are agreed on with the subject and approved". In the review, "there is self-scoring and scoring by the line manager. Contention is allowed, based on facts; there should have been queries preceding; (staff) can escalate issues and the policies are clear".

Whenever staff have a *complaint* or *conflict*, the managing director encourages them "not to go out and criticize" but rather to "bring it up in-house": staff have a right to say "I'm putting all this into this business; you have to treat me as a human being; take care of my interests". Everyone should feel "a sense of belonging" and "have somebody to run to". The open office system makes it easy for people to bring up any complaints. The prescribed procedure for each case is to "email your manager and copy someone higher, not to go above". Complaints are attended to promptly.

Regarding the *disciplinary system*, there is "no victimization; no firing without process". The prevailing freedom of expression observed during the interviews seemed to underline that this was indeed the norm for the company. In fact, in the minutes of a meeting during which the Managing Director had reprimanded someone for a lapse, the reprimand was recorded as an opinion.

Care for people is expressed in a number of ways. The company has a *family friendly* attitude, which is encouraged by Catholic social teaching (Guitián 2009). Staff are "encouraged to close early". This attitude is also shown in an effort to "relocate people to where their spouses live" and in "not employing those who cannot manage" a work-life balance.

With regard to *work conditions*, there is "on-the-job training", "helping people to get job satisfaction"; there are "monthly semi-social meetings and incentives to work"; it is a "suitable environment"; "customer service and politeness is important".

Along with many positive sentences we also find some employees who suggest some points to improve job satisfaction. For example, a staff member mentioned that "salary increase should be more often, perhaps twice a year, to encourage people" while also saying that "(it) is a good place", with a "comfortable working environment" "which helps morale".

At the inception of the company there was an atmosphere of impatience whenever people did not seem to "fit" into the organization. Later on, a "performance improvement programme as a one-off treatment" was instituted for such cases. If this does not work, the person is moved to another department to see if there is a better fit. In addition, "each person is assigned someone to mentor".

While "extra-budgetary approval is needed for anything outside" the budget, there exist "loan purses for employees beyond the contract"; and the company pays "rent for some people"; one of these was the IT manager whose rent was paid by the company for 2 years because he was finding it difficult to get accommodation in Lagos. More is done on a "personal basis". The owners also go out of their way to help personally, for example, a "guard complained of finding it difficult to move from house to office"; he was given "personal money for a motorcycle".

The company fosters the development of the people who work there in many aspects. The training budget for 2014 is about US$36,600. There is a standing rule: all supervisors and managers have to attend courses at least once a year. This has been the case for the past 4 years. Interactions with staff sent on executive education programs indicated that they were learning a lot and were happy with the experience. Consultants are also brought into the organization to train the staff in the premises, e.g. T-consult, Beautiful Minds, etc. In addition, there are constant in-house training programmes delivered by the Human Resources Manager – the company buys resources (e.g. instructional and educational DVDs) for him to use to carry out trainings in the different locations.

Non job-focused training includes in-company events such as the quarterly breakfast meeting – an event where staff (from the Connect, the dealership, the smart shop, etc.) make presentations about life issues. The presentations are expected to be non-work-related. Staff coordinate and arrange the agenda for these events. They also select a venue and set up the whole event. They are encouraged to look for venues that people may never have been to. For example, they hold them in big hotels that the staff would not otherwise have access to; to give them that access and to give them an idea of what happens there in those different spaces. Topics chosen for presentation by staff regularly include topics such as work-life balance, values of Kadick, etc. The theme for the first week of October 2014 was "being better – people moving from good (where we believe most people are) to being better." Kadick fosters talking about work and home because of the belief that "If you're good in your life generally, you would be better able to contribute to the organization".

Staff who make presentations that are outstanding in quality are nominated for further training by the Project Director. The Human Resource Manager then selects the appropriate program and sends them to attend it. A lady made a presentation on healthy living in the second quarter of 2014. It was a very good presentation. She was sent to a training programme in Lagos, at the School of Media and Communication of the Pan-Atlantic University. On her return, she made another presentation of what she had learnt in the training at the third quarter breakfast. She showed video clips of herself before and after the recent training programme. This has inspired the organization to want to send her for even more training even though this had nothing to do with her actual job role but rather with her life goals.[3]

---

[3] She had come into the organization saying that her career goal was journalism though she would like to work with Kadick for a while.

Top management have an attitude of permanent learning. In words of the General Manager there have been instances of "lessons not being assimilated among supervisors and managers who went through trainings". For example, one "manager of the Warri connect store was not doing well. He was moved to Lagos for a week to undergo a performance improvement programme[4] (PIP), in this case, a rigorous re-training programme on his work areas". A regional dealership manager accompanied him as a participant in the programme. The latter showed appreciable improvement. The former improved for a while and then deteriorated. Shortly afterwards, the company's trade partner, MTN, "recommended suspension on issues that they thought had been fixed though the PIP". Kadick demurred but "in the end they had to do it despite the pain; they had to do it because of their franchise agreement with MTN; but they effected a suspension with pay despite MTN recommending that it should be without pay". The man in question then made it clear that he was not planning to come back to work.

Regarding *integrity* issues and good example to staff, the interviewer heard sentences like these: "there's some money we don't want". "The company takes hits when necessary". The same policies apply to owners and staff when it comes to handling issues.

The company has *human values* and these are practiced and "enforced when contravened". One of the company's values is "discipline because anything of value requires discipline", for example, they insist that "things be documented properly: everyone must learn to use Outlook or send a mail". They also value "empathy in dealing with others; superior customer service; service as if it were your family", and integrity, "integrity is key in everything". There is a system of rewarding termed 'Kadick flag bearers' which evaluates the practice of these values. The flag bearers are given "gifts in the breakfast conference or lunch, etc.; no ... monetary rewards but always something". At one management meeting attended by the interviewer, it was observed that there was cordiality in treatment and a pleasant atmosphere. Staff were expected to have opinions, as the Managing Director told them, "you can't send in accounts without comments". Staff were reminded to "ask for help if you need it" and to "give feedback on progress". The consultant who was temporarily in the company to "handhold" new staff gave feedback of how this was going. The Managing Director expressed remorse for not attending the naming ceremony of a staff member's child.

To *promote harmony* within the organization, the management team organizes bonding activities, e.g. breakfast conferences. Reviews are held where people "talk about their problems". The owner-directors are "open to everyone's opinion and if it's superior, it will be taken up". Leadership is shared: "Responsibility is given to different people so that everyone is involved". This "creates buy-in from the people that have to do the major part of the work". The "open office" concept is also implemented physically. There is camaraderie. The interviewees responded positively; one was not on the list to be interviewed officially but spontaneously volunteered because he wanted to be part of whatever was going on.

---

[4]This was the regular medium used by the company for helping people to raise their performance levels.

In order to promote fairness, top management encourage staff to question themselves critically, posing questions like these: "Is it the truth?", "Is it fair to all concerned?", "Is it according to the rules?", "Would you like to be treated like that in similar circumstances?". Management decisions are taken with thought given to the people affected.

The important performance indices are "ability to grow; to take up responsibilities; commitment to the company's vision". The managers "study staff and reward each based on their impact" by giving "benefits, etc., e.g. professional courses; house rents; things not in your agreement – they come without previous agreement – interest free loan support to buy a new car – without service charges, etc. that a bank would charge; the company pays part of it for you; it's not just salary". "Salary is the agreement"; there are other "benefits that you reap that keep staff on".

To make up for lack of upward career progression since it is a small company, there is a lot of "job rotation" and "encouragement to get another job after five years". Hence, the company aims "to empower (staff) to be able to do it: use us as a springboard but remember to contribute. If you do not contribute, there will be nothing to bounce on". Top management also train staff in entrepreneurship; this is not directed at the bottom line but at personal growth, to prepare them for their future. The company also paid for computer school for one of the staff. In addition, employees are encouraged to develop and to showcase the talents that they have outside their work for Kadick. Late last year, a member of staff who demonstrated an aptitude for comedy and acting was flown to Lagos to attend an event; the AY show at Eko Hotel. It was her opportunity to travel by air for the first time in her life. The management is aware that some of their staff have never gone out of their immediate environment and they try to make this happen for them so that they can grow by interacting with other peoples in other environments. They want them to see the world is more than what they have around them.

To sum up, Catholic humanism is present at Kadick, not through eloquent declarations but a practical way, which includes policies, management systems and practices, and the whole culture. Although, like any company, Kadick is not perfect, it shows justice in most aspects, and it demonstrates authentic care and concern for the development of the staff. It is the passion of the top management to make an impact on the lives of the employees that pass through Kadick. Their initial thinking was "We cannot pay as much as they would like to earn. We cannot attract the more talented people who are drawn by the higher paying bigger companies. How else can we reward the people who come to us? Treat them with dignity and respect so that they will be happy. Train them so that they can work for us at a very high standard. Make them employable so that they can move to other organisations and do better". In return, employees demonstrated commitment, satisfaction and loyalty in their responses to the interviewer. One of the employees believes that the approach of Kadick will eventually bring dividends to the organisation, since they will inevitable grow "a network of people that may do business with them in future – who knows? Former employees are now in Shell, Mobil, First Bank, etc." He is full of admiration for Kadick's philosophy which he sums up saying that it is a company that believes that it "must make a difference in the lives of its employees, make them better people".

Agréments du jardin, an 'Economy of Communion'-Based Company

The second case study[5] illustrates the influence of Christian humanism in business in a different way. Some companies are organized on the basis of a conception of business that from the start is conceived as Christian. This is notoriously the case of companies that try to implement the principle of the 'economy of communion'. Before we present the short case study, some explanation about these principles will be useful.

The Economy of Communion

The economy of communion (EC) was set up in 1991 as part of the *Focolare* Movement.[6]

The project was launched by the founder of the Movement, Chiara Lubich, during a trip to Brazil where she observed that many of its members were living in poverty. She proposed creating a network of solidarity that goes beyond individual gestures of sharing. It therefore calls on companies to be part of a business model inspired by the early Christian communities. The project combines three objectives:

1. Bringing businesses into the hands of competent people capable of producing profits: there is therefore an explicit goal of economic efficiency.
2. Sharing the benefits by dividing them into three parts: one part for the needy, the destitute, the poor; another for the formation of "new men",[7] educated in solidarity and 'brotherly communion' to spread the word of the economy of communion – we will spell out in a moment what this means, and a third part must be reinvested in the company itself so that it can develop.
3. Developing, in light of this experience, an innovative way of conceiving the economy, one which is less individualistic and less conflictual and more based on cooperative relationships.

The Christian-Catholic foundations of this economic model are explicit and cannot be reduced to a declaration of good principles. They have a direct impact on how to distribute the profits but also on how to make them, that is, on the management of

---

[5] Contribution of Elena Lasida.

[6] Movement created in 1943 by Chiara Lubich. "Its purpose: to work cooperatively to build a more united world, following the inspiration of Jesus' prayer to the Father 'May they all be one' (Jn 17:21), respecting and valuing diversity. It focuses on dialogue as a method, has a constant commitment to building bridges and relationships of fraternity among individuals, peoples and cultural worlds" (source: http://www.focolare.org/usa/en/about-us/in-brief/, September 2014).

[7] 'And put on the new man, who according to God is created in justice and holiness of truth.' Ephesians 4: 24.

the company. The concept of 'communion' becomes the major organizational business principle.

This concept means basically that business relations, whether they are internal, i.e. within the company, or external, i.e. relation with other stakeholders, are conceived as relations within a community, as belonging to a same common project, rather than in terms of individual interests. Therefore, business relations are seen as brotherly, cooperative and reciprocal, rather than competitive and conflictual.

It is necessary, first, that the company is itself a community of people connected through values such as cooperation, trust, listening, love for truth, respect for skills, participation and mutual concern. This community of people, whose common project is to produce goods and services, is based on the recognition of the equal dignity of each of its members, beyond the roles and positions they hold. The dignity of each single worker permeates a common corporate culture. This culture not only takes into account the concrete working conditions but also the specific living conditions of life of each employee, including the protection of their health, their leisure time, and training and education.

However, communion is not limited to the internal organization of the company but also concerns its external relations. The communion is manifested primarily through the distribution of profits. This is where the project stands out dramatically compared to conventional business. Instead of focusing on the remuneration of shareholders, the model of the economy of communion shares profits between the development needs of the business, the needs of people in poverty, and the need to spread a culture of fraternity in society at large. This culture is a 'culture of giving': it emphasizes sharing with the poor, but it also aims to create collaborative relationships with all stakeholders of the structure. The company conceives itself as a member of a political community rather than a mere economic agent. It explicitly recognizes its social and societal function.

Finally, the economy of communion aims to renew our way of thinking about the economy. In this sense, several academic studies have already been produced, particularly in the context of the Sophia Loppiano Institute in Italy, a place of teaching and research associated with the economy of communion. The economist Luigino Bruni, professor at the LUMSA University of Rome, who coordinates the International Commission on the economy of communion has published several articles that clarify the position of the economy of communion in the history of economic thought.[8] An important element stressed in particular by Bruni is that the main contribution of the economy of communion is not so much the redistribution of wealth, but the way in which wealth is created and produced. In this sense the economy of communion project is not a philanthropic enterprise. Its aim is not to encourage the most generous entrepreneurs in profit sharing but to invent a new business model. The sharing is not so much about giving money: entrepreneurs share their talent, their creativity in problem solving, in creating new things, their ability to change the world in which they work. This is their vocation. The entrepre-

---

[8] See Bruni and Uelmen (2006) and the economy of communion website (www.edc-online.org) for references.

neurial ideal promoted by the economy of communion is social, not only economic. Its objective is to be evaluated according to its ability to manage social transformation. It is in this sense that Bruni talks about a form of governance of communion which aims to integrate the basic principles of Christianity.

The economy of communion movement is nowadays present in more 50 countries. According to the international website of the movement, there are more than 800 companies that are run according to the principles of the economy of communion, predominantly in Europe, particularly in Italy, and South America.[9] A guide to conducting a business under these principles is available, as are training and seminars in different continents. Established firms help new ones in the conduct of this ambitious project.

Agréments du Jardin, *as Example of Economy of Communion*

One example of a company that is managed according to the principles of the economy of communion is *Agrément du Jardin*,[10] a small firm in landscape gardening, based in the North of France. This company has existed since 1984. The current owner-manager, the son of the founder, has been running the company since 1989. The economy of communion movement started only in 1991, as noted, but the owning family has been connected with the Focolare movement since 1976. In fact, we could say that this company is, to some extent, an economy of communion firm *avant la lettre*, because its corporate culture was already very close to the current one before the principles of communion were fully implemented. According to the owner-manager, the economy of communion project came like an answer they were waiting for. They totally recognized themselves in the culture of sharing promoted by the economy of communion.

The owner-manager underlines that the principles of the economy should be applied *in liberty*. The annual distribution of the benefits and its division in three parts, in accordance with one of the principles of EC, is the object of a formal decision taken by the shareholders (the owner-manager and the co-owner, i.e. his sister).

The implications of the economy of communion principles in the management of the firm are numerous. First of all, according to the owner-manager, the relations with the employees are quite different from what is common in business. When people are hired by the firm, the owner-manager clearly explains that the firm is organized according to the principles of the economy of communion. Prospective employees do not necessarily have to support these principles, but the manager thinks that they have the right to know the specificity of the company to which they are applying. The owner-manager is quite confident of their employees' appreciation of the involvement in the EC. The fact that the profits are partly shared with the

---

[9] http://www.edc-online.org/en/eoc/how-itas-spreading.html
[10] The following description is based on an in-depth interview with Frédéric Dupont, the owner-manager of the firm, that took place on 10 September 2014.

poor gives more meaning to their work. Moreover, wages are slightly above the average wages in the sector and the employees also receive a bonus based on the general annual result. Evidence of the positive judgment by the employees is the fact that the turnover of employees is extremely low. The owner-manager underlines the crucial importance of this positive evaluation of the EC by the employees. He asks rhetorically: "what would our annual gift to the poor mean if my relations with the employees were bad?"

A similar logic is at work in the relations with the other stakeholders. Suppliers, for example, are considered to be long-term partners: if their products or services are of good quality, there is no reason to switch or to challenge their prices constantly.

The relations with clients are rather normal. The clients usually do not know – but some do – about the involvement of *Agrément du Jardin* in the EC. There is no label related to it, and it is not used as a marketing tool.

The relation with society at large is considered from the EC angle. It would be absurd to donate to the poor while at the same time not paying taxes and contributions to the social security system. The gardening sector is plagued by widespread black market transactions. However, the policy of *Agrément du Jardin* is a radical 'no' in this matter. The owner-manager estimates that his refusal to accept cash (for non-declared, i.e. tax free work) costs him 5 to 10 % of possible deals.

In general, the owner-manager compares what is usually indicated by the term corporate social responsibility (CSR), i.e. the relations with the stakeholders, with the visible part of a tree. It is the work deep down, at the roots, that determines this visible part. And sometimes these roots deliver unexpected fruits, in the sense that employees start to follow the principles of the EC. The owner-manager is proud to give the following anecdotic evidence. Every year, during the owner's holidays, one of the senior employees supervises the work, for which he gets a bonus. Last year, this person was helped to some extent by a younger colleague. When he was about to receive his bonus, he told the manager that he would rather give it to the helpful colleague this time.

From a financial viewpoint, the company has been thriving for 30 years. It is not growing spectacularly (it doubled its size in 15 years from 7 to 14 employees), but it has never faced major difficulties. People are obviously happy to work there and to share the benefits with those in need.

The very existence of firms that apply the principles of the EC is a challenge to the way the economy is often conceived in management classes and business schools. These firms seem to contradict the basic assumptions of the *homo oeconomicus* model which underlies rational management approaches: selfishness, strategic thinking, materialism, etc. And yet, as Luigino Bruni and Amélia Uelmen (2006) have shown, the logic of the EC is much closer to the way classical economists like Adam Smith conceived economic relations than one would expect. It is rather the recent neoclassical turn that has put the accent on individual economic maximizing of materialistic well-being. Although directly guided and inspired by Christian-Catholic humanism, the enigmatic results of these firms are likely to impress also people who do not share this background.

Auchan: From an Implicit Christian-Catholic Corporate Culture to a Structured Conception of Corporate Ethical Responsibility

The case study[11] presents the way in which business leaders of a retail company gradually clarify the ethical responsibilities of their company – in an ongoing discussion of particular cases. It is based on 15 years of experience as an external member of the ethics committee of the French retail company Auchan.[12]

In the Auchan case, the owning family had from the start the aim to do business in a way that was compatible with their Catholic family roots: respect for the dignity of the persons working for the company or otherwise involved in their business transactions (e.g. supply chain) is a basic principle, that constraints the scope of acceptable actions, but also inspires management. However, compared to the previous case, the business model as such is quite standard: Auchan is a retailer who wants to make profit, albeit in a responsible way.

Background

Auchan was created in 1961 as a single supermarket. Since then, it became a company which is running supermarkets and shopping malls in 16 countries with a business turnover of 62 billion Euros (2013). It employs 302,000 people, 160,500 of whom are shareholders (in 9 countries). Employees currently hold 11.2 % of the shares. The other shares are still owned by the (now hundreds of) members of the founding Mulliez family.[13]

The process of ethical reflection in the company did not start from scratch. If Auchan had a strong reputation for social responsibility from the start, and, moreover, developed a management style which strongly motivates employees by giving them objectives and responsibilities and, later, also by giving them the possibility to become shareholders and to take advantage of the growth of the company, this

---

[11] This section is an abridged and updated version of Demuijnck (2009).

[12] The description of this case is based on both a longitudinal participant observation (over 15 years) as a member of the ethics committee of this company and some in-depth interviews with the people who played a key role in the company's ethical decision making during this period. Personal notes taken by the author as well as the minutes of the meetings form the basic material for the following reconstruction. Three in-depth interviews with people who were involved in the committee from the very start complete the empirical research for this study. These people were informed of the research purpose of the interview. Auchan is a multinational company, established in 16 countries, but the study focuses on France, the home base of the company.

[13] Detailed information about financial results are to be found on www.groupe-auchan.com. The website also provides detailed information about Auchan's CSR and environmental policies. The yearly social and environmental report of the company is downloadable. For details about the shareholder family, one may consult Gobin and d'Herblin (2007).

reflected the commitment of the shareholder family to Catholic social teaching. In a nutshell, here are some of the key ideas of this teaching which are relevant in this context: Private property is morally correct if its ultimate aim is the 'common good' that is, roughly translated, if it is used in a socially responsible way. Making profit is a constraint for the survival of a firm, and therefore a legitimate aim, but it has to be done properly. Employees are considered as persons, i.e., beings with intrinsic dignity. Consequently, the principle of a morally defensible society based on private property also applies to these persons, hence the possibility offered to them to become owners as well.[14]

The Catholic background of the Mulliez family, who hold a large majority of the shares of Auchan, goes back to their parents and grandparents. They are direct descendants of, and related to, the families who were prominent owners in the once quite important textile industry in the Lille area. These families were deeply influenced by the more 'progressive' – at least in social matters – Catholic movement inspired by the *Rerum Novarum* encyclical. As a consequence the set of Christian values and Catholic social teaching formed the normative background of the 'culture' of the company.

From the 1930s on, most family members were – and some still are – strongly involved in a multitude of Catholic social movements.[15] Before the Second World War these movements were basically *La bourgeoisie catholique* (the Catholic bourgeoisie) and *Le réarmement moral* (moral rearmament). After the war the *Caux* movement and *l'Action catholique pour les independents* (ACI) became important, but today only the last two of these movements survive.[16]

Two types of meetings were organized by these movements. In the first type, the participants discussed practical issues about business. Out of these meetings grew the 'secular' *Centre des jeunes patrons* (Centre of young business leaders), that later became the still existing *Centre des jeunes dirigeants*, one of the leading militant movements in France in favor of CSR (Blasco and Zolner 2008).[17] The second type consisted of 'spiritual' meetings in which fundamental issues were discussed.

---

[14] For a detailed analysis of Catholic social teaching on wealth and income and their distribution, see Alford et al. (2006). Chapter 4 of this reader, written by Francis Hannafey, focuses on 'Entrepreneurship in Papal Thought' and is the most relevant for the issues dealt with here. It discusses excerpts of the encyclicals which are essential for the responsibilities of the owners of capital.

[15] Interview with Philippe Duprez, member of the Auchan ethics committee. Mr. Duprez has a great deal of documentation on Catholic employers' movements. Now retired, he was for many years the director of human resources of the company.

[16] The Caux movement changed its name to *Caux Initiatives of Change*. See http://www.caux.ch.

[17] Acquier et al. (2005) argue that, unlike what has happened in the US, CSR was conceived from the start as being disconnected from a religious background. This, I believe, should, be qualified to some extent. The separation of State and Church and the strong legitimacy enjoyed by public authority certainly had the effect that Catholic business leaders did not openly refer to their 'private' convictions (Boissonnat 1999). Yet, some of the most militant business leaders who defended strong opinions about the moral responsibility of companies during the last decades, such as e.g. Claude Bébéar (Axa) or Bertrand Collomb (Lafarge), are inspired by Catholic ideas and even a

One of the key themes of the latter debates was the idea that being born rich and having property was not a reason to opt for lazy hedonism. Consequently, Louis Mulliez, the grandfather of the founder of Auchan, argued during one of the meetings of the *Bourgeoisie catholique* in 1936 that ownership not only implies some advantages, but above all moral duties: the moral obligation not to become complacent in a privileged situation, but to take responsibilities with respect to the society as a whole. He further underlined the values of hard work, of living in a frugal way, and stressed that doing business in a moral way is a *calling*, a moral duty towards God and towards other people.[18] During this period, these duties were often interpreted in a quite paternalistic fashion (Ballet and de Bry 2001).

One could judge this information as somehow anecdotic, but according to the founders of Auchan, this mindset not only presented the mentality of the family in which they were educated, but the value system that they still consciously wanted to perpetrate when Auchan was set up.

The First Decade of Auchan

As a consequence, Catholic social teaching, and Catholic values in general, both progressive and conservative, were still a strong influence in the first decade of Auchan's development. A striking example of the more progressive sense is the employee shared-ownership that was developed in the early 1970s in Auchan. For more than 30 years the system has functioned very well and was referred to as an example to be followed during the political debates that preceded the recent (2001) law which stimulates employee savings and investment in stock.[19]

The leaders of Auchan introduced employee shareholding at a time when it was quite revolutionary on the basis of two considerations. First, the company was starting to make important profits, but, at the same time, it was quite demanding with respect to its employees. The leaders, who were also the shareholders, judged it as unfair not to share these results with the collaborators. Secondly, rather than increasing wages, they opted for sharing stock with the employees. Philippe Duprez, family member and at that time, i.e. 1971, head of Human Resources, relates that most family members were rather skeptical because they feared that they would no longer be the 'masters' of their businesses. But finally the family accepted the proposal, influenced by arguments based on papal encyclicals.[20] This recommendation appears, for instance, in *Quadragesimo Anno* (n. 28), where Pope Pius XI states:

secular movement such as the CJD (presented as one of the main actors by Alquier e.a.) has its roots in the Catholic movement. See also Berthoin Antal and Sobczak (2007) on the role of CJD.

[18] 'Y a-t-il encore en France une bourgeoisie catholique ?' *Epiphanie* XX, January 1936 (local journal of the *Bourgeoisie catholique* of Lille, France)

[19] Employee savings law, LOI n° 2001–152 du 19 février 2001 sur l'épargne salariale. See Balligand and Foucauld (2000).

[20] Interview with Philippe Duprez, member of the shareholder family and former Human Resources manager.

"It is entirely false to ascribe to the property alone or to the work alone whatever has been obtained through the combined effort of both, and it is wholly unjust for either, denying the efficacy of the other, to arrogate to itself whatever has been produced." But it is above all the more explicit *Mater et Magistra* that influenced the decision: "it is especially desirable today that workers gradually come to share in the ownership of their company, by ways and in the manner that seem most suitable" (n. 77). The following paragraph of *Mater et Magistra* was still presented, in a training session on business ethics focusing on the origins of the firm, in the 1990s: "But We have no doubt as to the need for giving workers an active part in the business of the company for which they work—be it a private or a public one. Every effort must be made to ensure that the enterprise is indeed a true human community, concerned with the needs, the activities and the standing of each of its members" (n. 91).

With hindsight, the former leaders admit that their Catholic values also led to more questionable judgments. For example, in those days, managers who divorced their spouse were considered to be less trustworthy and had more difficulties making a career in the company. But the important general point here is an obvious background assumption, which was beyond discussion, informed by these values, namely that the business should be run honestly with a deep respect for clients and employees.

Toward a Broader Ethical Framework

During the 1970s and the 1980s, the company grew rapidly, and, subsequently, preserving the 'values' became one of the worries of the shareholder family, albeit in a more secular way. Note, however, that the ideological history of the shareholder family was, until recently, evoked during training sessions, meaning that the Christian-Catholic background is not considered taboo. But the need for a broader ethical framework became obvious in a growing company with more and more employees from different backgrounds in a quickly evolving French society. As a result of these changes, a project to implement business ethics in the firm was initiated by the president (and major shareholder of the company) in the early nineties. The implementation was entrusted to the executives of the company. From 1992 onwards, the leaders of Auchan developed their particular approach to ethics. Initially there were two steps: the first consisted in creating a code of ethics. The ethics code of Auchan is clearly based on the model of stakeholder management. The people who wrote it had never heard of Edward Freeman's (1984) stakeholder theory but based their text on the idea that Auchan as a company has some responsibilities (beyond legal constraints) with respect to shareholders, employees, suppliers, customers and so on. With respect to each stakeholder, the commitments of Auchan are defined in a dozen fundamental commitments.[21]

---

[21] The code can be found in the annual reports on social and environmental responsibility, and can be downloaded from www.groupe-auchan.com.

The second step was the establishment of an ethics committee which would supervise compliance with the code. Initially, the operation of the ethics committee was very unclear. For example, the relationship between management and the ethics committee was not clear. Subsequently, the separation of duties was clarified: if a question is addressed to the ethics committee, the committee discusses it seriously and very openly, and then makes a recommendation that is returned to those who have decision-making power within the company. Later, the committee is informed about any decisions that were taken at that level.

The committee members are: the CEO of Auchan, one director of a supermarket, the head of the legal department, a person from the supply branch, the head of external communication, two shareholder family members, the executive in charge of sustainable development, the secretary general (who represents the president) and two external members (before 2006, only one external member sat on the committee). In addition to the permanent committee members, two or three other people are usually invited, in order to consult on a particular topic that is to be discussed.

Questions arrive at the committee in different ways. One source is mail on an ethical issue that is sent to the company by customers or by NGOs. But the committee also receives questions about the practices of sales, marketing, etc. that come from a host of employees, including executives and sales managers. Another source of questions is criticism in the media.

The stakeholder approach perfectly fits in with the range and variety of issues that have been submitted to the committee. The variety of the issues that were discussed is interesting. The following sample gives an idea of the type of questions or issues discussed:

1. What to do facing hostile reactions from customers about the fact that the supermarkets were open on a national holiday (8th of May, commemoration of World War II)?
2. Sexist discrimination among the employees (whether or not such discrimination exists and if so, what to do about it?)
3. Which rules to adopt to avoid customers becoming over indebted?
4. How to distinguish erotic literature (which is sold in the stores) from pornography (which is not sold in the stores) and how to display it in the shops?
5. Which videogames should not be sold (violence, racist allusions…)?
6. Which social standards should be imposed on textile suppliers in Asia, and what to do if infringements are observed?
7. Which profit margins should be applied to 'fair trade' products, if clients are willing to pay more for them than for equivalent standard products?
8. The amount of wasted fresh food, because of expired dates, and waste in general.
9. How to treat suppliers fairly in a reversed auction procedure?
10. Senior employees in hard working conditions.
11. Possible discriminations and how to avoid them.
12. How to limit the negative impact on the environment? To which extent is the retailer responsible?

13. To which extent are products with environment friendly labels really environ-
   mentally friendly?
14. How to deal with halal meat?[22]
15. Moral harassment and a whistle-blowing procedure.
16. Auchan's responsibility in the Rana Plaza catastrophe in Bangladesh.

The preceding lines provide an overview of the normative background against
which the ethics committee has been set up, the committee's composition and the
kind of questions that are treated during discussions.

From a methodological viewpoint, some issues arise. One is formal, and
addresses the question as to how the members of the committee proceed when they
discuss ethical questions. A related question is whether the manner in which they
proceed has evolved over the years, and if so how? In other words, can we observe
a learning process?

Incoherent Peacemaking Philosophy

The various debates on the above-mentioned (as well as many other) issues were
very interesting. We may leave the conclusions aside here – they were basically all
morally defensible – and rather turn our attention to making some remarks regarding the nature of ethical argumentation during these discussions.

A standard method of moral philosophy is to start with a set of principles. These
principles are applied to some particular issue and if they lead to shocking consequences, you should either bite the bullet – and accept these, thereby abandoning
your former opinions, – or you should conclude that something has to be changed
in your initial set of principles. Good arguments are supposed to let you draw sharp
conclusions, and we therefore explore arguments to find out if they will not lead us
to puzzling conclusions that hurt our intuitions at some point. The aim is to find the
point at which competing theories part company. James Sterba (2005) proposes an
alternative method which he calls 'peacemaking philosophy'. We should start with
the most acceptable, charitable interpretation of principles or theories, and then try
to reconcile them with the most acceptable and least controversial interpretation of
opposing theories. Sterba argues that doing so allows us to resolve many ethically
controversial issues: if, for example, utilitarianism and Kantianism are interpreted
in a not overly-radical way, they are more likely to point in the same direction.

Business people in ethics committees definitely practice peacemaking philosophy. In contrast to philosophers, they never attempt to drive a point to its limits in
order to find out where the principles that are invoked to justify a decision would
lead us to some surrealistic scenario (the kind which philosophers are fond of).

---

[22] 'Halal' refers to food that is acceptable for Muslims. It is especially related to meat: some animals are prohibited (e.g. pork) and concerning other animals there are strict rules on the way in
which animals have to be slaughtered.

Moreover, business people practice a quite 'incoherent' kind of peacemaking philosophy. This remark should absolutely not be read as some negative or disparaging judgment. I only want to stress the different perspectives: whereas philosophers are keen to point out deep, underlying paradoxes and conceptual complications, business people are happy to base their decisions on a robust consensus, notwithstanding the fact that this consensus is based on intrinsically contradictory principles.

For example, during one of the meetings, the discussion was about how to treat the 'elderly' among the employees respectfully. Again, the issue is about *voluntary* commitments beyond legal obligations: legally, people are declared 'able' or 'unable' by the *Médicine du Travail* (the national service which controls employees' health). Sometimes officially 'able' persons are physically less fit for some jobs than younger people. Arguments that were advanced in the discussion had a certain origin in the Golden Rule: 'what if you saw your father suffering on the work floor?' Other arguments were elliptic: 'we have to do with persons that belong to the Auchan community from the start and this should be respected'. But then the discussion switched quickly to the absurdity of the seniority principle, which makes the employment of older people relatively expensive. Now we can certainly discuss the seniority principle, but not necessarily on deontological grounds or on the basis of Catholic humanist values. In other words, the committee usually switches from a deontological to a consequentialist framework or it refers to Catholic humanist values ('dignity of persons', 'persons who belong to our community') without any bother.[23] The principles of both approaches are weakened so that an acceptable compromise becomes possible. Another example: it was argued that shops could be opened on a religious holiday if the employees who worked did so on a 'voluntary' basis (religious convictions ought to be respected). At the same time, voluntariness is stimulated by some extra pay, which implies that people's convictions are not *totally* respected: they have a price.

Even virtue ethics came into the picture a couple of times. In 1999, the popular TV station Canal Plus broadcast a documentary, during prime time, about a case of moral harassment in one of the Auchan supermarkets. The Auchan management was embarrassed by the accusations but admitted, during the ethics committee discussion, that it was obvious that the director did not have the appropriate moral virtues for his position.

In general, discussions tend to defend positions that seem acceptable, but it is far from certain that each of the principles that are supposed to underlie the positions would, ultimately, support them.

A final observation is the quite surprising strong personal identification with the firm. The use of the pronoun 'we' is constantly used during the sessions, which illustrates how most the managers – in any case those who were present in the ethics committee – consider the company as a community. When the first (negative) results of social audits organized in supplier companies in Asia were presented in 1997, the

---

[23] Takala and Uusitalo (1995) make similar observations about people in retailing companies.

CEO and the other members of the committee felt genuine shame.[24] Of course, the first and foremost worry was: "if a journalist published this, it would be catastrophic for our image". But beyond that, people said that they would no longer be able "to look at themselves in the mirror" if nothing serious was done about this situation. As a consequence, although people make clear distinctions between personal moral responsibilities and the responsibilities of the firm, they refer to personal feelings of shame when they judge their company's bad behavior.

Shifts in the Scope of Corporate Ethical Responsibility

The Auchan ethics committee gradually clarified the ethical responsibilities of the retail firm. Three elements together determined this evolution: (1) the growing scrutiny of retail companies by the general public and the media, (2) the shift in the underlying 'narrative' (Randels 1998) of the vision on ethical responsibility, and (3) the internal dynamics of the implementation of business ethics in the firm.

The first, external element is beyond the scope of this paper, and I will consequently focus on the factors internal to the company. Just one underlying assumption needs to be spelled out here: Insofar as a firm acts under the influence of external pressure, the primary motivation to try to implement ethical standards in the way of doing business is obviously the reputation of the company, that is, well-understood self-interest. For example, Auchan does not want to be "singled out" as a company that exploits children in Asia. Underlying this motivation to avoid a negative reputation and to create a positive one, there is a gamble: it is believed that customers would change their consumer behavior according to the reputation of the company. The challenge is, of course, based on an optimistic economic picture: to the extent that the purchasing power increases, the share of the income spent on food will decrease and consequently, people will focus less on the mere price of products. They will take into account other aspects to some extent, social and environmental ones. As a result, the company has an interest in preserving its reputation.

However, it has to be underlined that sometimes the ethical motivation clearly exceeds the concern for the reputation in the long run, and ethical issues are tackled independently of whether or not they may have reputational impact.

The change of the 'narrative' and the gradual disappearance of the *explicit* Catholic references influenced the scope of ethical concern. The internal dynamics of the ethics implementation also led to the acceptance of a broader realm of corporate moral responsibility including new topics, and, on the other hand, the more reserved reference to the Catholic background led to a diminished paternalist ethical concern for adult customers, which was present in the beginning. Still, some concerns of current executives of Auchan still reflect the Catholic background in topics

---

[24] Since then a whole set of measures have been taken to check and to improve the social conditions in which suppliers are obliged to produce. See the annual reports on the company's website for more details.

of cooperation in evil.[25] For example, the 2001 bestseller "The Sexual Life of Catherine M" by Catherine Millet, was not displayed on the shelves of the Auchan stores. Of course, you could buy it, because Auchan had no right to prohibit or limit the sale of the book, but the customer had to explicitly ask for it.[26] But when the ethics committee discussed the case, however, it recommended that Auchan adopt a less "paternalistic" policy regarding erotic literature. Millet's work would be on display nowadays, with the only restriction that it should be carefully placed out of children's reach. What happened on this point is that the notion of "cooperation in evil" – although this expression was not explicitly mentioned in the debate, the reluctance to sell the book expressed by some members was clearly based on it, – the committee lost *de facto* this notion, interpreting not cooperating to distribute erotic literature as "paternalism".

And yet, despite the fact that the owner family does no longer want to appear as proselyte, their Catholic humanism continues to influence the company, not only in an occasional restrictive concern like the one mentioned above, but in an unquestionable positive sense. They do so, first of all, by clearly supporting the ethics committee and by underlining its importance, but also by taking initiatives. In a more progressive vein, the two members of the Mulliez family who have a seat on the ethics committee surprised the committee with a survey they had set up (together with a Catholic priest) in the shops in the Paris suburbs. Their aim had been to find out whether there were, among the Auchan employees, people who belong to the group of the 'working poor', i.e. people who have a standard of living that is below the poverty line, despite the fact that they actually have a job. They found out that indeed some employees – single parents with part-time jobs – could not make a decent living with the wage they earned. A long discussion followed the presentation of the survey and one of the conclusions was that, in principle, part-time jobs should be *chosen*. In other words, all employees who want a full-time job should get one, and part-time jobs should be a matter of choice of the employee, not of the manager. This principle is now in the stage of implementation. Since the presence of customers in supermarkets is irregular and characterized by rush hours (evenings and Saturdays), the easy solution is to hire employees on a part-time basis. However, with some effort from the management, it turns out to be possible to deal with this irregularity without systematically relying on part-time employment. Interesting here is that the motivation to raise that issue was the idea that it seemed unacceptable to them, that some of 'our people', belonging to the Auchan family, lived in dire poverty. Obviously, their solidarity with these poor people was explicitly rooted in the Christian humanist idea of a company as a community. The debate, however,

---

[25] Catholic moral theology uses the term 'cooperation in evil' to refer to knowingly chosen acts which contribute to the sins of other persons. According to the Catechism of the Catholic Church (2003, n. 1737) bad effects of an action are imputable when there are foreseeable and avoidable.

[26] The French legislation constraints all booksellers to order on demand of their customers even a single copy of any published book. Therefore, booksellers cannot exert censorship and have to order books if customers order them (Law n° 81–766 of 10 August 1981, modified by law n° 85–500 of 13 May 1985).

was then further conducted in more secular terms, and it lead to the conclusion mentioned before.

As a consequence, the fact that the Auchan managers less often explicitly refer to Catholic values and (now) try to justify their decisions on grounds that are acceptable to all in a pluralistic society should not lead us to the conclusion that these Catholic values no longer play any role. For one thing, the set of values did not change radically. In 2008, the then CEO Philippe Baroukh surprisingly argued against the opening of supermarkets on Sunday, on the basis of the respect of "our cultural values".[27] Also, the role of the initial Catholic influence should not be underestimated: the ongoing dialogue would never have gotten off the ground if business behavior had not been understood as ultimately requiring an ethical component. The new implicit 'narrative' can only have some effect insofar as this basic vision is widely accepted.

Concluding Remarks

The picture I have sketched undoubtedly shows a rather positive image of Auchan as a company. However, a distinction should be made between the way in which topics are discussed and the daily decisions that are made within the company on the different lower levels of control. It is obvious that many decisions are not totally in line with the ethics code, and no member of the ethics committee would deny this. The reasons are obvious: conflicts between commercial objectives and respect of the rules, hasty decision making under stress, etc. An indication that reality is far from perfect is that the committee has thus far never lacked discussion topics.

However, the members of the committee all agree that under the influence of their debates, the different training sessions, and internal communication on the subject, progress has been made in many realms. From a more general perspective, one could ask whether the set of necessary and sufficient conditions that made this progress possible can easily be maintained in the future or transposed to other companies. Let us consider some of the key elements that were definitely necessary for this development to happen.

First of all, the period in which Auchan grew to its current size and in which its ethical steps were made was one of almost continuous economic prosperity and growth. Admittedly, the home market has matured in the last couple of years. However, this was compensated for by growth in foreign markets, at least in terms of shareholders' return on investment. Whether the management of the company would have been open-minded to the same extent in a tougher economic environment is an open question.

Secondly, the ethical discussions were set up and continuously supported by the shareholder family. Two points are especially important here. Firstly, one might ask whether the 'space of liberty' of the management with respect to ethical issues

---

[27] *Les échos*, 2 December 2008.

would be the same if the main shareholders were pension funds focusing on short term profits. Secondly, a growing worry of the shareholder family is that the next generation of inheritors – now there are already about 750 family shareholders – may not stick to the long term investments of the family business, and, therefore, might be willing to sell their shares.

Third, the simple fact of creating occasions to critically discuss the meaning of one's own activities is valuable *in itself*, regardless of the immediate consequences, since it fosters autonomous reflection. However, it is very likely that such reflection also positively influences decision-making within the company. As Lozano and Sauquet pertinently point out: "Unless there is space for reflection and justification, social and professional practices never automatically give rise to normative proposals that are unquestionable" (1999, 204).

Therefore, from a hermeneutic normative viewpoint, the process in which business leaders openly discuss and clarify the company's degree of responsibility for some particular issue, be it an issue directly related to their core business or a general social or environmental issue, is to be evaluated very positively.

Finally, the implicit ethical standards of the founders of the company, anchored in their Christian-Catholic value system were sufficient in a context in which the firm was small. It is important, in the interest of one's business, but also generally, to know that you should not cheat the client, that you should be respectful towards suppliers, even if you want to downsize commercial relations with them, etc. These topics remain important if a company grows of course, and they, therefore, constituted the main issues discussed in the first years of the ethics committee's existence. However, the important economic and social weight of big companies clearly demands a more explicit normative background and set of rules. What we have learned from the Auchan experience is that the creation of a forum in which these issues can be openly discussed is a crucial step. The importance of such a forum is not immediately related to what is decided in it, but its mere existence creates a dynamic process in which the company slowly but surely becomes aware of the specific responsibilities that can be attributed to big players in the market system. Business people who become used to ethical debates about their activities learn how to face them in an open and uncomplicated way.

Conclusion

The three cases we presented are totally different from each other. There is almost nothing in common between a multinational retailer of food and consumption goods, a services company in the telecom sector in Nigeria and a small SME in landscape gardening in France. Size, business model, cultural context, etc. of these companies are radically different. And yet the cases we presented reveal two crucial elements that are essential in these otherwise radically different companies: the commitment to respect employees and business partners as persons with a moral sense and the idea that a firm is also in some sense a community and not merely some people linked by a set of contracts. This is most obvious in *Agrément du Jardin*, the firm that embodies most explicitly Catholic humanism, not only in the way it is managed, but in its very mission statement. But the same values are to be found in the management of Kadick and Auchan as well, although both these firms operate in a context in which these values are difficult to implement. Auchan is an enormous multinational company in the very competitive environment of retail. Therefore, the size and the sector constitute a threat for the conception of the company as a community and the conviction that each employee is a person whose dignity should be respected. Until now Auchan has dealt with this threat in an exemplary way. Kadick operates in an African environment in which management is often authoritarian. Jackson (2004) relates this to colonial history and suggests that a more participative management style is perhaps less alien to traditional African culture as one would expect. Be that as it may, in the current African business world, a company in which people are respected as persons whose personal development is taken into consideration, and even are invited to speak up is rather uncommon.

References

Acquier, Aurélien, Jean-Pascal Gond, and Jacques Igalens. 2005. *Des fondements religieux de la responsabilité sociale de l'entreprise à la responsabilité sociale de l'entreprise comme religion*. Unpublished working paper (Cahier de recherche 2005–166), Toulouse: IAE.

Alford, Helen, Charles Clark, S. Cortright, and Michael Naughton. 2006. *Rediscovering abundance. Interdisciplinary essays on wealth, income, and their distribution in the Catholic social tradition*. Notre Dame: University of Notre Dame Press.

Ballet, Jerôme, and Françoise de Bry. 2001. *L'entreprise et l'éthique*. Paris: Seuil.

Balligand, J.-P., and J.-B. de Foucauld. 2000. *L'épargne salariale au cœur du contrat social*. Paris: La documentation française.

Berthoin Antal, Ariane, and André Sobczak. 2007. Corporate social responsibility in France. A mix of national and international influences. *Business and Society* 46(1): 9–32.

Blasco, Maribel, and Mette Zolner. 2010. Corporate social responsibility in Mexico and France. Exploring the role of normative institutions. *Business and Society* 49(2), 216–251.

Boissonnat, Jean. 1999. *L'aventure du christianisme social. Passé et avenir*. Paris: Bayard.

Bruni, Luigino, and Amelia Uelmen. 2006. The economy of communion project. *Fordham Journal of Corporate and Finance Law* 11(3): 645–680.

Catholic Church. 2003. *Catechism of the Catholic Church*. London: Random House. www.vatican.va/archive/ENG0015/_INDEX.HTM

Demuijnck, Geert. 2009. From an implicit Christian corporate culture to a structured conception of social responsibility in a retail company. A case-study in hermeneutic ethics. *Journal of Business Ethics* 84: 387–404.

Freeman, R.E. 1984. *Strategic management: A stakeholder approach*. Boston: Pitman.

Gobin, Bertrand, and Guillaume d'Herblin. 2007. *Le Secret des Mulliez – Révélations Sur le Premier Empire Familial Français*. Rennes: Borne seize (Editions la Borne Seize, s.l).

Guitián, G. 2009. Conciliating work and family: A Catholic social teaching perspective. *Journal of Business Ethics* 88(3): 513–524.

Jackson, Terence. 2004. *Management and change in Africa: A cross-cultural perspective*. London: Routledge.

Lozano, Josep M., and Alfons Sauquet. 1999. Integrating business and ethical value trough practitioners dialogue. *Journal of Business Ethics*. Part 2, 22(3): 203–217.

Melé, D. 2012. The firm as a "Community of Persons": A pillar of humanistic business ethos. *Journal of Business Ethics* 106(1): 89–101.

Melé, D. 2014. "Human Quality Treatment": Five organizational levels. *Journal of Business Ethics* 120(4): 457–471.

Melé, D. 2015. Three keys notions of Catholic humanism in economic activity: Human dignity. In *Human rights and integral human development*, Issues in business ethics, vol. 43, ed. D. Melé and M. Schlag, XXX–XXX. Dordrecht: Springer.

Naugthon, M. 2015. Thinking institutionally about business: Seeing its nature as a community of persons and its purpose as the common good, In *Human rights and integral human development*, Issues in business ethics, vol. 43, ed. D. Melé and M. Schlag, XXX –XXX. Dordrecht: Springer.

Naughton, M., and G.R. Laczniak. 1993. A theological context of work from the Catholic social encyclical tradition. *Journal of Business Ethics* 12(12): 981–994.

Randels, George. 1998. The contingency of business: Narrative, metaphor, and ethics. *Journal of Business Ethics* 17(12): 1299–1310.

Sandelands, L. 2009. The business of business is the human person: Lessons from the catholic social tradition. *Journal of Business Ethics* 85(1): 93–101. Re-printed in this volume.

Sterba, James. 2005. *The triumph of practice over theory in ethics*. New York: Oxford University Press.

Tablan, F. 2013. Human alienation and fulfillment in work: Insights from the Catholic social teachings. *Journal of Religion and Business Ethics* 3(1): 1–11.

Takala, Tuomo, and Outi Uusitalo. 1995. Retailers' professional and professio-ethical dilemmas: The case of finnish retailing business. *Journal of Business Ethics* 14: 893–907.

Index

© Springer Science+Business Media Dordrecht 2015
D. Melé, M. Schlag (eds.), *Humanism in Economics and Business*,
Issues in Business Ethics 43, DOI 10.1007/978-94-017-9704-7

CPSIA information can be obtained at www.ICGtesting.com
Printed in the USA
BVOW06*0816250315

393280BV00005B/9/P